That Religion in Which All Men Agree

The publisher gratefully acknowledges the generous support
of the Ahmanson Foundation Humanities Endowment
Fund of the University of California Press Foundation.

That Religion in Which All Men Agree

Freemasonry in American Culture

David G. Hackett

UNIVERSITY OF CALIFORNIA PRESS
Berkeley · Los Angeles · London

University of California Press, one of the most
distinguished university presses in the United States,
enriches lives around the world by advancing scholarship
in the humanities, social sciences, and natural sciences. Its
activities are supported by the UC Press Foundation and
by philanthropic contributions from individuals and
institutions. For more information, visit www.ucpress.edu.

University of California Press
Berkeley and Los Angeles, California

University of California Press, Ltd.
London, England

Library of Congress Cataloging-in-Publication Data

Hackett, David G.
    That Religion in Which All Men Agree : freemasonry
in American culture / David G. Hackett.
        p.   cm.
    Includes index.
    ISBN 978-0-520-28167-7 (cloth, alk. paper) —
    ISBN 978-0-520-95762-6 (electronic)
    1. Freemasons—United States—
History.   2. Freemasonry—United States—History.
3. Group identity—United States—History.   4. United
States—Religion—History.   5. United States—Social life
and customs.   I. Title.
HS515.R45   2014
366'.10973—dc23   2013025218

Manufactured in the United States of America

21 20 19 18 17 16 15 14 13 14
10 9 8 7 6 5 4 3 2 1

In keeping with a commitment to support
environmentally responsible and sustainable printing
practices, UC Press has printed this book on Natures
Natural, a fiber that contains 30% post-consumer waste
and meets the minimum requirements of ANSI/NISO
Z39.48-1992 (R 1997) (Permanence of Paper).

For Evie and Ben

Contents

Acknowledgments

"Where are the men?" I asked myself some years ago, while studying the membership lists of Albany, New York's early nineteenth-century churches. In 1830, 74 percent of that town's male work force did not belong to a church, and 72 percent of the members of its churches were women. City directory lists of Masonic lodges and their officers suggested themselves to me as holding possible answers.

I initially read my way into the literature on Freemasonry while looking for the existence of a male world that might broadly complement the Protestant women's sphere. As my research progressed, I saw larger implications. The fraternity's legendary history and ceremonial practices were part of a larger supernatural world inhabited by colonial men and women. Revolutionary-era Christian, republican Freemasonry had an influence on the creation of the United States that rivaled that of Protestantism. The brotherhood's private ceremonies were centrally involved in changing understandings of the body and sensory experience. Moreover, at different times Masonic beliefs and practices paralleled, interacted with, and diverged from not only white, mainstream Protestantism but also the black church, Native American world views, and immigrant Jewish and Catholic communal understandings. Though not a religion to its adherents, Freemasonry played a considerable role in the American religious past.

For assistance in my journey through Freemasonry, I thank the librarians and archivists who directed me to many of the materials for this book. The libraries of the Grand Lodges of Massachusetts, New York, Philadelphia, and Iowa were essential to this work. I am especially grateful to the librarian Bill Kreuger, who helped me find my way through the Prince Hall manuscripts at the Iowa Grand Lodge library in Cedar Rapids. Research visits to the American Antiquarian Society, the New York State Archives, the Schomburg Center for Research in Black Culture at the New York Public Library, the archives of Salisbury College in North Carolina, the First Congregational Church in Bedford, Massachusetts, and the Masonic Temple in Albany, New York, all provided needed materials. The Interlibrary Loan staff at the University of Florida, especially Janice Kahler, has always gone the extra mile in pursuing elusive materials.

I am grateful as well to a variety of sources for supporting this project. A National Endowment for the Humanities Fellowship and sabbatical homes provided by Princeton Theological Seminary's Center of Theological Inquiry and Princeton University's Center for the Study of Religion in America enabled the initial research. Daniel Hardy at the seminary and Robert Wuthnow at the university were gracious hosts. The Louisville Institute for the Study of American Protestantism supported a later year of research, which the Institute for Ecumenical and Cultural Research at Saint John's University in Collegeville, Minnesota suffused with Benedictine spirituality. Here again I was gifted with warm and caring hosts, in Patrick Henry and Killian McDonnell. I am thankful to Wheaton College's Billy Graham Center for a travel grant to visit its collections and to my home university, the University of Florida, for providing summer support and research leaves.

I also thank the academic audiences who listened to and engaged with my evolving project in ways that made it better. The residents at the Center of Theological Inquiry and the fellows and graduate students of the Center for the Study of Religion in America discussed my early workshop papers. It was a stroke of luck to have Nancy Ammerman, Jim Bratt, Peter Paris, and Albert Raboteau among these conversation partners in my sabbatical year. I presented successive papers at the annual meetings of the International Society for the Sociology of Religion, the American Academy of Religion, the Canadian American Studies Association, the American Studies Association, the Organization of American Historians, the American Society of Church History, and the International Conference on Freemasonry. I am grateful too for invitations to discuss my work at Yale University, the University of Chicago, Harvard University, the University of Notre Dame, Drew University,

Union Theological Seminary, the Center on Religion and Politics at Washington University, and the New York Grand Lodge of Free and Accepted Masons.

I have benefited from comments from and conversations with a number of colleagues and friends in addition to those already mentioned. Early on, Mark Carnes welcomed me into his home and shared his efforts to understand the burgeoning of late nineteenth-century fraternal orders. Cathy Albanese, Randy Balmer, and Mark Noll all offered advice and encouragement in the early stages. Laurie Maffly-Kipp and Grant Wacker provided important feedback on the initial draft of what became chapter 6, on the Prince Hall Masons. Fritz Detwiler, Joel Martin, Patrick Minges, and Joy Porter weighed in on chapter 7, on Native Americans. Jonathan Sarna and Daniel Soyer provided feedback on Jews and Freemasonry, while Chris Kaufman advanced my understanding of the Catholic Knights of Columbus (see chapter 8). Cathy Brekus, Jessica Harland-Jacobs, Paul Harvey, and Bob Wuthnow read whole drafts of the manuscript and offered constructive guidance. Within the Masonic fraternity, Mark Tabbert, the curator of the Masonic collections at the Scottish Rite Masonic Museum and Library, and especially S. Brent Morris, the editor of the *Scottish Rite Journal*, provided close readings of the penultimate draft. I am particularly indebted to Tony Fels for discussions of late nineteenth-century Freemasonry. Finally, it is a grace to have within the field of American religious studies good friends and colleagues who have offered words of encouragement as my research went down many a winding road. Beyond those already mentioned, Marie Griffith, Sam Hill, Brooks Holifield, Bob Orsi, Leigh Schmidt, Steve Tipton, and Tom Tweed have all rooted for this project, and I thank them for their support.

I first thought through the issues discussed in chapter 6 in an article in *Church History* ("The Prince Hall Masons and the African American Church: The Labors of Grand Master and Bishop James Walker Hood, 1831–1918," *Church History* 69, 4 [December 2000]: 770–802 . Copyright © 2000 American Society of Church History. Reprinted with the permission of Cambridge University Press.). I thank the editors for permission to reprint this essay in revised form here. This book has benefited from the superb copyediting of Juliana Froggatt and, at University of California Press, the careful guidance of Cindy Fulton and the consistent support of my editor Eric Schmidt. Together they carried the manuscript smoothly through to publication.

Here in Gainesville the circle of gratitude extends to my colleagues in the Religion Department, especially Vasudha Narayanan, Anna Peterson,

Manuel Vasquez, and Robin Wright. The department secretary, Anne Newman, has regularly gone out of her way to provide technical assistance. Nancy Savage expertly corrected the final page proofs. At home are Evie and Ben, whose entire lives have taken place during the writing of this book. It is to them and the joy they bring me that I dedicate it.

Introduction

Modern Freemasonry emerged from a milieu of early eighteenth-century London clubs, salons, and similar societies that were coming into existence in private, outside the control of the state. In 1709 the influential British social theorist Anthony Ashley Cooper, the third Earl of Shaftesbury, wrote a letter to a friend describing the emergence of these new forms of social life. Gentlemen who had previously upheld the "Sacred Truths" of the royal court, he recounted, were now meeting in "private" societies. There they engaged in wide-ranging conversations, "unravelling or refuting any Argument" so that greater truths might prevail. These "polite" societies, the English theorist observed, provided a new social space where urban gentlemen were free to discuss all manner of subjects, bound by private friendships characterized by "reciprocal tenderness and affection" that kept a studied distance from the solemn orthodoxies of state and church. These conversations, Shaftesbury warned, could take place only in private among gentlemen who knew one another well. To have such free interchange in public was "above the common Reach."[1]

By embracing one another as brothers joined by love rather than obedience to an authoritarian father, the members of these new societies conducted social relations in new ways. New ideas, put forward most notably by the Earl of Shaftesbury, held that people naturally got along with one another and were genuinely concerned for the well-being of others.[2] These innate sentiments could do naturally what the

I

heavy hands of the monarchy and the church could no longer do artifi-
cially through coercion. According to their 1723 constitution, the gentlemen who joined the Masonic fraternity saw themselves "as Brethren
upon the same level."[3] Within these affectionate bonds of brotherhood,
members subscribed only to "that Religion in which all men Agree."
No longer bound as "in Ancient Times" by the "Religion of the Country or Nation," Masons were free to pursue a variety of religious paths.
Politically, aside from an agreement to be "a peaceable Subject to the
Civil Powers," no orthodox position was required.[4]

Freemasonry's modern constitution, however, is rooted in ancient
foundations. Though binding itself to progressive rules and regulations,
the fraternity prefaced its constitution with a mythic history that traces
Masonic origins to ancient wisdom and occult knowledge. No longer a
medieval guild of stoneworkers, the brotherhood nevertheless retained
the symbolic language and secret ceremonies of initiation. Within the
secrecy of the lodge, members were free to entertain a variety of spiritual
perspectives.[5] Druids, pantheists, skeptics, and deists as well as Jews,
Catholics, and Protestants could all be found within the eighteenth-century fraternity. Indeed, the new, speculative Freemasonry embodied the
ideals of the age while allowing for alternative possibilities.

The purpose of this book is to weave the story of Freemasonry into
the narrative of American religious history. Freighted with the mythical
legacies of stonemasons' guilds and the Newtonian revolution, English
Freemasonry came to colonial America with a vast array of cultural
baggage, which was drawn on, added to, and transformed in different
ways in its sojourn through American culture. This study argues that
from the 1730s through the early twentieth century, the religious worlds
of an evolving American social order broadly appropriated the changing beliefs and initiatory practices of this all-male society. For much of
American history, Freemasonry was a counter and a complement to
Protestant churches and a forum for collective action among racial and
ethnic groups outside the European American mainstream. As a widely
available resource for organizing social relations and ideology, Freemasonry provides an interpretive lens through which to reframe our understanding of the American religious past.

This book comes at a time when the transformation of the field of
American religious history has opened new areas of inquiry. In the past
thirty years, a divinity school–based concern with the intellectual history of European American Protestants has given way to a religious
studies interest in African Americans, Native Americans, Jews, Catho-

lics, and other peoples and practices outside the domain of the Protestant middle class. Much of the new scholarship cuts across boundaries of gender, class, and region while paying particular attention to ritual and popular religion. Like most of the older American religious history, until recently the story of American Freemasonry has been a tale of middle-class European American northeastern male Protestants. Since the 1990s, however, a multicultural story of African American, Native American, Jewish, and Catholic Masons has emerged. In different ways, each of these groups employed elements of Freemasonry to navigate their way through a largely European American society. By assessing the appropriation of Freemasonry within and outside the European American mainstream, this study contributes to the ongoing effort to broaden and diversify our understanding of American religious history.

Although Freemasons rarely claimed that their fraternity was a religion, many both within and outside the brotherhood recognized its religious character. The society's modern constitution states that Masons cannot be atheists.[6] While denying that Freemasonry was a religion, most members appear to have been comfortable calling the order a handmaid of religion (that strove to make men better). Outside the fraternity, in 1972 Sydney Ahlstrom, the then-dean of American religious historians, observed that "for many they [the lodges] seemed to satisfy social needs and a yearning for rites and ceremonies that Protestantism lacked. For many others they seem to have provided a religious alternative to the churches."[7] More pointed were Freemasonry's major Catholic and evangelical religious opponents, who accused the fraternity of creating a veritable church of the Antichrist.

Since Masons did not understand their beliefs and practices as constituting a religion, to claim that Freemasonry was a religion imposes an interpretive lens that inevitably distorts Masonic practices. Once the brotherhood is declared to be a religion, then how *religion* is defined determines what in the fraternity is described as religious. As Jonathan Z. Smith has pointed out, "'Religion' is not a native term; it is a term created by scholars for their intellectual purposes and therefore is theirs to define."[8] Moreover, we know that academic definitions of *religion* were first developed in the context of colonialism and deployed as justifications for the marginalization of some social groups.[9] When academics employ the term to identify the idioms of people who claim not to be religious, these definitions can't help but skew our understanding of those practices.[10] However, the fact that the category of religion is inflected with power does not render it useless. Rather, we can explore how this category was rejected and transformed by Masons and mobilized against them by others in the American religious arena to make boundaries and create identities. But this exploration cannot take place without some conceptualization of what we are talking about. To reap the analytic benefits of placing American Freemasonry into the context of American religious historiography, we need to adopt a broad and flexible definition of *religion* that can allow for the inclusion of a variety of voices. To that end, in this book I define *religion* as shared ideologies and practices that help people become human in relation to transcendent realities.[11] By expanding and complicating the terrain of American religious history to include a group not usually seen as a carrier of religious beliefs and practices, this book intends to show how Freemasonry's American history contributes to a broader understanding of the multiple influences that have shaped religion in American culture.

Freemasonry's quest for primeval truth, for example, helps to reveal an enduring attraction to ancient wisdom throughout the American past. Fragments of broader, older ways of believing and acting, some predating Christianity, suffused colonial Protestantism.[12] Studies of early nineteenth-century Protestant primitivism, in turn, have unearthed a yearning to restore the church's ancient foundations.[13] Inquiries into early Mormonism have revealed its occult and hermetical origins.[14] Explorations of African American race histories, the Cherokee Keetoowah Society, Jewish efforts to create a modern Ararat, and antimodernism at the end of the nineteenth century have uncovered searches for intense spiritual experience among the archaic, medieval, and Eastern sources of the past.[15] Freemasons participated in all of these pursuits.

In its efforts to cross political and religious boundaries, Freemasonry rivaled Protestantism in influencing the creation of the new American society.[16] As one of the oldest and most pervasive American voluntary associations, Masons were more successful than the members of any other colonial organization in joining together disparate political and religious leaders. While regional denominational disputes stymied Revolutionary War chaplains, Masonic military lodges built ties among Continental Army officers. Perhaps even more than the Protestantism that emerged from the Revolution, a newly Christian and republican Freemasonry became closely identified with the new American nation. Where colonial leaders had invited Protestant ministers to sanctify their assemblies, by the early days of the new republic, American citizens were calling on Masons to bless their new institutions.

At the end of the eighteenth century, the fraternity began to develop its private, ritual life. Though scholarship has most frequently seen the expanding economy's creation of boundaries between public and private as most influencing women's lives, these changes had far-reaching effects on both men and women.[17] Emerging alongside rather than replacing the public activities of the lodge, Masonic ritual life contributed to the creation of a male private sphere that preceded the appearance of a private world of piety and domesticity among nineteenth-century Protestant women. Compared to colonial Freemasonry, in which men of good breeding and upright character attained the honor of membership as a means of entry into "polite" society, the early nineteenth-century version was a private world of warmth and intimacy, separated from an increasingly cold, competitive, and uncertain public sphere, with rituals that spoke to the struggles and anxieties of young men living amid widespread social change. In creating these rituals, moreover, Masons contributed to a new understanding of the inner, "true" self, which could be realized only through emotional assault on outward defenses. Where studies of women and Protestantism have described the evolution of a pious women's domestic sphere that encompassed the church, the growth and development of Freemasonry's rich ritual life suggests the parallel evolution of a private haven of intimacy and ritual among growing numbers of men as the century progressed.

Though divided by gender into church and lodge, respectively, women and men were nevertheless joined together within a larger relational system. The masculine world of Freemasonry could never be totally separated from the feminine domain of the home. Moreover, late nineteenth-century efforts to resolve the tensions between lodge and home suggest a growing interest in closer cooperation between men and women. In contrast to scholarship that has emphasized antagonism between the sexes, this inquiry finds a growing acceptance of Freemasonry within the churches and an accommodation of women in lodge activities.[18] Between the brotherhood's female auxiliary, who supported it, and the radical evangelical women who attacked it were the great majority of Protestant women, who said little about Freemasonry. More than a story of the subjugation of women by men, relations between the sexes involved challenges to and accommodations of each other's understanding of social life.

When placed alongside American Protestantism, the changing ideas and practices of the Masonic brotherhood suggest a religion not well known to the field of American religious history. At its eighteenth-century origin, the modern fraternity endorsed the Enlightenment theory which holds that people are naturally concerned for one another's well-being. In the hands of influential Anglican clerics, this inclusive new social vision placed less emphasis on revelation and more on reason. In the revolutionary period, Freemasonry joined Protestantism in adopting the republican and democratic impulses of the new American society. Ministers from the leading Episcopal, Unitarian, and Congregational denominations joined the fraternity, which made internal efforts to Christianize its beliefs and practices. The ritual exposures of the Anti-Masonic movement, however, broke the identification of the postwar fraternity with the special providence of the new American nation, leading the fraternity to retrench to a more general Protestant conservatism. Though consistent with the rationalism, commonsense realism, and antirevivalism of antebellum liberal Protestantism, Freemasonry diverged from the expansive mood it fostered. The optimistic faith in the immanent love of God that pervaded the new society stood strikingly apart from the brotherhood's awareness of human limitations.

The Protestant themes running through the history of American Freemasonry should not obscure the fact that other than atheism, the modern constitutions proscribed very little with regard to religion. Moreover, with no central authority imposing ideological orthodoxy, what it means to be a Mason has always been susceptible to cultural shifts, regional variations, and individual interpretations. Over the course of their brotherhood's fabled history, Masonic writers have generally worked to reflect the religious ethos of a lodge's particular setting. Yet despite this apparent conformity to surrounding religious life, Freemasonry carried within it a vast array of cultural elements that paralleled and diverged from Protestant religious beliefs and practices. Moreover, beyond the European American, old-stock, cultural Protestants who composed the great majority of the fraternity's North American adherents, the African Americans, Native Americans, Jews, and Catholics who joined the brotherhood adapted its resources to their particular needs and desires.

Excluded from European American Masonry, African Americans formed the Prince Hall Masons in the late eighteenth century. The records of this black fraternity have become a site for expanding our knowledge of African American history. Scholars have employed this resource to better understand black class formation, the construction of African American masculinity, and the institutions of black civil society.[19] Through a consideration of the origins of African American

Masonry and the African Methodist Episcopal Church (AME) in North Carolina, I suggest that this fraternity not only came into existence alongside and complementary to black churches but also, like the churches, provided symbolic, ideological, and organizational resources for African Americans to resist racism and find their way through contested terrain of American civil society.

Native American interactions with Freemasonry similarly date from the late eighteenth century. Older approaches to Native American history have understood Freemasonry, when mentioned at all, as part of a larger, "civilizing" process that emphasized the inevitable assimilation of Native tribes into the values and practices of white society. More recent approaches, in contrast, have stressed Native American resistance to Euro-American hegemony.[20] Moving with this more recent historiography, I hold that Native Americans adapted Masonic ideals and practices as part of a larger effort to both preserve Native identity and employ new spiritual resources to confront the challenges of accommodation to American society. At the turn into the twentieth century, moreover, when white, middle-class Masons were drawn to Native American wisdom in their quest for primeval truth, modernizing Indians sought within Freemasonry a means for finding their place in middle-class American society.

Jews and Catholics have an even longer history of membership in the Masonic brotherhood. Jews were admitted shortly after the creation of the modern fraternity's 1723 constitution, while Catholics formed the original medieval membership of what was then a confraternity of practicing stoneworkers. In the nineteenth century, Jews rose to prominence in the fraternity, while a series of papal attacks warned Catholics away from fraternal involvement. By the late nineteenth century, I argue, the desires of immigrant Jews and Catholics for organizations that responded to their needs both to assimilate into American society and to retain their ethnic and religious identities resulted in the creation of their own fraternal orders based on the Masonic template.

THE PUBLIC SPHERE

Beyond the ways in which Freemasonry has shaped and been shaped by American culture, this study explores its participation in the "public sphere," the realm of social life where citizens set aside coercive external religious and state authority and individual status distinctions to create collective opinion through rational communication. As conceived and developed by the German theorist Jürgen Habermas, the public sphere allows for its participants to arrive at a consensus based on "the authority of the better argument," which might then become the public will. In Habermas's formulation, the public sphere emerged in the late seventeenth century from the struggle against arbitrary state authority. Using England as his case study, he argues that the development of "rational-critical" debate grew out of the movement of people and ideas in London clubs and societies. Mediating between society and the state, private clubs were instrumental in the formation of the public sphere, and their modes of discourse necessary to the creation of public opinion. Through the rapid establishment of print media, especially newspapers, and private societies characterized by literary and critical discourses, this "classical public sphere" spread through eighteenth-century Britain, France, and Holland. It continued, Habermas holds, until the latter half of the nineteenth century, when the power of large corporations, the rise of state interventions, and social fragmentation eroded the independence of public opinion and undermined the legitimacy of its institutions.[21]

Consistent with Habermas's conception of the public sphere, Freemasonry was one of a variety of "polite societies" that formed in English and American cities between the 1690s and the 1760s. These voluntary organizations nurtured sociability through amiable conversation, literature, and polite pleasures. In contrast to older notions of hospitality, which reinforced traditional ties of family, ethnicity, church, and local community, the new sociability practiced by these societies promoted friendship and common interests among disparate people in the emerging public spaces of coffeehouses, taverns, and elegant homes. David Shields has persuasively argued that the various colonial American private and polite societies—including Freemasonry—helped to hold the social order together in an era that had moved beyond hereditary aristocracy yet came before the development of the middle class.[22]

To differing degrees and at different times, the cultural template of Freemasonry gave shape and content to the American public sphere. Emerging in coastal cities in the 1730s, the first American Freemason lodges were participants in a nascent American "polite" society. In a colonial America where, unlike Habermas's conception of eighteenth-century England, religious discourse predominated, Masons contributed to a rationalization if not a secularization of the emerging public sphere. In the early nineteenth century, the brotherhood created a white male private sphere, apart from its well-regarded public face, that paralleled and at times dueled with a white women's private sphere fractured by class and religious divisions. In the 1820s, the immediate and widespread emergence of Anti-Masonry witnessed to the rapid expansion of the public sphere through newspapers and other print media. The movement of late nineteenth-century affluent, educated women into the public sphere, moreover, can be viewed through the lens of the emergence of female affiliates, such as the Eastern Star wives of Freemasons. Beyond these and other involvements in the public sphere, this study discusses how African Americans, Native Americans, Jews, and Catholics each created "counterpublic" forms and uses for Freemasonry in a rapidly expanding and diversifying nineteenth-century American society.[23]

SCHOLARSHIP ON AMERICAN FREEMASONRY

This book comes at a time of growing appreciation for the impact of Freemasonry on major developments in American life. Earlier historians dismissed the fraternity as too obscure or exotic to have substantially influenced the course of events. Some explained away Anti-Masonry as social paranoia.[24] Social scientists, in turn, focused on the fraternity's sociological and economic benefits while taking little interest in Freemasonry's beliefs and practices.[25] Compounding the problem has been the historical writing of Masons themselves, which has been primarily concerned with the origins and meaning of the fraternity's social and ritual life and less interested in the lodge's interactions with the surrounding society. Recently, however, Masonic writers have demonstrated a broader understanding of Masonic history, while a new generation of historians has contributed to a growing appreciation of the influence of Freemasonry on American life. This study draws together much of this new scholarship while advancing arguments that offer a more complete picture of the influences of Freemasonry on American culture.

Since the mid-nineteenth century, Masonic antiquarians have produced multivolume chronicles, regional histories, and more narrowly focused monographs. In America, this includes the regional histories and related works of Albert Gallatin Mackey (South Carolina), Edward T. Schultz (Maryland), Charles T. McClenachan (New York), and Julius F. Sachse and Norris S. Barratt (Pennsylvania). Each of these histories, and the more general early twentieth-century overviews provided by Melvin Maynard Johnson and Jacob Hugo Tatsch, makes selective use of what is still a massive amount of undigested individual and Grand

Lodge records, sermons, and orations.[26] In Great Britain, the landmark work is Robert Freke Gould's *History of Freemasonry*, first published in the 1880s and edited by Dudley Wright in 1936. The midcentury British team of Douglas Knoop and G. P. Jones produced the best histories of early modern Masonry, while the University of Saint Andrews historian David Stevenson has written the most authoritative account of the brotherhood's origins in Scotland.[27] Two Masonic research journals, the longstanding *Ars Quatuor Coronatorum* (founded in 1886) and the more recent *Heredom* (founded in 1992), have published articles and reprinted primary materials on a wide range of topics. Within the past two decades, a new generation of American Masonic historians has produced a more scholarly literature. The best of these include Wayne A. Huss's Pennsylvania Grand Lodge history, Mark A. Tabbert's overview of American Freemasonry, and two volumes edited by Brent Morris and others that bring together essays by Masonic antiquarians and professional historians.[28] With the 2007 inauguration in Edinburgh of the annual International Conference on the History of Freemasonry, this intermingling of Masons and academic scholars has grown.[29]

Just as Masonic writing has more thoroughly engaged the available sources and broadened in scope, since the late 1970s scholars have shown a growing interest in the American brotherhood's social and cultural significance. In 1977, Dorothy Ann Lipson published her pioneering study *Freemasonry in Federalist Connecticut, 1789–1835*. In that book, she establishes that the revolutionary-era fraternity provided a sense of corporate identity for an emerging class of men whose entrepreneurial and political activity, mobility, and latitudinarian spirit conflicted with the verities of the old Connecticut "standing order." Lynn Dumenil's 1984 *Freemasonry and American Culture, 1880–1930* focuses on how the late nineteenth- and early twentieth-century ideology of Masonic writers mirrored the religious and moralistic content of American society's concerns and values while providing a "sacred asylum" from the immoral, competitive, and commercial world beyond the temple. In 1987, the American religious historian Anthony D. Fels finished his dissertation, "The Square and the Compass: San Francisco's Freemasons and American Religion, 1870–1900," which traces the religious parameters of the late nineteenth-century San Francisco brotherhood. Two theory-driven books appeared in 1989. In *Constructing Brotherhood: Class, Gender, and Fraternalism*, the sociologist Mary Ann Clawson uses a neo-Marxist approach to explore the relationship between fraternalism and conceptions of class and gender. She argues that the social and ideological resources of fraternalism provided a basis for unity among men of different social statuses. At the same time, in their efforts to preserve male autonomy, these all-male societies offered an alternative to female domesticity. An interpretive framework informed by gender theory and cultural anthropology guides *Secret Ritual and Manhood in Victorian America*. In this provocative book, Mark C. Carnes delves into the content of late nineteenth-century fraternal rituals to argue that the growth of these orders can be largely attributed to their providing rites of passage from the domestic world of women to the masculine workplace.[30]

The book you are reading is most indebted to Steven C. Bullock, for his 1996 *Revolutionary Brotherhood: Freemasonry and the Transformation of the American Social Order, 1730–1840*, a watershed in historians' efforts to articulate the impact of Freemasonry on colonial and early nineteenth-century American society and culture. Bullock's study was the first to trace the contours of American Masonry's early history. It argues that colonial Freemasonry exemplified the cosmopolitan ideals of provincial elites and was then transformed by the artisanal ideals of liberty, democracy, and public virtue. Employing the methods of quantitative social history and ethnographic cultural history, Bullock sees the fraternity as shaping and being shaped by momentous developments in nineteenth-century America, including democracy, individualism, sentimentalism, and the emergence of public and private spheres. Moreover, the fraternity provided resources for artisans, women, African Americans, and churches to respond creatively to extraordinary social changes. Rather than explain away the motives of Masonic brothers and those opposed to them, Bullock takes their beliefs and activities seriously and through this approach provides the most convincing argument to date for the social and cultural significance of early American Freemasonry.[31] Though the early chapters of my book build on many of Bullock's insights, my interpretation diverges from his in placing American Freemasonry in the context of the religious history of the period.

Recent years have brought the beginnings of an exploration of the influence of Freemasonry beyond the white middle class. The sociologists Theda Skocpol and Jennifer Lynn Oser have statistically documented the origins and development of African American fraternalism.[32] Nick Salvatore, Joanna Brooks, Cory D.B. Walker, and Stephen Kantrowitz have argued for the significance of fraternalism in the late nineteenth-century

American black community.[33] Philip J. Deloria, Joy Porter, and Patrick N. Minges have researched Freemasonry among Native Americans.[34] Daniel Soyer has explored the development of Jewish fraternal orders, and Christopher J. Kauffman has written on the Catholic Knights of Columbus.[35] These and other studies are bringing into focus the wide-ranging influence of Freemasonry on American culture and society. The efforts of these scholars and others to understand fraternalism have provided valuable pathways in my attempt to incorporate Freemasonry into the narrative of American religious history.

. . .

My telling of the story of American Freemasonry now unfolds in two parts. The first includes five broadly chronological chapters focusing on the European American fraternity. The second part consists of three thematic chapters, on African Americans, Native Americans, and Jews and Catholics. The book ends with an epilogue on developments since 1900.

The first chapter of part 1 begins with the grand arrival of Freemasonry in colonial coastal cities as part of the Anglicization of colonial life. I review the origins and multiple meanings of the society prior to its arrival before considering the influence of Masonic ideals and practices on the colonial elite. Crossing political, ethnic, and religious boundaries, the fraternity's social ideals and initiatory practices provided the basis for common ground among elite European American men. Moreover, the brotherhood contributed to the rational religious discourse of the nascent public sphere. At the same time, because it drew from Christian and non-Christian sources, the Masonic world view provided resources for the larger religious world that many eighteenth-century Americans inhabited.

The second chapter considers the transformation of the fraternity in the revolutionary period and its impact on the nascent American society. Beginning in the middle of the eighteenth century, a growing number of working men, outside the elite, joined a new and more democratic, "ancient" variant of the fraternity and directed it toward an embrace of the republican ideals of the new American society. "Ancient" military lodges more than Protestant chaplains knit together the officers of the Continental Army. Masonic military parades and public rituals, culminating in President George Washington's laying of the cornerstone of the new nation's capital with full Masonic trappings, signaled the identification of the fraternity with the new American society. At the same time, enlightenment influences on religious thought expanded the boundaries of Christianity to include Freemasonry, while the fraternity made efforts to become more Christian. Positioned to the left of orthodox Calvinism and its evangelical descendants and to the right of Enlightenment rationalism, a more overtly Christian and republican Freemasonry was seen by many as embodying the values of the new American society.

After the Revolution, the fraternity began to evolve its private, ritual life. The abbreviated initiations of colonial days now became lengthy dramas shrouded in layers of deepening meaning. The new ritual quest for primeval truth was part of a larger Christian Restorationist, Primitivist, and Mormon attraction to ancient wisdom. The third chapter begins with the origins and development of these new degree rites, their relationship to John Locke's epistemology, and their contribution to a new psychology of the self, which could be reached only through emotional assault. The Masonic use of strong emotions to reach an inner self occurred at the same time that the revivalists of the Second Great Awakening sought to break open the hearts of "sinners." Moreover, both the new rituals and the new evangelism anticipated the romantic embrace of emotion to reach the depths of one's identity. Further, at a time when some leading women were attracted to the fraternity's public embrace of republicanism and Christianity, the lodge was becoming a place of private retreat from the public world, broadly paralleling the development of women's private, pious, domestic sphere.

At the peak of the fraternity's influence, in the 1820s, the lodges were brought to their knees by the purported murder of someone who threatened to reveal their secrets, in what became known as the Morgan affair. Within a matter of months, as the fourth chapter recounts, Freemasons were "revealed" to be a political and religious threat to the "common man" and evangelical Christianity. The ensuing Anti-Masonic campaign, spurred by an expanding print culture and a democratizing ethos, laid bare a larger battle over Christian identity. At the same time that radical evangelicals sought to purge Masons from their churches, the fraternity's liberal religious themes were gaining ascendance within most Protestant churches. The conflict over Freemasonry further revealed developing class and religious divisions within "women's sphere."

In the late nineteenth century, a chastened Freemasonry continued its growth, though now within a profusion of new fraternal orders. Though never again to hold a prominent place in American public life, the brotherhood continued to cultivate and elaborate a private world of ritual meaning separate from the tumult of early industrial capitalism and the pious, female world of the home. Over time, the fifth chapter suggests, these two gendered worlds moved more closely together. By the end of the century, though the fraternity's antimodernist beliefs and practices diverged from the liberal Protestantism of the time, few Christians remained noticeably opposed to Freemasonry. The early twentieth-century remasculinization of some Protestant churches underscored this acceptance of, even attraction to, Freemasonry.

Beyond the European American middle class, African Americans, Native Americans, Jews, and Catholics appropriated Freemasonry for their particular purposes. The sixth chapter begins the second part of the book by turning to the nexus of African American Freemasonry and black churches in the late nineteenth century. Prince Hall Masonic lodges originated in the northern cities of Boston and Philadelphia in the late eighteenth century. After the Civil War, they were planted throughout the South alongside newly established African American churches. In North Carolina, the male membership and leadership of the African Methodist Episcopal Zion Church closely overlapped with that of the state's Prince Hall lodges. In fact, the Northern missionary James Walker Hood was both the bishop of the North Carolina Conference of the AME Zion Church and the grand master of the North Carolina Grand Lodge of Prince Hall Masons. Though these two interwoven social institutions were at times at odds with each other over relations between church and lodge, women and men, and the impact of the Holiness movement, together they provided black Americans with ideological and ritual resources that countered white racial narratives of African American inferiority. Moreover, unlike European American Masons and their churches, Prince Hall Masons worked with black churches in a common African American struggle to oppose racism and determine their destiny in American society.

The seventh chapter's tale of Native Americans and Freemasonry begins with the Mohawk leader Joseph Brant's 1776 journey to London, where he joined a Masonic lodge. Brant and subsequent Native American Masons employed the resources of Freemasonry to advance the interests of their people. Following the mid-nineteenth-century forced removal of southeastern Indians to the "Indian Territory" of what became Oklahoma, most of the area's Native American leaders joined the fraternity. The "civilization" program that the Washington administration initiated and which continued until the presidency of Andrew Jackson promised acceptance to Native Americans in return for their assimilation to the ways of European American society. Freemasonry was part of this process. At the same time, Native Americans appropriated Freemasonry in an effort to make use of new spiritual assets to retain their Indian identity and help steer their way through the challenges of living in the new American society. By the late nineteenth century, when Native American leaders were assimilating to white society and joining Masonic lodges, European American fraternalists were pursuing Native American wisdom, some going so far as donning Indian costumes and creating what they thought to be Native American ceremonies. For these members of the white middle class, Native American ways offered one means of responding to the dislocations of the modernizing American social order. For modernizing Native Americans, in contrast, Freemasonry provided an avenue for finding their place in early twentieth-century American society.

The eighth chapter turns to the involvement of Jews and Catholics in Freemasonry. Cosmopolitan English Jews became members soon after the 1723 formation of the modern fraternity, and their presence in the brotherhood grew in tandem with the expansion of participation of Jews in European and American society. In colonial America, Jewish Masons joined lodges founded within Jewish coastal settlements. After the Revolution, Jewish elites expanded beyond coastal cities and were chosen as leaders in the fraternity. Catholics, in contrast, trace their Masonic origins to medieval stoneworkers' guilds. In the early 1800s, American lodges included men from the upper reaches of the small immigrant Irish, English, and French Catholic communities. After the large-scale Irish, German, and Italian immigration in midcentury and the enforcement of new papal condemnations, American Freemasonry's attitude toward the Catholic Church began to change. The presence of Jews and Catholics in the Masonic fraternity was at times unsettling, and by the second half of the nineteenth century the needs of new immigrants for organizations that fostered a commitment to America while retaining Old World ethnic and religious identity led to the creation of exclusively Jewish (B'nai B'rith) and Catholic (Knights of Columbus) orders from the ideology and initiatory rituals of Freemasonry.

In the early twentieth century, as the epilogue briefly recounts, Freemasonry adopted the characteristics of a modern service club. New emphases on life insurance and recreation challenged an older embrace of honor and noble purpose. New interests in practical community involvement undercut the pursuit of deep and personal moral truths through ritual drama. Today the fraternity, like many American civic associations, is in decline.[36] Along with voluntary organizations throughout society, it has seen membership plummet. For much of American history, however, the Masonic lodge helped to shape a diverse and expanding religious culture. How all of this came about is the story to which we now turn.

PART ONE

European American Freemasonry

CHAPTER I

Colonial Freemasonry and Polite Society, 1733–1776

At sunrise on the morning of December 27, 1738, the "firing of guns from several ships in the harbor" to announce the festival of Saint John the Evangelist awakened the people of Charleston, South Carolina. At ten o'clock, the city's Masons, clothed in jewels, aprons, white gloves, and stockings and preceded by a small band, paraded through the streets to the site of their Grand Lodge meeting, at the home of James Graeme, the soon-to-be chief justice of the province and their provincial grand master. At eleven o'clock, the brotherhood processed to the Anglican church, where they sat in their separate section of pews and listened to their brother the Reverend Mr. Durand praise the fraternity's values of mutual love and benevolence. "In the same order" they then marched on to the house of Thomas Shepherd, a leading attorney, for "a very eloquent speech on the usefulness of societies" and an "elegant" dinner. This was followed by an invitation to a brother's ship, where several toasts were given, "saluted by the discharge of 39 guns." The evening concluded "with a ball and entertainment for the ladies."[1]

In the second quarter of the eighteenth century, reports of grand parades of gentlemen Masons began to appear in the newspapers of colonial coastal cities. In New York, the order of procession was carefully described:

> First walked the Sword Bearer, carrying a drawn sword; then four Stewards with White Maces, followed by the Treasurer and Secretary, who bore each a crimson damask cushion, on which lay a gilt Bible, and the Book of

Constitution; after these came the Grand Warden and Wardens; then came the Grand Master himself, bearing a truncheon and other badges of his office, followed by the rest of the Brotherhood, according to their respective ranks—Masters, Fellows Crafts, and 'Prentices, to about the number of fifty. . . . We hear they afterward conferred a generous donation of fifteen pounds from the public stock of the Society to be expended in clothing the poor children belonging to our charity school; and made a handsome private contribution for the relief of indigent prisoners.[2]

In Philadelphia, the officers and members of the Grand Lodge procession included the governor, the mayor, a chief justice, a college provost, the secretary of the Provincial Assembly, other leading men of Pennsylvania, and Deputy Grand Master Benjamin Franklin.[3] For colonial spectators, these "very grand show[s]" carried out with "grandeur and decorum" announced the elite social standing of Freemasons.[4]

The immediate impetus for these conspicuous displays came from the instructions and actions of the London Grand Lodge. James Anderson's *The Constitutions of the Free-Masons*, modern Freemasonry's founding rules and principles, printed in America in 1734 by Benjamin Franklin, instructs the brethren to hold the "Annual Communication and Feast, in some convenient place on St. John Baptist's Day, or else on St. John Evangelist's Day, . . . in order to choose every year a new Grand Master, Deputy and Wardens."[5] As early as 1721 the London Lodge enacted these instructions through elaborate public processions. Jewels, swords, and other regalia were adopted by the lodge or given to it as gifts by the noble grand masters.[6] The origins of these and other eighteenth-century public processions have been traced to late medieval towns where large religious parades involving most of the inhabitants displayed the hierarchical structure of their leadership. After the Reformation, those processions that continued to exist relegated the townspeople to spectators of the urban oligarchy of town leaders parading to church or court. Carried out with a theatrical self-consciousness—complete with ornamented clothing, polished gestures, and the new civic authority symbols of swords and maces—the processions of eighteenth-century England were designed to separate the townspeople from their leaders by exhibiting the power and structure of the new elite. Along with these public displays came similar ritual appearances in church and occasionally a gala ceremonial to stage grand displays of the rulers' generosity.[7] Colonial American Masonic festivals emulated all of these activities, though in somewhat different circumstances.

The appearance of the American Masonic fraternity accompanied the eighteenth-century development of colonial commercial cities. Between 1690 and 1740, the older seaport towns of Boston, Philadelphia, and New York and most of the newer coastal market hubs of Charleston, Savannah, Baltimore, Annapolis, Albany, New Haven, and Portsmouth experienced an expansion of trade that gradually drew them into the Atlantic marketplace. By midcentury, American coastal towns had become comparable to British provincial ports in economic activity.[8] Led by a growing demand for colonial exports, linked to an expanding commercial empire, protected and promoted by a strong imperial system, and endowed with an abundance of natural resources, the economy of British colonial America created an affluence capable of supporting an urban social order that was becoming more British. Social differentiation in America was always less developed than in Britain, and the colonies certainly had nothing comparable to the legally privileged English aristocracy. Yet as early as the 1720s in Boston, New York, and Philadelphia and by the 1760s in the newer colonies, a noticeable elite of merchants, lawyers, and government officials began a self-conscious effort to imitate British institutions, values, and culture rather than celebrate their American traits.[9]

Freemasonry was part of this Anglicization of colonial life.[10] Between 1733 and the revolution, the United Grand Lodge of London warranted more than one hundred lodges in the colonies' seaport towns.[11] By 1772 the fraternity's membership was about five thousand, including several hundred of the coastal cities' most important men.[12] As Steven C. Bullock has demonstrated, nearly all of Boston's and Philadelphia's Masons came from the most prestigious and highest-paying occupations. The majority (more than 60 percent) were merchants, responsible for the colonies' rapid commercial development. Professionals—including lawyers, government officials, physicians, and a few ministers—made up the second-largest group (14.4 percent in Boston and 21.2 percent in Philadelphia). The number of eighteenth-century lawyers and government officials grew in tandem with urban development and the increase of imperial authority. Less than 10 percent of Boston's and Philadelphia's Masons were artisans, and most of these worked at high-end crafts, such as clockmaking and silversmithing, which brought them into sustained contact with gentlemen.[13]

Meeting in genteel taverns apart from the common people, going in groups to the theater, and emulating the stylish new houses, dress, and manners of their British counterparts, Freemasons participated in a "refinement of America" that brought European styles and customs to the upper reaches of eighteenth-century American society. The new social code was signaled in such words as *polite, civil,* and *urbane* and manifest in the appearance of large, richly furnished homes with central staircases and many rooms. Along with these elegant houses came balls, tea parties, and formal entertainments where men and women of similar background and breeding met to display the dress, manners, and speech characteristic of the English upper class.[14] Masons displayed such genteel behavior in their studied arrivals and exits from church and in the formal, self-conscious displays of their processions. Within these elegant homes and well-appointed taverns, new private societies began to emerge. Variously devoted to literature, the arts, theater, or just good eating and free conversation, "polite" societies helped to create common bonds among the elite. What David S. Shields has described as a nascent public sphere of free conversation among relative equals first emerged in America among these societies in emulation of similar developments in England.[15]

The social ideals and organization of Freemasonry contributed to this great project of civility that enabled men of varied ranks and callings to set aside their differences and join together in polite conversation and common activities. More than an exclusive club within polite society, however, Freemasonry was the most successful colonial organization in crossing political, ethnic, and religious boundaries among leading affluent white men. By creating no formal membership barriers based on religion or politics, the colonial brotherhood helped buffer the divisive forces that threatened the social order of the new commercial centers. Moreover, in embracing freedom of thought and religious toleration yet requiring faith, the fraternity contributed to the rational religious discourse of the emerging public sphere. At the same time, by continuing to include elements of its pre-Christian past, Freemasonry participated in the broader supernatural world that encompassed colonial religious life. Before looking more closely at colonial American Freemasonry, a review of the origins and multiple meanings of the society prior to its arrival in America is necessary for understanding its beliefs and practices as they were called on, transformed, and created anew in the fraternity's journey through American culture.

ENGLISH ORIGINS

When Freemasonry first came to America from England, in 1733, it had already taken on the character of a noblemen's club while retaining to some degree the traditional features of a medieval institution connected to an artisan culture. The modern history of the society begins with the establishment of the premier Grand Lodge of England, in 1717. By this time the membership of Masonic lodges had shifted decisively from "operative" tradesmen skilled in the craft of masonry to "non-operative," "accepted," "admitted," or "speculative" noblemen and gentry.[16] Abandoning the regulation of the building trade, the new Masonic fraternity now met in taverns and contributed to articulating the ideas of the English Enlightenment. Members of the Royal Society, created to foster the new sciences, played a key role in organizing the modern fraternity and accounted for more than one-quarter of lodge membership in its first decade.[17] At the same time, Freemasonry retained myths of origin and secret rituals of initiation. To understand the fraternity's multiple meanings, it is necessary to briefly consider its early history.

The craft guild of Freemasonry began in Britain around the time of the Norman Conquest (1066), when kings, nobles, and church leaders embarked on building stone castles and cathedrals.[18] As fully qualified craftsmen free to enjoy the rights and privileges of the guild, masons were referred to as freemasons, much as other skilled tradesmen were sometimes called, for example, free carpenters or men granted the rights of citizenship in a town were called freemen.[19] Like the members of other guilds, freemasons had a mythical history stressing the antiquity and importance of their craft, held banquets on their fraternity's patron saint's day, initiated new members into their fictive brotherhood, and limited entry to the trade to men who had been properly trained in its mysteries, its skills and techniques.

The constitutions and ordinances from London's fourteenth- and fifteenth-century Mason's Company describe a hierarchical organization of apprentices and master craftsmen who retained a distinctive clothing (apron and gloves) and religious practice. Persons admitted to the fellowship were "to be clad in one clothing . . . convenient to their powers and degrees" and were to wear it every year when attending Mass on the Feast of the Four Crowned Martyrs, after which they were to have dinner or "honest" recreation. This feast day honored the martyrdom of four Roman stoneworkers killed by Diocletian for refusing to abandon Christianity.[20] Other masonic guilds were known to celebrate the feast day of Saint John the Evangelist or Saint John the Baptist.[21] All versions of the company's constitutions, moreover, contained a provision demanding secrecy, such as the following: "You shall keep secret the obscure and intricate parts of the science, not disclosing them to any but such as study and use the same."[22] These were trade or technical secrets intended to enforce membership requirements against the growing number of competitors in a time of building expansion.

Although nearly all early modern trades asserted high standing and great antiquity, the fact that masons created the vast stone cathedrals, arguably the most awe-inspiring human works in the Middle Ages, distinguished their claims from those of other medieval craftsmen. Unlike workers whose tools and products tied them to a local market, the masons involved in such large-scale projects were drawn from a relatively wide region. Assembling this regional labor force on a local work site necessitated the drawing up of detailed rules that would help to create shared values and standards of behavior both on and off the job. Among other things, these codes of conduct stipulated how masons should treat one another. For example, their requirements included not taking work from others or underpaying fellow masons, choosing only suitable persons to be apprentices, and respecting confidences and trade secrets.[23]

In the available manuscript constitutions, these charges follow an elaborate legendary history of the guild that traces the origin of masonry to geometry—the source of all knowledge. In the fourteenth and fifteenth centuries, this mythical prehistory was intended to be read out or recited at meetings, especially when entrants were admitted to the craft. The manuscripts open with brief invocations or prayers addressed to God the Father, the Son, and the Holy Ghost. The narrator then characteristically launches into the subject by presenting the "worthy Craft of Masonry" as rooted in "Geometrye," which is the foundation of "the seven Liberall Sciences." The origins of geometry are then traced to the children of Lamech, mentioned in Genesis. The founder of geometry was Jabel, Lamech's son who, fearing God's punishment, inscribed his discovery on stone pillars that could survive fire or flood. After the Great Flood, Hemarynes (Hermes), a great-grandson of Noah, discovered the pillars and from them retaught the sciences to humanity. Next, Abraham and his wife Sarah went to Egypt and taught the seven sciences to the Egyptians, including Euclid. Euclid then instructed King David during the latter's sojourn in Egypt. On his return to the Holy Land, David gave these charges to the masons who began building the Jerusalem Temple, whose construction continued under his son Solomon. Solomon sent for workers from other countries, whom he charged to spread the craft to France and England (later rites of initiation took place in an allegorical Solomon's Temple). Eventually, it was said, the

English king Edwin compiled both this prehistory and the guild's codes of conduct, and his books became the constitutions themselves.[24]

In the seventeenth century, Scottish masons working from these constitutions created catechisms for their rituals of identification and initiation, which collectively became known as the Mason Word. Although it was customary for craft guilds to maintain constitutions detailing their rules and legendary histories, masons not only had extensive codes of conduct and an elaborate legendary history but also, unlike other guilds, evolved an extensive ritual life. Again, this may have been due to the prominence of the craft and the need to guard trade secrets among a regional labor force. The early Scottish catechisms dealt with the admission of candidates to the two grades of mason known as Entered Apprentice and Fellow Craft. These rites probably existed prior to that time and may have been created out of earlier practices of the craft.[25] Though fragmentary and diverse in their contents, the surviving catechisms usually include questions and answers to ascertain the identity of another craftsman, culminating in the recognition of a secret or words, and rites of initiation that instructed the two grades of masons in the secrets of the Word.[26]

Both rites of initiation were said to involve a "great many ceremonies," which the surviving catechisms keep largely hidden from outsiders' view. Emphasizing secrecy, the Entered Apprentice investiture involved the recitation of the craft's legendary history, while the Fellow Craft rite explained the significance of the letter G—for both *geometry* and *God*—and its place in the Temple of Solomon. The ceremonies took place within the Mason's lodge, which could be their guild, their workplace, or the setting for their ritual return to ancient Egypt.[27] Though the scattered evidence of the catechisms does not give a clear picture of the early rites, the "work" to which the master put the masons in the lodge presumably symbolized the building of the temple. Among religious people of that time, "building the Temple" meant creating the kingdom of God.[28] Post-Reformation influences also appear to be present, in the use of the singular form of *word*. Scotland's new Calvinist churches emphasized the truth of the "Word of God" as revealed in scripture. Scripture itself was often referred to as "the Word." Such phrases as "in the beginning was the Word" invoked powerful sentiments of mystery and ultimate truth. In the Wisdom of Solomon, a favorite among Masons, "God made all things by his Word, and his Word killed all unbelievers."[29]

References to building the temple and the Mason Word, David Stevenson has suggested, also intimate that the rituals of seventeenth-century

Scottish Freemasonry may have emerged partly as a reaction to some of the changes that the coming of Protestantism brought to Scotland. As is well known, the Reformation fundamentally changed Christian religious beliefs and practices. Catholicism sanctifies life's passage with seven sacramental rituals that give social significance to the stages of life's journey. Protestantism shifts the emphasis from the ritualization of life's journey to particular beliefs and individual faith. Compared to the richness of Catholic ritual life, the practices of the new Protestant churches were barren. This was particularly true in Scotland, where there was a decisive break with the pageantry of the old church. By suddenly eliminating so much of the ritual and spectacle of the Catholic Church, the Scottish Reformation of 1560 may have created a profound sense of loss in many people.[30]

It is noteworthy, then, that the appearance of the Mason Word in Scotland coincided with the Calvinist Church's destruction of the religious aspect of trade guilds. For members of trade guilds, the pageantry and processions that marked the feast days of their organizations' patron saints were the high points of the year. The Protestant leader John Knox sneered at the "priests, friars, canons, and rotten Papists, with tabors and trumpets, banners and bagpipes," who processed through Edinburgh in 1558 on Saint Giles's Day. Reformation, in one respect, meant the suppression of the guilds' religious practices. Though their members continued to attend church in groups and begin meetings with short prayers, the guilds no longer participated in the religious festivals of the Christian year nor maintained altars dedicated to their saints. This reaction against ceremony may have contributed to the counterreaction of the majority of Edinburgh's leading craftsmen, who steadfastly remained Catholic following the 1560 Reformation. It is probably more than a coincidence, moreover, that within two generations an elaborate pageantry and ritual life emerged within Scottish Masonry.[31]

Aside from the innovations of the Mason Word, by the seventeenth century, secrecy was increasingly associated with the Scottish lodge. This was partly a legacy of the craft's medieval past, when it kept the mysteries of its operative trade to itself, but also reinforced by the late Renaissance passion for ancient, esoteric truth.[32] Though belief in the power of occult knowledge was declining by the eighteenth century, many educated Britons still believed that ancient mysteries might be retrieved and so reveal God's deeper truth.

It was from within the broader environment of hermeticism and Rosicrucianism that nontradesmen started to seek out the Masonic guilds.

Hermeticism began with the interweaving of metallurgical traditions and ideas gleaned from Gnosticism, Platonism, and Egyptian theology in Greco-Roman Egypt. Its magical practices were believed to have the power to turn base metals into gold and mere humans into immortals. The Renaissance recovery of ancient texts led to a new exploration of the supposed revelations of the divine being Hermes. Combining hermeticism with tales of an occult brotherhood, Rosicrucianism sparked the search for secret tablets, originally discovered in the tomb of the mystic Christian Rosencreutz, whose inscriptions revealed ancient mysteries.[33] Early seventeenth-century Scottish Masons, in particular one William Schaw, the master of the king's works, were imbued with the reforming and mystical hermeticism of the late Renaissance. Schaw was an intimate of the Stuart court of the 1590s, to which the Renaissance hermeticist Giordano Bruno carried the ancient wisdom. Schaw, in turn, brought hermeticism to the lodges of the 1590s.[34] The years around 1600 saw the peak of hermetic striving for spiritual rebirth based on secret knowledge and mystical societies. This was also the time when the legendary history and hidden ritual practices of Freemasonry began attracting large numbers of nonmasons.

What first drew them were statements contained in the old manuscript constitutions.[35] The legendary histories traced Masonic origins to both the author of Biblical wisdom, Solomon, and the source of occult knowledge, Hermes. Furthermore, like the ancients, the craft guild transmitted its knowledge not through books but through symbolic language and secret ceremonies. For late sixteenth- and early seventeenth-century Britons seeking primeval wisdom and occult knowledge, Masonic statements and ceremonies suggested a means of entry into the esoteric truths of the ancients. Elias Ashmole and Sir Robert Moray were among the first nonmasons initiated into the English and Scottish lodges. Ashmole, who was interested in hermeticism and the Rosicrucian brotherhood, joined and eventually became the master of his Edinburgh lodge. A few years later, in 1646, Moray, who had a great interest in alchemy and number mysticism, was admitted to a lodge at Warrington, Lancashire. Both men were founding members of the new scientific organization, the Royal Society.[36]

The late Renaissance glorification of mathematics and architecture similarly attracted men interested in planning and design. Renaissance thought associated architecture with the articulation of moral values, in the sense that buildings give concrete expression to society's ideas about how to construct social life.[37] For the fraternity, economic reasons played a role in the admission of nonmasons. As early as the 1670s, lodges in Scotland and England were offering "honorary" membership in their "ancient" society to prosperous gentlemen willing to offer infusions of capital for renovations and other building projects. Gradually, then, the guild evolved into a society that retained something of the old while adding the interests and values of the higher classes of men who eventually came to dominate it.[38]

Some of the men behind the founding of the modern Grand Lodge, in 1717, reflected their time of cultural change, when the Enlightenment emphasis on order, rationality, and science existed within an older longing for the deeper truths of ancient knowledge. William Stukeley, an early lodge master, was a fellow of the Royal Society, a member of its council, and a censor of the College of Physicians. He was also an Anglican priest, a cofounder of the Society of Antiquaries of London, and so deeply drawn to the stone circles of Stonehenge that he created his own "temple of the Druids." This occult yearning drew Stukeley to the "Mysterys of masonry, suspecting it to be the remains of the mysterys of the antients."[39] Similarly drawn to both Enlightenment reason and primeval truth was the scientist Sir Isaac Newton, whom Stukeley claimed as a "countryman" and a friend.[40] Newton's *Principia*, while establishing the foundations for later mechanistic science, also asserted that all of its discoveries could be found among the mysteries of occult knowledge and biblical wisdom.[41] This mixing of traditions was characteristic not only of the London circles surrounding Newton and his Masonic friends but of the larger Enlightenment project too.

The seeming anomaly of Enlightenment thinkers embracing ancient wisdom can be explained by keeping in mind that Enlightenment thought emerged within older cosmic and theological understandings of the world. The Enlightenment effort to identify a finite field of inquiry accessible to the human mind took for granted that a larger field of knowledge lay outside human investigation. John Locke's pivotal *Essay Concerning Human Understanding* sought to carve out from this larger metaphysical and divine external world an area limited to only that which the human mind can know. What some have identified as the darker side of the "modern," "rational" Enlightenment and worked to explain away as the residue of earlier, magical thinking was in fact the larger epistemological world that it inhabited. Galileo's battle against the church is one obvious example of the new way of thinking existing within an older paradigm. Rather than a progressive movement of order, reason, and science that gradually replaced ancient forms of knowledge, the evolution of modern thought is better characterized as shifting between the two opposing impulses of modern reason and ancient wisdom. The persistence of "ancient," "primitive," and "anti-modernist" thought within and beyond the American Masonic fraternity, as we shall see, is not an anomaly to be explained away but rather a reflection of the Enlightenment's failure to completely eclipse earlier metaphysical and divine ways of understanding the place of human beings in the world.[42]

Despite the mixing of new and old knowledge among Newton and the Masons of his generation, the men who created modern Freemasonry came from the next generation, of Newton's followers, and emphasized modern science over ancient mysteries. These included such men as Jean-Théophile Desaguliers, a Huguenot refugee trained in Newtonian science at Oxford who took holy orders in the Church of England and served as the grand master of the Grand Lodge in 1719.[43] Unlike Newton, Desaguliers and his brothers lived in an increasingly cosmopolitan London society, where enlightened thinking and polite social practices led to the creation of a new form of Masonic brotherhood.

The social reasons for the popularity of modern Freemasonry are rooted in large transformations that began in London and reshaped social relations. In the eighteenth century, the city experienced growing social diversity and a threefold increase in population. In this milieu, nobles, gentry, craftsmen, and strangers moved about without the communal or kinship bonds of earlier village life. In response to this anomie, clubs rapidly appeared, providing a means of re-creating the intimacy of local bonds by bringing gentlemen and aristocrats together in private tavern rooms for feasting, discussion, and singing. Lodge meetings, like those of these clubs, often took place amid the food and drink of a private tavern, where members "clubbed" together to cover the expenses.[44]

The new perception of a natural harmony among the members of this redefined social world aided this easy mixing of nobles, gentry, merchants, professionals, and master tradesmen. By the early eighteenth century, Thomas Hobbes's despairing vision of a selfish humanity that only coercion could control was losing its power. He produced his description of the Great Chain of Being, in which all of society was ranked and each level was in charge of those below and obeyed those above, amid the conflicts of the mid-seventeenth-century Civil War, but the concept no longer worked in a society driven by commercialization and torn by political and religious dissent.[45] The development of urban centers, a widening market, and population growth and movement made it increasingly difficult for the monarchy to assert control over the merchants, noblemen, and professionals of the new protocapitalist order. As early as the 1640s, the development of printing allowed for the circulation of previously secret political petitions and the beginnings of public debate.[46] Following the Glorious Revolution of 1688–89, the establishment of the first cabinet government marked a new stage in the development of the state's parliamentary authority. At the same time, the growing Deist movement and its rejection of the power of revelation increasingly countered High Church Anglican demands for religious obedience and the suppression of dissent. Where Hobbes had asserted that only complete submission to authority would avert conflict, the Third Earl of Shaftesbury and other progressive social theorists saw in human nature a "benevolence" that knit society together through sympathy and a natural desire for community.[47] Like the new world of Newtonian science, the new society could rely on simple and natural processes to work.

In 1709, Shaftesbury traced the emergence of this sentiment of benevolence to what he termed "private society." He composed his treatise in "defence" of the "liberty of the Club" as a letter to a friend of "court breeding." As recently as 1668, Charles II had sought unsuccessfully to outlaw English coffeehouses, for their association with free thought and political debate. Against the state-controlled ritualistic behavior of the royal court, which sought to fix an authoritarian and court-centered hierarchy of power, Shaftesbury argued for the "polite" behavior of the new private clubs, which were founded on the new freedom of expression.[48] "All politeness," as he put it, "is owing to liberty." Against the "temper of the pedagogue," which "suits not with the Age," the English nobleman endorsed the sociability of the club, where prevailed "a freedom of raillery, a liberty in decent language to question everything, and an allowance of unravelling or refuting any argument, without offence to the arguer." Through this new polite behavior, club members were able to "polish one another, and rub off our corners and rough sides by a force of amicable collision," resulting in a greater virtue. Moreover, by titling his treatise "An Essay on the Freedom of Wit and Humour," Shaftesbury made clear that these attributes, as well as theatricality and satire, had the serious purpose of enabling the expression of ideas under the imposition of the authority of church or state: "If men are forbid to speak their minds seriously on certain subjects, they will do it ironically. If they are forbid to speak at all upon such subjects, or if they find it really dangerous to do so; they will then redouble their disguise, involve themselves in mysteriousness, and talk so as hardly to be understood, or at least not plainly interpreted, by those who are dispos'd to do 'em a mischief." These "speculative conversations," Shaftesbury further warned, could take place only with the "mutual esteem" of "gentlemen and friends."[49] More coercive forms of social control would be necessary to tame the common people.

By the early eighteenth century, professionals and noblemen were employing the polite behavior and free conversation of private societies to forge a common culture, differentiating themselves from the lower orders. Modern Masonry was an expression of this new elite social vision. The fraternity drew its members from the growing middling ranks of men who had separated themselves from the rest of society through their professional training, education, or greater wealth yet were not among the landed gentry or nobility.[50] Its 1723 constitution offered a new way of imagining social relationships, by seeking to inspire "true friendship among persons that must else have remain'd at perpetual Distance." Unlike the members of a Hobbesian hierarchical society, Masons were to treat one another as equals. Holding their society together was not the coercive power of a patriarch but rather the natural benevolence of brothers. "All preferment among Masons," the new constitution said, "is grounded upon real worth and personal merit alone."[51]

Such equality, however, was reserved for gentlemen, men who could afford the fraternity's special clothing and expensive fees, and deference continued to be given to nobles. In 1721, "great Joy at the happy Prospect of being again patronized by noble Grand Masters, as in the Prosperous Times of Freemasonry," met the election of the Duke of Montagu to this post.[52] A revision of the guild's mythic history that posthumously granted the title of grand master to England's kings reinforced such "memories" of olden times. As with its attraction to both the new science and occult knowledge, the modern fraternity looked forward while retaining something old.

The constitution of 1723 elaborated the new vision of the fraternity and remained, throughout the eighteenth century, the document to which all official lodges subscribed. Written by the Scots Presbyterian clergyman James Anderson, it "digested" the older charges in what he called a "new and better method."[53] Complaining of "gross Errors" in the legendary histories, Anderson updated the list of former grand masters to include not only the kings of England, thereby linking its political history with the development of Freemasonry, but also Augustus Caesar.[54] The kings included the first Stuart king of England, James I, who imported the Augustan style of architecture from Renaissance Italy. Instead of the medieval architecture celebrated in the old constitutions, which brought to mind the now unfashionable pursuit of occult wisdom, the 1723 history heralds Augustan aesthetics, which suggested the order and symmetry of the Newtonian universe and the new Enlightenment social theory.[55]

Similarly, the new constitution transformed the guild's instructions on religion and politics. Previous constitutions began by invoking the Trinity and contained the injunction that masons shall be obedient to God and the Holy Church. Anderson instead makes no specifically Christian belief obligatory. "A Mason is oblig'd, by his Tenure, to obey the moral law; and if he rightly understands the Art, he will never be a stupid Atheist nor an irreligious Libertine."[56] Taking the latitudinarian view shared by moderate Anglican priests and Protestant dissenters, Anderson pledged the fraternity to a position midway between a parochial High Church Anglicanism and an unbelieving natural religion.[57] In doing so, he stepped away from his Presbyterian convictions and his recent sermons decrying both Deists and Unitarians.[58] No longer obligated by their fraternity to submit to the religion of the nation, Masons were told to keep "their particular Opinions to themselves" while affirming a common belief in the transcendent.[59] By encouraging its members to step outside their religious convictions, the new fraternity proclaimed a religious harmony among all men while prescribing very little. Although the constitutions' call for men of "whatever Denominations or Persuasions" to join the fraternity suggests that this "religious harmony" was intended to encompass no more than doctrinal differences among Christians, as early as 1731, Masonry's formerly obedient servants of "the Church" had admitted Jews into their fellowship.[60]

Political involvement was similarly open. Previous constitutions commanded all masons to "bee true men to the Kinge without any treason or falsehood."[61] Now, aside from an agreement to be "a peaceable Subject to the Civil Powers," no political position was required.[62] At the same time, Whig party leaders were among the early members of the modern fraternity, and Anderson's history reflected their advocacy of a strong constitution and court-centered government.[63] Similarly, he, Desaguliers, and their brothers established a Grand Lodge governed by rules and statutes requiring all lodge members to submit to the authority of their elected officers and all lodges to pledge their loyalty to the Grand Lodge.[64] Neither wholly subordinate subjects of a king nor dangerously radical liberals, the members of the new fraternity submitted to its constitutional government, which embraced social stability while celebrating the brotherhood as a model for a well-ordered, cooperative society.

Presenting itself as a harbinger of the new social vision, the fraternity allowed its members considerable latitude in their political and religious convictions. As Shaftesbury argued, the genius of the private club was that it kept a playful distance from the solemn orthodoxies of state and church.[65] Meeting in the King's Arms, the Apple Tree, and other upscale London taverns, lodge members enjoyed long evenings of ritual toasts, "sumptuous" feasts, "innocent mirth," entertaining orations, and the business of welcoming "noblemen and gentlemen of the first rank" into their order.[66] At the same time, by creating a constitutional society that its members could alter through majority vote, the modern fraternity experimented with the reformation of civil society. It further enhanced its progressive image by embracing the new, liberal spirit of religious toleration. Although popular Newtonianism, with its frequent references to God as the Universal Architect, came to dominate Masonic rhetoric, amid the secrecy of the lodge, members were free to entertain a variety of spiritual perspectives. Like the antiquarian William Stukeley, who said that he entered the fraternity in search of "the remains of the mysterys of the antients," a wide array of Druids, Deists, Jews, Protestants, and Catholics were members of the English fraternity. On the whole, however, as participants in the liberalizing mainstream of early eighteenth-century English society, the gentlemen and nobles of Freemasonry reinforced the progressive ideals of constitutional monarchy and religious toleration.

COLONIAL AMERICAN FREEMASONRY

The Freemasonry that came to America in the 1730s brought this extensive collection of cultural baggage, which the encounter with local culture reworked and transformed. Between the 1730s and the 1760s, Masonic lodges were one of a variety of "polite" societies that formed in America's coastal cities. These private clubs included Saint Andrew's, Saint George's, and other British immigrant societies; the Beefsteak Society, the Calve's Head Club, and other eating clubs; various literary, theatrical, and philosophical societies; and predominantly female salons and tea tables. Dedicated to the pleasures of amiable conversation, the arts, and good eating, these societies promoted the common interests of relative strangers in the new public meeting spaces of taverns, coffeehouses, and well-appointed homes. At a time when urban social relations were moving beyond the traditional ties of family, ethnicity, church, and local community, Freemasonry was among the new social forms that anticipated the rise of the American middle class.[67]

Since 1990, several colonial historians have adopted and refined Jürgen Habermas's theoretical framework of the public sphere to explain these social developments in America while not paying particular attention to religious life. Michael Warner's *The Letters of the Republic* (1990) makes the case for the significance of an emerging print media in the establishment of a secular eighteenth-century public sphere. He holds that through a burgeoning array of newspapers, pamphlets, and broadsides, print was both a carrier and an expression of a new republican ideology. David Conroy's study of taverns in eighteenth-century Massachusetts, *In Public Houses* (1995), investigates their role in the creation of secular public space. In *Civil Tongues and Polite Letters* (1997), David S. Shields argues that colonial polite societies were vehicles for producing horizontal relationships among the elite.[68] Taken together, these books suggest that a new language of secular discourse was taking hold through print and the new societies. I argue—in contrast to the secular focus of these studies, a tendency characteristic of Habermas's European public sphere—that debates over religious ideas suffused the public sphere that emerged in America by the 1740s.[69] The late colonial period saw an intermingling of secular and religious discourse.

Although Habermas held that the totalizing worldview of premodern religion stood in an inverse relationship with rational criticism, whereby religion must decline if enlightenment were to progress, his theoretical framework of an exclusively rational public sphere does not sufficiently acknowledge the pervasive presence of religion in the colonial world. There, unlike in England, the metaphysical authority of the monarchy was an ocean away.[70] Instead, Reformed Protestant and Anglican establishments held varying degrees of religious authority across the colonies. A flexible Calvinism that was capable of including both the orthodox and the revivalist sides of the Great Awakening informed most eighteenth-century Christianity.[71] At one of its extremes was a small minority of Catholics, and at the other the various advocates of Enlightenment religion, while all stood apart from Native American religions and the African gods of eighteenth-century slaves.[72] Within this broad religious culture, moreover, magical beliefs and practices, some older than Christianity, persisted.

Not only was British metaphysical authority an ocean away, but so too was the English Parliament. Thus colonial assemblies and especially local governments shaped political society. As David D. Hall has argued, rather than cohesively united by the absolute authority of the monarchy, religious and political authority in colonial America were "remarkably local and decentralized." Moreover, unlike England, eighteenth-century America had no "broad distribution of printed matter." As a result, its "social and political criticism were never fully differentiated from the language and practices of radical Protestantism."[73]

Timothy H. Breen first described this "religious public sphere" as "an intellectual space in which allegedly disinterested writers employing their reason in the name of the people might criticize and shape popular religious assumptions."[74] Beginning with the controversies that came to be known as the First Great Awakening, Americans engaged in public, print debates over religious matters. Frank Lambert has argued that the itinerant evangelist George Whitefield initiated these disputes by demanding that the forum for religious controversy be moved from the private, clerically controlled pulpit to the public arena of print, where literate men and women could make reasoned judgments and arguments.[75] Accusations that the upstart evangelicals spoke in uncouth language while employing rhetoric and emotion rather than reason resulted in their making efforts to dispute in the language and reasoned logic of polite society.[76] In moving from the private expression of religious convictions to public, printed efforts to persuade readers of the truth of their beliefs, writers on all sides of the issue learned to frame their arguments to appeal to the common sense of their readers. As the Boston antirevivalist John Caldwell warned, "Understand with your own Understanding; see Evidence before ye believe or judge."[77] Moreover, this paralleled ongoing secular debates over bank fraud and related issues, and in both cases, more and more colonial Americans adapted to polite society's insistence that individuals make informed, well-reasoned decisions in an expanding marketplace of ideas.[78]

Whatever the character and significance of the American public sphere, it first appeared among the less than 5 percent of the population that lived in coastal cities.[79] By the early eighteenth century, every major port city had at least one coffeehouse or tavern, which served as nexuses for extra-local news and information and, like elegant homes, a site for the new sociability. Within the decorum of this nascent polite society, strangers met, circulated manuscripts and published materials, engaged in and discussed literature and the arts, and entertained alternative visions of social and religious life. Gradually, a small but influential number of colonial elites fashioned a new and experimental realm of social life where they worked to bridge differences through civility and congenial conversation and find common cause in a wide variety of pursuits. Sheer joy, entertainment, and the members' delight in one another's company, David S. Shields has argued, were as much the purpose of these societies as any other motive. However, while providing a common ground of private pleasures for a coalescing upper class, they foreshadowed, with their multiple forms of communication and social relations, the emerging public.[80] By the 1760s, this congenial realm of elegance and polish gave way to the sober reason and morality of a rapidly expanding public sphere, in which the new print media joined growing numbers of citizens in dialogue over questions surrounding revolutionary social change.

Freemasonry established its first American lodge, in Philadelphia in 1733, within the social and cultural milieu of polite society. By the 1740s, Philadelphia and the similarly old and large urban centers of Boston and New York had several lodges, while inland seaports founded their first lodges in the following decades (Albany's, for instance, in the 1760s). Masonic membership was a means of entry into polite society. Lodge meetings were held in the elegant private rooms of upscale taverns, where gentleman habitually gathered for dinners and entertainment. Deliberately expensive fees attracted the "man of merit" while discouraging "those of mean Spirits, and narrow, or Incumber'd Fortunes."[81] Those who were "well known" by the brothers were immediately admitted to candidacy; others were required to wait one month while "proper inquiry" was made into their character and behavior. James Anderson's *Constitutions* instructed lodge members to "avoid all slandering and backbiting and talking disrespectfully of a person" and instead to treat one another "with much courtesy." Individual lodges required members to appear in "decent cloathing" and refrain from obscene language, excessive drink, and indecent behavior. They were to participate in lodge rituals with the utmost "solemnity" and offer the master of the lodge "due reverence." An escalating series of punishments, beginning with fines and culminating in banishment, met infractions of this gentlemanly code.[82] Though Freemasonry was a society with secrets, entry into the fraternity was intended not as a withdrawal into private life but as an opportunity for gentlemen to demonstrate and refine the social manners of the upper class.

Freemasonry also helped to shape the structure and discourse of the emerging public sphere. In its efforts to harmonize the divisive forces of nationality, religion, and politics, the fraternity helped to create a new social order that brought together leading affluent white men of different ethnic and religious backgrounds. The social philosophy and organization of Freemasonry were part of the "new civility," which enabled persons of different ranks, callings, origins, and occupations to put aside their differences and engage in congenial communication and common activities. The fraternity's encouragement of free thought and religious toleration yet requirement of faith, moreover, contributed to the rational religious discourse of the emerging public sphere. Civility involved not only improved taste and manners but also a mutual tolerance and open-mindedness that encouraged individuals to employ reason and evidence to arrive at their religious convictions. At the same time, Masonic Christianity shared with much of the colonial religious world a faith laced with magical and mystical elements of archaic origin. Amid its movement toward Enlightenment forms and ideals, the brotherhood maintained elements of its ancient past.

FREEMASONRY IN COLONIAL ALBANY

The early history of the first Masonic lodges in Albany, New York, provides a window onto the emergence of this community-wide organization. Prior to the 1760s, Albany was an overwhelmingly Dutch settlement over whose economic, social, and political life merchant family networks maintained control. Arising in vertical relationship to the town's horizontal social order were those inhabitants who mediated between the largely homogeneous town and the increasingly heterogeneous provincial population.[83] Most of the inhabitants traced their origins to the arrival of a large group of Dutch settlers in the 1660s, whose descendants primarily determined the beliefs and practices of the town through the 1760s. Beginning with the English takeover of the Netherlands' colony as part of the Glorious Revolution of 1688, however, members of the Schuyler and Cuyler families, among others, took the lead in learning the English language and mediating between the town and extralocal commercial and political interests. They and others in the province "who brought with them the French and English languages, soon acquired a sway over their less enlightened fellow settlers."[84]

Although polite society barely took hold in Albany (which had no institutionalized private societies of any description prior to establishment of the Masonic lodge in the 1760s), Anne Grant's *Memoirs of an*

American Lady traces its emergence.[85] Grant's recollections of her child-hood in the Albany of the 1760s portray colonial Dutch Albanians as "children of nature" who, unfortunately, lacked "good breeding." In conversation, for example, they were "limited in regard to subjects." Of the "substantial luxuries of the table . . . they knew little." Dominating the town's moral framework was the Dutch Reformed church, which stood at its center and counted nearly all of the townspeople as members. Grant observes that public worship was often "mechanical," though the townspeople never doubted the "great truths of revelation."[86]

Indeed, participation in the beliefs and practices of Reformed Calvin-ism was the most enduring collective social action of the colonial Dutch community. Estate inventories of Albany's Dutch householders reveal catechisms written by the town's ministers, the Bible, and little other reading material. As late as 1771, the town's persistent old ways included the occasional and rudimentary schooling of children; the lack of newspapers with knowledge of the outside world; and a determina-tion to keep out of town those who might undermine its way of life.[87] Though certainly not "elegant and polished," Grant concluded, the Albany Dutch "were at least easy and independent."[88]

Providing the leaven of polite society in Albany were the Schuylers and several other interrelated "inhabitants of the upper settlement," who once a year went to New York City. There, "at a very early period a bet-ter style of manners and polish prevailed . . . than in any of the neighbor-ing provinces." This "pleasing and intelligent society" was most in evi-dence around the British governor, where "a kind of a little court kept." Grant favorably describes Sir Henry Moore as a "show governor" whose "gay, good natured, and well bred, affable and courteous" demeanor seemed primarily intended "to keep the governed in good humor." The government house was the scene of frequent "festivities and weekly con-certs." Within this circle, Grant describes the Schuylers and other leading Albany families as "conscientious exiles," allied through intermarriage and upbringing to the "primitive" Albany settlers yet committed to the "liberality of mind and manners which so distinguished them from the less enlightened inhabitants of their native city." Grant praises Catalina Schuyler, the matron of the Albany Schuyler home, for the "singular merit" of being able to move between "this comparatively refined soci-ety" and "the homely good sense and primitive manners of her fellow citizens at Albany, free from fastidiousness and disgust."[89]

The locus for polite society in Albany and the site of an emerging public sphere was the Schuyler home, called the Flatts, which was a few miles outside town. The house was "an academy for the best morals and manners." In 1709, Philip Schuyler, Catalina's husband, had returned from London with a small library of newspapers and books that were apparently read throughout the extended family. Catalina was said to begin and end each day with Scripture and spend no less than several hours in "light reading, essays, biography, poetry, etc." Under the supervision of Catalina and Philip, the family hosted meetings with provincial leaders, strategy sessions with British army officers, and assemblies where peace treaties or alliances were worked out with various nations. In these endeavors, Grant recalled, the Schuylers pointedly mixed "serious and important counsels with convivial cheerfulness, and domestic ease and familiarity." Dinner parties regularly included the family, close friends, visitors "of worth or talent," military guests, and "friendless travelers." The talk around the table was "always rational, generally instructive, and often cheerful." Frequently a "new set of guests" arrived in the afternoon for tea. Catalina and Philip also presided over a "Lyceum" at their home, where "questions in religion and morality, too weighty for table talk, were leisurely and coolly discussed; and plans of policy and various utility arranged." The larger purpose of social life at the Flatts, Grant acutely observed, was to employ "the rays of intellect . . . to unite the jarring elements of which the community was composed, and to suggest to those who had power without experience, the means of mingling in due proportions its various materials for the public utility."[90]

Despite the incubation of polite society in the Schuyler home, as late as the 1740s, Albany remained a place where, according to the visitor and Master Mason Alexander Hamilton, "there was no variety of choise, either of company or conversation."[91] Large-scale change began in 1754 with the arrival of refugees from the French and Indian Wars, who almost doubled the town's population, from eighteen hundred to three thousand. The arrival of as many as fourteen hundred officers and soldiers, all of whom were quartered in Albany homes, followed in 1757.[92] Among these troops were officers who were "younger, and more gay," and, Grant tells us, encouraged the formation of "a sect . . . among the younger people, who seemed resolved to assume a lighter style of dress and manners, and to borrow their taste in those respects from their friends." This rustling of polite society among his younger church members "alarmed and aggrieved" Theodorus Frelinghuysen Jr., the town's Dutch minister. The eldest son of the Dutch minister who had helped begin the Great Awakening in New Jersey, Frelinghuysen focused his wrath on the manners and entertainments of the young British officers, who "were themselves a lie" and therefore deeply threatened the "truth" of Dutch life. In keeping with his Reformed Calvinist convictions, Frelinghuysen declared that those who, in the name of politeness, gave themselves over to the vainglory of fashionable display, the levity of wit, the consumption of luxurious goods, and the idleness of dancing and gaming faced the terrors of divine judgment.[93] The Common Council efforts to get rid of these invasive people, through unequal taxation and selective enforcement of laws, aided the minister's crusade.[94]

Nevertheless, a 1760s wave of Scots-Irish and English immigrants and subsequent economic growth transformed the community from an isolated trading post into a bustling commercial center. These developments provoked new economic tensions between wealthy "gentlemen" and landless poor; social and religious divisions among the town's three ethnic churches (Presbyterian, Anglican, and Dutch Reformed); and political divisions between the newcomers and the largely Dutch Common Council. Albany's two colonial lodges were the first cultural institutions outside the churches to appear in the community. What became Union Lodge in 1765 was originally a British military lodge, which had arrived with the troops quartered in the city over the winter of 1757–58. Masters Lodge was founded in 1768. The new fraternity attracted leaders from throughout the community, though it drew heavily from British newcomers.

Though more than two-thirds of Albany's prewar Masons were of British descent— including the most prominent Scots-Irish and English merchants, some of the non-Dutch members of the Common Council, and the ministers of the Presbyterian and the Anglican churches—a number of Dutch merchants, aldermen, and church members joined them. For the members of the two Reformed churches, joining the lodge, with its freedom of thought and religious toleration, meant setting aside denominational convictions. At the same time, the inclusion of Presbyterian, Anglican, and Dutch Church members in the fraternity, where only a generation earlier the Dutch had steadfastly resisted the imposition of an Anglican church on their town, was a watershed of interethnic cooperation and a harbinger of postwar interreligious fellowship. Although the more affluent and older Dutch were less willing to join the lodge than their English, Scots-Irish, and Yankee peers, Albany's Masonic fraternity was the first local society to bridge the community's ethnic and religious divisions.[95]

The membership of Albany's first Masonic lodge suggests Freemasonry's emergence as part of the town's expanding public sphere. Richard Cartwright was the master of the first lodge, which met in his tavern, the King's Arms, one of only two in town. He had been a British soldier stationed in Albany, and after completing his service, he joined its Saint Peter's Anglican Church and established his tavern. The King's Arms was a focal point for the postal service, land and lottery sales, the boarding and stabling of visitors, political meetings (including the first meeting of the Sons of Liberty), and monthly gatherings of the Masonic lodge. Entering into this largely British social setting were younger-generation Dutchmen, such as Leonard Gansevoort. Descended from one of the original Dutch families and having married up into the affluent and polite Cuyler family, Gansevoort was a Dutch Church officer and later a member of the local Committee of Correspondence. The brotherhood also welcomed men like the Scots-Irish immigrant Matthew Watson, who came to Albany in the 1760s, worked as a tailor, and became an elder of the Presbyterian church, and the Boston-born merchant John W. Wendell, who became a member of the Common Council and served as a trustee of the Presbyterian church. Despite the Calvinist convictions of their respective Dutch Reformed and Presbyterian churches, men such as Gansevoort, Watson, and Wendell entered Freemasonry in Albany. The democratizing social practices and benevolent social philosophy of the "polite" society nurtured in the Schuyler home had foreshadowed this mixing together of established British soldiers, Scots-Irish and Yankee immigrants, and the rising generation of Dutch town leaders. In 1768, the members of this newly formed brotherhood, some of whom would play key roles in the Revolutionary War, paraded their importance to the community in a Saint John's Day march from the King's Arms to Saint Peter's Church.[96]

Though Albany Masons could be found on either side of the emerging revolutionary fervor, together they displayed a heightened civic consciousness. Beginning in 1766 with the violent local reaction to the British imposition of a new tax on newsprint and continuing with the formation of the local Sons of Liberty and the later election of a Committee of Correspondence to the Continental Congress, Albany Masons held leadership positions in opposing British rule. Similar to the Masonic constitutions, the constitution of the Sons of Liberty of Albany pledged allegiance to "his most sacred Majesty King George the Third" while reserving the right to democratically elect the group's officers.[97] Prominent Dutch and British Masons, including the young Leonard Gansevoort and the alderman Peter W. Yates, were elected to the Committee of Correspondence. Yates also served as a delegate to the Continental

Congress and, after the war, become the town's most famous anti-Federalist. Members of the local lodges were similarly conspicuous in the leadership of the Albany militia and the town's Continental Army regiment. Tory sympathizers could also be found among the lodges' members. They included former British soldiers, whose lives their Masonic brothers on the Albany Commission for Detecting and Defeating Conspiracies scrutinized for Loyalist activities, most notably Richard Cartwright, the innkeeper who hosted the first local lodge meetings. He fled to Canada in 1778 after refusing to take a loyalty oath. While the majority of Albany's Masons supported the American side, most significant here is the active participation of lodge members in debates over the direction of their civil society.[98]

POLITE CHRISTIANITY

The social history of Albany's Masons offers one example of Freemasonry's widespread success in creating common ground across political and religious boundaries among elite white men. By the middle of the eighteenth century, market expansion, population growth, and non-English immigration had intensified political disputes, which the religious divisions that developed following the Great Awakening further exacerbated. Throughout the seaport towns of colonial America, Masonic lodges worked against this factionalism by including in their membership elite men of different backgrounds. One Anglican cleric and Masonic leader said, "When our MASTER CHRIST shall come again to reward his faithful Workmen and Servants; He will not ask whether we were of LUTHER or of CALVIN? Whether we *prayed* to him in White, Black, or Grey; in Purple or in Rags; in fine Linen, or in Sackcloth; in a Woollen Frock, or peradventure in a *Leather Apron*. Whatever is considered as most convenient, most in Character, most in Edification, and infringes least on Spiritual Liberty, will be admitted as good in this Café."[99] Baptists, Lutherans, Presbyterians, Quakers, Anglicans, Catholics, and even Jews, among others, were admitted to Freemasonry.[100] Although not all of the elite joined—both the Quakers of Philadelphia and the Puritans of New England were less evident among the brotherhood—no other late-colonial institution, notably political parties and Christian churches, encouraged so many white male political and religious adversaries to find common ground.

Part of the attraction of Freemasonry to the newly cosmopolitan elite was the fraternity's embrace of Enlightenment ideals of sociability and benevolence. Its belief in promoting friendship "among men that other-wise might have remained at perpetual distance" suggested that human beings naturally enjoyed one another's company because of their innate sentiments—perhaps even a sixth sense—of benevolence, what Shaftes-bury called a "moral sense."[101] What mattered most, according to John Locke's widely read *Some Thoughts Concerning Education*, was "respect and good will to all people."[102]

In setting aside religious differences in favor of "that Religion in which all Men agree," Masonic thought also resembled the latitudinar-ian movement in the Anglican Church.[103] Influential clerics sought to include a wide range of nonconformists in their fellowship by emphasiz-ing rational religion as a basis of agreement and minimizing the impor-tance of revelation. Missionaries whom the Anglican Society for the Propagation of the Gospel in Foreign Parts (SPG) sent to America were to begin instructing their charges with the principles of reason and nat-ural religion.[104] The common colonial Masonic practice of processing into an Anglican church and listening to a sermon prepared for the occasion suggests a substantial overlap in the Masonic and Anglican world views.

The Church of England was the established church in six of the orig-inal thirteen colonies and second only to New England Congregational-ism in number of churches through much of the eighteenth century. Anglicans were most heavily concentrated in the populous Chesapeake Bay provinces and the Atlantic coastal towns stretching from Port-smouth, New Hampshire, to Savannah, Georgia. There the church's welfare was assured not only by the authority of the crown, parliament, and a long tradition but also by the support of those who found in its broad and generous orthodoxy a religious home that allowed for a soci-ety with more culture and tradition than the rest of America afforded at the time. By the middle of the eighteenth century, Anglicanism, the pur-suit of knowledge, and religious toleration were commonly linked.

Colonial ministers and adherents of the Church of England believed that God habitually conveys his goodness through the proper order of society and the moral behavior of his people. The missionaries of the SPG and the books distributed by the Society for the Promotion of Christian Knowledge spread such values of the moderate English Enlightenment as free will, reasonableness, and correct moral behavior to the colonists. These placed Anglicans at odds with Congregational-ists, Presbyterians, Dutch Reformed, and other Calvinist churches, whose teachings were far less optimistic about human ability and the possibilities of individual salvation. Similarly, the Church of England's embrace of liturgy, sacraments, authority, and correct formulations of dogma resulted in tensions with the simplicity, democracy, and egalitarian spirit of the Quakers, not to mention the enthusiasm and disorder of the First Great Awakening. Obedient to God, king, and the "proper" ordering of church and society, the colonial Church of England provided American colonists with close ties to English culture, customs, and Enlightenment ideals.[105]

The agreement to worship in Anglican churches and listen to Anglican clerics on Saint John's Day suggests that many members of the colonial brotherhood were also members of the established church.[106] Trinity Church in Boston, Christ Church in Philadelphia, and the other new, grand Anglican churches, with their high steeples, organs, and rich interior decorations, were the favored sites for Masonic services. Samuel Seabury, the first American bishop, and William Smith, a rector of Christ Church, were among the many Anglican Masonic clerics who extolled the virtues of the lodge. Some, such as the Reverend Samuel Howard of Maryland, delivered the Saint John's Day sermon while serving as a lodge grand master. Others, such as Charles Inglis of New York, never joined a lodge but willingly addressed Masonic audiences.

The Saint John's Day sermons continued the medieval heritage of divine worship on patron saint's days and the Anglican custom of the charity sermon. In Britain the charity sermon was a well-established institution by the middle of the eighteenth century. Freemasons and other benevolent organizations set aside a day for these festivities, selected a popular preacher (when one could be induced to undertake the task), and supported the event by assuring a large congregation of members—and a consequently large offering for the poor, the needy, and the sick. The well-known evangelist George Whitefield preached the first American Masonic charity sermon, on June 24, 1738. "I was enabled to read prayers and preach with power before the Freemasons," he wrote in his diary, "with whom I afterward dined." Whitefield preached at Solomon's Lodge at Savannah to raise funds for an orphanage. The earliest printed Masonic sermon was Reverend Charles Brockwell's *Brotherly Love Recommended*, delivered at Christ Church, Boston, on the Festival of Saint John the Evangelist in 1749 and published the following year.[107] Brockwell, who served as "His Majesty's Chaplain in Boston," had been a Mason since 1740 and rose to senior grand warden by 1753.

The fifteen Saint John's Day sermons published prior to 1780 have a similar structure and content, emphasizing mutual love, charity, and the need for virtuous behavior. According to their preachers, the purpose of Freemasonry is to encourage human beings' innate love for others so that it extends outward in circles of mutual benevolence, transcending divisions, like those of religion, and ultimately including all of humanity. The intention of the society, Rev. Brockwell stated, is "the uniting of men in the stricter bands of love; for men, considered as social creatures, must derive their happiness from each other." Preaching after the enthusiasms of the Great Awakening, Brockwell cautioned that this love should not grow "hot or cold in our inclinations" but proceed "upon the steady principles of Reason and Religion."[108] Moreover, in contrast with those whose affections diminish according to proximity, extending to family and neighbor but rarely further afield, Freemasons enlarge the operation of their sympathy through mutual bonds. As another orator put it, "Friend, parent, neighbor first it will embrace, / Our country next, and next all human race."[109] Latitudinarian clerics of the seventeenth century also well knew this model of extending social harmony. What distinguished the society of Freemasonry was that it went beyond Christianity in joining all humanity in mutual benevolence. This "blessing of universal love" was especially needed, said the latitudinarian cleric Thomas Pollen of Newport, Rhode Island, to overcome "a monstrous diversity of religious tenets . . . a furious clashing in worldly interests, and an unchristian enmity between rival families, [that] are rending the very bowels of a society in pieces."[110]

Banding together in a brotherhood of cosmopolitan and respected gentlemen, Freemasons presented themselves as a cultivated elite coming together for the common good. Charity flowed from this benevolence and could follow an expansive path. Though the fraternity's charity was intended particularly for its members, on Saint John's Days and in times of community distress Masons extended financial aid to those in greatest need. In 1740, the Charleston fraternity gave two hundred and fifty dollars to assist the survivors of a citywide fire; on Saint John's Day in 1767, a single lodge gave one hundred pounds for the relief of New York City's poor.[111]

To differing degrees, all of the Saint John's Day ministers believed that Freemasonry was a Christian organization. John Rodgers of Berkshire County, Massachusetts, prefaced his remarks by saying that he did not know a great deal about the Masons, yet from what he had read he "presumed" they were Christians. Others, such as Brockwell, saw Jesus as the "Patron of our Society." Or, as Pollen put it: "This society . . .

follows the steps of their master Christ, whose design was in that blessed society himself instituted."[112] The common assumption was that to be a good Mason one must be a good Christian. "For what duties are mentioned in the Gospel, are not adopted in your Book of Constitutions?" argued Zabdiel Adams of Lancaster, Massachusetts. "There you are required to fear God . . . love the brotherhood, honour all men, and to submit to the government under which you live."[113]

Masons demonstrated their commitment to Christianity by carrying Bibles on gilt cushions in their processions and, on occasion, refusing to celebrate the Saint John's Day festivities without a clergyman present.[114] Moreover, virtuous action for Christians and Masons appeared to be one and the same. As "children of the same God, candidates for the same Heaven," Masons were told that it was their duty to "enlarge the narrowness of men's understandings, to smooth the roughness of their wills, and to level the unevenness of their passions."[115] Such actions measured their growth in Christ. Nevertheless, what it meant to be a Christian and what it meant to be a Mason was not always clear in colonial society, reflecting not only a confusion in the relationship between moderate Anglicanism and Freemasonry but a larger difficulty in the "polite" society in which both parties participated.

One way of investigating this confusion is to look at the tensions and accommodations between the two kinds of courtesy books that began to appear in colonial libraries and bookshops in the early eighteenth century. These widely read manuals are another indication of the spread of polite society among the elite. Instructions for youth are part of a vast literature in Western civilizations going back to classical times.[116] Books on manners and the equally popular books on morals had different origins and intents. Manners books were copies of older English and, before that, French instruction books, which were imbued with instructions for proper behavior in the courts of medieval royalty. Their purpose was to provide instruction in the cultural practices of aristocratic European society.[117] The Earl of Chesterfield's *Letters to His Son*, one of the first and most popular of these books—published in eighteen American versions prior to 1800—devoted whole chapters to such topics as "the perils of bad enunciation" and "the policy of discreet reserve" as steps in a young man's minute instruction in proper behavior in polite society. In his book, Chesterfield says little about divine punishment or God as the final judge of bad behavior, rather threatening his son with the hell of exclusion from "what is agreeable and pleasing in society."[118] In contrast, books on morals have a Christian heritage.

Richard Allestree's *The Whole Duty of Man*, which went through one hundred editions in as many years, is divided into chapters to be read aloud every Sunday.[119] It taught young people the virtues associated with a proper Christian upbringing: submission to God, obedience to parents, pure thoughts, continual acts of piety and charity. Acting in a manner pleasing to society and the danger of ridicule for not doing so have no place in it. As Richard Bushman has argued, these two types of guidebooks "stood apart from one another," leaving the reader to resolve the disparities. In practice, the eighteenth-century elite appear to have created a common moral system from them. At times, as with *The School of Good Manners*, the two approaches were literally bound together into a single book.[120] For the colonial gentry, good manners expressed a Christian regard for the happiness of others. At the same time, as polite Christians, they regulated their piety as carefully as their bodies, to restrain, for example, the emotional excesses of evangelical religion.

In their Saint John's Day sermons, Anglican clergymen urged this polite model of Christian virtue on the gathered congregations of Freemasons. To them, good breeding entered into the assessment of proper Christian behavior. By cultivating a "courteous, pitiful, and sympathetic temper," Adams said, you "shall reflect an honour both on your Christian and Masonic profession." Failure to act in love toward one's neighbor, another said, was in "contempt of common sense and good breeding" as well as "defiance of the feelings of humanity and the laws of God." To behave in an "unworthy" manner, Brockwell declared, "casts a reflection" on "the reputation" of not just the individual but the brotherhood as a whole: "People will be very apt to frame their conceptions of it from the conduct and deportment of those who are its members."[121]

For the colonial gentleman, to become a Mason was to share in the values and behavior of America's emerging elite, including a moderate Anglicanism shaped by the courtly manners of polite society. In this period, as affluent people attempted to discipline themselves and their children in the modes of genteel conduct, they divided themselves from all who refused to embrace the new principles. Especially repugnant were those whom Brockwell termed the "vulgar," who, with their dirty hands, slovenly clothes, and ungainly speech, appeared crude and debauched, a lower order of life. Following the Great Awakening, Brockwell derided the "convulsions into which the whole country is thrown by a set of Enthusiasts . . . [who] strole about haranguing the admiring Vulgar in extempore nonsense."[122] In contrast to these disruptive revivalists, Masonic gentlemen showed polite consideration of their peers and a caring condescension toward their inferiors.

THE RELIGIOUS PUBLIC SPHERE

One early Masonic encounter with the revivals of what came to be known as the Great Awakening occurred in Charleston, South Carolina.[123] On December 27, 1739, that city's lodge held its annual Saint John's Day celebration, complete with public processions and an evening of balls and entertainments.[124] The following Sunday the itinerant evangelist George Whitefield arrived to conduct several days of preaching. Soon thereafter, he pointedly asked Alexander Garden, the Anglican commissary, if the latter had delivered "his soul by exclaiming against" the pompous "assemblies and balls" held for the entertainment of the town's upper class. Garden was taken aback by the insubordination of the young Whitefield and admonished him, "Must you come to catechize me?"[125] He then tartly told the young preacher that there was "no harm" in these entertainments of polite society, especially when compared with the "Mobb-Preachings, and the Assemblies of his Institution," where "Men and Women" built "up one another in Conceit of their being righteous" while "damning" the morality of "all others."[126]

Over the next several months, in pamphlets and in the pages of the *South Carolina Gazette*, Charleston Protestants waged a battle over the Great Awakening. Whitefield initiated this debate by challenging Garden to a "public exchange" on the doctrinal validity of the Grand Itinerant's preaching. As Whitefield put it, "It would be endless to enter into . . . a private debate," where each would repeatedly offer his own point of view. Rather, the "publick" should be informed of their positions through "the press." Then they could let the "World judge" who was right.[127] As Frank Lambert has argued, Whitefield's successful challenge resulted in moving the arena of religious disputes from private conversations among ministers to public, print debates among a literate and increasingly translocal readership.[128] In these public debates, Garden in turn demanded Whitefield give reasoned rationales rather than a florid, emotional argument "without sufficient evidence or proof to support it." The young preacher was too accustomed to using a "jingle of words, not serving to instruct, but to intangle and amuse the minds of the weak and unwary populace."[129] As others dismissed Whitefield as a "Zealot" who "composes not Sermons like a Man of

Letters," supporters of the Grand Itinerant came to his defense, arguing that the evangelist's sermons were "agreeable to the dictates of reason; evidently formed upon scripture; exactly correspondent with the articles of the establishment."[130] Whitefield admitted that in a public debate, his arguments had to be based on reason, even though "what seems a reason to me, may not be deemed so by another."[131] As the debates of the Great Awakening continued through the 1740s, both sides made efforts to frame their arguments in the reasonable, lettered language of polite society. As a result, the religious public sphere that Whitefield helped to create constrained him—and others—by obligating all writers to offer arguments based on reason and objective evidence.

Benjamin Franklin, the printer and Masonic provincial grand master, worked with Whitefield to expand this religious public sphere. Franklin printed more pamphlets for and against the revivals than any other colonial printer, despite the fact that Whitefield's evangelical revivalism stood at odds with Franklin's Masonic Christianity.[132] An Episcopalian upbringing but little involvement in the Presbyterian church he joined as an adult informed Franklin's beliefs. His biographers portray him as a moderate Deist, sufficiently religious to propose that a clergymen pray over the deliberations of the Constitutional Convention. "The System of Morals" left to us by Jesus of Nazareth, he told the Yale president Ezra Stiles, was "the best the world ever saw or was likely to see." Yet Franklin also believed that the Christian moral system had become "corrupted." Moreover, with regard to Jesus, Franklin had "some Doubts as to his divinity."[133] In contrast to the Philadelphia printer's lax church attendance and moderate Deism, his Masonic career, which spanned a period of almost sixty years, was extensive. Inducted into Saint John's Lodge of Philadelphia in 1731, he was elected lodge secretary, junior grand warden, provincial deputy grand master, and grand master of Pennsylvania in his years as a Mason. In 1734, Franklin published the first American edition of James Anderson's *Constitutions*. His newspaper frequently included Masonic items. In 1755, Franklin prominently participated in the dedication of Freemason's Lodge, the first Masonic building in America.[134] While serving as an American representative to France in the 1760s, the printer-turned-diplomat became deeply involved in the learned Masonic society known as the Lodge of Nine Sisters.[135] This consistent, long-term involvement with the fraternity at least suggests Franklin's acceptance of Freemasonry's universal moral teachings. In a 1738 letter to his mother, he defends the fraternity as having "no principles or practices that are inconsistent with religion and good manners."[136] Though Franklin and Whitefield stood apart in their religious perspectives, both believed in settling religious disagreements in a public forum, where thinking men would decide the truth of writers' rational arguments.[137]

The men attracted to Freemasonry in the midcentury First Great Awakening encouraged the rational communication of the emerging public sphere. These included the printers who, with Franklin, inaugurated the first newspapers in Charleston and Boston. In 1731, Franklin sent his lodge brother and printing apprentice Thomas Whitehurst from Philadelphia to Charleston with a printing press, which soon published the *South Carolina Gazette*.[138] In that same year the Harvard-educated printer and eventual provincial grand master Jeremy Gridley founded Boston's *Weekly Rehearsal*. The past grand master Isaiah Thomas states in his *History of Printing* (1810) that the *Weekly Rehearsal* "was carried on at the expense of some gentlemen who formed themselves into a political or literary club and wrote for it. At the head of this club was the late celebrated Jeremy Gridley, who was the real editor of the paper."[139] In the 1730s, the printer and Mason Thomas Fleet began publishing the *Boston Gazette*, which soon carried Masonic news items. In 1739, it ran a defense of Freemasonry that underscored the fraternity's vital role in the "Search after Truth" through the communication of knowledge. "By exercising our Tho'ts, and by . . . communicating to our Fellow Creatures we afford them Aid in their Search after Truth. . . . Let every Lover of Reason . . . stir himself up, and put forth all his Powers for setting up such Societies for the investing the Mind with Learning and true Knowledge."[140] In the seven short years after the formal establishment of Freemasonry in colonial America, several hundred men in the new lodges of Philadelphia, Boston, Charleston, and New York joined these first colonial printers. Many were in the forefront of colonial efforts to establish institutions of higher learning. They included the Harvard-educated Massachusetts governor Jonathan Belcher, who founded Princeton University; the original members and early trustees of the University of Pennsylvania; the first president of the American Philosophical Society; and the organizers of the Philadelphia Library Company. These were men not unlike Gridley, whose "extensive Acquaintance with Classical and almost every other part of Literature, gave him the first Rank among Men of Learning."[141] Within a religious discourse that embraced rational communication as the basis for moral behavior and the ordering of society, the colonial fraternity taught men how to create a society based on Enlightenment principles. As the public sphere rapidly expanded in the 1760s, these habits came to characterize the civic workings of the emerging American society.

"MYSTERIES AND HIEROGLYPHICKS"

Despite Freemasonry's contributions to colonial society, some continued to question whether it really was Christian. The Reverend John Rodgers pointed to the "strong prejudices . . . against your fraternity" that were "charged to the . . . excesses [of intemperance and profanity] said to be committed" at lodge meetings. He went on to say that there are "those among you, who indulge yourselves in the habitual neglect of the known and great duties of religion."[142] Others worried over the Masons' adulteration of the Gospel with "foreign mixtures."[143] Zabdiel Adams said, "The very notion of your dealing in mysteries and hieroglyphicks is enough to raise cruel suspicions in many persons."[144] These suspicions were warranted.

On June 24, 1734, for example, the Reverend Charles Brockwell argued that not only did Freemasonry predate Christianity but the Christian story veiled Freemasonry's deeper meaning. He began his oration by informing the members of Boston's Saint John's Lodge that Saint Paul was a Mason. This fact, he argued, was clear to the brotherhood but not to "the learned . . . interpreters of Scripture" who were not Masons and therefore "could not possibly conceive the apostle's true meaning." In Corinthians, for example, when Paul mentions his experiences "in the Body or out of the Body" and of the "third heaven or paradise," he is speaking elliptically about the Masonic degree ceremonies. Rather than reveal the deeper Masonic secrets to outsiders, Brockwell asserted, Paul spoke to his fellow Masons in code through the Christian story. This hidden language of Masonry, moreover, "remain'd unaffected and Intire" when "God confounded the common language of mankind, at the Building of Babel." This is "a language which none but Masons are capable of learning, a happiness which none but Brethren are capable of enjoying."[145]

Most Saint John's sermons stressed polite Christianity, yet Brockwell's oration suggests a divergence between it and Freemasonry. Though few outsiders seemed concerned about this at the time, the fraternity had not only its own myth of origin but also its own calendar, which marked time from the creation of the world rather than Christ's birth. Lodge minutes were dated 5750 rather than 1750, for example, to mark the imagined date, four thousand years prior to Christianity, when the world began.[146] Secret words, symbols, and rituals enshrouded the lodge in an aura of mystery. The three rituals of initiation—Entered Apprentice, Fellow Craft, and Master Mason—had little to do with Christianity and continued to be the primary business of lodge meetings. "Working the craft" through these rites gave the assembled brotherhood a common experience that deepened their commitment to one another and to the fraternity's ideals but perhaps not to the Christian Church. Margaret C. Jacob has suggested that the apparent contradiction between the fraternity's enlightened Christianity and the emphasis it placed on its pre-Christian past might best be seen as evidence that it was "living" the rise of Enlightenment thought and practice in the colonial religious world. In her view, these heterogenous elements indicate the less than straightforward manner in which Freemasonry, and for that matter the whole of society, became modern.[147]

By the late eighteenth century, such heterodoxy was more the exception than the rule in the American religious landscape. As David D. Hall has demonstrated, in the seventeenth century, European immigrants lived in a broader, older "world of wonder," laced with the debris of other systems of thought, some older than Christianity. Witchcraft, apparitions, other unearthly phenomena, and supernatural explanations of natural occurrences such as comets, hailstorms, earthquakes, sudden deaths, and monster births pervaded colonial culture.[148] By the beginning of the eighteenth century, this expansive, eclectic early modern view began to give way, especially in the upper classes, to denominational institutions that worked to expand their reach in colonial society while separating Christianity from other magical beliefs and practices.[149] The trend toward social consolidation, Patricia U. Bonomi has shown, resulted everywhere in the emergence of religious organizations "as significant centers of stability and influence" and in the enhancement of religious authority.[150] The number of churches in the seven largest Protestant denominations increased more than sevenfold between 1700 and 1780, resulting in a widespread sacralization of the colonial landscape.[151] Amid this growing Christian consolidation, pluralism, eclectic beliefs, and occult practices persisted.

Given the complexity of the eighteenth-century religious world, it is not clear what hold the rituals and beliefs of the lodge had on colonial Masons. Following the Revolution, a number of new religions did emerge that claimed Masonic origins. As early as 1788, a society of Druids formed within one Masonic lodge by rejecting all forms of Christianity and embracing the sun worship of the ancient Druids.[152]

Later on, the Mormons appropriated Masonic elements.[153] Yet it was not until the early nineteenth century that Masonic ritual life in either England or America was standardized. As one Masonic historian wrote, "The ritual was in a more or less fluid condition during this period."[154] In Boston, for example, it was common for members to complete only one or two of the three degree rituals.[155] After examining the minutes of several colonial lodges, another Masonic historian concluded that "the ceremonies were brief and possibly not overly impressive."[156] For colonial brothers, consistent procedures and meaningful ceremonies appear to have been less significant than the members' participation in polite society.

. . .

On the eve of the American Revolution, Catalina Schuyler, the doyenne of Albany's polite society, was increasingly melancholy. Her hopes of a "golden age" in her country now "grew weaker." Though she shared in the joy of the community on the repeal of the Stamp Act, she noted that this action "produced little gratitude " toward the British authorities. She was chagrined over the behavior of the town's young people, who had "abandoned their wonted sports" and instead "amuse[d] themselves with breaking the windows and destroying the furniture of . . . suspected . . . stamp-masters." Even more disruptive of her mannered world was the decline in "polite" visits to her home by the provincial gentry, who were now "succeeded by Obadiah or Zephaniah, from Hampshire or Connecticut, who came in without knocking; sat down without invitation; and lighted their pipe without ceremony; then talked of buying land."[157] Because Mrs. Schuyler firmly believed that "increase of wealth should be accompanied with a proportionate progress in refinement and intelligence," she refused her table to these "petulant upstarts." As the revolution approached, she saw "nothing on all hands but a choice of evils."[158]

By the 1760s, an expanding public sphere characterized by rational communication carried on in print had eclipsed America's colonial polite society. Balls, plays, and other entertainments now gave way to republican discipline. Private meetings in elegant homes and taverns became less frequent than public gatherings that brought together a broad expanse of the rising generation who would lead the coming war effort. The new print media engaged a progressively larger and more literate population in public dialogue on momentous questions concerning the future of the social order.[159] Though some, such as Catalina Schuyler, believed that the colonists "had not cohesion nor subordination enough among them to form, or to submit to any salutary plan of government," others, such as the Freemasons who joined the Albany Committee of Correspondence, created republican organizations devoted to the war effort.[160] Masons could be found on both sides of the war question, but all came from an organization that encouraged a new civic awareness. In the revolutionary period, growing numbers of ambitious and politically active men entered the fraternity and worked to identify it with the men and ideals of the newly emerging American society. For many brothers, the order's old ideals of tolerance and benevolence provided a vision for the new American society. At the same time, new emphases on republican values, morality, education, and Christianity became hallmarks of a once again transformed fraternity.

CHAPTER 2

Revolutionary Masonry

Republican and Christian, 1757–1825

Historians of religion point to republicanism and democratization as central developments in American religious life in the revolutionary era. Beginning in the 1760s, a new republican ideology that incorporated both Christian and Enlightenment ideas into its hegemonic framework expanded Christian ideas of liberty and community to encompass not only the church but the nation as well. Though American Protestantism was not constitutionally connected to the legal structure of the state, it did come to align itself with the new American nation. At the same time, a host of evangelical populists led a religious revolt against the learned clergy, decorous congregations, and centralized authority of the dominant Anglican, Presbyterian, and Congregational churches, which resulted, by 1850, in the numerical triumph of Baptists and Methodists. The revivals that erupted in the 1790s were part of a tumultuous democratic revolution in American religion, coincident with a broader revolt against elite domination throughout the culture. Although the Protestantism that emerged from the Revolution was closely identified with the new American nation and its democratic spirit, so too—and perhaps even more so—was a more overtly Christian and republican Freemasonry.[1]

In the middle of the eighteenth century, changes in Freemasonry were closely related to transformations in American society. Beginning in the 1750s, a large number of mechanics, lesser merchants, and military men proposed a new form of Freemasonry, which they termed Ancient.

These ambitious and politically active men transformed the fraternity. Embracing the ideals of virtue and merit, the brotherhood now proclaimed itself to be in the vanguard of new efforts to build a republican society. By the 1790s, as their order expanded rapidly throughout the interior, Masons described it as embodying the republican values of morality, education, and Christianity.

A growing convergence of Christianity and Freemasonry around Enlightenment ideals marked the first quarter of the nineteenth century. In the Revolutionary War, military lodges were more effective than Christian churches in building ties among Continental Army officers. Avoiding the extremes of both sectarianism and nonbiblical rationalism, following the war Freemasonry attracted ministers and other members of liberal-leaning denominations, leading to a high incidence of Episcopalians, Congregationalists, and Unitarians among its leaders. At the same time, Bible readings and Christian prayers and rituals entered more overtly into lodge meetings. In contrast to the colonial period, when civic ritual had centered on the monarchy and the church, with Christian ministers blessing public institutions, in the postwar era, following the revolutionary shift to republican ideals and symbols, Masons were increasingly called on to solemnize public enterprises, even going so far as to lay the cornerstone at the foundations of Christian churches.

As Alexis de Tocqueville has stated, intermediary institutions between the authority of the state and the will of the people stabilized the emerging American republic, by working to create and shape public culture.[2] Freemasonry was one of these organizations, which emerged from eighteenth-century polite societies that transformed following the revolution into institutions that played a significant role in shaping public opinion. Many of the leading advocates of American independence were attracted to the Masonic brotherhood, whose efforts to bring together men from different regions and backgrounds in an increasingly republican and Christian framework they saw as a harbinger of the new American society.[3] Masonic symbols and ceremonies thus came to be employed in public rituals, closely identifying the fraternity with the new American nation. Though soon to be contested by gender, class, and racial criticism, Freemasonry encouraged nationalist rhetoric and practices that contributed to the larger effort to create a common social discourse. At the same time, orthodox Calvinists warned of a Masonic infiltration of government and church that threatened to undermine the full and free participation of all Americans in civil society. Yet until the fraternity's unraveling, following the Morgan affair of 1826, Freemasons weathered these criticisms through their close association with brothers such as George Washington and their prominent participation in the civic ceremonies of the young republic.

FROM MODERNS TO ANCIENTS

On the evening of June 24, 1737, Benjamin Walker, a sugar baker, peeked into a tavern window to see what was transpiring at a meeting of the Boston Masonic Lodge. Earlier that day the lodge had taken to the streets for its annual Saint John's Day procession. Walker noted in his journal, "Great Numbers of people of all sexes and sizes [assembled] to see them walk thro the streets."[4] Men such as him, who stood below the rank of gentleman, could not go behind the honorable society's closed doors. By the end of the century, however, urban craftsmen and country gentlemen whose broadening aspirations attracted them to the status and sophistication of Freemasonry would dominate this society that had previously brought together the most prominent men in America's seaport towns.

The catalyst for this transformation was a dispute over proper ritual procedures between two factions in British Freemasonry. In the 1740s, the novelty and fashionable appeal of English Freemasonry had begun to fade. The number of lodges declined. Satires and mock processions lowered the dignity of and public respect for the fraternity. Ineffective and indifferent leaders, apathetic members, and exhaustion from rapid expansion all figured in what one London Mason termed the order's "low repute."[5] In the midst of this weakness, the London Grand Lodge denied membership to several journeymen Irish Masons living in London because they could not demonstrate knowledge of ritual changes made by that body to keep out imposters. Infuriated by this rebuke, in 1751 a group spearheaded by this Irish faction and led by Laurence Dermott, a journeyman painter who had been the master of a Dublin lodge in 1746, met to organize a rival Grand Lodge.

Calling themselves Ancients, after their desire to restore the original degree rituals, the insurgents named the existing London Grand Lodge members Moderns for tampering with the fraternity's essential ceremonies. Dermott then effectively exaggerated the matter to give the impression that the Moderns had so far departed from the sacred and unchanging rites and customs as to be illegal and unauthorized.[6] His new book of constitutions, the *Ahiman Rezon* (Help to a Brother), while otherwise closely following James Anderson's *Constitutions*, chided the Moderns for their ritual innovations, neglect of the Saint John's Day feasts, perfunctory ceremonies, and irregular times of meeting. In contrast, the *Ahiman Rezon* emphasized stricter ritual observances and tighter administrative practices.[7] By all accounts, Dermott was a forceful character and able administrator who gained prestige for the new fraternity by receiving official recognition from the Grand Lodges of Ireland and Scotland. Serving as grand secretary of the new lodge for thirty-five years, he eventually cajoled, bullied, and molded the Ancients into an equal to the premier Grand Lodge. One measure of his success was the acceptance by the London Grand Lodge of its new name—in its own minutes.[8]

Though the immediate occasion for the indictment of the Moderns lay in a dispute over rituals, social differences underlay the rise of Ancient Freemasonry. Dermott later described the original members as "Men of some Education and an honest Character but in low Circumstances." The 1751 membership rolls indicate that most were "mechanics," journeymen painters, shoemakers, and tailors, of a similar character to those who had earlier established the lodges for Masonic craftsmen. One of the new Grand Lodge's first acts of business was to provide support from its charity fund for members in debtors' prison. In his *Ahiman Rezon*, the Ancients' grand secretary expanded the pool of eligible Masonic candidates beyond the affluent elite by stipulating only that members of the Ancient fraternity be freeborn men, "upright in body and limbs," free of debt, and "endowed with an estate, office, trade, occupation or some visible way of acquiring an honest and reputable livelihood."[9] He then took steps to democratize the organization by requiring the election rather than the appointment of all Grand Lodge officers.

The Ancients' more humble rank encouraged their expansion abroad, often through regiments in the British Army interested in forming military lodges that were issued traveling warrants. These bodies provided Masonic fellowship for lower ranks of soldiers, who could not, like their superiors, mingle in polite society. In its first decades of existence, the Ancient Grand Lodge sent more than one hundred military lodges to the British colonies, particularly North America, where it warranted forty-nine traveling lodges during the French and Indian War.[10] These military lodges admitted local civilians, each group of whom, when the regiment moved on, applied to the Ancients for a warrant for a stationary lodge.

The first Ancient lodge established in America, however, grew out of a lodge originally chartered by the Moderns in Philadelphia in 1757. The majority of the original petitioners to Philadelphia's Lodge No. 4 appear to have been British immigrants, including soldiers then stationed in

Philadelphia, who were Ancient Masons, a fact of which the Moderns were initially unaware. Once formed, the new lodge accepted other Ancient British Masons and adopted the Ancient manner in admitting new members. By August of 1757, the Pennsylvania Grand Lodge had received reports of these irregularities and responded by sending investigators. Lodge No. 4 did not receive these interlopers fraternally, remarking in its minutes that the visitors "behaved as spies in an enemy camp." Summoned before the Grand Lodge committee, the officers of No. 4 willingly "plead[ed] Guilty" to being Ancients. As a result, the warrant of No. 4 was recalled less than six months after it had been issued. "Determined never to forsake the good old way," the insurgent members were soon granted a warrant from the London Ancients, in 1758, becoming Ancient Lodge No. 1. Tensions continued between the two groups when one Modern, Solomon Bush, a prominent Jewish Freemason who was going to London on other business, refused to carry the Ancient lodge's payment of its fees to the Ancient Grand Lodge.[11] Following the establishment of their Lodge No. 1, Philadelphia's Ancients created a Grand Lodge in 1761 and grew rapidly. In contrast to the four lodges warranted by the local Moderns between 1730 and 1758, Philadelphia's Ancients warranted more than fifty between 1761 and 1785. Lodges working under the Moderns rapidly declined, ceasing to exist altogether about 1793, when their hall was sold and the proceeds donated to the city as a fund "to furnish the poor with wood."[12]

In 1774, the London Ancients issued a decree that any lodge in the world with a warrant from the Moderns should be deemed unworthy of association with the "Ancient Community" and its official sanction from the London Grand Lodge of Ancients canceled.[13] This was in keeping with Dermott's dictate in the *Ahiman Rezon* that "ancient Masonry contains everything valuable amongst the moderns, as well as many other things that cannot be revealed without additional ceremonies."[14] This claim seems to have been generally accepted, in some instances even by Moderns. In 1778, the Episcopal clergyman William Smith, having served for many years as the grand secretary and grand chaplain of the Pennsylvania Moderns, submitted himself to be "healed" in an Ancient ceremony. By 1785, as many as nineteen hundred men had been initiated into lodges warranted by Philadelphia's Ancient fraternity.[15] By 1800, the national Ancient fraternity encompassed all eleven American Grand Lodges, whose five hundred subordinate lodges included an estimated twenty-five thousand members. Together these men constituted about 3 percent of the adult white male population and a substantially higher percentage of those with property and the means to pay the fraternity's fees.[16] In addition, these numbers do not include the late eighteenth-century expansion of the fraternity into the African American community through the creation of Prince Hall Masonic lodges (see chapter 6).

The triumph of the Ancient fraternity was part of a large transformation of American society that challenged old social divisions between the elite and common people. In the second half of the eighteenth century, a movement of increasingly sophisticated and politically aware urban artisans emerged and became vigorously involved in efforts surrounding the coming war.[17] At the same time, rising leaders of country towns and villages were developing political and economic standing and a growing cosmopolitanism.[18] Masonic membership was particularly attractive to each of these groups because it provided them with social prestige and a means for creating community with the elite. Masons could be found on both the American and the British sides of the Revolution, but the growing prestige of the Ancient brothers and the involvement of American officers in local and military lodges led to the close identification of the order with the American cause.[19]

Freemasons were central to the war effort. They accounted for 69 of the 241 men (29 percent) who either signed the Articles of Association, the Declaration of Independence, the Articles of Confederation, or the Constitution or served as generals in the Continental Army or as General Washington's aides or military secretaries. Such luminaries as Washington, Benjamin Franklin, and John Hancock were Freemasons. Forty-two percent of the generals commissioned by the Continental Congress and led by Washington were or became Masons.[20] These men were often actively involved in ten military lodges whose membership drew overwhelmingly from the ranks of commissioned officers. Like the British military lodges, these gatherings of American soldiers provided identity and mutual support. Unlike the ineffective and parochial Christian chaplains, the Continental Army's military lodges provided common beliefs and rituals that reinforced the validity of the emerging American society. By the war's end, the largest of these lodges counted several hundred officers among its members.[21]

MILITARY LODGES

Military lodges were more effective than Christian ministers in building ties among Continental Army officers. The Christian chaplaincy in the

Revolutionary War began with a disorganized system of volunteer preachers. Gradually, the Continental Congress extended its influence to include chaplaincies, which it slowly developed into an organized system.[22] In practice, however, chaplains were few in number and transient in service. In January of 1776, only one-third of the army's regiments had chaplains.[23] Among the 117 ministers who worked as chaplains, only one remained in service throughout the war, while the majority did not stay more than ten months.[24] Though some chaplains served as regular soldiers, the great majority sheltered themselves in private homes or with staff officers. During marches they were ordered to stay at the rear of the vanguard.[25]

Few, transient, and set apart, the chaplains were additionally frustrated in their work by the soldiers' pervasive drunkenness, profanity, and widespread lack of interest in religious services. On July 4, 1775, the day after Washington took command, he reminded the army that the Articles of War forbade "profane cursing, swearing and drunkenness" and imposed on all officers and men when not on duty "punctual attendance on Divine Service to implore the blessing of heaven upon the means used for our safety and defence." In spite of this, he found it necessary throughout the war to reiterate the obligation of men and officers to attend divine services. But an apparent indifference on the part of the chaplains encouraged soldiers' apathy. On February 15, 1783, Washington issued lengthy general orders against relaxed discipline and expressed particular astonishment at the behavior of chaplains, who had "frequently been almost all absent at the same time."[26]

Organized Christianity also suffered from denominational antagonisms. Almost one-half (48 of 115) of the chaplains with known denominational affiliations were Congregational ministers from New England, some of whom protested Rhode Island's appointment of the Unitarian minister John Murray because of his ultraliberal and heterodox views.[27] Virginia frontiersmen, in turn, deplored the predominance of Anglican clergymen (nine of ten) in their state's delegation and the absence of ministers from their dissident Baptist faith.[28] In June of 1777, Washington addressed Congress at length on this knotty subject. Fearing the outbreak of religious disputes if men were compelled "to a mode of Worship which they do not profess," he concluded that it would be best if each regiment had a voice in choosing a chaplain of its own "religious sentiments."[29]

At the same time that an ineffective structure, persisting indifference, and localism impeded the work of organized religion, officers were attracted to the new nationalistic fervor particularly evident in the sanctity of the military funeral. As the Connecticut Congregational chaplain Ammi Robbins put it, "There is something more than ordinarily solemn and touching in our funerals, especially an officer's; sword and arms inverted, others with their arms folded across their breast stepping slowly to the beat of the muffled drum."[30] These officers' funerals were often accompanied by Masonic rites, which, at least one historian reports, army chaplains frequently performed.[31]

While no systematic comparison of chaplains' names and Masonic membership records has been conducted, anecdotal evidence is suggestive. The Congregational minister and Connecticut Line Brigade chaplain Abraham Baldwin offered a "polite discourse" to a meeting of all military lodge leaders in a New Jersey Presbyterian church.[32] The Presbyterian minister Andrew Hunter was both chaplain to the New Jersey Brigade and the worshipful master of its military lodge.[33] By the winter of 1782, moreover, the military lodges had become so well established that Washington granted a request from Israel Evans, New York's Presbyterian Brigade chaplain, to erect a public building outside army headquarters on the banks of the Hudson near Newburg for both divine services and lodge meetings. That spring, the building, known to Masons as the Temple, was the site for both Christian worship and the initiation of officers into the mysteries of Freemasonry.[34]

In contrast to organized Christianity, the military lodges sought to overcome local differences. Unlike the regional religious biases of New England Congregationalism or Virginia Anglicanism, the lodge's commitment to "all men" regardless of region or denomination provided a basis for community beyond local boundaries. The fraternity's emphasis on social distinction based on merit rather than birth similarly worked against local prejudices. Moreover, the lodges provided social space for war-weary officers from all over the colonies to relax and enjoy one another's company. The fraternity's commitment to creating a society based on an affection among men that transcended differences suggests an anticipation of the new republican society that the army's officers were fighting to create.[35]

The meetings of military lodges were usually held when the army was resting in camp between campaigns. Eleven Connecticut regimental officers in Roxbury, Massachusetts, for example, formed American Union Lodge during the army's encampment in Boston in the winter of 1776. The lodge subsequently moved with the army through Connecticut, New York, and New Jersey. Charged in their warrant from the

Grand Lodge of Massachusetts to promote "the utmost Harmony and Brotherly Love" among themselves and to be "very cautious of the Moral Character" of prospective members, the new lodge founders agreed to set about their "masonic work" of proposing, examining, and ritually admitting new recruits in the evening of the first, second, and third Tuesdays of every month and in extra meetings when warranted. The lodge held thirty-one meetings in its first six months. At the Battle of Long Island in August of 1776, however, ten members were either killed or captured, and the lodge was forced to close. It held only one meeting between March 1777 and February 1779, but it admitted thirteen new members and initiated twenty candidates, all commissioned officers, between 1776 and 1779.[36] In the winter of 1779, the lodge, led by Worshipful Master General Samuel Parsons, met in the army's winter quarters, along the banks of the Hudson opposite West Point.[37]

Beyond individual lodge meetings while the army was in camp, the winter of 1779 saw representatives from all ten military lodges come together to propose a unified American Freemasonry. More than one hundred high-ranking Masonic military officers were present in Morristown, New Jersey, for that meeting, including Generals Washington and Mordecai Gist and Colonels Alexander Hamilton and Thomas Proctor. Their petition, to be presented to several provincial grand masters, requested the creation of a national General Grand Lodge, which would "preside over and govern all other lodges of whatsoever degree or denomination." By eliminating distinctions between Moderns and Ancients, standardizing practices, and correcting abuses, the new Grand Lodge would encourage "frequent communion and social intercourse" among brethren throughout the country so that Masonic "morality and virtue may be far extended."[38] Though the proposed Grand Lodge never came into existence, the unanimous support for this petition among the military's leading Masons suggests both Freemasonry's emerging power to provide a common bond among military leaders and its support for the new American nation. As the war continued, the symbols and rituals of Freemasonry, which united men of diverse backgrounds, also reinforced the patriotic effort to create a public sphere of unity in the emerging American society. Wartime Masonic processions first displayed this development.

FREEMASONRY AND THE NATION

At West Point in June of 1779, a procession of thirty members of American Union Lodge, joined by more than seventy visiting brothers, celebrated the Festival of Saint John the Baptist. Led by a "Band of Music with drums and fifes" and displaying the "Bible, Square and Compass," the company marched to the "Red House," where "His Excellency George Washington and his family" and a "number of gentlemen" joined them. Following a sermon, an address to the "Brethren in particular," and a dinner, toasts were drunk to "Congress" and the "Arts and Sciences," and a special toast, reported to occur at all Masonic events in the war years, was drunk to slain Masons, on this occasion including the military leaders "Warren, Montgomery, [and] Wooster." After the celebration, Washington, "attended by the Wardens and Secretary of the Lodge," returned to his barge while the musicians played "God Save America." "Three cheers from the shore" accompanied the announcement of his departure, which were "answered by three from the barge, the music beating the 'Grenadier's March.'"[39] Following this impressive gathering, a new military lodge named after Washington was formed and eventually inducted more than two hundred Continental Army officers.[40]

Such celebrations underscored the growing identification of Freemasonry with Washington and the new American nation. The general had first taken part in a public Masonic function just six months earlier. Following the departure of the British from Philadelphia in June of 1778, the Philadelphia Grand Lodge organized a great Masonic celebration of this event, to be commemorated on Saint John's Day, December 28. On that day, nearly three hundred Masons participated in a grand procession, with "his Excellency our illustrious Brother General Washington" taking the grand master's position of greatest honor.[41] The march ended at Christ Church, where the city's two most prominent Anglican clergymen conducted the religious services. Rev. Dr. William White, later the first bishop of Pennsylvania, gave the prayer, and Rev. Dr. William Smith, now an Ancient Mason, dedicated his sermon to General Washington.[42] Afterward a collection was taken for relief of the poor, which raised four hundred pounds—a large amount for the times.

This celebration substantially enhanced the fraternity's prestige. The regal and orderly public procession of more Masons than had ever been seen together in America signaled the brotherhood's size and significance. One historian has observed that the number of Masons in Philadelphia in 1778, 571, was larger than the membership of any other voluntary society in the city at that time.[43] The large sum that the fraternity collected for the poor supported its image as a charitable organization actively responding to the needs of the city's destitute. However, it was the order's association with Washington and the cause of the United States that clearly marked a turning point in its evolution. From this point forward, Washington endorsed the society's activities through his prominent presence in the members' public activities and private correspondence. As a Masonic ode commemorating his participation in these ceremonies exulted,

See Washington, he leads the train,
'Tis he commands the grateful strain;
See, every crafted son obeys.
And to the godlike brother homage pays.

Over the next few decades, Masonic sermons, addresses, and orations reverently associated Washington, Masonry, and the ideals of the new nation.[44]

This convergence was particularly apparent to Masonic observers of Washington's presidential inauguration in New York City in 1789. For that ceremony, General Jacob Morton, the marshal of the festivities and the master of Saint John's, the city's oldest Masonic lodge, brought the Bible from the altar of his lodge. Robert R. Livingston, the chancellor of the state of New York and the grand master of its Grand Lodge, administered the oath. Afterward, Washington "reverently" kissed the Bible, which was later returned to the lodge. A memorial leaf was folded at the page the president had kissed, and in subsequent years the Bible became the lodge's most sacred memento.[45] At least one Masonic historian thought that Washington's inaugural address—with its acknowledgment of his hopes and fears, his appeal to the divine ruler, and his examination of the requirements of the Constitution—reflected Masonic principles.[46]

The sanctification of the new nation through Masonic rituals was even more public in President Washington's participation in the Masonic ceremonial laying of the cornerstone of the nation's Capitol in 1793. For that formal occasion, the president clothed himself in the apron and insignia of a Mason and processed solemnly with hundreds of brothers through the city in a grand Masonic parade. Arriving at the southeast corner of the Capitol, he laid on the cornerstone a silver plate commemorating his presidency and inscribed, "In the thirteenth year of American independence . . . and in the year of Masonry, 5793." He then covered the plate with the Masonic symbols of corn, wine, and oil. The corn dedicated the Capitol to the Grand Architect of the Universe and to Masonry, the wine to virtue and science, and the oil to universal charity and benevolence. The "whole congregation" then "joined in reverential prayer, which was succeeded by . . . a volley from the military."[47]

Joseph Clark, the grand master of Maryland, articulated the significance of the event in his address at the laying of the Capitol's cornerstone, comparing it to the "like work" of laying the cornerstone of King Solomon's Temple. From that ancient ceremony, Clark observed, had come the flowering "of our honourable, and sublime order." Similarly, he prophesied, after this ceremony, "Architecture, Masonry, Arts, and Commerce will grow with rapidity inconceivable to me." With Freemasonry as its cornerstone and the incomparable Brother Washington modeling Masonic virtues, Grand Master Clark envisioned the new American nation as embodying the deepest Masonic values.[48]

The symbols and rituals of Freemasonry, self-consciously used by the leaders of the new American republic, provided visual support for the new government's legitimacy while encouraging public acceptance of the fraternity as an embodiment of the ideals of the new society. The spread of cornerstone ceremonies in the early years of the young republic affirmed this relationship. Beginning with Washington's laying of the cornerstone at the Capitol in 1793, government leaders turned to the brotherhood to sanctify public undertakings. The state capitols of Massachusetts and Virginia each received Masonic blessings.[49] As the economy expanded, the fraternity anointed bridges and the Erie Canal locks and sanctified public higher education in cornerstone ceremonies at the University of North Carolina and the University of Virginia. In 1818, several thousand spectators turned out for the Massachusetts Grand Lodge's dedication of Boston's new Massachusetts General Hospital.[50] Such practices extended to the nation's churches. For example, in 1826, "the cornerstone of the new Episcopal Church, at Carlisle, Penn. [w]as laid . . . with *Masonic rites*, by Cumberland Star Lodge, No. 197— assisted by Harrisburg, Chambersburg, and Lansingburg Lodges, and many of the fraternity from other places. . . . The Chambersburg paper remarks: 'Is this not a novelty . . . to find Masons engaged in laying the corner stone of a place of Christian worship, at the request of its pastor and congregation?'—It is: and we see in the fact, an era approaching of more liberal opinions respecting, and kindly disposition towards, that ancient and honorable fraternity."[51] By the 1820s, not only Protestants but also Catholics and Jews were calling on the brotherhood to bless their houses of worship.[52] The height of the fraternity's popularity may have been the Marquis de Lafayette's tour of the United States in 1824–25, which went through all twenty-four states over thirteen months, accompanied by Masonic processions, dinners, cornerstone layings, and intense media coverage.

Like so much of postwar Masonry, these ceremonies had their origins in England but were given new meaning in the American context. Eighteenth-century English Masons had evolved rituals for the consecration of new lodges. Their ingredients, including grand processions, a royal arch, prayers, engravings, striking a mallet, and corn, oil, and wine, were transported into the new American rites.[53] At the Bunker Hill memorial consecration, for example, hundreds of New England's brethren, clothed in full regalia, marched behind a military escort and in front of governors, congressmen, and the president of the United States and through a lofty, triumphal arch on which was inscribed "The Arts pay homage to valor." When the cornerstone was raised, the Massachusetts grand chaplain prayed that "the Grand Architect of the Universe grant a blessing on this foundation stone" and the grand treasurer placed a silver plate engraved with the names of the grand master and local officials beneath the cornerstone, on which the grand master poured corn, wine, and oil while praying to the "bounteous Author of nature . . . [to] grant to us all in needful supply the Corn of nourishment, the Wine of refreshment, and the Oil of joy." He then "struck the stone thrice with his mallet and the Honours of Masonry were given." An oration and a concluding procession followed.[54] The Masonic consecration of American public enterprises adapted older rituals that prepared English lodges for the practice of Freemasonry, to celebrate the new American republic.

This appropriation was part of a larger effort to create a national popular political culture in the years following the Revolution. Working against the regional, racial, ethnic, class, and gender diversities of postwar America, the civil ceremonies of Freemasonry, like the new Fourth of July parades, speeches, and toasts, were elements of a spontaneous attempt to delineate the borders of a common though contested public world.

As David Waldstreicher has argued, emerging efforts by various groups, including African Americans and women, to create a common understanding of American society through public events and print culture worked to resolve the many paradoxes of localism and nationalism, plus racial and gender identities, that characterized the early years of the young republic. Though Waldstreicher does not discuss Freemasonry in this context, the central role that it played in postwar public events offers evidence of its contribution to what he calls "the true political culture of the early Republic." While the white, male, and affluent character of the fraternity's members obviously worked against the creation of a truly inclusive society, the nationalist rhetoric and practices that the brotherhood encouraged and engaged in contributed to the effort to produce a common social discourse within perpetually negotiated borders.[55] This was particularly apparent in the fraternity's appropriation of republicanism.

REPUBLICAN MASONRY

Republicanism has always been more an ideal than a description of society. The concept began with Niccolò Machiavelli and other political theorists of the Italian Renaissance and was later developed through Montesquieu's belief that all governments rest on their subjects. For these social theorists, what makes the law effective in despotic governments is fear; what makes the law effective in a republic is virtue. In the seventeenth-century English Civil Wars, social thinkers employed the term to envision new ways for governments to provide for the well-being of their people. As previously discussed, the Earl of Shaftesbury and other late seventeenth- and early eighteenth-century English republican thinkers responded to Thomas Hobbes's vision of a hierarchical society held together by coercion by putting forward the idea of natural benevolence and sociability. They believed that people naturally get along with one another and are concerned for the well-being of others. Such universal benevolence, however, was possible only for gentlemen. Ordinary people would have to submit to more coercive forms of social control. Following the Revolution, Americans took the English theorists' attempt to justify the rule of the gentry and enlarged it to become a means of holding together the whole of society. Social order and well-being in the new American republic would rely on the virtue of all citizens.

Revolutionary-era American spokespersons drew deeply on the libertarian thought of English social theorists in their embrace of republicanism as a set of political and social attitudes to guide the new world they believed they were creating. History, they held, revealed an eternal struggle between the forces of liberty and the forces of power. Preserving a republican government meant protecting liberty from the perpetual aggression of power. Without the authoritarian government or hierarchical restraints that supported earlier nations, American republicans believed that the character of the people rather than the force of arms would determine the health of their society. Virtue, including the repudiation of self-interest through the acceptance of moral rules, undergirded the new society. Hence, American republicanism meant maintaining private and public virtue, social solidarity, and vigilance against the corruptions of power.[56] As the new nation came into its own, moral training in the republican virtues became a particular concern of the Masonic fraternity.

Because the brotherhood embodied the older Enlightenment ideals of benevolence and sociability and the new American commitments to patriotism and democracy, the call to Freemasonry became indistinguishable from the call to American citizenship. In charging his brethren to act out their Masonic "duties and virtues," one late eighteenth-century orator put it this way: "We are now blessed with a free, independent and equal government, founded in theory upon principles the most beneficial to society." Masonic duty therefore required that "every benevolent principle, be cultivated by us . . . in seeking the general good of the whole."[57] Similarly, George Washington, responding to an address from the Pennsylvania Grand Lodge praising his nation building, saw the new government as at its best in realizing the ideals of Freemasonry: "To erect upon a solid foundation, the true principles of government, is only to have shared . . . in a labor, the result of which, let us hope, will prove, thro' all ages, a sanctuary for brothers, and a Lodge for the virtues."[58] Not only did Masonic duty now require the fulfillment of the duties of American citizenship, but, conversely, the realization of the "true principles of government" meant the embodiment of Masonic virtues.

Following the Revolution, Masonic leaders put renewed emphasis on the order's long-held moral teachings and their new republican meaning. Benevolence and sociability, the hallmarks of the English theorists, were institutionalized. "Our institution asserts . . . the natural equality of mankind," the grand master and future New York governor De Witt Clinton said in 1793.[59] "From the beginning of time to the present day," Brother Benjamin Green echoed to his Marblehead, Massachusetts, lodge in 1797, "the Free Mason's lodge . . . has ever been considered . . . a nursery of . . . love and good will to mankind."[60] By seeking to extend their values to the larger social world, moreover, the brothers came to see their fraternity as a harbinger of a new social order. In the late eighteenth and early nineteenth centuries, Masonic leaders frequently spoke of the fraternity as a "school of virtue" dedicated to the "cultivation and extension of the principles of morality, good will and virtue."[61] Though the order had always encouraged spreading its values to society at large, it now gave particular emphasis to the claim that the development and practice of Masonic virtues were "precisely the duties" that every "man owes to his brother."[62]

This new Masonic emphasis on moral improvement came at a time when the disestablishment of religion was undercutting the role of churches as moral teachers. Prior to the Revolution, nearly all of the thirteen colonies had either tax support for ministers or religious tests for public office. To a great extent, the Anglican, Presbyterian, and Congregational churches were the established teachers of public morality. Following the separation of church and state, a period of growing pluralism and sectarianism ensued. By 1815, a variety of pan-Protestant moral improvement societies had emerged, anticipating the moral reform movements of later decades. Just after the revolution, however, Freemasonry was the only established institution whose rejection of particular religious and political requirements and embrace of "universal" moral teachings allowed it to reach out to all citizens. As the "sacred asylum" and repository of republican virtue, the order appeared to offer a higher plane, beyond the confusions of postwar religion, that embodied the principles of the new American society.[63]

What influence the Masonic "school of virtue" had on the moral tenor of the new society or on Masons themselves is difficult to determine. Though the fraternity heralded the need for moral improvement, this very emphasis suggests the difficulties perceived in attaining it. In contrast to English social theorists who believed that moral benevolence was a natural capacity only of gentlemen, revolutionary Americans staked their new nation's success on the ability of its entire citizenry to embody private and public virtue. Rather than applaud the success of the people in demonstrating this morality, many Americans emphasized the need for more moral training. "The laws of nature are to be found in the human heart," Clinton said, yet they are mingled "with those black and hostile passions which harass society."[64] To overcome these "dark passions," another Masonic spokesperson said, each lodge member "solemnly promised" to watch over his brother and, when needed, "remind him . . . of his failings, and aid his reformation."[65] References to the "failings and offences of our brethren" are sprinkled throughout Masonic orations.[66]

In addition to supporting republican virtues, postwar Masonic spokespersons revived interest in scientific learning and education. Prior to the society's migration to America, the cultivation of the arts and sciences was a hallmark of Freemasonry. The English legendary histories trace the institution to Hermes, Euclid, and other originators of these fields. Both the Enlightenment emphasis on order, rationality, and science and the seemingly purer wisdom of the ancient world fascinated the founding members of the English Grand Lodge. Yet neither ancient wisdom nor Newtonian science were of much concern to colonial Masons, whose chief preoccupation was consolidating their elite social class through fraternal love and honor. Following the Revolution, however, American Masonic leaders revived their fraternity's identification with the learned men of the past and in so doing aligned it with the onward march of civilization. "It is well known," Clinton stated in 1793, that Freemasonry "was at first composed of scientific and ingenious men, who assembled together to improve the arts and sciences." Locating these men in long-ago antiquity, when "knowledge . . . was restricted to a chosen few," he explained that "when the invention of printing had opened the means of instruction to all ranks of people, then the generous cultivators of Masonry communicated with cheerfulness to the world, those secrets of the arts and sciences."[67] This retrieval of an older emphasis on arts and sciences helped to establish the fraternity as central not only to the advance of civilization but to the transmission of knowledge as well. The Masonic movement was "one of the ancient founders of schools," Brother John H. Sheppard lectured the Grand Lodges of New Hampshire and Maine in 1820. "The liberal arts and sciences" were "taught in Lodges," whose "brethren imparted instruction to their children and others."[68]

Masonic leaders asserted this new interest in learning at a moment when cultural indifference toward education and public schooling was not yet overcome. Against the "apparent indolence of men of learning, and the small benefit the community seems to derive from . . . academical institutions," Sheppard argued that "such characters and such institutions are infinitely important in the support of a republican government."[69] Acting on this conviction, New York's Grand Lodge created a free common school for Masonic children in 1810, a time when all other schools were either pay, sectarian, or both. By 1817, with the expansion of public interest in common schooling, the state took over patronage and supervision of the Mason-sponsored Free School.[70]

As no less than patrons of the arts and sciences and founders of schools, postwar Masonic leaders saw themselves as essential to the success of the American experiment. Yet their efforts to identify the fraternity both with the onward march of civilization and as a "school of virtue" devoted to the improvement of morals appear to have been more successful rhetorically than in practice. There is some evidence that the emphasis on education encouraged some lodges to support outside educational activities. Lectures on learned topics were also occasionally presented in the lodges. Yet apart from the requirement of second degree members to memorize a short overview of the seven liberal arts, there is no evidence of any lodge creating a regular course of study, much less a systematic school of learning, in this period.[71] What is certain is that claims about the fraternity's support of moral and mental improvement pervaded the order's private and public meetings. And however realized in practice, postwar Masonry's celebration of republican morality, science, and education did separate the fraternity and its members from the narrow localisms of family, church, and region and link them to the larger, cosmopolitan world of the American republic. As believers in the fraternity as the "primordial" source of learning and education, Masonic leaders saw earlier than many the need for "mental improvement" in support of republican institutions.[72]

The Masonic expression of these republican ideals at a time of national expansion contributed to the dramatic increase in the number of American men who entered the fraternity. Between 1800 and 1820, the American population nearly doubled, from 5.3 to 9.6 million, and spread rapidly to the west.[73] By 1821, nine new states contained a quarter of the American population. In the first quarter of the nineteenth century, the American Masonic fraternity grew more than threefold, from an estimated twenty-five thousand members, primarily in the urban East, to an estimated eighty thousand nationally. This represented an increase from about 3 percent of the adult white male population in 1800 to about 5 percent of the 1820 number (the percentage of Masons among those with the leisure to attend the fraternity's gatherings and the resources to pay its initiation fees was even larger).[74] In 1824, Freemasonry was described as "powerful" in every state of the union. Its members identified as "men of rank, wealth, office and talent . . . effective men, united together . . . in the legislative hall, on the bench, [and] in every gathering of men of business."[75]

During this Masonic heyday, the fraternity's civic role replaced that of Christian churches in the colonial period. Prior to the Revolution, Congregational, Presbyterian, and especially Anglican clergyman were called on to bless the public enterprises of the monarchy's subjects. The revolutionary overthrow of hierarchical society, the separation of church and state, and the rise of republican ideology punctured the sacred canopy of the Christian Church. Into this void stepped a newly democratic, patriotic, benevolent, and republican Freemasonry, which willingly offered its symbols and rituals as a means for rebuilding society's foundations.

CHRISTIAN REPUBLICAN MASONRY

In the revolutionary era, American Protestantism incorporated republican and Enlightenment ideas into an expanding framework that closely identified the church with the nation. Between 1763 and 1789, the meanings of Christian "liberty" and "righteous community" came to embrace not only the church but the nation as well. Though the church was never tied to the constitutional structure of the state, American Protestantism and republicanism became closely interwoven.[76] Similarities between their principles, moreover, led to the pervasive assumption that republicanism not only expressed Christian ideals but should be defended with Christian fervor. This was particularly true of Calvinist Christians and their evangelical heirs, yet it was also so for the early proponents of liberal Protestantism, whose distinctive ethos was then emerging from the influence of Enlightenment thought on Calvinist Christianity. Though orthodox and liberal Protestants would soon be at loggerheads, all came together in the first quarter of the nineteenth century in the belief that the success of the American republic depended on the moral education of its people.

In these early years of the American nation, Enlightenment influences similarly expanded the boundaries of Christianity to include Freemasonry. As we have seen, prior to the revolution, colonial Masons had an ambiguous relationship with the Christian religion. Their 1723 constitution instructed Masons to leave "their particular Opinions to themselves" and instead to adopt only "that Religion in which all men agree."[77] Some defended the order as inherently Christian, others believed that it transcended Christianity, and a few were fascinated with ancient, esoteric wisdom, but most appear to have seen the fraternity as representing universal moral principles rather than particular religious claims. While these multiple views continued into the early national period, Freemasonry was increasingly seen as working to realize the temporal ends of Christianity. This had to do with changes in both American Protestantism and the fraternity.

In the revolutionary period, Enlightenment thinking led to the development of a Protestant liberalism that, while not denying the reality of supernatural forces, brought the power of reason to bear on religious judgments. The indigenous religious liberalism of Unitarianism, for example, had its intellectual and social origins in a small group of Congregationalist clergy in the Boston area who took offense at the "enthusiastic" religion that George Whitefield was spreading in the 1730s and 1740s.[78] Such men as Charles Chauncy and Jonathan Mayhew were uncomfortable with a Calvinist frame of reference shaped by the belief that human beings are essentially sinful and can attain salvation only through an act of grace. In contrast, American liberal Protestantism asserted the human capacity to create a just and benevolent world. "Reasonable" Christianity provided the religious foundation for Enlightenment beliefs about humanity's ability to construct, improve, and abide by the rules of a safer and more caring environment.

The emergence of liberal Protestantism expanded the boundaries of Christianity to include the ideology of colonial Freemasonry. The latitudinarian movement in the Church of England, in particular, employed Newtonian science to stake out an understanding of religion between the extremes of Catholicism and atheism or religious indifference. Reason and science rather than faith and revelation lay at the foundation of latitudinarian belief and practice. This Anglican view was widely adopted by colonial American Masons, including clergy.

In the early nineteenth century, Protestant ministers and other members of a variety of denominations joined Freemasonry, with the great majority of its new leaders coming from the Unitarian, Episcopalian, and Congregational Churches. The brotherhood met this attraction with efforts to link itself more overtly with Christian faith. Standing to the left of sectarian Calvinists and their evangelical heirs yet to the right of Enlightenment rationalists, Christian Freemasonry appeared to respond to a widely shared desire to reimagine the character of American society as it emerged from the revolution.

The Unitarians James Thompson and William Bentley were characteristic of the Protestant ministers who joined the fraternity following the war. When he was ordained in 1804, the Harvard-educated Thompson stood, "like many of the New England clergy, on that indistinct and wavering line between Calvinism and Unitarianism, sometimes called moderate Calvinism." In that same year, the Barre, Massachusetts, native was present when the appointment of a liberal to the Hollis Professorship of Divinity marked the end of orthodoxy at his college. "Following discussions attendant on the inauguration of Dr. Ware as Hollis Professor," Thompson was said to have become "completely emancipated from Calvinistic . . . theology." He joined his local lodge shortly thereafter and later served as the grand chaplain of the Massachusetts Grand Lodge.[79] Bentley had a similar story. In his youth in prewar Salem, Massachusetts, and at Harvard during the war, he was described as a "decided and earnest Calvinist." Following his ordination and permanent settlement in Salem's Second Congregational Church in 1783, he "renounced Calvinism" and soon became an "avowed Unitarian." Two years afterward, Bentley joined his local lodge, later serving as state grand chaplain.[80]

The twenty-four ministers who served as Massachusetts Grand Lodge chaplains between 1797 and 1825 followed similar courses. Twenty were raised in the strict-to-moderate Calvinism of the Congregational Church and later helped form its liberal wing (five) and the liberal Unitarian (twelve) and Universalist (three) Churches. The majority of these grand chaplains, including two of the four Episcopalians, attended Harvard College. Nearly all were ordained within a few years of finishing college and joined their local lodge around the same time.[81]

These clergymen were benevolent and educated, concerned more with the moral and mental improvement of society than with the dogmatic sectarianism of Calvinist churches. Believing in the universal benevolence of God and universal salvation, these liberal ministers avoided theological controversies and supported the formation of interdenominational societies to advance social morality and education. These were men such as the Unitarian John Pipon, whose sermons were always "sound" but "never doctrinal" and who avoided "the topics of dispute which divided the religious community" while offering to all a "general benevolence" which "lost none of its strength by diffusion."[82] Or the Concord Unitarian Ezra Ripley, whom one congregant, the Transcendentalist Ralph Waldo Emerson, described as "adopting heartily, though in its mildest forms, the creed and catechism of the fathers" and who worked ardently for the temperance cause.[83] Some went so far as the Reverend Joseph Richardson, who declared "all religious creeds or formulas [to be] of human device" and thereby "unfit to be regarded as substitutes for the Christian life."[84] Well-educated themselves, they sat on school committees, helped form the American Education Society, and joined the Massachusetts Historical Society. With the ministers and other members of other denominations, they helped create local and national Bible societies, the Society for the Propagation of the Gospel, and numerous benevolent and charitable institutions intended to serve the community as a whole.

For these leading liberal ministers, their local Masonic brotherhood complemented and supported the larger purposes of Christianity. There they found men like themselves, from their community, from their church, who were similarly interested in mental and moral improvement. The brothers, in turn, often placed these clergymen in positions of authority. In addition to serving as grand chaplains of the Massachusetts Grand Lodge, several were deputy district grand masters; the Universalist Paul Dean became the grand master of the Massachusetts Grand Lodge, while Thompson had a lodge named after him.[85]

In their Masonic discourses, these ministers repeatedly placed the temporal work of the lodge within the greater spiritual purpose of Christianity. The Congregational minister Ezekiel L. Bascom argued that while Freemasonry was committed to improving social morality, it, like other "religious and moral societies," "rises or falls" to the degree that "piety to God" is "the reigning principle of our hearts."[86] The necessity of personal and social "regeneration for the enjoyment of the blessing of holy union," the Congregational minister and brother Clark Brown concluded, "render[ed] Masonry important, as well as Christianity necessary."[87] For these Christian Masonic clergymen, the lodge was, in an often-repeated phrase, "the handmaid" of Christianity, working toward its temporal ends while not usurping Christianity's larger spiritual objective. As Bentley bluntly declared in an address to his local Salem lodge, "the object of Christianity and Masonry never can be the same." Christianity's aim is "the advancement of personal virtue always above the state of society in common life. It proposes its highest rewards in a future existence, and directs all its associations to this end." In contrast, "our institution provides immediately for the friendship of life and manners through the world."[88]

Although the majority of early nineteenth-century Masonic clergy appear to have been Unitarian, Episcopal, or Congregational, the fraternity had some evangelical Baptist and Methodist leaders. The Baptist revivalist Joshua Bradley, known for his *Accounts of Religious Revivals in Many Parts of the United States from 1815 to 1816*, was also the author of *Some of the Beauties of Freemasonry*.[89] The Methodist Solomon Sias was the publisher of his denomination's newspaper *Zion's Herald* in the 1820s and the prelate of an advanced degree, the Encampment of Knights Templar. In 1820, he brought his evangelical convictions into the lodge, reminding his fellow Masons that "the rude and sinful state of man . . . is early impressed on the mason's mind; and the necessity of change of heart and life" is "clearly pointed out."[90] Men such as Bradley and Sias believed in human depravity and the need for an experience of conversion yet were also, like their Baptist brother John Gano, "of a liberal mind, and esteemed pious men of every denomination."[91]

Baptist missionaries and itinerant Methodists, tied to a system that relocated them every few years, may have joined the ubiquitous fraternity to help them accommodate to their constant movement. The Masonic membership of the fiery populist "Crazy" Lorenzo Dow, perhaps the most well-known and well-traveled Methodist itinerant, is further evidence of the attraction of the brotherhood to evangelical preachers. Unkempt in appearance, rough in manner, and guided by inner lights and vision, Dow had a passionate preaching style, often accompanied by hysterics and falling on the ground, that would seem the antithesis of the studied decorum of the gentleman Mason. Yet in 1830 he was introduced to a Maryland lodge meeting as a "visiting Brother." Addressing the lodge, "Brother Dow" exhorted his fellows "to show that Masons can be good men as well as good Christians."[92]

The presence of evangelical ministers in the fraternity suggests the wide appeal of postwar Masonry. The broad reaches of "Masonic Christian" theology included both evangelical convictions of human depravity and liberal confidence in human benevolence yet shared a common desire to improve the moral condition of the American people. Some ministers, moreover, may have joined the fraternity as an act of patriotism, some because it provided a measure of immunity from the dislocations and uncertainties of an increasingly mobile population, and some for social, economic, or political reasons.[93] The available evidence, however, suggests that a fit between liberal theology and Masonic ideology was the primary reason. American thought moved toward Freemasonry's Enlightenment ideals following the Revolution. Because of its embrace of all Americans and advocacy of mental and moral improvement, Masonry became central to some Christians' religious values. Though never enjoying the acceptance of all Christians, the fraternity was a significant force on the religious landscape in the early years of the republic. This was due to the expansion of not only liberal Protestantism to include Freemasonry but also the Christianization of Masonic beliefs and practices.

Ever since its 1723 constitution had demanded religious toleration, Masonry had kept its Christian content in the background. At their medieval origins, the English guilds were fervently Catholic brotherhoods watched over by patron saints. On the feast day of their saint, these artisans, carrying candles and dressed in their distinctive workmen's clothing, marched to the church where they maintained a separate altar and sanctuary light for their saint. Following Mass, the brothers gave alms to the poor and processed back to their hall for the annual election and feasting. Even after the Reformation and the 1723 constitution's adoption of religious toleration, Freemasons celebrated the saint's days of John the Baptist in June and John the Evangelist in December. In colonial America, processions to Anglican churches, with participants clothed in the white aprons and gloves of "speculative" Masons, and blessings and prayers from Anglican Masonic clergymen were fairly common on these occasions. Though a sermon, usually called a charity sermon, now replaced the Mass, the distribution of alms to the needy, the election of officers, and a banquet usually followed. In the early nineteenth century, ministers and churches from a greater variety of denominations were chosen to, respectively, address and host these festivals, yet the curious phenomenon of a nonsectarian institution keeping two ancient Catholic saints' days persisted.

The religious toleration of the 1723 constitution, written by the Presbyterian clergyman James Anderson, similarly walks an ambiguous line between universalism and Christian faith. This document's famous charge "Concerning God and Religion" states, "A Mason is oblig'd by his Tenure to obey the moral Law; and if he rightly understands the Art, he will never be a stupid Atheist, nor an irreligious Libertine. But though in ancient Times Masons were charged in every Country to be of the Religion of that Country or Nation, whatever it was, yet 'tis now thought more expedient only to oblige them to that Religion in which all Men agree." Though asking only that members accept "that religion in which all men agree," in the lengthy history that is also part of the constitution, Anderson notably interweaves the history of Masonry with biblical history, celebrating the birth of "God's Messiah, the great Architect of the Church."[94]

About fifty years after the publication of the 1723 constitution, William Preston's *Illustrations of Freemasonry* (1772) forcefully reasserted the fraternity's belief in universal religion. This book provides details of the style and form of Masonic ceremonies and was widely read over the next half century. Here Preston wrote, "The distant Chinese, the wild Arab, and the American savage, will embrace a brother Briton. . . . The spirit of the fulminating priest will be tamed; and a moral brother, though of a different persuasion, engage his esteem; for mutual toleration in religious opinions is one of the most distinguishing and valuable characteristics of the Craft. As all religions teach morality, if a brother be found to act the part of a truly honest man, his private speculative opinions are left to God himself."[95] Yet around the same time, the English Mason William Hutchison published a less well-known work, *The Spirit of Masonry* (1775), that just as forcefully asserts the fraternity's Christianity. "It is not to be presumed," he wrote, "that we are a set of men professing religious principles contrary to the revelations and doctrines of the 'SON OF GOD', reverencing a Deity by the denomination of the God of Nature, and denying the mediation which is graciously offered to all true believers. The members of our Society at this day, in the third stage of Masonry, acknowledge themselves to be CHRISTIANS."[96]

Given this ambiguous legacy, the postwar Christianization of Masonry amounted to a more overt linkage of Christianity and Masonic membership. Though clergymen had previously held prominent positions in the fraternity, the position of grand chaplain was now institutionalized and regularly called on their ministerial gifts. Massachusetts established this office as early as 1797.[97] Connecticut did the same in 1815 with the appointment of the Reverend Roger Searle of the Episcopal Church, who then opened and closed Grand Lodge sessions with a "very solemn and impressive prayer" that became a new form of ceremonial.[98] Prominent in processions, often between the grand master and the steward who carried the Bible, grand chaplains were now called on to pray over cornerstones and administer the dedicatory corn, oil, and wine, their prayers, blessings, and sermons becoming regular, Christian elements in Masonic proceedings.

Other Christian elements now appeared in the order's ritual life. In New York, members prayed that "our new brother . . . may, with the secrets of Free Masonry, be able to unfold the mysteries of Godliness and Christianity." New York's Grand Lodge also condemned "the transaction of any business" on the Sabbath.[99] In Connecticut, the Grand Lodge considered a request that all prayers used in initiations be "offered through Jesus Christ, as the common Savior and mediator between God and man."[100] In sum, by the early nineteenth century, leading brothers such as John Crawford, Maryland's grand master, were arguing that "Masons should abandon the idea that their only concern is to perfect the religion of nature" and instead realize that only through "intimate acquaintance with the holy writ" could they become worthy Masons.[101]

CHRISTIAN OPPOSITION

Despite Masonry's Christianization, not all churches endorsed the Enlightenment-leavened Christianity of the postwar lodge. While the

fraternity's promotion of Christian piety, interdenominational cooperation, and benevolence reflected the ideology of liberal denominations, it
also challenged the sectarian claims to exclusive religious truth and the
congregational loyalty of the more orthodox, Calvinist churches. In
New England in particular, where church and state had been tightly
interwoven, the fraternity's perceived irreligion and separation from
church life came under attack. In the last years of the eighteenth century, Calvinist Congregational leaders tried to yoke the American fraternity with the Bavarian Illuminati and targeted the lodge as a source
of the many far-reaching changes that had occurred in society since the
mid-seventeenth-century heyday of the Puritan faithful. At the same
time, orthodox ministers protested the brotherhood's secrecy, encouragement of social amusement, and belief in natural religion. Though
this opposition did not effectively prove the flaws in Freemasonry to
orthodox parishioners, it did make Calvinist clergy aware that the lodge
was not only attracting men from their churches but also withdrawing
new areas of their parishioners' lives from pastoral guidance.[102]

American Christian opposition to Freemasonry had its deepest roots
in colonial Puritan beliefs in not only the sovereignty of God and the
depravity of mankind but also the political and religious leadership of
God's elect. In the colonies of Massachusetts and Connecticut, only
"visible saints," church members who were thought to have experienced God's saving grace, could hold political power. Because the convergence of republicanism and Christianity in the revolutionary era
expanded the Christian ideas of liberty and community to encompass
not only the church but the nation as well, orthodox emphasis on the
Christian meanings of this new ideology led conservative Calvinists to
defend the new republicanism with religious fervor. Both the Puritans
and republicans saw history as a struggle between good and evil. The
Calvinist opposition of Christ versus Antichrist paralleled the republican battle between liberty and tyranny. Most Calvinists and republicans
similarly saw the good society as free of corruption, either of sin (Calvinists) or of power (republicans). As these two views began to merge
during the Revolution, orthodox Christians and their evangelical heirs
employed the language of republicanism to defend Christian truth and
congregational loyalty.[103]

This was particularly true in the colonies of New England as the
closed, corporate character of their theocracies, established in the seventeenth century, began to unravel. Following the revivals of the First
Great Awakening, Calvinist ministers' longstanding worries over sinful

behavior increased. Worldliness, the Enlightenment tolerance of skepticism, and a loosening of doctrinal standards contributed to this unease. Next came the political instability, economic turmoil, drinking, cursing, and other signs of moral depravity of the revolutionary years. Then followed the outbreak of the French Revolution and the fear that outsiders espousing subversive beliefs were seeking to overthrow the new institutions of American society.[104] For New England's Calvinist ministers, steeped in a federal covenant theology, the defense of their society, which God had chosen for his own designs, necessarily meant that the church must speak out. At the end of the eighteenth century, Calvinist leaders in New England and elsewhere began to organize a reform movement to conquer the evils of sin and foreign tyranny that now appeared to them to threaten American society.[105]

The ground was thus prepared for the sermon that the Congregational minister Jedidiah Morse gave in Charlestown, Massachusetts, on May 9, 1798, a day set aside by President John Adams for "solemn humiliation, fasting and prayer." Morse was a graduate of Yale, had studied theology with Jonathan Edwards the Younger, and held to New Light theology, which affirmed that the revivals of the 1740s were a work of God. Morse began his sermon by voicing Calvinist republican worries over the social danger of growing irreligion. Directing his attack specifically at such anti-Christian works as Thomas Paine's *The Age of Reason* (1794), Morse declared, "Atheism and materialism are systematically professed. Reason and Nature are deified and adored. The Christian religion, and its divine and blessed author, are not only disbelieved, rejected and contemned, but even abhorred." Morse went on to assail those who employed "reviling and abuse" to malign state leaders and the clergy who, in keeping with the Calvinist belief in the alliance of church and state, had done what they could to support and vindicate the government.[106] The Charlestown pastor then delivered his bombshell accusation that there was "reason to suspect that there is some secret plan in operation hostile to true liberty and religion." Based on his reading of a book on European conspiracies by the Scottish scientist John Robison and little other evidence, Morse declared that the Bavarian Illuminati and their branches in this country were conspiring to subvert both independence and Christianity.[107] Coming at a time of political turmoil, this salvo began two years of newspaper controversy and pulpit pronouncements concerning the repute of Freemasonry.[108]

Though Morse's sermon contained no references to Freemasonry, Robison's work describes an underground society in Germany, the

Illuminated Masons, or Illuminati, who had spread their influence through Masonic lodges. Created, according to Robison, to overthrow both state and church, the Illuminati had been a secret influence in the French Revolution. When his sermon was printed, Morse explained in extended footnotes that his attack was directed not against Freemasonry but against Illuminism, which was "a vile and pestiferous *scion* grafted on the stock of simple Masonry." Further, he believed that these corruptions could not have entered this country, where the immortal Washington stood at the head of the Masonic fraternity and the Masons of New England "have ever shown themselves firm and decided supporters of civil and religious order."[109] Indeed, the Charlestown pastor demonstrated his support for the order by addressing Concord's Corinthian Lodge just two months after the May speech.[110]

Despite these exculpations, Morse's identification of the Illuminati as the cause of continuing social disorders began a growing indictment of American Freemasonry. Soon thereafter, Yale's Congregational president Timothy Dwight fanned the fire by publicly declaring that American Freemasonry was involved in a conspiracy with the destructively radical Bavarian Illuminati. A champion of the Connecticut New Light Calvinist establishment, Dwight was on a campaign in 1798 to eradicate Enlightenment skepticism and irreligion from his college, his denomination, and anywhere else he found it, including "secret" societies. In his Fourth of July sermon that year, he pointedly lambasted the Masons for providing a clandestine place where "every innovator" could "attack every doctrine and institution, however guarded by law or sanctity."[111]

New England Masonry responded promptly to the disparagements of Robison and his American followers. On June 11, 1798, the Grand Lodge of Massachusetts composed a loyal address to President Adams that expressed alarm at the "illiberal attacks of a foreign enthusiast, aided by the unfounded prejudices of his followers," which were "tending to embarrass the public mind with respect to the real views of our society."[112] The Unitarian minister and Masonic apologist William Bentley followed with an assault on those clergy "who play the shuttle-cock of faith, with the dexterity of expert gamesters, and have the art of making the multitude fly with its feathers." Singling out Morse, he concluded that "we must leave Robison to an inquisitive public and forgive a worthy divine who has noticed the book, and has made our order ridiculous."[113]

Regardless of these and other denials, continuing agitations by the orthodox clergy and the press appear to have had some effect. One

Rhode Island Mason admitted publicly that the fraternity was suffering from "a temporary odium." In Massachusetts, another lamented that Morse's charges had considerably embarrassed the order. Another worried over a loss in membership. Statistical evidence for eight Boston-area lodges from 1794 to 1802 does show a dip in membership in 1799, yet it was one from which the fraternity rapidly recovered following its public role in George Washington's funeral in December of that year.[114]

Despite the Illuminati fury, the prominent and unchallenged position of Freemasons in both Washington's funeral and the many public processions that marked the passing of the nation's first president dampened criticism of the order.[115] Not only were Masons accorded places of honor in these ceremonies, but Washington was remembered as a Mason who wore the fraternity's apron and sash at the laying of the Capitol's cornerstone and who praised the brotherhood's embodiment of the values of the new American society. One Masonic orator asked, "If our principles and doctrines . . . destroy the bonds of nature and of government; how could Washington, that *Perfect Man*, when his feet were stumbling upon the dark mountains of death, say, 'I am ready to die,' until he had warned the world to beware of the Masonic institution and its consequences? He was a thorough investigator, and a faithful follower of our doctrines."[116] Following the ex-president's death, the Illuminati-fueled attacks on the fraternity rapidly declined. For how could Freemasonry be anything but noble if Washington had been among its members? Publicly proud, republican, and Christian, early nineteenth-century Masonry claimed to stand in the vanguard of the emerging American society. In this same period, it was developing elaborate and private ceremonies that responded to new trends in American society.

CHAPTER 3

A Private World of Ritual, 1797–1825

In the early nineteenth century, American Freemasonry developed an extensive ritual life. The perfunctory ceremonies carried out in rented rooms of colonial taverns now took as much as several hours to perform, in elegantly decorated sanctuaries in permanent lodge buildings. Ceremonial dress, dramatic action, sensual imagery, mysterious symbols, and symbolic objects now came into play. This was especially true of the new Royal Arch degrees, which were higher than those previously available and whose initiatory steps advanced a select few along a path of moral and spiritual enlightenment toward the discovery of ancient wisdom. These rituals led the brotherhood back to its seventeenth-century longing for ancient wisdom and forward to romanticism's search for one's true identity through deep feelings. Candidates were introduced to what they believed to be primordial truth, from the beginning of time; at the same time, the new ceremonies employed violent emotional attacks to break down the initiate's defenses and allow him to arrive at an interior self.[1] This new emphasis on ritual encouraged the creation of a separate ceremonial world.

The transformation of Masonic rituals contributed to several significant developments amid the religious pluralism and social disorder of the early nineteenth century. In its emphasis on the recovery and restoration of ancient truth, postwar Masonry resembled Protestant primitivism. In the early nineteenth century, a variety of religious groups—including the Mormons, the Disciples of Christ, and the Landmark

Baptists—embraced efforts to restore the church's ancient foundations. This impulse signaled the failure of Enlightenment attempts to advance reason over primeval wisdom. At the same time, the revivalists of the Second Great Awakening sought to penetrate to the hearts of "sinners" and to provoke strong emotions in their congregants, who would thus reach their inner selves. Though taken from ancient times, Freemasonry's new rituals paralleled such forward-pointing tendencies in Evangelicalism. The evolution of this ritual world also contributed to the early nineteenth-century emergence of private spheres. Though historians have given much attention to the gradual development of a female world of pious domesticity apart from public life, the creation of Freemasonry's ceremonial life carved out a parallel realm for men. Taking place alongside rather than replacing the lodge's public purposes, the new rituals marked a new movement of men between a homosocial private world and participation in public life. In the early years of the republic, this movement was paralleled by the efforts of women to enter into public life, as educators, editors, and moral reformers. Though Masonic men continued to be prominent in public life, as the century progressed, both Freemasons and elite women became identified with their respective intimate private worlds.

NEW RITUALS

The impetus for the revision of American Masonic ceremonies originated in England. Prior to the transformation in 1717 from a guild of craft masons to a fraternity of gentlemen, operative masonry had but the "meagre ritual" of two rites "intended to embody merely methods of recognition." The new speculative Masons expanded these into three degree ceremonies.[2] By the 1760s, however, some believed that the elementary nature of the new rites, coupled with the convivial ethos of the lodge, had resulted in their being "sunk into oblivion" through "inattention."[3] To remedy this situation, William Preston, an editor by trade and the master of several London Ancient lodges, worked with his friends to gather old Masonic documents, corresponded with Masonic leaders, and observed lodge ceremonies throughout England. He collated what he found, added his own thoughts and observations, and then worked his material into a system.[4] Though forbidden to reveal the content of his three degree rites, which would have been "violating the Laws of the Order," Preston designed his *Illustrations of Masonry* (1772) to "illustrate" that the "Craft" was intended to teach moral lessons and improve the character of its members through lectures and ceremonies.[5] For the next hundred years, the many American editions of this work provided the foundation for American Masonic ritual life.

Preston's rituals for the three degrees—Entered Apprentice, Fellow Craftsman, and Master Mason—collectively known as Craft Masonry (and later as Blue Lodge Masonry, in reference to the traditional color of the regalia in lodges derived from English or Irish Freemasonry), took place in a large rectangular lodge room, which the candidate learned was a representation of King Solomon's Temple. Solomon's Temple itself was modeled on the tabernacle that the ancient Israelites had erected following their flight from Egypt. A Bible was placed on an altar in the middle of the room, beside replicas of a craftsman's square and compass, and laid open to a passage appropriate for the evening's "labor." Seated around the room were the lodge members, clad in respectable clothing and white aprons, the latter often trimmed in blue and bearing an embroidered "All-Seeing Eye" of God.[6] The major officers sat in designated chairs, the engraved metal pendants on their embroidered collars symbolizing their offices. Prior to the Entered Apprentice ceremony, the candidate was asked to, among other things, take his left arm out of his shirt sleeve, to expose his left breast, and empty his pants pockets. A rope, or "cable-tow," was then placed loosely around his neck, with one end dragging on the floor behind him, after which he was blindfolded. "Neither naked nor clothed," the candidate was now prepared for his journey. The lights in the room were extinguished so that only the glow from the three candles placed around the altar could be seen. Slowly the present faded from view, and before the candidate's eyes an imagined scene from the past appeared.[7]

Each of the three basic rituals lasted more than an hour, with the classic elements of a rite of passage now clearly present. These included the candidate's "separation" from his normal life, experience of "marginality" through symbolic actions that intensified his physical and mental disorientation, and final "integration" into his new social identity as a member of the Masonic brotherhood.[8] As the candidate proceeded in his travels around the room, often being led in circles, he was stopped at certain points to hear a lecture, respond to questions, kneel in prayer before the central altar, or hear a passage from Scripture.

The key moment of these ceremonies occurred when the stimulation of the candidate's senses linked his emotions and intellect. At the beginning of the Entered Apprentice rite, for example, the point of a compass met the blindfolded candidate's bare breast. The senior deacon then sternly warned him of the necessity of keeping secret all that was to follow: "As this is a prick of your flesh, may the recollection of it be to your mind and conscience, and instant death in the case of revolt."[9] The fear that likely accompanied the stab of his breast was intended to heighten the candidate's awareness and call to mind for some time to come the deacon's solemn warning. As he progressed through the degrees, some sensory stimulation intended to link a rush of feeling with the order's ideals accompanied each lesson that the candidate received. Such trials taught the initiate the history of the order, the meaning of its key symbols, and his moral responsibilities as a Mason. At the end of the Entered Apprentice ritual, the cable tow was removed, the candidate restored his clothes, and an oath of loyalty and investment with his apron and working tools integrated him into his new social identity. The admonishment to secrecy that first worked to separate the candidate from his previous social role now united him more closely to the group. For those who experience this integration into the brotherhood, the Masonic leader John Vanderbilt said in 1808, "nothing can be more binding, nothing more sacred or more pious."[10]

Early nineteenth-century Masons believed that the symbolic education of the three degree rituals was "peculiarly calculated to impress the mind with a deep sense of eternal things."[11] Though some might see the symbols as "selected by caprice, and arranged to make a show," according to John Sheppard, the lodge master of Portland, Maine, "the furniture, the ornaments, and the jewels of a Lodge, all convey moral lessons." Indeed, "everything in the Masonic hall" was an instrument "of the mind[,] to retain knowledge and communicate it to others."[12] These images made an impression on the senses. Reflecting the Lockean epistemology of his day, elaborated by David Hartley and what became the British associationist school, Preston's rituals were founded on the premise that sensations are the source of the mind's ideas. According to Preston, "Every thing that strikes the eye more immediately engages the attention, and imprints on the memory those circumstances which are accompanied with serious and solemn truths."[13] Extending Locke's principle of association, Hartley argued that even moral ideas are learned through sensory stimulation and strengthened by repetition.[14] Therefore, the greatest sensory stimulation accompanied the rituals' greatest moral lessons. When asked to offer a coin to the lodge in the Entered Apprentice rite, for example, the candidate would find nothing in his pocket and be seized with guilt. At this point the master admonished, "Let this ever be a striking lesson" to assist any brother in a like condition whom he might encounter.[15] For early nineteenth-century American Masons, frequent repetition of the three central rites in the regular induction of new members, coupled with a new emphasis on their precise performance—through attention to detail, memorization of key teachings, and standardization of ritual content—assured their deepening impression on the brothers' minds.

The popularity of Preston's rituals in America underscores the widespread adoption of Enlightenment theories of knowledge in the postwar fraternity. John Locke's epistemology and Isaac Newton's science were foundational to the Enlightenment thinking that eclipsed classical assumptions about the human mind and the universe in much of Britain and America in the late eighteenth and early nineteenth centuries. Classical thinkers assumed that the elements of the universe obeyed the commands of a divine presence. In Newton's cosmology, in contrast, scientific principles, not God's actions, explained the universe. The planets moved not because God so commanded but because of their gravitational pull and relative weight. Though created and sustained by divine powers, the universe was not in itself moral. In like manner, Locke created a new model of the mind, which he saw as endowed not with innate ideas but with the power to make ideas out of its impressions. For centuries, people had believed that the purpose of knowledge was to discover objective, transcendent truth. Against this classical tradition, Locke asserted that the essences of things cannot be known. In his *Essay Concerning Human Understanding* (1690), Locke proposes that the receipt of sense information about the "primary qualities of things"—solidity, motion, number—and the more subjectively perceived "secondary qualities"—color, texture, odor, taste—produce generalizations, or "ideas."[16] All we can ever know, according to him, are the ideas that our senses create and that reside in our circle of consciousness. Preston's rituals, based on these assumptions, presented a new moral pedagogy to early nineteenth-century American Masons.[17] Rather than resting in the belief that innate ideas about God govern the human mind, Enlightenment thinkers held that moral knowledge is to be found through the ideas developed from sensory impressions. As Benjamin Gleason, the first grand lecturer hired to inculcate the new rituals, said, "The work is now changed! It is improved! . . . We are now upon the Voyage of Experiment!"[18]

While most members of the American fraternity were satisfied to complete just the three Craft degrees, a considerable number were drawn to discover the further mysteries taught by the new upper grades of the ritualistic progression. The development of these higher degrees can be traced to two sources. The York Rite rituals originated in the English mid-eighteenth-century elaboration of the third, or Master's, degree into what later became a seven-degree system culminating in the Royal Arch degree. Recall that the original reason the English Ancients gave for their split with the English Moderns in 1751 was anger over this degree tinkering. Nevertheless, it was the Ancients who continued these revisions. What became known as the Scottish Rite was the second source of the higher degree ceremonies. The Scotsman Andrew Michael Ramsay, who became the grand orator of the Grand Lodge of France in 1740, inspired these. Chevalier Ramsay rejected the operative origins of Freemasonry and instead traced the society's birth to Palestine at the time of the Crusades. Religious and military themes took the place of architecture in the degrees invented by those he inspired, leading to the incorporation of the Orders of Knighthood into the expanding degree system.[19] Through Ramsay's influence, elaborate regalia, staging, and new sacred elements entered the lodge's system of symbols. The late eighteenth-century transmission to America of parts of these two evolving higher degree systems by different people and at different times, plus the ongoing creation of unrelated rites by individual entrepreneurs,[20] made for ritual chaos until the arrival of Thomas Smith Webb's pivotal *Freemason's Monitor, or Illustrations of Masonry* in 1797.[21]

Working with the eighth edition of Preston's *Illustrations* and adding a considerable amount of new material, Webb, a printer from Albany, New York, created what became the most widely read and influential manual for early nineteenth-century American Freemasonry. In this volume, Webb acknowledges that his material on the first three degrees is "principally taken" from Preston's work, with some minor alterations.[22] To this he added materials that he gathered on his visits to lodges in Boston and Philadelphia, plus his own thoughts and elaborations. Beyond Preston's three symbolic degrees, Webb introduced the Royal Arch degree, which had spread unevenly throughout the American Ancient lodges in the latter half of the eighteenth century. What in later editions became the new Royal Arch system of four additional degrees culminating in the Royal Arch ceremony proliferated in America after 1800. In some areas, by 1820 there was one Royal Arch chapter for every two lodges. Gradually, Webb's revised York, or American, Rite evolved into a series of degrees extending beyond the Royal Arch and including the Knights Templar. The second part of the book includes information on a separate progression of eleven degrees, titled the Ineffable Degrees of

Masonry, which were part of the Scottish Rite. Although different people brought elements of these "French" rituals to America prior to the Revolution, the creation of the first Supreme Council of the Ancient and Accepted Scottish Rite of Freemasonry, in Charleston, South Carolina, in 1801, most firmly established their presence in America.[23] Webb also devoted six chapters to "Observations on the Orders of Knighthood," including the Knights Templar, the Knights of Malta, the Red Cross, and several minor orders. As an evolving all-purpose manual, what became known as the Webb-Preston Work went through eight editions and sold more than sixteen thousand copies by the time of its author's death in 1819.[24] By the 1820s, most American Masons had passed through the three basic rituals, and a majority of the leadership had proceeded to the Royal Arch degree of the American Rite, while a much smaller minority had participated in the less firmly established rituals of the Scottish Rite.[25]

This rapid development of postwar American Masonry's private ritual life occurred at the same time that the fraternity's public structures were changing to accommodate the need to expand and regularize their activities. As we have seen, in the first quarter of the nineteenth century, the membership of the American Masonic fraternity increased more than threefold, from twenty-five thousand members largely in the urban East to eighty thousand brothers spread from the coast to the country's western expansion as far as Missouri.[26] Bureaucratic expansion accompanied this unprecedented growth. Where previously there had been only local lodges and state Grand Lodges, now most towns had Royal Arch Chapters, while in most cities one or two Knights Templar Commanderies could be found. Each of these new layers of Masonic activity had its own hierarchy of officers and was subordinate to its respective state and national Grand Chapters and Grand Commanderies.[27] At the same time, the supervision of local lodge activity spurred the creation of new offices. In Massachusetts, the lodges were divided into twelve districts, each with a deputy grand master.[28] In New York, inspectors were appointed to promote uniformity in lodge procedures and collect dues.[29] In South Carolina, and eventually throughout the American fraternity, holders of the new position of grand lecturer instructed the brethren in the proper performance of their rituals.[30] In many states, fundraising committees were established to build permanent lodge buildings. Further regularization resulted from the creation of rules governing fees, meeting times, proper procedures, and the like. In 1811, at the end of a busy term as Massachusetts's grand master when many of these reforms were enacted, the printer Isaiah Thomas exulted to his brethren that "order and regularity prevail and many serious evils are corrected."[31]

The growth and regularization of the Masonic fraternity paralleled the postwar evolution of voluntary societies, churches, and political parties. Following the revolution, benevolent and educational societies, upstart denominations, and political parties all developed translocal organizations that separated them from local societies. The tasks of spreading information and standardizing procedures demanded the creation of extensive organizational infrastructures. The wide-scale and inexpensive distribution of printed material, the need for traveling agents and paid staff, and the centralization of authority all encouraged the growth and rationalization of national societies.[32] This was the case as much for such interdenominational voluntary organizations as the American Bible Society and the American Sunday School Union as for the Federalist and Democratic-Republican political parties. Among the churches, the ascendance of Methodists and Baptists through a democratization of leadership and worship styles, revival methods, and adaptive organizations similarly demonstrated the need for new structures to harness the growth and freedom of the postcolonial era.[33] Similar to all of these evolving national organizations, the Masonic fraternity was expanding and regularizing its public activities. But unlike these societies, the fraternity was also developing a private, inner life. While Freemasonry's public face claimed that it exemplified and led the nascent American society, its new and involved ritual life differentiated it from other groups. The simple colonial rituals of initiation to polite society were now enshrouded in a private world of intimate friendship and deepening meaning.

The touchstone for the development of the fraternity's ritual life was the Master Mason degree. Though this initiation ceremony was similar in structure to those of the first two degrees, it introduced a new flair for the dramatic that also characterized the higher rites. Whereas the first degree provided basic instruction in the beliefs and practices of the order, and the second degree elaborated on the fields of knowledge that constitute Masonic learning (science, polite learning, the seven liberal arts, geometry, architecture, the five senses, etc.), the third degree focused on the loss of the knowledge of God and efforts to achieve its restoration. The need to achieve this restoration, Masons held, was the impetus for the creation of the higher degrees.[34] Without this restoration, Webb and his followers believed, "the masonic character cannot be complete."[35]

Following a reenactment of the central elements of the earlier degrees, in the third degree ritual the candidate was reblindfolded and performed the story of the murder of Hiram Abiff, the Master Mason of King Solomon's Temple. The candidate, in the role of Abiff, was asked for the secret Word by three ruffians. When he refused, he was seized by the throat and given violent blows until he was left for dead and "buried" in a canvas bag. Like the earlier rituals, the third degree sought to achieve a connection between the heart and the mind of the candidate (and vicariously of all those present) through the stimulation of the senses. In the ceremony, ritual music, chanting, attractive and alarming objects, poetic dialogue, prayer, tactile movements, and confrontations all worked to this end. The physical confrontations between the candidate and the three ruffians unsettled him. The "fatal" blow was a hit with a soft bag, which knocked him backward to the floor. The third degree ritual also left the candidate in a state of liminality for twice as long as the first and second. For much of this time he was socially invisible, playing the part of a dead man wrapped in canvas. Following this extended marginality, he experienced reintegration with a greater force than in the first two degrees. With Abiff dead and all hope of recovering the Master's Word lost, Temple workmen (members of the lodge) surrounded the candidate in the role of the slain mason. Then the prodigious effort of King Hiram of Tyre (the senior warden) and King Solomon (the master of the lodge) raised the "dead" candidate, in whose ear was whispered the Word that would substitute for the one that had been lost. At this moment the blindfold was removed, and after the lodge master's lecture on the significance of all that had occurred, the candidate was recognized as a Master Mason.[36]

The higher degrees continued the dramatic escalation of the third degree, employing elaborate costumes, props, and action to take candidates on arduous pilgrimages from the sterile present into the ancient past in search of deeper meaning. The most popular of the higher degree ceremonies, that of the Royal Arch, began with three candidates thrown to the ground, tied together, blindfolded, and then told that they must "travel through rough and rugged ways, and pass through many trials" to respond to God's charge that they rebuild the Temple at Jerusalem. In their journey, they crossed wild rivers, penetrated dark forests, and were confronted with live fire and treated as "strangers." In the physical space of the lodge ritual room, they had "a good deal of difficulty" repeatedly crawling through a gauntlet of men who forcefully kneaded "their knuckles upon the necks and backs of the candidates." The initiates then made their way through a "rugged road" of "blocks, and logs of wood, old chairs and benches." Finally, passing through the brightly colored veils of the Temple hung in the lodge room, they met "a dazzling light" and accepted the "High Priest's" offer of work on the Temple, "no matter how servile or dangerous." At the end they discovered a hidden vault below a trap door, where one of their number, lowered by rope "even to the risk of [their] lives," found the long-lost Ark of the Covenant. Congratulated for their accomplishments and adorned with Royal Arch aprons trimmed with scarlet, they were left to wonder how the ark had gotten there. "You must go higher in Masonry before you can know," they were told.[37] Webb regarded the Royal Arch degree as "indescribably more august, sublime and important, than all which precede it; . . . the summit and perfection of ancient masonry."[38] Taken together, the mysterious symbolism of the higher degrees not only further integrated those who persevered through them into the membership and most frequently leadership of the brotherhood but also promised Masons that they might finally arrive someday at "the source of all those virtues which we have so often been told it is our duty to practice."[39]

These strange, secret ceremonial practices created by early nineteenth-century Masons, so different from colonial rites, were responses to a changing social world. Following the Revolution, the balance of the American economy shifted, from the subsistence agriculture of the countryside to the emerging mercantile and early industrial capitalism of the new urban centers. In 1776, U.S. cities with more than five thousand inhabitants numbered less than a dozen; by 1850, there were about one hundred and fifty. In the eighteenth century, Americans had organized their economy in hierarchical patterns modeled on the family. The seasonal, task-oriented, family-centered work that characterized both the farm and small artisan shops reflected these hierarchical ideals and deference of the colonial period. Following the War of 1812, the transportation revolution and the rapid expansion of the marketplace dismantled this model of economic production, physically separating master craftsmen and merchants from their workers and giving rise to a contractual capitalist system. Rather than being treated as dependents in an extended family, workers were now relative strangers valued for their productivity in a fluid marketplace of time-disciplined labor. In this context, a growing number of mobile and propertyless young men struggled to attain the stability and status of their colonial forebears.[40]

Webb's journey was characteristic of this generation. Born the son of a poor Boston artisan, he struggled to support his mother and sisters after his father's early death, suffered several business reversals, and lived in four states before achieving gentleman status. As Steven C. Bullock has argued, the men who were most invested in the new rituals, and so rose to positions of leadership, had similar experiences. What best defined them was neither wealth nor social status but Masonic interest.[41] Responding to Webb's descriptions of a cold, selfish world marked by uncertainty and struggle, they took to his new rituals, which helped them to connect with what they believed to be a primeval religious certainty while granting them a private status far removed from the public cultural world of colonial gentlemen.

The development of Freemasonry's private world was part of the early nineteenth-century emergence of private spheres where individuals increasingly received greater recognition. In the 1830s, Alexis de Tocqueville noted the tendency of "each citizen to isolate himself from the mass of those like him and to withdraw to one side with his family and friends," so creating a "little society for his own use."[42] Scholars of women's experiences have emphasized the effect of this bifurcation of social life on women, though men were influenced as well.[43] As Jan Lewis has argued for Thomas Jefferson's Virginia, in America the breakdown of gentry dominance amid the growing difficulty of achieving financial independence undercut the republican call to civic virtue. Where previously the society's leading men had devoted themselves to public service, now they began to withdraw from politics to serve their families first.[44] Moreover, historians of the family agree that in the early part of the nineteenth century, the decline of patriarchal authority was accompanied by the rise of more equal, companionate relationships between husband and wife and the encouragement of "indulgent" child-rearing practices, which resulted in a new and time-consuming emphasis on love rather than obligation and duty as the core of family relationships.[45] At this time, therefore, changes in the economy, the social order, and the family contributed to an expanding private life. In this context, a growing number of elite women became identified with the pious and private world of domesticity, while affluent men retreated to the new ceremonial life of Freemasonry.

PRIMEVAL WISDOM

An aura of mystery and the pursuit of a hidden wisdom that only a few might come to know enshrouded Freemasonry's higher rites. Postwar Masons believed that they were recovering an ancient wisdom that speculative Masons had lost. Thomas Smith Webb described the Royal Arch degree as bringing "to light many essentials of the craft, which were for the space of 470 years buried in darkness."[46] Although hermeticism and the supernatural had been primary emphases of the earliest British speculative Masons, they were marginal adornments to the rationalism of the colonial British and American lodges. Scattered amid colonial lodge publications are occasional references to "essential secrets," yet there is little to suggest that mystical practices were avidly pursued at that time.[47] Only gradually did postwar Masons recover the connection to ancient wisdom. The fullest realization of sophisticated hermetic knowledge was in the Scottish Rite degrees, but these were not broadly available until the 1820s and not popular until the 1850s.

Yet for those willing to read between the lines, early nineteenth-century Masonic manuals provide intimations of hidden, ancient truth. Ever since the 1723 appearance of the order's modern constitution, Masonic publications regularly reprinted the brotherhood's lengthy mythical history, which attributed Freemasonry's origins to multiple influences predating Christianity. According to this history, the fraternity arose at the beginning of time, when Adam, "our first parent, created after the Image of God, the great architect of the Universe," had the knowledge of "Geometry, written on his Heart." The story then traces the losing and the refinding of this ancient art, which Masons believed to "involve many religious truths," ranging from the Hebrew Scripture's accounts of Noah's Ark and the Babylonian exile on through to Greece, Rome, and eventually medieval England. Along the way, it identifies such biblical luminaries as Moses and King Solomon as Master Masons. Yet it also recognizes innumerable pagan "priests and mathematicians," the builders of the great Egyptian pyramids, the Greek mathematicians Pythagoras and Euclid, and eminent men as far away as "India" and the "African nations" as learned in "the good Science." Not only Jews and Christians but also Egyptians, Greeks, Indians, Africans, Druids, and various unnamed practitioners of the "Royal Art" populate this account, providing the reader with multiple tributaries beyond the Bible that ultimately lead back to God's inscription of Masonic wisdom on Adam's heart.[48] The diversity of this heritage led Thomas Paine to conclude that Masonry "is derived from some very ancient religion wholly independent of, and unconnected with that book [the Bible]."[49] Webb's *Freemason's Monitor* speaks of a "mystery" to be engaged "which requires a gradual progression of knowledge." It would teach initiates with eyes to see the true meaning of "hieroglyphical figures" and "allegorical emblems" that had been communicated "from the most remote periods of antiquity."[50]

The promise of initiation into ancient mysteries was most apparent in the Scottish Rite version of the Royal Arch ritual. This ceremony was built around a vision thought to have been experienced by the prophet Enoch. Enoch, the sixth son in descent from Adam, wanted to know the name of God so that he could be restored to the prelapsarian perfection of Adam. God appeared to Enoch in a vision and, wanting to reveal his name, sent Enoch to the top of a mountain, where he beheld a triangular plate of gold inscribed with some characters, which he was admonished never to pronounce. Enoch then built an underground temple of nine arches that hid the plate. Ages passed until Solomon's architects came upon Enoch's temple while building a similar temple to God and discovered the mysteries on the golden plate.[51] The Enoch legend involves a restoration of both primordial truth and an original priesthood. Like the members of the spiritually powerful Hebraic priesthood, the Royal Arch high priest was to be "a priest forever after the order of Melchizedec."[52]

This emphasis on a return to primeval wisdom and the restoration of an original priesthood resembles the impulses of Protestant primitivism. Despite the Enlightenment's forward embrace of reason, order, and science eclipsing ancient ways of knowing, persisting currents within and outside Christianity continued to assert that the human pilgrimage must reach back to the primitive "first times" of pristine purity to find the secrets of life. Passages in the Bible with recurrent themes of longing to return to the Garden of Eden, restore the covenant with God, and renew an original kingdom of God aided this desire.[53] Such early nineteenth-century religious groups as the Churches of Christ, the Landmark Baptists, the Christian movement, and the Mormons embraced the ideal of restoring the ancient church by recovering the Christianity of the first apostles. Prior to this period, the Anabaptists and other sixteenth-century radical reformers had advocated a return to the "primitive" church. This crusade first came to America with the Puritan attempt to reform the Church of England by embracing the biblical ideal of a Christian commonwealth. Throughout the colonial period, Edwin S. Gaustad has argued, there was a strong "sentiment of restoration" that included a determination to leap the darkness of centuries and re-create the pure church of the first Christians.[54] This desire reemerged amid the religious pluralism and social disorder of the post-revolutionary era, when various churches argued that to embrace the "old ways" was to establish a clear and reliable certainty amid the confusion surrounding contending versions of Christianity. Though these groups disputed exactly what was the essence of Christianity, they were united in their belief that the first Christians embodied a sacred authority and truth that subsequent generations had lost.[55]

Like these primitivist churches, the Freemasons of the early nineteenth century sought to return to an ancient wisdom that had "escaped" the "ruins" of time and been preserved in its original "integrity and purity." In 1818, Grand Chaplain Salem Town lectured the Grand Lodge of New York on the brotherhood's belief that the principles of ancient Masonry "were coeval with the creation of the material world." Following the history in the order's modern constitution, Town believed that prior to the building of King Solomon's Temple, the fraternity existed only in religious and moral ideas found throughout the known world.[56] The building of the Temple, he believed, marked the institutionalization of these ideas, through the formation of the operative brotherhood. Both Masonic books and exposés of the period reported this conviction, that the principles of Freemasonry could be traced backward from Solomon to Adam, while the building of Solomon's Temple had inaugurated and preserved its organization and rituals. As an ancient institution founded "on the Rock of eternal ages," Freemasonry had withstood the ravages of time and retained the capacity to offer its candidates the opportunity to "enter into the celestial lodge above, where the Supreme Architect of the Universe presides . . . [in] endless eternity."[57]

In their new emphasis on restoration, Masons engaged in a revisionism that was characteristic of the times. In 1820, Thomas Jefferson completed his "enlightened" revision of the New Testament, which eliminated "irrational" doctrines while reducing the gospels to Jesus's moral teachings. In 1833, Joseph Smith finished his revision of the Bible, which, in contrast to Jefferson's alteration of the text to suit his Enlightenment preferences, dwelled on and expanded its ancient and mysterious elements. Rather than work within the parameters of scholarly translations, the Mormon prophet sought to understand the original inspiration of the Bible's prophets and so come to understand the ways of God.[58] In this effort, he was influenced by what he had come to know of the Masonic restoration, which had a significant impact on the creation of Mormon beliefs and practices.

The Mormon religion that Smith inspired borrows heavily from Masonic symbolism. Mormon temples display such emblems as the beehive and the All-Seeing Eye. Temple garments include an apron with a compass and a square. Progress in the Mormon priesthood has substantial parallels with progress through the lodge's degree system. Both Mormons and Masons invoke the power and primacy of the priesthood of Melchizedek. Most obviously, the story of the discovery of the Book of Mormon on golden plates in a stone vault on a hilltop echoes the Enoch myth of Royal Arch Freemasonry.

The origins of Masonic influences on the Mormon religion have been traced to the early nineteenth-century prevalence of the fraternity in the regions of Vermont and upstate New York where the religion began. In 1823, the year of Smith's first encounter with the angel Moroni, who would lead him to the hidden tablets that contained the Book of Mormon, he was living in a milieu where Masonic manuals were readily available. Friends and family had joined the fraternity, and a fascination with hermetic teachings fueled his interest in treasure hunting.[59] By 1835, in Kirtland, Ohio, Smith was telling his followers of a coming ritual of "endowment" that would provide them with spiritual powers. At that time, he was performing ceremonial purifications of the body and anointings of members of the priesthood following biblical patterns. After the community moved to Nauvoo, Illinois, in 1839, Smith became a Freemason. He was initiated as an Entered Apprentice in the Nauvoo Lodge on March 15, 1842, and the next day underwent the degree rituals of Fellow Craft and Master Mason. He then participated in lodge meetings and was involved in thirteen enactments of these degree ceremonies in the weeks just before he formally introduced, on May 4 and 5, the new endowment ceremony to his trusted circle of Nauvoo Masonic friends.[60]

Although this ritual contained such non-Masonic elements as the washings and anointings from the Kirtland ceremony, early Mormon leaders believed that it constituted a Mormon restoration of Masonic rites. Many of Smith's closest Mormon associates were long-time Masons, including eleven of the original twelve apostles. By October of 1842, 253 Mormons had joined the Nauvoo lodge, a number larger than the total membership of all the other Illinois lodges combined.[61] Mormon leaders were deeply involved with the establishment of the Nauvoo Lodge and active workers in instituting its Masonic rites in the spring of 1842. These included James Cummings, who recalled that Smith seemed "to understand some of the features of the [Masonic] ceremony better than any Mason and that he made explanations that rendered the rites much more beautiful and full of meaning."[62] Smith was quoted as believing that there was a "similarity" between the Mormon and Masonic priesthoods, though the latter had become "degenerated."[63] Like the Royal Arch degree, the Mormon endowment ceremony restored the "lost word" and the Temple ritual in the building of the next (Mormon) temple, allowing candidates to pass through a "veil" and become anointed in the Holy Order of the High Priesthood. Smith apparently believed that Masonic rites were an apostate form of priesthood that survived from Solomon's Temple and had now been restored in the Mormon ceremony. His successor, Brigham Young, taught that though King Solomon had founded Freemasonry and built his Temple to give endowments, he was prevented from doing so. As Young explained, "One of the High Priests was murdered by wicked and corrupt men . . . because he would not reveal those things appertaining to the Priesthood that were forbidden him to reveal until he came to the proper place."[64]

So great were the similarities between Masonry and Mormonism that one Mason who joined the temple spoke of Mormon ritual in terms of Masonic restoration, claiming Mormonism as the "the true Masonry." As Heber C. Kimball stated, "The Masonry of today is received from the apostasy which took place in the days of Solomon, and David. They have now and then a thing that is correct, but we have the real thing."[65] The new endowment ceremony, by restoring what had been lost, was a purer form of ancient Israel's Masonic rites. Although most of the Mormon hierarchy were Master Masons when the Latter-Day Saints arrived in the Salt Lake Valley in 1847, Young decided not to petition for a Masonic lodge in Utah because he believed that the rituals of the Mormon temple had superseded those of Freemasonry.[66]

While primitivism broadly conceived characterized Freemasons and Mormons, both of these movements, as well as the Protestant primitivist groups of the early nineteenth century, were also looking toward the future. By seeking to restore ancient ways, primitivism in its many forms was a strategy of reform "built around," as W. Clark Gilpin has argued, "the idea of an historical lapse."[67] Primitivists believed that society had lost its way and could find it again only by returning to its original purpose. By measuring present immorality and confusion against the sacred paradigms of the past, they were not so much opposed to the idea of progress as seeking to shape the future according to their vision. The name chosen for Smith's Church of Jesus Christ of Latter-Day Saints suggests this forward movement. The Masonic invocation of ancient wisdom carried similar impulses toward change. On the one hand, the embrace of hermeticism and the supernatural appears to repudiate the rationalism and scientific thinking of the

Enlightenment. Secret knowledge hoarded by private societies and kept in subterranean vaults ran against the Enlightenment belief in openness and the spread of information. On the other hand, the higher degrees pointed forward to a new emphasis on deep feeling to reveal one's "true" identity.

ROMANTICISM

Freemasonry's new rituals both reflected and advanced new ways of thinking about human identity. By the early eighteenth century, John Locke's mechanical model of the human mind as developing through the creation of ideas in response to sensory stimuli had led Enlightenment thinkers to believe that human consciousness could be educated and relied on for guidance. Followers of Locke increasingly emphasized the role of feeling in this process. Scotland's David Hume notably advanced the idea that in the experience of sympathy, human beings possess a reliable basis for moral judgment.[68] Hume's countrymen Francis Hutcheson and Thomas Reid argued for the Christian nature of this "common" or "moral" sense. They held that feeling transcends reason not only because it makes a deeper impression on the mind but also because it perceives interrelationships that the logical process cannot grasp.[69] By the middle of the century, Edmund Burke claimed in his widely read treatise on the sublime that the deepest feelings are experienced through encounters with the vastness or terror of nature.[70] Such sublime feelings, Immanuel Kant believed at the century's end, originate in the human mind.[71]

For many Enlightenment thinkers, sublime emotions were those that moved the mind beyond its grasp. Not only nature but great literature, such as that of John Milton, William Shakespeare, and the Bible, induce this vigor, by expanding the mind through the realization of its deepest feelings. In the early nineteenth century, the romantic Samuel Taylor Coleridge asserted that "deep thinking is only attainable by a man of deep feeling."[72] When Thomas Smith Webb referred to Masonry's higher degrees as sublime, he was indicating just this capacity to evoke these deepest of human responses in the candidate. The new rituals contributed to this evolving understanding of the human psyche in the methods it employed to break down the individual's defenses to get to the sublime feelings at the core of human identity.

As previously discussed, the higher degree rituals take the initiate on a journey marked by physical assaults and sharp emotions in pursuit of deeper truth. Already in the third degree, the initiate was blindfolded, roughed up, and left for dead. He experienced the distress of abandonment and the assurance of acceptance. For those who continued on this journey, the physical challenges and emotional trials only increased. In the Royal Arch degree, the candidate passes several times through a "living arch" of members who press their knuckles on his back, and he eventually finds himself prostate on the floor and having to force himself through "like a man swimming." Chairs, tables, and other obstacles litter his journey along "rough and rugged roads." Lowered "ten feet" by ropes into a secret vault, he is then "violently" jerked upward. Throughout this ordeal of several hours, it is never clear whether the "weary sojourner" will have the mettle to survive, much less pass through the four "veils" that enshroud the "sacred tabernacle." The rituals of the postwar fraternity sought to penetrate the candidate's "false" exterior through such physical and emotional assaults. Pain and struggle, fear, abandonment, and awe were all tools directed toward altering men fixed in their ways, opening them to deeper truth.[73]

These early nineteenth-century Masonic methods were similar in some ways to the "new measures" that the evangelist Charles Finney employed in his efforts to reach the spiritual heart of sinners. Like the new Masonic rituals, Finney's approach signaled a decided shift from previous practices. His theology, in the words of the religious historian William D. McLoughlin, "clearly mark[ed] the end of two centuries of Calvinism and the acceptance of pietistic evangelicalism as the predominant faith of the nation."[74] In contrast to all previous approaches to religious renewal, moreover, Finney famously asserted that a revival of religion "is not a miracle, or dependent on a miracle, in any sense. It is a purely philosophical result of the right use of the constituted means."[75] Rejecting colonial Calvinism's belief in God's unknowable sovereignty and arbitrary grace, Finney not only accepted the Enlightenment advances that allowed for a better grasp of the physical and psychological laws of nature but also believed that it was God's plan that they be employed to evangelize the world. In the mid-1820s, he began his revival work in western New York. Finney emphasized the place of human effort in obeying divine commands to promote religious awakenings through his new measures: setting aside a period of days for "protracted meetings" of constant prayer, fasting, and worship, which sometimes lasting through the night; employing a dramatic, extemporaneous preaching style frequently directed at specific, named sinners; and calling individuals forward to sit on an "anxious bench" where they were publicly exhorted to decide on immediate submission to God.[76] As heirs to Enlightenment ideas on the nature of the universe and the individual, both Finney and the early nineteenth-century Masonic ritualists embraced the importance of individual effort. As pioneers in what became therapeutic efforts to break down the personality's "false exterior," they all experimented with forceful psychological techniques to reach what Finney called "the spiritual heart." Yet they had an even more intimate connection: Finney had been a Mason.

Finney's participation in Freemasonry preceded his conversion to Christianity. He joined the order in Connecticut in 1813 at the age of twenty-one, a time when, by his own account, he was "almost as ignorant of religion as a heathen."[77] Throwing himself into the ritual life of the lodge, Finney soon became a Master Mason. In 1818 he went to Adams, New York, to study law. There he joined the local lodge, became its secretary, regularly attended its meetings, and "paid the strictest attention" to its rituals. Finney converted to Christianity in 1822 at the age of twenty-nine but did not leave the Masons until just before his ordination in 1824. Though much later in life he firmly denounced Freemasonry's "unchristian practices," he said nothing against the fraternity in the Anti-Masonic uprising of the late 1820s. He attributed this silence to his still feeling bound by the secret oaths of the order.[78] Given the virulent attacks on the brotherhood following the disappearance of William Morgan in 1826, he probably also felt it wise not to disclose that he too had been a Mason.

Though there is no evidence of a direct relationship between Finney's Masonic participation and his embrace of Christianity, Mark C. Carnes has pointed to similarities between Finney's classic account of his conversion and the Master Mason ritual. In each instance there is a period of wandering, a desire for secrecy—as Finney put it, "away from all human eyes and ears"—and a search for "greater light."[79] Finney's heterodox theology, moreover, was similar to the Freemasonry of his period in combining the colonial Calvinist belief in human depravity with the early nineteenth-century embrace of human efforts to attain salvation. And like the Masonic ritualists, Finney believed that new means were now required to "break the chains of pride" and "uncover the delusions of the human heart."[80]

The evolution of Freemasonry's ritual life contributed and responded to developments in the reorganization of the inner life of Americans following the Revolution. The Lockean epistemology underlying the Webb-Preston system advanced the belief of many educated Americans that knowledge of morality and abiding wisdom are developed though sensory impressions. The new rites responded to the convictions of young men who, like the leaders of the emerging Protestant primitivist groups, looked to the past for wisdom amid the social uncertainty and religious pluralism of the early nineteenth century. Yet the innovative techniques that the degree ceremonies employed to break down the individual's defenses and reveal the sublime feelings at the core of human identity were, like Finney's new measures, harbingers of the therapeutic culture.[81] Faced with the confusion of the emerging modern society, some saw the cultivation of their inner life as providing the otherwise missing certainty of deep feeling in a changing world.[82] The quest for secret wisdom in the lodges led to the creation of an elite white male private sphere that paralleled the developing private domestic world of early nineteenth-century affluent white women.

"THE ITCHING CURIOSITY OF MOTHER EVE"

Around the end of the eighteenth century, several friends of Hannah Mather Crocker, a leading Boston matron, told her that they were "very anxious" because their husbands were becoming Masons. They worried not only about their men being away until late in the evening but also that the lodge might harm their husbands' "moral and religious sentiments." A daughter of the Reverend Samuel Mather and a granddaughter and great-granddaughter of the Puritan divines Cotton and Increase Mather, respectively, Crocker was related through her mother to the royal governor Thomas Hutchinson. She married the Harvard graduate and Revolutionary War captain Joseph Crocker in 1779 and raised her ten children while living in her parents' Boston home. Despite her background, Crocker seems to have had very limited schooling. It was thought sufficient at the time, she later wrote, "if women would even read and badly write their name." Following her husband's death in 1797, Crocker began in earnest to pursue her education. At about this time her anxious friends approached her. Deciding to investigate the intentions of Freemasonry, she soon reported her "great joy" in discovering "the value of the institution." At some point thereafter, the women created a female lodge, "founded on the original principles of true ancient masonry, so far as was consistent for the female character," and complete with their own "tokens, signs, and word." Saint Ann's Lodge existed for several years, with Crocker as its presiding "mistress." In 1810, she sent a series of letters on Freemasonry to a newspaper to defend the educational, benevolent, and Christian intentions of the institution.[83]

Crocker and her friends were among a new generation of what historians have identified as "republican mothers."[84] Elite women such as the members of Saint Ann's denounced what then passed as female education, which fostered dependency instead of producing self-reliant women who could contribute to the political independence of the nation. Crocker and her friends saw their lodge as an improvement society. In 1810, she wrote that the "prime inducement for forming the lodge was a desire for cultivating the mind in the most useful branches of science, and cherishing a love of literature; for at that period, female education was at a very low ebb." Confronted with the belief that women were "mere domestick animals" for whom education was unnecessary, the women of Saint Ann's asserted that they could "no longer bear a cramp of genius" and instead sought through their association to "rouse" themselves "to thought."[85] In 1818, Crocker published her *Observations on the Real Rights of Women*, one of the earliest arguments for female education yet one in which the author carefully points out that she is not looking for a dispute between the sexes: "It would be morally incorrect and physically improper" for women to trespass "on masculine ground." Instead, she asserts that "the culture and improvement of the female understanding will strengthen the mental faculties, and give vigor to their councils" and thereby contribute to the success of a "free, federal, and independent nation."[86]

Republican mothers like Crocker were trying to bring together a colonial, hierarchical understanding of separate spheres with a new republican appreciation of autonomy and individualism. Within the confines of the domestic realm, the ideal republican woman was to become self-reliant and literate. She would take seriously her political task, of educating her sons in civic virtue. By the 1830s, such women moved beyond the education of their sons to write and organize moral reform movements to teach all men the virtues of republicanism. Recognizing that their work served larger social and political purposes, they moved the older understanding of the woman's sphere closer to the world of men.[87] In forming a female lodge, Crocker and her republican women friends were appropriating what they knew of Freemasonry to advance their education and thereby—to their minds—the interests of the nation. Saint Ann's existence, though short, suggests that following the Revolution, transformations in the lives of elite white men and elite white women moved their worlds closer together.[88]

By justifying an advanced education as necessary for them to fulfill the social and political requirements of their gender and not as an end in itself, republican mothers broadened the arena of women's perceived responsibilities for the greater good of the new society. Following the Revolution, Americans understood civil society to include any gathering of private citizens whose basic freedoms of speech, press, and assembly the law protected. Though republican women accepted their exclusion from the male realms of politics and business, they rapidly expanded their influence in what became the feminine arena of civil society.[89] As Mary Kelley has argued, the efforts of Crocker and her contemporaries to establish female academies and seminaries resulted in women developing the ability to create a "subjectivity in which rights and obligations of citizenship were fundamental to their sense of self." By connecting their private selves to public duty, elite women were able to project themselves into public life. In the 1830s, women schooled in the more than 180 female academies that had appeared since 1790 emerged as teachers, writers, and moral reformers in a public, civil, female social space that stood between the family and the state. Because they pursued advanced education as essential to fulfilling their role as republican mothers, these women believed themselves to be morally obligated to instruct all men in republican virtue.[90]

As an apostle of this "gendered republicanism,"[91] Crocker looked to the model of Freemasonry for guidance. In her letters defending the order, she emphasizes its educational, benevolent, and Christian strengths, all areas of particular interest to republican woman. Most attractive to Crocker was the fraternity's renewed focus on "Science and Literature." By emulating its efforts to "enlarge the mind," Saint Ann's, she believed, "gave the first rise to female education in this town." In her estimation, "the Masonic society" was also "preeminent on the list" of groups devoted to "charity and benevolence." Benevolence, for Crocker, meant the tendency to "expand the heart" by promoting the "happiness of our fellow creatures." This naturally led people to come to the "aid" of "poor persons." Seemingly following the brethren's lead, Crocker observed, elite women at the turn of the century had formed "a number of societies" for the relief of the "poor." Christianity was a third area of converging interest. Crocker lauded the fraternity for providing a system of thought that led inevitably to her belief in "JESUS CHRIST, who is *the chief Corner Stone* of the Christian profession." Finally, in Crocker's view, both the postwar fraternity and this new generation of elite women shared the embrace of these ingredients as necessary to the "freedom and independence" of the new American nation.[92]

For their part, lodge members were delighted with this female acceptance. In 1815 they republished Crocker's letters with a preface by the Congregational minister and leading Boston Mason Thaddeus M. Harris, who complimented her for rising to a level "superior to all jealousy on the account of the exclusion of her sex" to "happily" state the "merits of Freemasonry."[93] Crocker's letters were a welcome vindication at a time when some women had become interested in joining the fraternity. In the colonial period there was little if any suggestion that women objected to their exclusion from what was then a social club for the elite men of polite society. Though colonial understandings of gender placed greater emphasis on the hierarchical relationship between men and women rather than their separation into public and private spheres, nearly all social life then was segregated by sex.[94] As late as 1797, William Bentley, a Massachusetts minister and Mason, asserted that "it is not a want of confidence that has kept our sisters from our association, but the established order of Civil Society."[95] The need to assert this "established order," however, suggests the difficulty of its maintenance.

In the revolutionary era, a new understanding of society most frequently associated with the political thinking of John Locke gradually took hold. The origins of revolutionary thought cannot be easily traced to any one intellectual tradition, be it the Enlightenment, classical republicanism, Protestantism, or some other.[96] Moreover, scholars working in the dominant theoretical framework of women's spheres have been taken to task for an inattention to the "complexity and change" in women's lives prior to 1800 that foreshadowed the dramatic changes in their historical experience in the mid-nineteenth century.[97] By this time it is easier to see a public-private divide and a domestic female sphere than to trace the origins of this outcome back through the various ways of thinking and behaving available in the late eighteenth century. Given this complexity, what is now most apparent in the new political thinking was a conceptualization of society that originated in ancient Greece and Rome, was adapted by Locke, and saw the state as not modeled on but in opposition to the family. The state consisted of men of equal status, while the family was composed of males and females divided by hierarchies of gender, age, and wealth. Locke's contribution was to bring together the ancient ideal with the contemporary reality of seventeenth-century England. There the most significant male relationships were with other men, outside the family, in the realm of politics and society, while women's most significant interactions were in the family, where both genders were present. The importance of this new political thinking for postwar Americans was that it imagined a society divided into a public world of men and a private world of women and the family.[98]

This idea was connected to a real though gradual structural change in the American family that occurred first among the literate, commercial urban population. In the late eighteenth century, affluent women were no longer sharing parental responsibilities with servants, their husbands, or their husbands' workers. As Ruth H. Bloch has shown, the critical development was "the gradual physical removal of the father's place of work from the home" because it meant that he no longer had continuous contact with his children.[99] With the withdrawal of the father and other parental figures, the responsibility for raising the children gradually centered almost entirely on the mother. Outside this urban elite, of course, poor white women did menial labor and slave women worked in the fields. Yet the new responsibilities of elite white women dovetailed with the new political thinking to create a new cultural understanding of women's roles. With their new duties, both imposed and voluntary, affluent women forged a new identity as republican mothers, serving as guardians of private morality and public virtue.

The Masonic responses to elite women's interest in the fraternity—what one brother termed the "itching curiosity of mother Eve"—suggest this changing understanding of women's roles in the new American social order.[100] The most traditional were assertions that women should not be Masons because gender segregation characterized the whole of civil society. "It might be asked in return," the Amherst, Massachusetts, Master Mason Samuel Dana said, "why [women] are not chosen governors, councillors and senators."[101] Without this separation, the Philadelphia grand master James Milnor echoed, "the powerful attraction of female charms placed constantly before us, might lessen our attention to [our] obligations."[102] But there were others in the fraternity who argued as early as 1811 that it was "wrong to deny that the fair sex are capable" of higher learning.[103] Though few would go as far as Crocker, who in 1818 stated that "the author of nature has endowed the female mind with equal powers and faculties"—although she also said that women should steer clear of "masculine ground"—some Freemasons and republican women appear to have been rethinking gender roles.[104] Gradually, however, the ideology of separate spheres took hold, resulting in what one Mason identified as "an admirable partition of qualities between the sexes."[105] Public and private, political and social, reason and emotion were increasingly gendered and opposed. Yet within the boundaries of domesticity, women continued to attend female academies and seminaries and employ their knowledge to influence civil society through their roles as teachers, writers, and members of societies for moral reform.

The shift in elite women's self-understanding was apparent in their reasons for not seeking membership in Freemasonry. Around the time that Crocker declined to enter the male domain of the lodge, "A Lady in Worcester" gave a decidedly different reason for not wishing to join the fraternity. In her *Observations on Freemasonry*, Abigail Lyon writes of seeing no reason to become a Mason, for she had already been "initiated" into the virtues of the fraternity "at my birth." The "science of Masonry . . . refines the understanding, softens the manners, blends together every virtue of the human heart"—qualities, in her estimation, women already have "in our composition."[106] We have already seen that a particular public purpose of the postwar fraternity was to improve the moral character and behavior of men. What is new here is the suggestion that women need no such improvement.

This new estimation of women's nature is apparent in the reprinted British and indigenous American publications that the urban elite read between 1785 and 1815. With the new focus on mothers as primary caregivers, authors increasingly questioned men's moral authority. Rather than ridiculed as women's emotionalism, the feelings of the heart became the foundation of their superior virtue. Advice literature on the education of children, which had previously addressed fathers, was now almost exclusively directed at mothers. The preparation necessary for motherhood became an argument for female education. At the same time, Enlightenment beliefs in the tabula rasa of the newborn's mind overcame Calvinist assertions of infant depravity. Clergymen now spoke of the critical role of woman's love in turning not only sons but husbands too away from selfishness and toward virtue by instilling affection in their hearts. By the 1830s, the serious educational requirements and broad social usefulness of the calling to motherhood were widely accepted.[107]

The idea that women already possessed the "softness" of heart that was one goal of Masonic training entered Masonic apologetics with a flourish. Consider this extended example from an 1820 oration that Brother S. B. T. Caldwell delivered in Middleburg, Virginia:

> Ye lovely fair, whose unrivalled virtues predominent sway o'er the hearts of men: Ye tender *mothers*, whose maternal affection fondly watched our

infantile slumbers, and tenderly guarded our juvenile days, from the thorny paths of vice: . . . It is not, my fair hearers, because we deem you unworthy to wear our honourable badge . . . neither is it because the working tools of our profession are too ponderous for your delicate forms, that we draw the veil which hides from your view the mysteries of our order. No! No! It is not *you* we distrust; but *ourselves*. . . . It is an acknowledged fact in the philosophy of human nature, that the feelings, the affections, the sensibilities and the sympathies of your sex are more easily awakened to the piercing cries of suffering humanity than are those of ours. The adventitious aid of mystic institutions, therefore, is not necessary to urge you to deeds of charity and benevolence, nor the use of symbols to lead you to virtue. "Your own hearts are the lodges in which *virtue* presides, and the dictates of her will be your only incentive to action."[108]

Such exaggerated praise for the newly innate virtues of elite women as moral mothers watching over private morality and alleviating public suffering provided the brotherhood with a new argument for keeping them from joining the fraternity. Ann Douglas has seen similar praise by men of the natural virtues of elite women as a "compensatory etiquette" whereby politeness and reverence suggested atonement as much as recognition. Affluent mothers who focused their energies on their children and, through benevolent societies, orphans and the poor were honored for the moral sanction they gave to the self-interested business activities of early nineteenth-century capitalists.[109] Yet while male rhetoric sought to fix women in their new social role, affluent women, as a rising group looking for increased power and influence, pursued this new status as a site from which they could assert their newly ascribed moral authority to influence civil society. Whether or not this rhetoric convinced women to steer clear of the fraternity, new understandings of women's roles placed their interests uncomfortably close to the public interests of Masons. This often led orators to emphasize less the refinement that resulted from Masonic membership and more the hard labor of operative masons and the travails of military life.

The converging interests of postwar Freemasons and affluent urban mothers suggest that both men and women were moving between a homosocial private world and a larger public sphere. In the first quarter of the nineteenth century, Freemasons were involved in both the public worlds of politics and business and the intimacy of private rituals. At the same time, mothers of the revolutionary generation were taking on a new identity as educated, self-reliant citizens, which drew them to the public values of a republican and Christian Freemasonry. Pushing the boundaries of their domestic sphere, republican mothers were rooted in the home yet, through their interest in the moral education of their society in republican virtue, moving closer to the public world of men. Though women persisted in their efforts to influence civil society from the private sphere as editors, educators, and reformers and Masons continued to be prominent in public life, as the century progressed, both groups were increasingly identified with their respective pious havens of intimate friendship.

CHAPTER 4

Anti-Masonry and the Public Sphere, 1826–1850

By the 1820s, American Freemasonry had created a space for itself apart from the authority of established churches and civil government and between the social worlds of public and private life. Surveying the American scene in the 1830s, the Frenchman Alexis de Tocqueville contended that in a nation devoid of established hierarchies, the abundance of voluntary organizations contributed to the stability of democracy. "In order that men remain civilized or become so," Tocqueville remarked, "the art of associating must be developed and perfected among them in the same ratio as equality of conditions increases."[1] Early nineteenth-century Freemasonry was among a bevy of voluntary organizations in civil society that shaped and were shaped by the public-spirited republican virtue of the postrevolutionary era.

Seen from the perspective of Anti-Masonry, however, the brotherhood was a secret cabal of politically connected, secularizing, affluent men deeply threatening to the common man and evangelical Christianity. Indeed, in New York's "burned-over district," the center of Anti-Masonic rage, Masons were overwhelmingly merchants and professionals who controlled a majority of the positions of political leadership and held liberal or no religious affiliations.[2] Though similar protests against the fraternity's hegemony had been mounted as recently as the Illuminati affair of the century's turn, the new attacks took place in an increasingly democratic public sphere, spurred by a rapidly expanding print culture. In an era that celebrated the common man, hierarchical degree ceremonies and aristocratic titles looked woefully out of place. New attacks on the society's secrecy and blood oaths, purportedly binding the members primarily to one another rather than to republican government, gained traction. Mingled with these were the testimonies of Masonic apostates whose lurid descriptions of surrogate religious ceremonies that blasphemed Jesus were proclaimed with revival fervor. Democratic public meetings and mob actions voiced these charges in local communities, where village elites had previously controlled the social order. Newspapers and pamphlets then carried news of these developments beyond the towns to a growing regional and national audience, mounting popular opinion against the fraternity.

The ensuing battle over Freemasonry uncovered larger struggles over Christian identity. Radical Anti-Masons sought to purge the brotherhood from their churches, only to find that American Protestantism widely accepted the fraternity's liberal themes. Rather than stamping out secularization and reasserting sectarian authority, Anti-Masonry revealed the churches' widespread complicity in the individualism and other market-oriented values of the new social order. At the same time, the conflict between defenders and critics of Freemasonry opened up divisions in the emerging ideology of domesticity. Though opposition to Freemasonry was well within the bounds of women's church-related effort to safeguard the home, leading Masonic wives' support of the order complicated the early gendered protests against it.

. . .

Freemasonry's difficulties burst forth in western New York in 1826, when William Morgan, a Mason, threatened to publish Masonic secrets. Though such rituals had been publicly disclosed as early as 1730, Morgan promised to reveal the secrets of the higher York Rite degrees. Before he could do this, he was kidnapped, never to be heard from again. The following year, after repeated failed efforts to discover his fate and bring the perpetrators to justice, the Morgan affair ignited a fire of protest that engulfed the northern states. New Grand Lodges as far west as Illinois and Michigan were damaged and weakened. Masonic activities in the established strongholds of Massachusetts, New York, and Pennsylvania were dramatically reduced. Fear of reprisals led to the cancellation of annual parades and banquets. Individual fraternity members were scorned by their neighbors, denied seats on juries, and refused church membership. New York, Connecticut, and Vermont wrote laws to outlaw the order. Only seventy-five of the five hundred lodges active in New York in 1825 continued to function, while the national population of Masons declined dramatically, from a high of one hundred thousand in 1826 to a low of forty thousand in 1835. In the short span of a decade, the northern fraternity had been brought to its knees.[3]

Anti-Masonry emerged in the context of the early nineteenth-century democratizations of politics and religion that culminated in the Jacksonian era of the common man. Following the revolution, respect for the hierarchical authority of a local elite gave way to an embrace of the democratic power of ordinary Americans.[4] In the public sphere, national efforts to influence the opinions of ordinary people overtook the leadership of established local elders. Political leaders could not survive without responding to the will of the people. At the same time, the structures of American Christianity were democratized. As Nathan Hatch has argued, evangelical populists led a religious revolt away from the old deference to clergy, learned theologians, and centralized external authority and toward a new endorsement of individual religious experience and a practical Christianity molded on the image of ordinary people. As the population dramatically expanded and moved westward, "America's nonrestrictive environment," Hatch stated, "permitted an unexpected and often explosive conjunction of evangelical fervor and popular sovereignty."[5] Nowhere was this more apparent than in the burned-over district of western New York, where in Batavia, Genesee County, newly settled New Englanders driven by revival zeal and a passion for equality confronted the Masonic abduction of Morgan.

The Masons of Genesee County were an identifiable subgroup in a general population that shared a Yankee cultural background and the broad American commitment to public virtue and morality. Although the three hundred members of the county's three Masonic lodges were active in all occupations and represented all income levels, Kathleen Smith Kutolowski has shown that four-fifths were merchants and professionals at a time when 93 percent of the Genesee work force was involved in farming. Many of these "merchants, artisans, attorneys and physicians" lived in the county's two major villages. Though not "unusually wealthy," these entrepreneurs were the men most likely to have the resources and time that membership in the brotherhood required.[6] Dorothy Ann Lipson's analysis of Freemasonry in Federalist Connecticut similarly found early nineteenth-century Masons to be disproportionately drawn from commerce, manufacturing, and the professions, with the added insight that these were usually young men, 80 percent having taken their first degree between the ages of twenty-one and thirty.[7] For young, upwardly mobile men adrift from the traditional moorings of hometown, family, and occupation and living amid the tumult of an increasingly market-oriented society, Freemasonry offered—among other attractions—the refuge of like-minded friends. Or, as the Anti-Masonic Baptist minister John G. Stearns put it, "the ultimate design of Masons, in uniting their talents and raising a fund, was to promote the good of their own connexions."[8]

Early nineteenth-century western New York Masons also stood apart from the evangelical Protestantism of their neighbors. By the early 1820s, Kutolowski has shown, some 85 percent of Genesee County's ninety-four churches could be characterized as part of a Baptist, Presbyterian, and Methodist evangelical majority. While Freemasons were among the members and ministers of these denominations, the great majority "clustered in a handful of Episcopal parishes," several had helped found the area's four Universalist churches, and a third of at least one lodge's members had no religious affiliation. This was at a time when church membership was increasing dramatically as a result of revival fervor.[9] In Connecticut, Lipson noted, "as Freemasonry grew in popularity and spread along the inland roads to relatively remote agricultural communities it was associated with a nascent demand for change in the tone and style of the Puritan communitarian heritage, a symptom of a new and growing latitudinarianism."[10] Paul Goodman's analysis of Anti-Masonry in the New England states, moreover, concludes that the order "attracted members from various denominations with a high incidence of Episcopalians, Unitarians, and Universalists among the leaders." In contrast, "religious Antimasonry appealed especially to Christians who clung strongly to Calvinist roots, particularly conservative Congregationalists, Presbyterians, and Baptists and others who adhered to an older, communitarian religious tradition that placed a high value on uniform beliefs, revealed religion, and sectarian exclusivity."[11] Though the contours of individual Masons' worldviews cannot be determined, it appears that the early nineteenth-century brotherhood adhered to a perspective at odds with that of its evangelical neighbors.

Nonetheless, these differences in occupation and religious orientation alone are not sufficient to explain the sudden rise of Anti-Masonry. Print attacks on the order can be traced as far back as 1698.[12] Samuel Prichard's exposé of the fraternity's rituals, *Masonry Dissected*, was first published in 1730.[13] (Ironically, it remained in print for more than fifty years primarily because Masons purchased it to help them memorize the rituals.) Attacks on the brotherhood continued after its arrival in colonial America. Boston's newspapers ridiculed its pretensions while denouncing its secrecy for hiding immoral practices.[14] One generation prior to Morgan's abduction, guardians of New England Puritanism had declared that Freemasonry was involved with the Bavarian Illuminati in a secret conspiracy to overthrow American churches and government. Despite dire warnings from Yale University's Timothy Dwight, Boston's Jedidiah Morse, and other Puritan stalwarts, there was little evidence of European uprisings troubling relations between the church and the lodge. Though open conflicts over the beliefs and practices of Freemasonry occasionally arose, local clergy were inclined not to stir up controversy over an organization that prominent laymen supported.

The Morgan affair brought into public view the potential threat of Freemasonry to the democratizing ethos of the early nineteenth century. In the months following Morgan's disappearance, politically connected New York Masons prevented its effective investigation. Members of the fraternity were among the judges and juries in the twenty trials that decided the fates of the alleged abductors. All but four were acquitted or given short jail terms. As one observer reported, "Sheriffs, witnesses, jurors, and even judges upon the bench, were bound by secret oaths which they considered more sacred than their oaths of office,—to espouse the cause of a brother Mason and defend him whether right or wrong."[15] Indeed, beyond their occupational and religious differences from their neighbors, Masons held three-fifths of the county's positions of political leadership despite their minuscule share of the electorate.[16] The early political historian Jabez D. Hammond suspected that Masons held a majority of New York's political offices: "Legislative, judicial and executive officers, from presidents and governors to deputy marshals and constables . . . reverend senator to the town meeting orator, were, I religiously believe, a majority of them free masons."[17] The first Anti-Masonic attacks thus accused Masonic politicians of placing their allegiance to the fraternity ahead of their commitment to republican government.

As the order's involvement in the legal machinery delayed the justice for which the citizenry clamored, the spotlight turned to the very existence of a secret society in a democratic nation. At a time when Americans were demanding openness and equality, was there really any place for a brotherhood whose members were set apart from the rest of society and bound by loyalty only to one another? Pseudoaristocratic elites flaunting grandiose titles looked badly out of touch with an era that celebrated the plain attributes of the common man. Soon after Morgan's abduction, "more than a hundred different meetings, and probably more than a thousand such, were held in the infected territory."[18] At these gatherings, citizens conducted investigations, organized demonstrations, and passed resolutions, such as this one from the New York town of Eiba: "That they would not support any person for any office, either in town, county or state, or any minister of the gospel who is a member of the fraternity."[19]

Religious fervor mixed with political outrage now surrounded the fraternity. Elder David Bernard, the pastor of a Baptist church near Batavia, was so angered by the conduct of Masons that he became the first minister to renounce the fraternity after Morgan's abduction and probable murder. Like subsequent clergy who repudiated the brotherhood,[20] Bernard recounted an earlier attraction to it: "Soon after I commenced the service of Christ, Free Masonry was commended to my attention as an institution from heaven; moral, benevolent, of great antiquity, the twin sister of Christianity, possessing the patronage of the wise, the great, and good, and highly important to the ministers of the Lord Jesus. Wishing to avail myself of every auxiliary in promoting the glory of God and the happiness of my fellow men, I readily received the first three degrees." Though later troubled by the "awful oaths" of obligation he had taken, which promised a grisly death to any who broke them, Bernard continued to believe that there was "substantial good in the order," going so far as to pursue the "higher orders of mysticism" that he thought the Royal Arch degree contained. Morgan's murder lifted the veil from his eyes. "I compared the murder of Morgan and the conduct of the fraternity in relation to his abduction with the oaths and principles of the order, and became fully satisfied that to continue longer in the institution was not my duty." With a moral verve characteristic of the times, Bernard not only renounced the order but set out to "reveal its secrets, oppose its influence, and use my exertions to destroy it."[21] His *Light on Masonry*—a compendium of descriptions of the fraternity's rituals, reports on the Morgan affair, and a history of Anti-Masonry in New York—became the movement's most widely read publication.

As the firestorm grew, Bernard instigated a convention of nineteen Baptist churches that officially resolved to have "no fellowship" with brethren who did not "completely abstain" from Freemasonry.[22] This became the prototype of many subsequent convocations to revile the fraternity and demand action against it. Evangelical enthusiasts denounced the movement with the same conviction, emotional preaching, and dire warnings of impending doom heard in the region's omnipresent revivals. Going beyond the antirepublicanism that had prompted the first Anti-Masonic protests, ministers and laymen from several denominations—now better informed of the content of fraternal rites—accused the brotherhood of attempting to make itself appear sacred by distorting biblical passages in its rituals. The resurrection of Jesus in particular was seen as mocked and blasphemed, in the symbolic death, burial, and raising of the central figure of the Masonic third degree rite. Horror was expressed at the torturous deaths, described in Masonic oaths, that would result if any dared to defy their secret obligations to the order.[23] In the eyes of its opponents, Masonic rituals, myths, and symbols were being used as a surrogate religion.[24] Already there were local instances of Masonic funeral rites taking the place of church services.[25] At minimum, the new religious Anti-Masonry found traction in the growing conviction that the fraternity was irreligious. Though its earlier characterization as part of an external European conspiracy that threatened Christian republicanism had not taken hold, after 1826 a large and growing number of American citizens were alert to the internal menace of a malevolent Freemasonry that sought to destroy their churches and democratic communities.

Though successful as a political movement, Anti-Masonry had a divisive effect on New York's evangelical churches. As one observer noted, "The fiercest contentions arose in local churches; clergymen were dismissed, or compelled to resign their pastoral charges; fellow-members of churches refused to partake of the sacred elements of the supper at the same table; and, in one instance, a clergyman bearing the curse of Freemasonry, was personally assaulted in the pulpit. From single churches, the spirit of proscription entered many ecclesiastical bodies, threatening to produce a wider field of spiritual disunion and desolation."[26] Most successful were the Baptist churches in the western region of New York. Led by the crusading ministers Stearns and Bernard, aided by the Baptist emphasis on local church governance, and driven by a persisting revivalistic impulse, these and other Baptist churches in the state "took the lead" in passing tough resolutions requiring unqualified renunciation of Masons, resulting in the excommunication of ministers and laymen and schisms between and within some associations and churches.[27]

The New York State Baptist Convention and the more eastern Baptist associations chose to remain silent on the issue, while other associations and churches agreed to less binding resolutions. Presbyterian ecclesiastical discipline led that denomination to take a definite but careful

Anti-Masonic stance. Though individual western presbyteries required the "ministers and members" of the churches under their immediate charge "to dissolve their connection with Freemasonry . . . and explicitly to signify the same to their Christian brethren," the larger Synod of Genesee, concerned more with the "peace and order of churches," denounced "all indiscriminate censuring and impeachment of the motives and characters of brethren merely because they have belonged . . . to the institution."[28] Calls for church harmony and order met demands for radical action. When the Presbyterian prelate Lebbeus Armstrong preached his renunciation sermon on Freemasonry as "a Work of Darkness," for example, his trustees "determined to lock the doors of the house of worship against him on all further occasions."[29] The Methodist hierarchy similarly refused to allow the controversy to disturb their ministry, avoiding all contact with Anti-Masonry at the ecclesiastical levels. There is no evidence of Methodist actions against Masonry at either the annual sessions of the Old Genesee Conference or the sessions of the General Conference. While strident Anti-Masons promoted the crusade through their churches, the evangelical denominations had no uniform response.[30]

Thwarted in their efforts to rally evangelical organizations to their cause, Anti-Masonic leaders held a series of independent conventions, free from the obstruction of church hierarchies and Masonic church members. According to the contemporary observer William Stone, at such a meeting in LeRoy, New York, on March 6, 1828, "the character of Anti-masonry began to change" and the "Anti-masonic party first received . . . its political 'form and pressure.'" Because the movement's "effervescence" was "gradually subsiding," religious Anti-Masons such as Stearns and Bernard deferred to Anti-Masonic politicians led by Thurlow Weed, who was neither a church member nor interested in a religious crusade.[31] Opposition to Freemasonry now evolved into a political party dedicated to keeping Masons from office and finally eliminating the fraternity. Reflecting on this turn of events several years later, Benjamin Cowell, a "moral Antimason" from Rhode Island, said that while he originally opposed combining religion and politics in this way, he became convinced "that the only way we have left to put down masonry is the BALLOT BOX. We must make it a political question and put it down by political means."[32] The dramatic decline of the order by the mid-1830s suggests that these political efforts were successful.

The rise of Anti-Masonry helped move the focus of the American public sphere away from local arenas controlled by educated, enlightened gentlemen and toward national efforts to influence the opinions of ordinary people.[33] Locally influential Masons led the order's initial response to the Morgan affair, using political, economic, and social pressures to suppress dissent in their communities. Against these traditional mechanisms of control, both political and religious Anti-Masons held public meetings to build broad, community-wide support. No longer solely the domain of bourgeois clubs and polite discourse, the public sphere now expanded to include an array of citizens who gathered in outdoor spaces, on street corners and town squares, and spoke in raucous speech that defied the literary standards of rational communication.[34] As one Masonic observer reported, citizens gathered "in almost every town" to express "the most angry vituperations" and pass "the most inflammatory resolutions" against the fraternity.[35] Angry rhetoric and crowd action led an increasing number of ordinary people to question the order's previous high regard and join in efforts to remove its members from churches and political office. Anti-Masonic sermons, traveling lecturers, and pamphlets advanced the cause. Nearly one hundred Anti-Masonic newspapers soon mushroomed into existence, spreading the news and sensationalizing the lengthy investigation of Morgan's abduction.[36] People who previously knew little about the fraternity were alarmed to hear of its sinister activities and worried about its threat to the national welfare. When the crusade entered the political arena, it moved farther and faster than any previous American social reform movement, creating a political party whose branches multiplied throughout the northern United States.[37] Though the Anti-Masonic Party was not successful in eliminating the order and itself went out of existence by 1832, the larger movement against Freemasonry succeeded in removing the fraternity from its postwar pedestal of public acclaim.[38]

CHRISTIAN IDENTITY

The battle over Freemasonry revealed larger struggles about what it meant to be a Christian in the newly emerging American society. Evangelical Protestantism arose in the ferment of the postwar reorganization of religious life. Beyond festering divisions among the old denominations and the birth of new churches, all postwar religious life was affected by the movement away from Calvinist beliefs in the innate depravity of humanity and toward more "reasonable" commitments to human ability.[39] New political mandates to respect individual rights and personal liberty became matters of Christian duty. Social reforms emphasizing education and temperance turned into benchmarks for measuring the arrival of the millennium. As churches came to accept the individualism, upward mobility, and materialism of the new market-oriented society, they competed with one another for members, while the authority of their ministers steadily declined. Though New England's theocracy had long ago eroded, it was not until the early nineteenth century that these new patterns of thought and action became apparent.[40]

Given these changes in religious life, it is tempting to see "infidel" Freemasonry's "serpentine" penetration of the life of the churches as responsible for introducing the worst elements of the post-revolutionary order, and the evangelical Anti-Masonic response as a reassertion of sectarian beliefs, clerical authority, and antisecular values. But the evangelical churches were complicit in accepting the values of the new social order. As James Turner has argued, the triumph of evangelical religion was rife with irony, as these churches embraced many of the secularizing trends yet called them Christian: "Even while damning Deists, church leaders swallowed the Deist conception of a natural-law God. Even while lauding the converted heart, they absorbed the maxim that belief in God rests on intellectual assent to a demonstrable proposition. Even while preaching the blood of the Lamb, they devoured the Enlightenment's moralism and its God bound by human morality. Ritual cannibalism purports to transfer the life-force of a slain enemy to the voracious victor. In this case it worked."[41]

At the same time that the most rabid Anti-Masons were seeking to rid their congregations of Freemasons, the fraternity's liberal themes, especially its amorphous Deism and disinterest in doctrinal and sectarian differences, were becoming acceptable trends in Protestantism. The silence of nonevangelical denominations on the validity of the order and the equivocal oppositional voices of evangelical denominations suggest this acceptance of secularizing developments. Moreover, disputes over Freemasonry threatened to divide congregations against themselves, undermining church order. Ronald P. Formisano has found that rather than a struggle between two distinct groups, the battle over Masonry in Massachusetts was "essentially cultural and religious, between descendants of the Puritans who were very similar in socio-economic status, and in many ideas and enthusiasms, but whose values clashed in fundamental ways."[42] Masonic church members were as interwoven in their communities, and even in subgroups of these communities, as those who opposed them. Hence, churches not only were becoming more tolerant of Masonic ideology but also wished to avoid the controversy rather than threaten their order and harmony.

After 1830, the official denominational literature of New York no longer discussed Anti-Masonry. As already noted, the Presbyterians were only cautiously opposed to Freemasonry, and the Methodists took no official interest in it. As the Anti-Masonic movement turned toward political solutions, its religious former leaders took up other causes. Stearns became an apologist for the Baptist faith. Bernard served in various agencies, including the American Bible Society, the American Baptist Home Missionary Society, and the American Baptist Union. Signaling a broad trend in Baptist churches, the congregation in Carroll, New York, which had vehemently opposed Freemasonry, now saw the effort to eliminate the brotherhood as a political matter, outside the church's jurisdiction. The congregation now asked only that its Masonic members not "speak of those things that are done by them in secret."[43] The 1830 "Report on the Effect of Freemasonry on the Christian Religion," presented to the National Anti-Masonic Convention, further suggests this tacit acceptance. While offering the usual criticisms of the order, the report bends over backward to excuse the decision of church members to become Masons: "To have become a freemason, with good motives, is a misfortune, not a crime." Moreover, many people had become members before the Morgan affair and so were "as ignorant of the unrevealed iniquity of the institution . . . as those who never passed the threshold of a lodge." Given this situation, the report advised, "Let us not censure the hesitation, or chide the tardy action of Christians who are yet members of the institution; but invite their attention, and leave them to the influence of time and their own reflections."[44] Eventually, most churches followed this course of action. Despite the Anti-Masonic crusade, a more circumspect Freemasonry persisted there.

WOMEN AND THE ANTI-MASONIC CRUSADE

In addition to revealing larger struggles over Christian identity in the new society—struggles that the matter's suppression generally resolved—the conflict between defenders and critics of Freemasonry signaled early fault lines in the emerging ideology of domesticity. In the first half of the nineteenth century, the families of western New York's immigrant New Englanders began transitioning from the corporate economy of the countryside, with its patriarchal authority structure, to the middle-class structure of the market towns, in which women presided over a private sphere of children, morality, and religion.[45] Women now joined Protestant churches at a rate double that of men.[46] Church discipline fortified their moral authority in the domestic sphere, and church-based reform movements gradually became a means of extending their perceived maternal traits outside the household. Beginning as early as the end of the eighteenth century, elite Protestant women formed benevolent associations for the relief of indigent women and children. By the 1830s, evangelical women were conspicuous in temperance and antislavery efforts.[47] The campaign against Freemasonry took place in the midst of this larger transition.

Though opposition to Freemasonry could certainly be seen as within the bounds of pious women's efforts to protect the home, allowing for private, ad hoc attempts to influence men to abandon their membership, and there is scattered evidence of female protests, there was no such sustained public female movement.[48] Following Morgan's abduction, women in one Genesee County town defended their home life against the dissolute behavior of Masonic men, exclaiming that "the time and money spent in Masonic orgies is robbing their families and connexions of their natural and just claims, and is calculated to excite distrust and create discord in families."[49] Around the same time, the only verifiable women's Anti-Masonic meeting took place in nearby Wheatland Township, New York, and passed resolutions against the order.[50] At least one Anti-Masonic newspaper, moreover, sympathized with the Masonic wife, "left in solitude, left in the shades of night, ignorant of the employment by which her husband is engaged."[51]

Yet these early gendered attacks, suggesting emerging tensions surrounding the new sexual division of labor, are complicated by contemporaneous support for the order by leading Masonic wives. Sarah J. Hale, the editor of *Godey's Lady's Book*, the most widely circulated periodical in Victorian America, was emblematic of these women. Her influential opinions on female manners and morals moved gradually from the earlier Enlightenment ideology of women's intellectual equality with men, articulated by such authors as Hannah Crocker, to a mid-nineteenth-century affirmation of female moral superiority that sanctioned activism. Speaking for a generation of women who made gendered difference the driving justification for expanding their influence, Hale argued that although the home firmly bounded their place, women's moral superiority called them to a larger role in reforming the nation's public life.[52] Yet in contrast to the scattered voices of evangelical women who complained about the order, Hale had nothing but praise for Freemasonry.

Throughout her career, Freemasons nurtured and supported Hale. In 1813 she married David Hale, a rising lawyer who was soon the master of his local New Hampshire lodge. When he suddenly died in 1822, leaving her with five children to raise, Masons stepped in to assist in the publication of her first poems. In 1828, John Blake—the chaplain of the Massachusetts Grand Lodge, an Episcopal priest, and the editor of the *Episcopal Register*—invited Hale to Boston to edit his *Ladies' Magazine*, which Louis Godey bought and merged with his *Lady's Book* (later named *Godey's Lady's Book*) in 1837.

In 1830, when Anti-Masons attacked Boston's King Solomon's Lodge for its failure to complete the Bunker Hill Monument commemorating American resolve in the Revolutionary War, Hale responded by not only praising the brotherhood's "kindness and liberality" but also organizing like-minded women to create a merchandise fair that eventually raised sufficient funds to complete the monument.[53] Her appeal "to the Women of New England," published in the *Ladies' Magazine*, helps us to understand the perspective of those women who supported Freemasonry. Joining Hale on her "Ladies Executive Committee" were the affluent wives of leading Bostonians, including Mrs. Jonathan Chapman, the wife of the then mayor, and Mrs. John C. Warren, whose husband's grandfather Major and Grand Master Dr. Joseph Warren famously died at Bunker Hill. The campaign raised an astounding, for the 1830s, thirty thousand dollars. In her appeal, Hale made clear to her mostly female readers that she was not requesting "any infringement of that feminine propriety which they should scrupulously retain when coming before the public." Only "females, and children of both sexes under the age of twelve years" should contribute, solely as an "opportunity" for "mothers, to awaken in their children's hearts the love of country, of social order, and the refined enjoyment of doing good." For wasn't it, Hale observed, the "true value of money to use it for purposes that purify the affections, improve the intellect, and strengthen and exalt the best feelings of our nature"? While the Masons' Bunker Hill Monument Association noted that Hale's efforts were "condemned by some, because the women were 'stepping out of their sphere,'" it nevertheless concluded that under her leadership, these women were simply taking action out "of their own innate capacity for good."[54] Despite the Anti-Masonic crusade of the 1820s, Freemasonry found support in the 1830s among affluent Masonic wives such as Hale, who influenced the formation of the values and behaviors of other middle-class women.[55] In this early period, not only had organized female opposition to Freemasonry not yet coalesced, but there were also divisions among women over the virtues of the order.

. . .

Following the Anti-Masonic crusade, the fraternity retreated from public view. In western New York in the 1840s, few members of Genesee County's two persisting lodges held political positions or prestigious jobs, while close to half were farmers. The one continuing Masonic attribute from earlier days was members' affiliation with nonevangelical churches.[56] Elsewhere, grand public processions of Masons largely disappeared and would only return in the 1850s. The cancelling of these displays of power helped keep the fraternity out of the public eye and so reduced anger at its exclusivity and isolation from the rest of the community.[57] Masonic prohibitions on alcohol use in the lodges and the building of new lodges at a distance from taverns furthered this effort, as did the reemphasis of state Grand Lodges on long-standing rules forbidding the discussion of religion or politics.[58] Fear of another popular uprising also led the fraternity to moderate its claims of a special relationship with Christianity and instead accentuate a general Protestant conservatism. Beyond these internal changes, by the 1850s new religious and sectional threats shifted the focus of those who had feared a Masonic takeover of American democracy. The arrival of swarms of Irish Catholics and the conspiracy of Southern slaveholders became far greater dangers to the new society than the machinations of a weakened fraternity.[59] At the same time, a liberalizing climate made Masonry's religious principles more acceptable in the eyes of the churches. By the mid-nineteenth century, the Jacksonian-era assault had severed the fraternity's unique claims to the moral and religious leadership of the new nation.

CHAPTER 5

Gender, Protestants, and Freemasonry, 1850–1920

Over the last half of the nineteenth century, the chastened Masonic fraternity recovered its losses in membership and grew at a pace that resulted in more than 5 percent of the adult native white male population joining the brotherhood by the century's end.[1] This occurred within a large burgeoning of all manner of fraternal orders in what came to be called the Golden Age of Fraternity.[2] As the century progressed, industrialization, urbanization, and immigration shattered well-established patterns of family, work, and religious life. Outside the home, women and men sought new gender-defined associations, African Americans and new immigrants responded to the erosion of traditional communal networks by forming new organizations, and native-born Americans created societies to reform themselves and "outsiders."[3] By the 1910s, the great majority (59 percent) of America's voluntary associations were fraternal organizations.[4]

In this great profusion, Freemasonry occupied a distinctive position as the oldest and most respected of the middle-class orders. Though the fraternity did not reachieve the public prominence of its post–Revolutionary War days, it did continue to provide its members with an intimate private world of brotherhood, ritual meaning, and entertainment apart from the competitive marketplace and the female-dominated home. As the nineteenth century progressed, however, accommodations between women and Masons resulted in the growing convergence of their social worlds. By the end of the century, only a small minority of

Protestants and official Catholicism remained opposed to Freemasonry. Though the attraction of some Masons to antimodern beliefs and practices marked a clear boundary between the fraternity and late nineteenth-century liberal Protestantism, Masons appear to have been so welcome by the early twentieth century that some churches began borrowing from the fraternal framework as part of a broad-based remasculinization of American Protestantism.

THE GOLDEN AGE OF FRATERNITY

Like Freemasonry, the new fraternities provided men with a sense of order and group belonging in response to an expanding society built on mobility and individualism.[5] Men who had recently arrived in a city could create the kinds of face-to-face relationships and values formerly associated with family and community. Immigrants could find both the close-knit bonds of their hometowns and socialization to American values.[6] Through lodge membership, businessmen could make contacts, cultivate credit sources, and gain access to a nationwide network. Moreover, lodges provided essential economic benefits at a time when families could no longer rely on communal and kinship networks and before the advent of government-sponsored social welfare.[7] Whatever the racial, gender, or ethnic makeup of these societies, all were committed to moral uplift and self-improvement. In late nineteenth-century America, this meant inculcating into their members the middle-class values of sobriety, thrift, piety, industry, self-restraint, and moral obligation. Finally, through distinctive regalia, grand titles, and in some cases an ever-ascending hierarchy of degrees, late nineteenth-century fraternal orders responded to the various desires of Americans to join exciting new groups, increase their social prestige, imaginatively use leisure time, and satisfy spiritual needs.

New fraternal orders began to emerge as early as 1819. In that year, the British immigrant Thomas Wildey founded the Independent Odd Fellows of North America after advertising in his Baltimore newspaper for fellow immigrants who had joined the English Odd Fellows before coming to America. In 1834, the first indigenously spawned fraternal organization, the Improved Order of Red Men, evolved from a Baltimore-centered "tribe." Claiming descent from the Sons of Liberty and the Boston Tea Party, the Red Men employed what they believed to be Native American rituals and regalia to create a Masonic-like brotherhood. Following the Civil War, Americans made use of the now readily available Masonic manuals to produce their own "ancient" histories and ceremonies.[8] The Knights of Pythias (est. 1864), the Benevolent and Protective Order of Elks (1866), the Ancient Order of United Workmen (1868), the Ancient Arabic Order of the Nobles of the Mystic Shrine (1871), the Knights of Honor (1873), the Royal Arcanum (1877), the Knights of the Maccabees (1878), and the Modern Woodmen of America (1883) were all formed on the Masonic model.[9] Conversely, Freemasons pushed beyond the limits of their organization to create new fraternities. Masons who wanted to move beyond the lodges' new ban on alcohol and require the more aggressive pledge of total abstinence founded the Sons of Temperance in 1842. By the 1850s, this new society temporarily eclipsed Freemasonry in membership. After the Civil War, individual Freemasons created the Patrons of Husbandry (the Grange) for farmers, the Ancient Order of United Workmen for skilled craftsmen, and the Grand Army of the Republic for Union veterans.[10]

Membership in more than one fraternal organization was common and apparently desirable, especially among the leadership. In 1897, W. S. Harwood, writing for the *North American Review*, concluded that five and a half million of the nation's nineteen million adult men were members of at least one of its seventy thousand fraternal lodges.[11] Working with Harwood's statistics and reducing his numbers to account for multiple memberships, Anthony D. Fels has estimated fraternal membership to be about four million in 1896, compared with about two million (male and female) unionists in 1904 and 7,400,000 male members of Protestant religious denominations in 1906.[12] Hence, fraternal orders enrolled more men than labor unions and more than half as many men as Protestant churches. Moreover, their form permeated society, with the orders for immigrants, African Americans, and women (which were often referred to as fraternal[13]) taking on the trappings of fraternalism.

New arrivals from Europe quickly found their way into these societies. Between the Civil War and the nativist campaigns that coincided with the upsurge of southern and eastern European immigration, many orders not only admitted newcomers but also allowed local lodges to operate in their native tongues. Jews in particular became a significant presence in Freemasonry and other orders, while Catholics, despite the papal ban on joining fraternal groups, also made their way into these societies. However, the limits of Masonic religious neutrality and a desire for self-determination led Jewish Masons to help organize B'nai B'rith in 1843 and Catholics to create the Knights of Columbus in 1884.

Immigrants also brought over their old ethnic organizations, such as the Irish Ancient Order of Hibernians, and, once here, created associations of people from the same hometown. Known as landsmanshaftn, these became the most popular form of organization among eastern European Jewish immigrants. Though the rites of ethnic orders were similar to those of the mainstream societies, they were often used for different purposes. The Hibernians, for example, focused their ritual on the cause of Irish nationalism. In contrast, the Irish Knights of Columbus sought to reconcile their Catholicism with an ardent Americanism. As Daniel Soyer has argued, immigrant initiation rites "aimed largely at reconciling lingering loyalties to native lands, languages, and religions with the deep desire to integrate fully into American life."[14] The foes of immigration, in turn, churned up nativist sentiment through such new societies as the Order of United Americans (est. 1844), the United American Mechanics (1845), the Order of the Star-Spangled Banner (1849), and the Brotherhood of the Union (1850).

Despite this relative openness to European immigrants, mainstream American fraternalism consistently excluded African Americans. Racial segregation was accomplished on the basis of not only appearance but also formal stipulations that all members must be white. The resulting black fraternal movement both diverged from and paralleled white models. Indigenous organizations such as the Good Samaritans, the Nazarites, and the Galilean Fishermen emerged in the black community, growing out of mutual aid societies that worked closely with the black churches as both resources for black autonomy and barricades against white racism.[15] Rooted in the same milieu yet more closely following a white model were the African American versions of the Knights of Pythias, the Grand United Order of Odd Fellows, and the Prince Hall Masons. The latter two were large organizations with a decided impact on black social life after the Civil War and in the Southern states where blacks were a large portion of the population (see chapter 6). Another difference between the black and the white fraternal movements was their gender relations. Among the white middle-class, women were largely in the churches and men in the lodges. There was a greater overlap in the black orders, where a common struggle against racism and for self-determination was paramount: more men in the churches and a sustained female involvement in the fraternities.

Women's societies also developed in the late nineteenth century. The largest of the independent women's groups were the Women's Christian Temperance Union (est. 1874), whose agenda expanded to a variety of social issues; the General Federation of Women's Clubs (1890), which formed from the leadership of local clubs; and the single-issue reform societies, the Anti-Saloon League and the National American Woman Suffrage Association. Perhaps half a million women chose to enroll in these and mixed groups, missionary and mutual aid societies, and women's auxiliaries to fraternal organizations.[16]

After the Odd Fellows created the Order of the Daughters of Rebekah (1851), Freemasons founded the Order of the Eastern Star (1855), whose membership was open to the female relations of Master Masons. Other orders followed suit. By 1900, the Eastern Star had more than two hundred thousand members.[17] Like other women's associations of the period, the women's auxiliaries expanded their members' sphere of public activity. Such affiliated orders, however, remained subordinate to their male counterparts. Admission was allowed not on a woman's individual merits but because of her kinship with a fraternal man. This was characteristic of a male-dominated social order which recognized women primarily by their family relationships.

GENDER AND FREEMASONRY

In the pantheon of late nineteenth-century fraternalism, Freemasonry occupied a distinctive niche of middle-class respectability. Though theirs was similar to other mainstream orders in primarily including native white men of British and northern European stock and excluding women and African Americans, Masons saw themselves and were seen by others as the best of the middle class. Over time, the new fraternities were perceived as having distinctive socioeconomic ranks. Immigrant fraternities and mutual benefit societies were at the low end of the spectrum. The Knights of Pythias's blue-collar following placed it in the lower middle class, while the Odd Fellows comprised "the great middle, industrial classes."[18] At the top stood Freemasonry, whose membership was primarily drawn from the professions, merchants, and white-collar occupations.[19] While Masonic membership was available to men of all classes, the dues, regalia costs, and other fees placed it beyond the reach of most workers.[20] And although members were not required to have an education, mastery of the degree rituals required some measure of literacy, as well as leisure time. Perhaps more important than the occupational profile of the lodge was the extent to which members identified with the middle class and enshrined bourgeois sensibilities. Against the Odd Fellows' 1890s claims to a larger membership, the Masons held that theirs was of a "better sort." In their efforts to attract and retain "respectable" men, the order built striking new temples in the best locations of America's cities and towns.[21] Far from a suspect cabal of subversives, late nineteenth-century Masonry believed itself to be a socially prestigious organization. For many American men, the Masonic square and compass on one's watch chain was a recognizable sign of middle-class respectability.[22]

While claiming an elite status, Freemasons shared with other American mainstream fraternal orders an identity based on the exclusion of women. As previously discussed, the separation of elite women and men into different spheres began after the Revolution and reached its clearest definition by the late nineteenth century. This new gender-based system gave women both a restricted domestic sphere and a potentially empowering outlet for their moral energy: women's societies. Hence, the woman's sphere was both an adjustment to and a criticism of the new urban, industrial order. Like domesticity, fraternalism also accommodated and was critical of the emerging society. As Mary Ann Clawson has argued, both saw the need for a sphere of life where concern for others would extend beyond self-interest. Moreover, each saw in the creation of kinship relations—as in fraternalism's "brotherly bonds of affection"—the possibility of imposing collective moral restraints. At the same time, however, the male sphere of fraternal orders conflicted with the female sphere of the home. In opposition to the new conception of womanhood, which portrayed women as distinctively pious and caring, fraternalism challenged the importance of the family by claiming that an all-male brotherhood could make men moral. Freemasonry in particular, against the claims of an increasingly feminized Protestantism, provided men with both institutional solidarity and a defense of their moral autonomy.[23]

As the nineteenth century progressed, much of American Protestantism became identified with women's concerns. Displaced from the center of community life, churches now competed with social, professional, and political organizations for male members, while women defined themselves in religious terms. In the early nineteenth century, women joined churches in far greater numbers than men, accounting for as many as 78 percent of all converts in the Second Great Awakening.[24] At the start of the twentieth century, women were 61 percent of all Protestant church members and more than two-thirds of Protestant churchgoers.[25] Their preponderance in the pews inevitably influenced Christian theology. Orthodox Calvinist images of a paternal, authoritarian God gave way to liberal assurances of a maternal, affective, and nurturing Jesus. On the one hand, this shift enshrined the home and sanctified motherhood.[26] Yet on the other hand, women employed the association of femininity and religiosity to advocate for the moral reform of society.[27] "As society progresses," one Congregational minister said, "woman's work becomes more and more in the home, from which centre it moves outward."[28]

Over the course of the nineteenth century, women moved slowly but deliberately into the public sphere through participation in maternally themed voluntary societies. These associations imitated the male societies that their brothers and fathers created, following similar patterns of organization and procedure, yet were unlike them in employing the private domestic imperative of motherhood, the inculcation and reform of moral behavior, to justify their engagement in public activity. Though forbidden by convention from full participation as equals in the public sphere, women engaged in their own forms of expression and communication to advance issues of particular concern to themselves and their families. In this way, growing numbers came to embody an alternative civil society, what some have called a "counterpublic," that now contended with the prevailing male public sphere for acceptance and influence.[29] Though less-privileged women and women of color were often restricted in their protests to supporting male-dominated activities, Mary P. Ryan has shown that women of all backgrounds found a variety of ways to access public life.[30] The encounter of women with Freemasonry provides one window onto these struggles between genders in the expanding yet predominantly middle-class public sphere.

As the female "cult of domesticity" grew in much of American Protestantism in the second half of the nineteenth century, it inevitably conflicted with the masculine world of fraternal orders. Despite Freemasonry's 1850s revival as a temperance-minded, civic self-improvement association, its claim that an all-male brotherhood could make men moral went against changing notions of women's capacities and purpose. Emboldened with the moral authority of the domestic sphere, suffragists challenged men's political power, female moral reformers attacked social vice, and a growing number of women entered public life through higher education. At the same time, the sacred, private world of the lodge came under attack. Woman had many reasons to be suspicious of the fraternal lodge. The ideology of the domestic sphere provided them with a moral authority whose realization depended on men accepting domestic constraints. Long evenings spent at the lodge

allowed men to escape women's influence. Oaths and secrets undermined the sanctity of marriage vows. Female suspicions, in turn, met
with male resentment of women's increasing dominance in the church
and the family. The conflict between these two viewpoints resulted in
continuing Anti-Masonic tension long after the demise of political Anti-
Masonry.[31] By the 1870s, activists such as the suffrage leader Matilda J.
Gage concluded that the real purpose of fraternal orders was to "set one
sex against another."[32]

This antagonism between middle-class white men and women nevertheless occurred within a larger relational system. The masculine world
of the lodge could not be completely cut off from the feminine world of
the home. Moreover, the many efforts to lessen the tensions between
lodge and home indicate a growing desire for closer cooperation between
men and women. As the century progressed, Freemasons responded to
the encroachment of women on their domain by attempting to incorporate women and their interests into lodge activities. Masonic wives were
invited to lodge lectures and banquets. Separate "Home" and "Wom-
en's" departments began to appear in the pages of Masonic periodicals.
And women were symbolically admitted into the fraternal system
through the new Order of the Eastern Star auxiliary. Although this was
officially independent of the fraternity's all-male structure, its acceptance
of Masonic female relations, much to the consternation of many fraternal members, suggests some accommodation. Moreover, by the 1880s,
the Eastern Star sought a greater role for women, albeit within the
bounds of male authority. By the end of the century, the social worlds of
men and women were coming closer together.

The justification for excluding women from the fraternity drew on
contemporaneous understandings of the sexual division of labor, in
which men were breadwinners who went out to confront the harsh realities of public life and women remained at home, protected from the
world's dangers. In 1849, for example, the Masonic leader William
Hunter, addressing a Saint John's Day gathering in Louisiana, went out
of his way to "assure you ladies, that it is not because we fail to appreci-
ate your high moral and intellectual worth, or your ability to keep our
secret, that you are not permitted to share in our rights and privileges. . . . But it is because we respect women most in her own peculiar
sphere, not mingling with the crowd, but in retirement; not busying
herself with the affairs of communities, but with her household relations." There were "dangers," he warned, in wandering too far from
the domestic sphere. Should a woman "be seen at night in our lodges,"

apart from "the natural protection of a brother, husband, or father, . . . our respect for her would be diminished, and we should consider her as much out of place, as if she were . . . leading a band of soldiers to carnage and bloodshed."[33]

Though women were excluded, Masonic apologists held that their lodge activities were ultimately intended to benefit women. It was "for you," one said, that "the golden harvest of Masonry be gathered."[34] Though away from their homes, Masons claimed that through their lodge work they not only maintained a "deep and abiding" interest in their female relations but also went out of their way to provide aid to Masonic widows and orphans "which relatives, or friends, or churches cannot or care not to bestow."[35] As they had since early in the century, apologists also claimed that women had no need of Masonic moral training, because they inherently possessed superior virtue. When all of these arguments proved less than convincing, Masonic writers reverted to the assertion that the society's "ancient landmarks" expressly forbade the admission of women. "Anxious as we may be, and *are*, to please, accommodate and render happy our kind sisters, we have received the institution upon certain express and stipulated conditions; and we cannot violate these without being guilty of breach of compact, and a forfeiture of all our rights under it."[36]

Despite this resistance, around the middle of the century, efforts were made to respond to the persisting interest of women in the fraternity while maintaining the lodge's male autonomy. Some Masonic leaders began to invite women to attend lectures and banquets at the lodge, while the editors of fraternal magazines began to address a female audience. The editor of the *Mystic Star* wrote, in "Women's Interest in Masonry,"

> Though the ritual of Masonry may not be revealed, and though the degrees may not be conferred upon woman . . . our magazines contain that which illustrates the real worth of Masonry, and *we think* these magazines should have departments devoted to the interests of home and woman. We hope soon to be able to make our Home Department, what we desire in this respect. We are happy to be assured that it is already highly prized by many of our lady readers. We have had the thanks of several of the brethren for the effect it has already had on their wives, in subduing prejudices, and inducing more respect for the institution.[37]

The most imaginative effort to reconcile fraternalism and the claims of domesticity was the creation of the Order of the Eastern Star. Its original purpose was to enable the female relatives of Master Masons to identify themselves as such and so realize the support of the order. Since the 1840s, both men and women had expressed a desire for Masonic protection for their female relations who were traveling or in distress. As "Ida," a Masonic wife, described the problem in the *Mystic Star*, "In traveling lately with a very sick friend, we found ourselves in a large city, perfectly friendless, and unable, from the great crowd of visitors, to procure rooms suitable for an invalid, we addressed a member of the Masonic Fraternity, stating our near relationship to Brothers high in standing, and we received from him every assistance and kindness possible; but it would have been a great pleasure had we been able to show some credentials, *entitling* us to the courtesies so freely bestowed." She then suggested that beyond gaining some symbolic recognition, female Masonic relations might also form an organization for the "purposes of social enjoyment and the furtherance of benevolence, as well as our lords and masters. We do not, by any means, wish to be understood as requesting to be admitted as working members of the Craft, on a footing with the Fraternity, but simply as a subordinate branch, acting under instruction, and furnished with a sort of countersign which will serve to prove our genuineness."[38] Responding to such proposals, in 1855 the Freemason Rob Morris created the Order of the Eastern Star.[39] Over the course of the late nineteenth century and despite often strenuous fraternal objections, Morris, some of his Masonic brothers, and their female relations evolved an auxiliary body of the fraternity that provided women access to an organization and a ritual that affirmed their domestic virtues and supported the charitable purposes of Freemasonry.

The structure of the Eastern Star was characteristic of a male-dominated social order that recognized women only by their family relationships. Eligibility for membership depended entirely on a woman's status as a wife or daughter of a Master Mason and not on her individual qualities. Eastern Star members did not become Masons, and no Masonic governing body approved the women's order. Moreover, men could join this "women's" order, and in fact, Master Masons had to be present for a chapter to convene. However, the new organization did offer the female relatives of Masons the opportunity to participate in an expanded public sphere. Clara Barton, the founder of the American Red Cross, said that she joined the order because "my father was a Mason; to him it was a religion, and for the love and honor I bear him, I am glad to be connected with anything like this." From this first step outside the home, Barton soon created her relief organization.[40]

Nonetheless, male Eastern Star officeholders had greater influence than their female counterparts, and chapter meetings usually took place in the male lodge, under the leadership of a worthy patron and a worthy matron (often a husband and wife). Unlike the dramatic structure and content of Freemasonry, the Eastern Star conferred only one initiation degree, which moreover did not impart new morals or duties to the candidates. Instead, the five-part female ceremony, written by men, affirmed the "female" values of the domestic sphere by tying biblical heroines to the virtues of obedience, devotion, fidelity, faith, and charity. The order's manuals, moreover, explicitly state that only those who "believe in Jesus Christ" can be members. In sum, the Eastern Star merely confirmed that women achieve virtue only through family roles, their church, and their relationships to men.[41]

Seen from one perspective, it would appear that Masons created the Eastern Star primarily to deceive their female relations. In this vein, Mark C. Carnes concludes that "the entire enterprise" of the ladies' degrees "was founded upon an elaborate but seemingly transparent deception" that deflected women's attention from the secret workings of the lodge.[42] Indeed, as one Masonic periodical declared, "the conferring of said degrees on women is calculated to deceive and mislead them, and is therefore improper."[43] Yet as Clawson holds, this view does not sufficiently take into account either the "depth of male opposition or the commitment to feminine advance of the order's members."[44] Throughout the late nineteenth century, prominent Masons ridiculed "hairpin" Masonry and often excluded Eastern Star chapters from meeting in their lodge rooms. As recently as 1921, the grand master of the old Masonic stronghold of Pennsylvania decreed that "within six months," any member "identified with the order of the Eastern Star . . . sever all relation therewith."[45] Underlying the perception that the auxiliary was an elaborate ruse was the deep-seated, long-standing opposition of some Masonic men to female involvement in fraternal activities. At the same time, the conscious efforts of female Eastern Star members to advance their rights in their organization signal their participation in a larger late nineteenth-century movement for greater involvement in public life.

The feminist advances of the Order of the Eastern Star can be more easily understood in the context of the evolution of women's organizations in the late nineteenth century. Although by midcentury some women were involved in the temperance, abolition, and incipient suffrage movements, most female public activities were local and circumscribed by church organizations. Moreover, mixed-gender public groups raised troublesome questions about the propriety of women having a vote, much less a role in leadership.[46] According to its 1876 constitution, a grand patron and a grand matron were to govern the Eastern Star's Grand Chapter. The Grand Chapter "exercised all its executive powers," including that of forming new chapters, while the grand matron presided at meetings, enforced all legislation, and appointed all committees. Women held ten of the Grand Chapter's sixteen offices, and two men and two women represented each individual chapter. At the local level, the grand patron normally presided over the conferring of degrees but could invite the grand matron to do so.[47] At the very beginning of the Easter Star's organization, therefore, women presided over meetings, enforced legislation, appointed committees, held a voting majority, and could confer degrees. Some measure of the size of this women's advance can be seen in the 1873 comment of the order's historian that "a considerable number of sisters insisted that they should not vote" and needed to be persuaded that they now had that right.[48]

In the last quarter of the century, the Eastern Star made significant changes in its constitution that reflected a greater appreciation of women's abilities. This was a time when groups such as the Woman's Christian Temperance Union and the General Federation of Women's Clubs were coming on to the national stage. Well aware of these advances in public participation, Elizabeth Butler, in her 1878 grand matron's address to the order's General Grand Chapter, held that one purpose of the organization was to educate woman "to the idea that she may stand side by side and on an equality with man in any position which her ability proves her power to maintain, without detracting from her womanliness." She then pointedly criticized the "sole executive power" of the grand patron as an "an unfair provision" and demanded that the grand matron have "concurrent supervisory duties."[49] By 1892, the constitution of the General Grand Chapter had been changed to read that the grand matron "shall exercise all executive powers."[50] Remarking on this advance, Grand Matron Nettie Ransford observed that "the continued prosperity of the Order assures you that it has not suffered although placed in the hands of sisters."[51] Similar advances were evident in the area of membership. By 1886, the order had decided that although a woman was able to join only because of her relationship to a Master Mason, in the event that he was for any reason evicted from the fraternity, her membership would continue, standing on her merits.[52] Celebrating such "intelligent progress," the 1883 grand patron decried the Masonic fraternity for rejecting the auxiliary by turning its "moss-covered back to every innovation of its . . . usages, and cling[ing] like an imbecile to its toys of the past."[53] Moving rapidly with the "spirit of the times," by 1910 the Eastern Star had nearly half as many members (47 percent) and more than a third as many chapters (39 percent) as there were Masonic members and lodges.[54]

There were of course limits to women's advancement in a mixed-sex fraternal auxiliary. The presence of men could inhibit the creation of female networks, otherwise a potential source of women's empowerment. Such forces were likely in play in 1895 when the Grand Chapter decided not to accept an invitation to join twenty prominent women's societies in the National Council of Women. The grand matron acknowledged that the council was "a gathering of intellectual, thinking women, contact with whom, cannot but elevate those uniting with them." While clearly recognizing the "benefits" to women that this "proposed alliance" would bring, the leadership of the auxiliary nevertheless decided that joining the National Council would divert it from "the real object of our existence," which was to serve the "charitable and social purposes" of the "Masonic parent."[55]

Perhaps the greatest contribution of the Eastern Star was its effort to bring the separate Victorian-era worlds of women and men closer together. As Grand Patron Benjamin Lynds put it in 1892, "Our Order, being founded upon a liberal basis, unites men and women who are comparatively strangers, often estranged from each other by the force of education and prejudice, in bonds of fraternal sympathy and love."[56] The auxiliary's insistence on a mixed-sex membership implied a critique of the segregated social life of both female domesticity and the male lodge. In this sense, the Eastern Star anticipated the Masonic development of a more couple- and family-oriented social life wherein lodges balanced their private banquets with picnics, sleigh rides, concerts, and other respectable entertainment. As one Wisconsin lodge member described the effect of the Eastern Star, "They have introduced a degree of social life into Masonry that astonishes and probably pains the old, old-fashioned Mason."[57]

PROTESTANT OPPOSITION

By the late nineteenth century, overt Protestant resistance to fraternal orders had narrowed to a few small Midwestern perfectionist and reformed denominations and conservative Congregational and Baptist factions in mainline denominations, whose total membership accounted for less than 5 percent of all Protestants.[58] These were such radical evangelicals as the Wesleyan Methodists, the Free Methodists, and the United Brethren, whose leaders had deep roots in antebellum reform movements ranging from women's rights and the abolition of slavery to peace, Sabbatarianism, and prohibition. They were joined by Scottish and Scots-Irish seceding Presbyterians whose conservative Calvinism placed a high value on communal purity, sectarian exclusivity, and a refusal to support any government not founded on Christian principles. Though there were differences among the denominations, and practices at times fell short of beliefs, all of these biblically oriented Protestants saw social reform as a strategy for purging both society and the church of all that denied God's will. Such perfectionist aspirations flourished between 1840 and 1865 in all the major denominations, especially in the trans-Allegheny settlements of the Midwest.[59] There the Baptists, Methodists, and other dissenting sects, less inhibited by an entrenched upper class, infused secular society with rigorous group discipline, egalitarianism, and practical idealism. For these evangelical reformers, attacking fraternal orders was a logical extension of their Christian principles.[60] The fulcrum of this resistance was Wheaton College in Illinois, where the National Christian Association (NCA) was founded, its weekly newspaper the *Christian Cynosure* was published, and the Congregational minister and anti–secret society leader Jonathan Blanchard was the president of the school and the association.[61]

Blanchard represented one tributary of a mainstream Evangelicalism that divided after the Civil War. He gradually separated from his longtime Congregational friend Henry Ward Beecher over the latter's willingness to adapt Christianity to late nineteenth-century culture. In contrast to Beecher's "worldliness," Blanchard insisted on holding to the more rigorous Evangelicalism of the antebellum period. While Beecher and his followers drifted toward liberalism, Blanchard returned to the unfinished business of Anti-Masonry.[62] Duplicating the format that antebellum reform movements had popularized, the annual meetings of the NCA involved three days of sharing devotions, hearing committee reports, passing resolutions, and listening to speeches. Its efforts included the formation of a short-lived political party that called for prohibition, the banning of lodges, Sabbatarian legislation, and an amendment to the Constitution proclaiming the United States a Christian nation. In addition, "agents," or lecturers, went throughout the Midwestern "rural districts where the industry and intelligence of the people make the lodges weak."[63] There they distributed tracts and exposés of fraternal rituals, signed up subscribers to the *Cynosure*, and spoke of the dangers of "oath-bound secret societies" that were planning to "overthrow the Christian churches and capture the government under which we live."[64] Like the Anti-Masonic crusaders of the 1830s, evangelical Protestants who had seized on Freemasonry as a master symbol for all that was threatening to replace an old social order based on republican and Christian principles, Blanchard believed that the churches bore considerable responsibility for the spread of the new orders. Unlike in the 1830s, only a small minority of Protestants supported the Anti-Masonic cause. The NCA newspaper had fewer than five thousand subscriptions at its peak.[65]

Along with the usual attacks on fraternal orders, first articulated by the earlier Anti-Masonic movement, Blanchard's Midwestern denunciation of the liberal religious leaders of the East reflected an emerging division in Evangelicalism. On November 14, 1871, for example, in the pages of the *Cynosure*, he accused the Boston Congregational clergyman Alonzo H. Quint of being a Mason.[66] The secretary of the Massachusetts General Association of Congregational Churches for twenty-five years, a founding editor of the *Congregational Quarterly*, and the secretary of the National Council of Congregational Churches, Quint was the principal author of the Congregationalists' "Burial Hill Declaration," which affirmed the essential unity of all Christians.[67] In clear contrast to Blanchard's rigorous perfectionism, Quint was willing to adapt to a religiously plural environment, reject the various total abstinence pledges that Blanchard considered essential features of the true church, and oppose a confrontational strategy for social change. He was also a Mason. In 1871, the same year when he was chosen to be the secretary of the National Council, Master Mason Quint was appointed the senior chaplain of the Masonic Grand Lodge of Massachusetts.[68] Beyond condemning Quint's Masonic membership, Blanchard attacked him as one of those "worldly leaders in the East who hated the reform efforts in the West." These were "men whose pulpits make no secret of denying the atonement," neglect the Bible, reject the law of the Sabbath, advocate billiards and baseball games, and collectively seek to swing the churches of Jesus Christ "off from his gospel and into conformity with the world."[69] Quint did not respond in any Christian publication but did apologize to the Grand Lodge of Massachusetts for this Blanchard "fanatic" who threatened the fraternity with political action and Masonic Christians with excommunication. From Quint's perspective, Blanchard was intolerant and bigoted, unable to see that any institution, such as Freemasonry, "which softens the acerbities of sects and parties" and "unites us as citizens and as men, is an Institution which we ought to cherish and defend."[70]

For the female supporters of the NCA, the attack on fraternal orders was both conservative and radical. Although Mark C. Carnes asserts that "the NCA's hopes of vanquishing the orders rested squarely upon the shoulders of evangelical women," those who supported the association had no greater voice than women in other midcentury mixed-gender public organizations.[71] All of the officers, agents, lecturers, and members of the NCA were men.[72] Women writers did begin to appear in the *Cynosure* by 1875, to offer such articles as "A Woman's Plea against Secret Societies." Yet as late as 1883, the editors asked, "Where are the heroic women to lead off the righteous crusade against secret societies?"[73] Compared to the Order of the Eastern Star, whose women held offices and took official action, the NCA appears to have discouraged female leadership and initiative. At the same time, it attacked fraternal orders not for challenging the moral authority of the female domestic sphere but for subverting the common effort of men and women to bring about a perfect society.

Outside the NCA, few evangelicals were willing to take on fraternal orders following the Civil War. A loyal following of fraternal men now permeated the professional, business, and political reaches of the "respectable" middle class. At the same time, the great majority of evangelicals had loosened their rigorous discipline and relaxed their more controversial calls for social reform. Blanchard and his followers, in contrast, found their identity in upholding the prophetic positions of the antebellum period. By the 1890s, however, these Midwestern perfectionists had begun to change their perspective. Though they still believed that the world was "on its way back to God," that way seemed less clear than it had in 1839, when Blanchard spoke of a linear progression toward the millennium, with each reform eliminating more and more evil until the realization of the perfect society. In 1891, however, he warned of "the horrors which must precede the overthrow of the abominations which remain, ere Christ can reign on earth."[74] Such millenarian thinking was characteristic of the deepening sense of cultural pessimism that settled over the radical evangelical movement by the end of the century.[75] As George Marsden has argued, Blanchard's radical Evangelicalism, with its postmillennial hopes of transforming the culture, gradually hardened into a premillennial, separatist fundamentalism that hoped at best to "restrain evil until the Lord returns."[76] This narrowing and hardening of the evangelical vision, moreover, resulted in a growing resistance to gender equality, biblical feminism, and women's involvement in social reform.[77]

Between the Freemasonry-attacking NCA and the order-supporting Eastern Star were the great majority of middle-class Protestant women, who were largely reticent about the fraternity. Among these women, the largest social reform organization was the Women's Christian Temperance Union (WCTU), led by Frances Willard. By the late nineteenth century, Willard's Methodist Episcopal Church had parlayed a growing doctrinal latitude and desire for respectability into the largest and the least Anti-Masonic evangelical congregation in North America.[78] For many of the women of this and other "progressive" denominations, Willard embodied "a new kind of womanliness." She was both a strong and independent social activist and a caring, gentle woman whose obvious piety maintained continuity with earlier, more domestic ideals of true womanhood.[79] Embodying both the domestic and the social activist ideals of the evolving "women's sphere," by the 1880s Willard and her followers had embraced a variety of reforms, including labor, prostitution, public health, sanitation, international peace, and women's suffrage, but not opposition to fraternal orders. Though Willard was a long-time family friend of the Blanchards', because she took a pragmatic approach to fraternal orders, the NCA and its radical evangelical colleagues strongly resisted her vision of a great reform coalition of labor, agriculture, and all temperance organizations, even encompassing groups committed to secrecy, such as the Knights of Labor and the Good Templars. This resistance ultimately led Willard to remove an NCA forum from a WCTU conference in favor of a presentation by the Knights of Labor.[80] Her presence at the Masonic cornerstone-laying ceremony for the Methodist-related Evanston Female College, where she served as president, further suggests her acceptance of fraternal orders.[81]

Unlike the NCA, which saw fraternal orders as the root of society's ills, the few middle-class Protestant women who spoke out against the lodges saw them as unwelcome diversions from social reform efforts. The radical suffragist Matilda Joslyn Gage, in an early address before the NCA, lamented the damage that her husband's lodge membership had done to their marriage yet saved her most pointed criticism for Freemasonry's refusal to admit women (she would have joined otherwise) and then, turning the tables, demanded that the NCA endorse female suffrage (which it soon did).[82] Despite dire warnings from the NCA about the damage that fraternal orders did to the "sobriety and rectitude" of men and women, large numbers joined these orders by the 1880s, suggesting that few were heeding these alarms.[83]

AN ALTERNATIVE RELIGIOUS WORLD

At the same time that Protestant women were seeking greater accommodation with the men of the Masonic lodge, many in the fraternity remained absorbed in its alternative religious life. In their late nineteenth-century bid for respectability, Masonic writers worked to shape the fraternity's worldview to reflect the moral and religious perspectives of the Protestant middle class. To make a broad-based appeal, the brotherhood at times reflected both the conservative and the liberal positions that resulted from the new theological and social pressures that late nineteenth-century urbanization, immigration, and evolutionary science placed on Protestantism.[84] On the conservative side, in 1888, Grand Lodges in Texas and Missouri expelled Masons "for denying the existence of God and the truth of the Bible."[85] Such actions reassured conservative Christians that the lodge affirmed their religious principles. On the liberal side, Masons appear to have been free to adapt fraternal perspectives to their own religious views and needs, short of unbelief. Given these conflicting viewpoints, the fraternity's primary public purpose was to present itself as an aid, or "handmaid," of the Protestantism of the respectable middle class. The available evidence, however, does not support this amiable portrayal. If Masons did indeed believe that the lodge supported the more important work of the church, then wouldn't a significant portion have been church members?

In his study of Freemasonry in Gilded Age San Francisco, Anthony D. Fels found that just 14 percent of the city's brotherhood in 1890 were enrolled in Protestant churches.[86] Nationally, only one out of seven white Masons (14.4 percent) in 1898 had progressed to the Knights Templar degree of the York Rite, which requires that one be Christian.[87] Although no other statistics relating church membership and Masonic affiliation are available for the late nineteenth century, at minimum these suggest that less than a majority of late nineteenth-century Masons were also church members. Moreover, consistent with the fraternity's earlier history, a plurality of San Francisco's Masonic clergy and laity were Episcopalians, closely followed by Unitarians. Freemasons were also found in nonevangelical churches in Lutheran, Congregational, Presbyterian, and Methodist denominations.

The convergence of Freemasonry and liberal Protestantism was most apparent in their common embrace of Enlightenment efforts to base religious authority on reason rather than revelation. Liberalism's favorable regard for the natural sciences was similar to the Masonic commitment to Newtonian science. And echoing the fraternity's hallmark belief in universalism, liberal Protestants moved toward a greater appreciation of the world's other religions. Both groups, moreover, rejected Evangelicalism's emotional piety while embracing the importance of a well-reasoned ethics. Even sharing these views, however, churches had different styles, and San Francisco's churchgoing Masons were among those most fond of order, tradition, and hierarchical authority. In that city especially they could be found in any of the major denominations that followed the Gilded Age trend toward stately new buildings, sumptuous furnishings, stained-glass windows, elegant organs, and a renewed appreciation of High Church liturgical forms.[88]

Despite their similarities, Freemasonry diverged from the expansive mood fostered by Protestant liberalism in the late nineteenth century while continuing its consistency with the rationalism, commonsense realism, and antirevivalism of antebellum liberal Protestantism. The Masonic emphasis on an orderly society aware of human limitations stood noticeably apart from the new, optimistic liberal faith in the immanent love of God that pervaded the new society. The liberals' metaphoric reading of the Bible and interest in biblical criticism contrasted with the fraternity's commonsense emphasis on discovering "self-evident" religious truths through the study of nature and Scripture. Further, in contrast to the liberal social gospel's outward concern for the poor, the brotherhood's charity remained focused largely on the needs of the brethren, their widows, and their children. Finally, although the new liberal interest in world religions appeared to overlap with the fraternity's embrace of the common ground of all faiths, Freemasonry's use of ritual elements from a variety of sources was intended to foster its own values rather than promote interreligious dialogue.[89] The development of fraternal rites, moreover, made clear that unlike Protestant ministers, who emphasized the moral power of the Bible, Masons taught morality through the practice of ritual.

The great majority of Freemasons experienced only the three-degree sequence of Craft Masonry, while a lesser though still considerable number passed through the four degree rituals of the Royal Arch Chapter. Both Craft and Royal Arch rituals were well established by 1820. Beyond the three Craft rites were two separate progressions of higher degree ceremonies. York, or American, Rite Freemasonry included ten degrees, sequences of which the separate Royal Arch, Royal and Select Master, and Knights Templar lodges conferred. The Ancient and Accepted Scottish Rite conferred Scottish Rite Masonry's twenty-nine degrees. While the three basic degrees of Craft Masonry continued to teach moral values and the fraternity's legendary origins to initiates, the higher degrees, intended to lead candidates through successive layers of trial and revelation to an ever-elusive truth, took on a long and complex life of their own. Though the new rituals have often been seen as the reason for the fraternity's revival, only a minority of the most dedicated pursued the higher degrees. By the end of the century, about one-quarter of all Masons were members of Royal Arch lodges and less than 5 percent had progressed through the thirty-two initiations of the Scottish Rite.[90] Higher degree recipients, however, were consistently among the fraternity's leadership and frequently held membership in the Odd Fellows, the Knights of Pythias, and similar orders that also offered a progression of higher degrees.

Fraternalists were not alone in using ritual drama to teach moral lessons. Early nineteenth-century revivals employed theatrical effects to convert sinners, and the midcentury temperance and abolitionist crusades found such dramatic stage performances as *Ten Nights in a Bar Room* and *Uncle Tom's Cabin* to be effective weapons in advancing their respective campaigns. By the 1870s, the appeal of the playhouse, the pondering of moral questions, and the intrigue of mystery were well established among a general public that was regularly treated to traveling theaters featuring biblical stories, Shakespeare, and contemporary dramas as well as vaudeville, circus, and minstrel shows.[91] Even before the advent of movies, a variety of entertainments offered the opportunity to escape into make-believe worlds. Similar to these theatrical developments, Masonic ritual evolved to provide moral instruction, dramatic entertainment, and escape into exotic worlds while creating bonds among the participants. For some, the "mysticism" of the higher degree rites exuded a "strange and powerful attraction." As one contemporary observer reported, for these most committed and influential fraternalists, "there is a peculiar fascination in the unreality of the initiation, the allurement about fine 'team' work, a charm of the deep potency in the unrestricted, out-of-the-world atmosphere which surrounds the scenes where men are knit together by the closest ties, bound by the most solemn obligations to maintain secrecy as to the events which transpire within the walls."[92]

The ritualists' rejection of the present in favor of a pilgrimage to the past suggests a repudiation of the theological ideas of liberal Protestant churches. In the higher degree ceremonies, an assumption of human failing and the need for suffering and tribulation with uncertain outcomes replaced the liberal view of humanity's goodness and innocence in celebrating life's pleasures. Candidates for the Royal Arch degree were described as "frail, dependent and needy creatures" afflicted with the "leprosy of sin." Living amid "the pains and calamities" of their everyday existence, they were instructed to persevere in their efforts to wring a deeper understanding from the esoteric symbols of the ancient past. In contrast to the reassuring domestic imagery of liberal Protestant ideas about death, the morbid scenes of the higher degrees tormented candidates with the probable gruesomeness of their end. The loving God of the liberal churches was nowhere to be found. Instead, candidates were instructed to take off their shoes and prostrate themselves before their "great, mighty, and terrible" God.[93]

One likely historical context for the interest of American middle-class men in the higher degrees is the late nineteenth-century search for more intense forms of physical and spiritual experience in reaction to what Max Weber called the "rationalization of Western culture."[94] According to T. Jackson Lears, the ethos of modernization, with its relentless demand for bureaucratic efficiency and worship of material values, haunted the traditional sensibilities of late nineteenth-century Americans. At the same time, liberal Protestantism's sentimental humanism seemed incapable of offering the gravity of "older, sterner" creeds. Lacking "spiritual ballast," leading members of the middle class experienced what Friedrich Nietzsche called "weightlessness," marked by vague moral distinctions and ambiguous spiritual understandings.[95] Seeking to free themselves from the tightening grip of positivist materialism, antimodern dissenters tried to recover intense experience through new and diverse fascinations with medieval Catholic piety, Oriental and other "primitive" cultures, traditional craftsmanship, strenuous exertion in militarism and the martial arts, agrarian lifestyles, depth psychology, and other interests that purportedly did not demand the suppression of so much of the individual's personality. The revival of liturgical forms of worship and traditional doctrines in some Protestant denominations was part of this diffuse movement, as was some of the Masonic interest in the higher degrees.

Among the sixty-six members of the "better-educated strata of the old-stock ruling class" who constitute the basis of Lears's study were several cultural leaders with Masonic connections. One, the Masonic brother and pioneering Orientalist Paul Carus, railed against liberal individualism by proclaiming the Buddhist tenet that "the existence of self is an illusion." His prodigious output of books and articles on Oriental mysticism and primeval knowledge signified a "quietistic withdrawal from a disenchanted universe."[96] In the same vein, Lears sees Harold Frederic's widely read *The Damnation of Theron Ware* (1896) as an indictment of the title character's vapid liberal Protestant gospel of moral and material ascent and an affirmation of the sturdier Old World Catholicism with which the novel contrasts it, personified by an Irish parish priest.[97] Samuel Clemens (Mark Twain) joined his local Missouri lodge at the age of twenty-six and remained a member there until his departure ten years later.[98] According to Lears, his writings portray a struggle between modern and medieval sensibilities. *A Connecticut Yankee in King Arthur's Court* (1889) comically contrasts the world of late nineteenth-century capitalism with sixth-century England. Similar to Huck Finn, the Arthurians are celebrated as "free from the self-consciousness, the restraints and decorum, of Victorian 'civilization.'"[99] Taken together, the writings of Clemens, Frederic, and Carus suggest that one significant attraction of Freemasonry to the old-stock middle class was its satisfaction of their antimodernist yearnings.

REMASCULINIZATION OF THE CHURCHES

While Freemasonry's antimodernist medieval gallantry and mystical rituals marked a clear boundary between it and much of American Protestantism, at the turn of the century the appeal to men of such trappings led to the creation of new brotherhoods in the churches to lure them in. In 1908, Edgar Blanchard, a descendant of the radical evangelical–turned–fundamentalist Anti-Mason Jonathan Blanchard, acknowledged that "many men who regularly attend their lodge meetings are seldom seen at the services of their church." He then praised the "impressive initiatory rites" of the lodge for fostering a "strong fraternal spirit" absent in the churches. Compared to these ceremonies, Blanchard lamented, those of the church were "weak." Moreover, "the lodge is conducted on strictly business principles," while "in the church ... there is a woeful lack of strictly business procedure, and affairs sometimes get into a chaotic state."[100] In response to such concerns, beginning in the 1880s, the Brotherhood of Saint Andrew (Episcopal), the Presbyterian Brotherhood, and the Brotherhood of Saint Paul

(Methodist) appeared, offering "deeply religious" and elaborate ceremonies and ritual degrees to churchmen.[101] Some of their members were
also leaders in the Men and Religion Forward Movement.[102]

The movement to inject manliness into Victorian religion that became
known as Muscular Christianity began as early as the mid-1800s in
England and took hold in America in the late nineteenth century. As
seen by the historian Clifford Putney, it was a response to the effete-
making "overcivilization" of young men in the cities, the harmful effects
of womanly sentimentality, and the need to reinvigorate "old-stock"
Americans to better compete against muscular immigrants. This white
native-born Protestant middle-class men's movement was also part of
the Progressive Era's embrace of the "strenuous" life and assertion of
the superiority of Anglo-Saxon identity.[103] Climaxing with the 1910–12
Men and Religion Forward Movement, the only widespread religious
revival in America that told women they were not welcome, American
Muscular Christianity drew its supporters first from ecumenically
minded, Social Gospel–leaning Protestants and then from conservatives
who were particularly concerned with the pervasive presence of women
in their churches.[104] The purpose of the Men and Religion Forward
Movement was to bring men back into religious life, through a businesslike organization that marketed a virile Christianity. The movement
especially embraced physical fitness, social reform, and the assertion of
male authority in the churches.[105] Though this short-term campaign
resulted in few male converts and Muscular Christianity receded in
importance by the 1920s, its adherents contributed to what Nancy F.
Cott has called the "persistent strictures and ideologies of male dominance" that prevailed in American society from 1910 to 1930.[106]
Whether because of a "more masculine" church environment of businesslike efficiency; greater attention to meaningful ritual; the assertion
of Anglo-Saxon identity; the embrace of physical fitness; the reclaiming
of male authority; or some other reason or combination of these, men
were returning to the churches.[107] Between 1906 and 1926, census figures show that the number of males in Protestant churches increased
6.4 percent, to 41.8 percent of all members. Some urban, middle-class
denominations reported greater increases.[108]

. . .

A Freemason who was born in the early 1800s and lived through the
century's end would have experienced momentous changes—from
the heights of the moral and religious leadership of the new nation to

the depths of the Anti-Masonic troubles and on through the fraternity's resurgence as a badge of respectability for the emerging middle class. The politically connected, nationally prestigious, republican and purportedly Christian fraternity he would have entered in the first quarter of the century retreated further into its private sphere in the second quarter, just as the majority of antebellum Protestant churches tacitly accepted its liberal themes. As the century progressed, Victorian Protestant women and Masonic men negotiated a greater accommodation of each other's social worlds. By the end of the nineteenth century, a new generation of young, outgoing middle-class men had entered the lodge and begun to change the fraternity from a sacred asylum into a modern, secular organization. Before considering this development, we must first expand the story of Freemasonry and American religious history beyond the experience of European Americans from Protestant backgrounds to include African Americans, Native Americans, Jews, and Catholics, all of whose appropriations of Freemasonry offer insights into our understanding of their respective religious histories.

PART TWO

Beyond the White, Protestant Middle Class

Freemasonry responded to the needs and desires of American men both within and beyond the white middle class. Though dominated by native born European American men from Protestant backgrounds, throughout the fraternity's sojourn through American culture it attracted Catholics, Jews, Native Americans and African Americans who appropriated the Masonic framework for their own purposes. Catholics were the original operative Masons, working on the great stone castles and cathedrals of the medieval period. Jews were admitted to the eighteenth century "modern" fraternity. In nineteenth century America, both these groups created from the Masonic template their own orders to respond to the needs of their immigrant brothers to both assimilate to American society and retain their Old World identities. In the middle of the nineteenth century, a growing number of Native American leaders joined the fraternity following the forced removal of Southeastern Indians to "Indian Territory", in the region of present-day Oklahoma. For these Native Americans and their turn-of- the-century forbearers, the fraternity provided resources to help them find their way through the challenges of living within the new American society. Finally, after the Civil War, African American Northern missionaries set about planting Prince Hall lodges and black churches throughout the South, that together worked to resist racism and encourage the self-determination of freed slaves. In their encounter with Freemasonry, each of these groups claimed the fraternity as their own while working to fashion its resources toward their own ends. This book now turns to the narratives of Freemasonry and African Americans, Native Americans, Jews, and Catholics and how each made use of the fraternity's beliefs and practices.

CHAPTER 6

The Prince Hall Masons and the African American Church

The Labors of Grand Master and Bishop
James Walker Hood, 1864–1918

In the late nineteenth century, James Walker Hood was the bishop of the North Carolina Conference of the African Methodist Episcopal Zion Church and the grand master of the North Carolina Grand Lodge of Prince Hall Masons. In his forty-four years as a bishop, half of that time as the senior bishop of the denomination, Reverend Hood was instrumental in planting and nurturing his denomination's churches throughout the Carolinas and Virginia. The founder of North Carolina's denominational newspaper and college, the author of five books, including two histories of the AMEZ Church, the appointed assistant superintendent of public instruction and a magistrate in his adopted state, Hood had a career that was representative of the broad mainstream of black denominational leaders who came to the South from the North during and after the Civil War. Concurrently, he was the superintendent of the Southern Jurisdiction of the Prince Hall Masonic Grand Lodge of New York and a moving force behind the creation of the region's black Masonic lodges— often founding them in the same places as his fledgling churches. At his death in 1918, the *Masonic Quarterly Review* hailed Hood as "one of the strong pillars of our foundation."[1] If Bishop Hood's life was indeed, according to his biographer, "a prism through which to understand black denominational leadership in the South during the period 1860–1920," then what does his leadership of both a Prince Hall Grand Lodge and the AMEZ Church tell us about the nexus of fraternal lodges and African American Christianity at the turn into the twentieth century?[2]

Scholars have noted but not substantially investigated the significance of fraternal orders for African American social life. At the turn of the century, W. E. B. DuBois saw hope for the uplift of blacks through "mastery of the art of social organized life" in them.[3] In 1910, Howard Odum ranked black fraternal orders equal in membership to the black church and "sometimes" more important.[4] According to the 1915 *Who's Who of the Colored Race*, two-thirds of the most prominent African Americans held membership in both a national fraternal order and a black church. Forty-two percent of those holding joint memberships were Prince Hall Masons, one-third of whom were clergymen or church officers.[5] Subsequent research has explored the economic, class, and political importance of these orders and their influence on black masculinity while documenting their continued pervasive presence in African American society.[6] Yet only recently have investigators ventured into the meaning of fraternal beliefs and rituals for African Americans or explored the relationship between fraternal orders and the black church.[7]

In addition to the tendency of historians to underemphasize rituals and beliefs, the study of black fraternal orders has suffered from a paucity of evidence. The otherwise prolific Bishop Hood left few references to his lodge membership. Unlike the primary materials of white lodges, which pose a problem not so much of finding as of understanding, those of Prince Hall lodges are hard to locate. This has to do partly with the scarcity of these records and partly with the still enforced secrecy of the order.[8] Nevertheless, several Prince Hall histories, some state proceedings, and a scattered national array of lodge information, members' writings, and newspaper accounts are available. In Hood's case in particular, reading the available annual proceedings of the North Carolina Grand Lodge alongside the minutes of the AMEZ North Carolina Conference allows us to observe similarities and differences between the two organizations and the role he played in each.

The activities of the Prince Hall Masons complemented the work of the AMEZ Church, this chapter argues, by providing the black community with additional symbolic, ideological, and organizational resources to resist racism and find its way through the contentious arena of American civil society. Hood's North Carolina Prince Hall fraternity drew a considerable portion of its membership from the rolls of his North Carolina denomination. Though different in their beliefs and ritual lives, the two organizations were structurally similar. The origins of their relationship can be traced to the post-revolutionary era, when both mutual benefit societies and the black church provided seedbeds of autonomy and bulwarks against the racism of white society. Following the Civil War, these two interwoven social institutions came to the South, offering black Southerners similar race histories that countered white racial images and provided meaning and hope for their lives. Bishop Hood appropriated beliefs from Masonry that complemented his missionary efforts, while his fraternity's practices created bonds among black men and helped them to become responsible members of the community. This marriage between the church and the lodge was not without conflicts, with outsiders in the Holiness movement, between church and lodge members, and between men and women. Still, compared to white Masons, Bishop Hood's Prince Hall members were active supporters of the church, in a common struggle against racism and for the self-determination of the African American community. Taken together, the black church and the fraternal lodge were central to the formation of what Joanna Brooks has called "a black counterpublic." In this social and intellectual space, African Americans struggled to reclaim their humanity from slavery and subsequent racial subordination.[9]

CHURCH AND LODGE

In late November of 1874, Bishop James Walker Hood presided over the weeklong eleventh annual gathering of the ministers of the North Carolina Conference of the AMEZ Church, in New Berne. Raised in Pennsylvania and ordained in New England, Hood was the pastor of a congregation in Bridgeport, Connecticut, when his denomination sent him as a missionary to the freed people of the South. In 1864 he arrived in New Berne, in coastal North Carolina, where he was appointed bishop in 1872, and by 1874 he had overseen the planting of 366 churches with more than twenty thousand members.[10] As a Northern missionary and church organizer, Hood operated in a milieu where most of the newly freed slaves were either completely unchurched or in need of additional structure and organization, at least from the Northern perspective, to purify their Christianity of the distortions of Southern white religion.[11] A religious conservative whose social activism stemmed from his belief that Christian conversion would lead to the elimination of oppression and social injustice, Hood urged his followers to pursue a "profound" commitment to Christ. This was especially important for ministerial candidates, whom the conference examined carefully for their "literary qualifications, their intemperate habits and filthy practices," and to whom the bishop directly appealed to honor the dignity of the ministry by living "holy and spotless lives." Following these remarks, Hood announced that prior to the evening's "love feast," the Masonic fraternity would lay the cornerstone at New Berne's new brick church.[12]

Five days later, the Zion leader journeyed to Raleigh, where he was feted as "Most Worshipful Grand Master" at the fifth annual proceedings of the Prince Hall Grand Lodge of Free and Accepted York Masons for the State of North Carolina. Shortly after his arrival in New Berne in 1864, Hood had followed through on his commission as the superintendent of the Southern Jurisdiction for the Prince Hall Masonic Lodge of New York by establishing King Solomon Lodge No. 1 there, the same town where he organized his first AMEZ church.[13] He organized his next three lodges in the towns of Wilmington, Fayetteville, and Raleigh, the sites of the largest AMEZ congregations.[14] In 1870, these four lodges formed the North Carolina Grand Lodge and unanimously elected Bishop Hood as their grand master. By 1874, there were eighteen Prince Hall lodges in the state, with 478 members. In his address that year to his "dear Brethren," Grand Master Hood sounded notes of encouragement that echoed—though in different language—the remarks he had made one week earlier to the AMEZ faithful. Appealing first to the "Supreme Grand Master" to bless their gathering "within these sacred walls," the Prince Hall leader pronounced that "the state of the craft in this jurisdiction is good." Most lodges were "composed of good, solid material, and, when the master's hammer has given [them] the necessary polish, [they] will form a beautiful structure," although a few, notably his namesake J. W. Hood Lodge No. 8, in Goldsboro, "lacked Masonic ability." The grand master reported that his best visit was to Pythagoras Lodge No. 6, in Smithville, most of whose "members are professors of Christianity." Hood urged that candidates for "the mysteries of Masonry" be "men of active minds" with, according to the Grand Lodge By-Laws, "a desire for knowledge, and a sincere wish of being serviceable to [their] fellow-creatures." A candidate must also be "free," "of good standing as a citizen," and have no physical deformity "so as to deprive him from honestly acquiring the means of subsistence." On the last day of the gathering, Grand Master Hood prayed to the "Supreme Architect of the Universe" to "guide and govern all we do."[15]

Accompanying Bishop Hood on his journey from New Berne to Raleigh were a number of his ministers, who also served under his direction as leaders in Prince Hall Masonry. The 1874 AMEZ conference minutes list 192 participating ministers. Sixty-four, or one-third, of these also appear in the available Prince Hall proceedings for the 1870s. They included one-third of the conference's ruling elders, some of whom held similar leadership positions in the Grand Lodge. In 1875, for example, Bishop Hood appointed Thomas H. Lomax as the presiding elder for the Charlotte District, one of six in the conference, and Grand Master Hood appointed him district deputy grand master for the Charlotte District, one of five that the Grand Lodge oversaw. Similarly, R. H. Simmons, a ruling elder throughout the 1870s, was appointed the grand pursuivant of the Grand Lodge, in charge of instructing members in the lore and practice of Freemasonry. Several elders held important committee positions in both the conference and the Grand Lodge. Still others were both ministers of churches and leaders of their local lodges. In sum, in 1874 one-third of the AMEZ ministers in North Carolina were members and often leaders in Prince Hall Masonry. These sixty-four men, in turn, accounted for more than 13 percent of the state's 485 Prince Hall members.[16] Since these figures do not include the untold number of church members who, like their ministers, followed their leader into the lodge, it appears that Grand Master Hood forged a substantial portion of the leadership and membership of North Carolina's Prince Hall lodges from the leaders and members of his North Carolina AMEZ denomination.

These groups had not only the same leader, an overlapping membership, and societies in many of the same towns but also similar organizational structures and an appeal for the same broad cohort of young African American men.[17] The annual meetings of both took place over several days and followed a rhythm of worship, business, and recreation. Central to each meeting was the bishop's or grand master's address and report on his preceding year's visit to individual churches or lodges. Both were rational, hierarchical societies governed by bylaws and central committees. Enduring committees in the conference included Credentials, Finance, By-Laws, and Complaints, which had their parallels in the Grand Lodge's Credentials, Finance, By-Laws, and Grievances committees. Considerable time in each annual meeting was given over to complaints or grievances concerning members. Those of AMEZ revolved around intemperance, adultery, irregular credentials, and "preaching erroneous doctrine." Grand Lodge penitents were more often assailed for being "dull and inactive," holding irregular credentials, or challenging Masonic doctrine. Finally, a major concern of both groups was the recruitment of able young men with "active intellects." AMEZ ministerial candidates were particularly scrutinized for their "clean" habits and Christian learning, while "good citizenship" and adequate employment were important criteria for becoming a Prince Hall Mason.[18]

Yet these organizations had fundamental differences. The AMEZ Conference was the ruling body of a denomination of Christian men and women who believed in the literal Gospel and worshiped according to the practices of Methodism. The Grand Lodge, in contrast, was the governing body of a secret group of men whose beliefs stemmed from a variety of seventeenth-century, medieval, and ancient sources, and regularly passed their members through three successive ceremonies of initiation. Hymn singing and sermons pervaded the Zion conference activities. Invocations of the Supreme Architect, secret rituals, and flamboyant public processions distinguished the Grand Lodge gatherings. The lodges themselves were named Hiram, Pythagoras, Widow's Son, Morning Star, Rising Sun, and even J. W. Hood to recognize important men and moments in Masonic lore. Unlike the Christian churches, whose members met to worship every Sunday, the lodges enacted their rituals twice a month, on weekday nights.[19] In moving from Sunday-morning church services to weekday-evening lodge meetings, Bishop Hood and other leading Masonic ministers climbed down from their pulpits, left their sanctuaries, took off their ecclesial robes, put on cloth aprons that often displayed the "All-Seeing Eye," donned embroidered collars and jeweled pendants signifying their office, entered lodge rooms decorated to resemble King Solomon's Temple, and assumed positions in a rectangle of elders. Given the significant differences of belief and ritual that separated the AMEZ Church from the Prince Hall lodges, how did Bishop Hood and his followers come to live in these intermingled worlds? To try to answer this question, we first need to consider the origins of these organizations and how each adapted to the needs and desires of African Americans.

ORIGINS

Both the Prince Hall lodges and the AMEZ Church emerged from the distinctive social milieu of free urban African Americans following the revolution. The earliest African American social institutions resulted from a mixture of black initiative and white discrimination. In Philadelphia, for example, Absalom Jones and Richard Allen created the Free African Society in 1787 as a mutual aid organization and a nondenominational religious association. Several years later, in perhaps the most famous event in African American religious history, Jones and others were forcibly removed from their prayer benches in Saint George's Methodist Church. Soon thereafter, Jones created the African Episcopal Church and Allen the African Methodist Episcopal Church. This incident of discrimination once led historians to emphasize racism as the reason for the founding of black churches. Albert J. Raboteau has countered this by pointing to the earlier desire on the part of Jones and Allen to create a separate religious association as equally important.[20]

The close relationship between mutual benefit societies and the black church as both resources for black autonomy and barricades against white racism continued throughout the nineteenth century. African mutual aid societies assisted the needy, especially widows and their children, in return for modest dues. They also provided social networks for a community in flux by offering information on jobs, mobilizing public opinion, and cultivating social bonds. Many of Philadelphia's societies were associated with black churches, and many of their names indicate the continuing identity of blacks with their African heritage—the Daughters of Ethiopia, the Daughters of Samaria, the Angola Society, the Sons of Africa, and the African Lodge of the Prince Hall Masons.[21] By the second quarter of the nineteenth century, Christian names for these associations predominated.[22] Out of the post-1820s Baltimore Mutual Aid Society, for example, grew at least three national societies: the Good Samaritans, the Nazarites, and the Galilean Fishermen.[23] By 1848, Philadelphia alone had more than one hundred mutual benefit societies with a combined membership of more than eight thousand, while in the South, similar groups, such as the Burying Ground Society of the Free People of Color of the City of Richmond (est. 1815), had appeared.[24] Many of the later societies, such as the New York Benevolent Branch of Bethel (est. 1843), grew out of churches.[25] Yet the example of the African mutual benefit society preceding the Christian church underscores the interweaving of African and Christian, secular and sacred, within and between these two primordial social institutions of African American culture.[26] These joint influences were again on display in 1797 when Jones and Allen established Philadelphia's African Lodge of Prince Hall Masons.

Freemasonry among African Americans began in Boston before spreading to Philadelphia. In 1785, Prince Hall and fourteen other black Bostonians were inducted into a British military lodge. Though their Masonic credentials were legitimate, the Grand Lodge of Massachusetts denied them admission, after which they applied to the Grand Lodge of

England, which recognized them as valid. In the early nineteenth century, a growing number of black lodges created the African, or Prince Hall, Grand Lodge and, like their white counterparts had done after the Revolution, declared independence from the Grand Lodge of England.[27] From these beginnings, the Prince Hall lodges developed and, from the outset, reinforced their claims to authenticity in the eyes of European Americans by largely following the beliefs and practices of European American lodges while asserting the African origins of the fraternity.

Like the European Americans who joined this English society and adapted it to their circumstances, African Americans found in the American Masonic fraternity a useful array of forms and ideals for adaptation to their social environment. Like other African American mutual benefit societies, Prince Hall Masonry offered its members economic aid and social connections. Unlike most other societies, it drew its members from the most "respectable" black families. The men who joined Philadelphia's First African Lodge, for example, were among the city's most affluent and long-standing black residents, even if their occupations did not rise to bourgeois status in their white neighbors' eyes.[28] Moreover, as the black equivalent of a prestigious white society, Prince Hall Masonry gained public recognition for its leaders and provided them with a stage for addressing the larger society. Like the many African American religious leaders who used the Declaration of Independence's trumpeting of equality to challenge racial inequality, Hall and his followers employed the fraternity's ideals of unity and brotherhood across racial and national lines to confront racism.[29] "Live and act as Masons," Hall charged his brothers, "give the right hand of affection and fellowship to whom it justly belongs; let their colour and complexion be what it will, let their nation be what it may, for they are your brethren and it is your indispensable duty so to do."[30]

At the same time, Hall, the Methodist minister John Marrant, the statesman Martin Delaney, and other early Masonic leaders claimed an African history for the order that provided a powerful moral vision for the emerging African American community. While historians hold that the first Masons emerged from medieval stonemason guilds, Masons, both white and black, trace the mythic origins of the fraternity to King Solomon, who they believe synthesized all previous wisdom into physical science and manifested it through the building of the Temple in Jerusalem. Black Masons, however, claim that the deeper truths that Solomon presented originated in a preceding African civilization. It was "the Africans," Delaney said, "who were the authors of this mysterious and beautiful Order."[31] By this interpretation, black Masons were able to claim the legacy of Masonic history as their own and contend that it was a heritage not of slavery but rather synonymous with freedom, liberty, and democratic government.

The published writings of Allen, Jones, Hall, Marrant, and other church and fraternal leaders contributed to the creation of a black print culture that responded to the black experience of slavery by reclaiming their collective identity. Speaking out against the white economic and political control of the public sphere, where African Americans were treated as no more than property, these early black leaders claimed for African Americans the right to determine their collective destiny and participate fully in American society. Emerging first among literate African American church and fraternal members in Philadelphia and Boston, this black counterpublic worked to create a social and intellectual space for black social criticism and debate apart from white supervision. The establishment of separate and protected institutions that resisted white appropriation and allowed for black self-governance aided progress in this effort.[32] In this context the secrecy of Prince Hall Freemasonry provided a buffer against white domination. Moreover, as we have seen, a counternarrative emerged in this early black brotherhood that allowed African Americans to claim a primordial place in the unfolding of civilization.[33]

The published speeches of the earliest Prince Hall leaders wove a familiar biblical and Masonic history while placing a new emphasis on the African peoples of ancient Egypt as the originators of true wisdom. In 1789, Marrant delivered the first of these addresses, to the African lodge of Boston. In his sermon for that year's festival of Saint John the Baptist, he revealed Egypt to be an Eden-like "paradise" and the Bible's African patriarchs Cain and Nimrod as the original Masons, to whom God had given knowledge of the craft. Marrant is best known for his 1770 conversion to Christianity by the evangelist George Whitefield in Charleston, South Carolina. When the American Revolution broke out, the British evacuated him to London, where he was ordained a Methodist minister. His Methodist supporters then sent Marrant to minister to the community of black Loyalists whom the British had moved to Nova Scotia. At this time he also ministered in Boston, where he became a chaplain of the first African Masonic lodge in America. In his 1789 Saint John's Day sermon, Marrant employed Bible passages from Samuel and Daniel and their interpretation by Josephus and "most of the [church] fathers" to conclude that "paradise did as it were border on

Egypt." He then said that in this Eden-like Egypt, following the fall of Adam, the "allwise God" put "into the hearts" of "Cain and his sons" the secrets of Freemasonry. Arguing against the dominant Masonic and Protestant narratives, Marrant located Masonic origins before the building of Solomon's Temple, in an Egypt where God, rather than marking Cain and Nimrod for their sinful actions, chose them to be the first human repositories of Masonic truth.[34]

A common desire to provide black people with an emancipatory history motivated Marrant and the many subsequent African American writers who creatively interpreted the past. By the 1780s, the new genre of race histories had emerged among African Americans intent on providing a moral and spiritual purpose to the history and future of their race. African American historians hoped to counter white racial images by reimagining the story of their community to provide both indictments of contemporary racial practices and self-fulfilling prophecies of racial unity. Following the revolution, these narratives were most publicly presented before mixed and African American audiences at freedom celebrations that highlighted African American contributions to the war, commemorated the end of the slave trade in 1808, and prescribed a more hopeful future. In the early nineteenth century, journalists, artists, statesmen, and others joined black ministers and Masons in a common effort to create a usable past from their collective memory and an expanding array of biblical, Masonic, classical, scientific, patriotic, and historical materials. Through public speeches, political commentaries, histories, short stories, and related publications, all of which an emerging black press carried to an expanding black population by the 1820s, authors combated racism with narratives that provided dignity, meaning, and purpose to the lives of African Americans. These publications were disseminated in the black community's gathering places of church, school, neighborhood, and home; among the growing numbers of mutual aid, fraternal, and related associations; and ultimately throughout the greater Atlantic world and north to Canada in diasporic exchanges among churches, lodges, and business contacts.[35]

The Prince Hall lodges contributed both ideologically and socially to the formation of the nineteenth-century black counterpublic. The addresses of the early Prince Hall leaders provided a counternarrative to European American history by placing the story of African American suffering at its center.[36] Public processions by lodge members into the centers of urban life, on the June feast day of Saint John the Baptist, in December to honor Saint John the Evangelist, and to observe members' funerals, similarly brought attention to the African American presence in civil society while challenging white control of public spaces. As social spaces, the lodges provided an arena for black self-governance apart from and against the dominant white public sphere.[37] Moreover, in these secret and protected private refuges, black men formed enduring bonds and new ideological tools in their common effort to influence white society. These contributions of Prince Hall men helped African Americans to claim a public social space from which to engage the civil machinery of European American society.

JAMES WALKER HOOD

Though we do not know for certain when and where James Walker Hood entered into the "mysteries of Masonry," the evidence suggests that it was in 1855, when, as a young man of twenty-four, he first traveled from rural Pennsylvania to New York City and found work as a waiter. In the mid-nineteenth century, New York, Boston, and Philadelphia were the principal centers of the fewer than thirty Prince Hall lodges then in existence. "Soon after I became of lawful age," the North Carolina Grand Lodge proceedings record Hood as stating, "I petitioned a regular Lodge, in due form, and my prayer was granted."[38] Around the same time that the future grand master became a Mason, he also entered the ministry of the black church.

Hood was born in 1831 into a religious family in rural southeastern Pennsylvania. His father, Levi, was a minister in the African Union Church, the very first black denomination, and his mother, Harriet, was a member of Richard Allen's Bethel AME Church. In 1855, during the young Hood's sojourn in New York City, he joined a small congregation of the African Union Church. In 1856, Reverend Williams Councy, the pastor of the congregation, granted Hood a preaching license. In the autumn of 1857, Hood relocated once again, to New Haven, Connecticut. This time he was unable to locate a branch of the African Union Church, so he joined a quarterly conference of the Zion connection, which accepted his license to preach. In June of 1859, the following conference year, the New Haven Quarterly Conference recommended that the New England Annual Conference accept the young minister on a trial basis. The annual conference consented to this request and appointed Hood to two stations in Nova Scotia. After two years there, he assumed the pastorate of a congregation in Bridgeport, Connecticut. Then, in 1863, members of the New Haven conference, many of whom were from New Berne, North Carolina, called on their bishop to send someone down to serve the newly emancipated people around New Berne in areas that Union forces had captured. Thus is was that in 1864, Reverend Hood set out on his mission to the South.[39]

Like many black denominational leaders, Bishop Hood believed that the black church had a providential role to play in society. His 1895 history of the AMEZ Church places this denomination's story in the larger epic of the African exodus from white churches following the revolution. The AMEZ denomination dates from 1796, when a group of black members protesting discrimination in the Methodist John Street Church in New York City organized it. They built their first church, Zion, in 1800, and from there emerged an African American denomination that continued to follow the Methodist form of administration. Hood saw the emergence of the African American church as both a reaction to white discrimination and an act of black self-determination. While decrying the efforts of white Methodists in the John Street Church to "maintain the inferiority of the Negro," he also believed that a "divine purpose" guided the late eighteenth- and early nineteenth-century movement of "colored members of all denominations" into "the Negro Church." As he put it, "In the unfolding of that Providence which underlaid the human meanness which produced the general exodus of the Afro-American race from the white Church, there have come and still are coming to the proscribed race benefits so rich, abundant, and glorious that the sufferings incident are not worthy of mention." Without the black church, Hood proclaimed, black people "would have had no opportunity for the development of [their] faculties, nor would [they] have had any platform on which to exhibit [their] vast possibilities."[40]

Though the founders of the AMEZ denomination had, according to Hood, "no fault to find with the doctrine or form of government" of Methodism, he and other nineteenth-century "race historians" adapted the history of the Christian church to serve the needs and desires of African Americans.[41] Using the genealogical tables of the Bible, the Zion minister identified Ham as the ancestor of blacks and traced the origins of major ancient civilizations such as Egypt, Ethiopia, and Babylon to peoples of Hamitic ancestry. Indeed, the Zionite insisted that the African race stood at the front ranks of the earliest civilizations of the world.[42] Like the Prince Hall reworking of Masonic history, this understanding of the Bible provided a positive vision for the emerging black community.

When Hood left Connecticut for North Carolina, he went as an emissary of perhaps the two most prominent, and deeply interwoven, social institutions of the Northern African American community: the Prince Hall Masons and the black church. Each had emerged following the Revolution and provided America's emerging black society with resources for its development and a defense against white racism. Both Hood's Masonic fraternity and his AMEZ denomination continued to observe the doctrines and practices of their white counterparts yet adapted their respective histories to remove the stigma of slavery and endow the past and the future with a significant spiritual and moral purpose. Bishop Hood was among the many Northern missionaries who saw God acting through the black church to uplift the black race. Grand Master Hood, in turn, saw the Masonic fraternity as an opportunity to embrace the dignity and humanity of a universal brotherhood. In the last decades of the nineteenth century, both societies became Southern institutions. As the senior bishop of the AMEZ Church, Hood presided over the growth of his denomination from 4,600 members in 1860 to 700,000 by 1916. At the same time, Grand Master Hood contributed to the Southern expansion of the Prince Hall Masons. By the turn of the century, there were more than 117,000 nationally, nearly two-thirds of whom were concentrated in the South.[43] Despite the common commitment of these prominent social institutions to the uplift of black Southerners, they had substantial differences. What was the relationship between the theology of the black church and the beliefs of Prince Hall Masons? And what were the practice and the purpose of Prince Hall Masonic rituals? Here again, Hood's story provides insight.

BELIEFS AND RITUALS

Bishop Hood's theology reflected the thinking of an era prior to the rise of science and the professionalization of history, when biblical paradigms and sacred histories pervaded the religious world view. By the 1880s, the scientific and intellectual currents that gave rise to Protestant liberalism were filtering into black religious communities through such journals as the *AME Church Review*, though apologies for Protestant orthodoxy were the most frequent response to these new ideas.[44] Hood was one of many contemporary black denominational leaders who defended the literal understanding of the Bible and stood against all changes in Christian doctrine. In the post–Civil War period, the Zion leader opposed Darwinian scientific theories, historical and critical study of Scripture, and the idea that salvation was possible outside

Christianity.[45] Although, by the turn of the century, African American intellectuals were praising the progressive New Negro, who had little use for sacred stories or biblical world views, Bishop Hood and his fellow race historians continued to solace African Americans with representations of their race that countered disparaging white narratives.[46]

Like many of these accounts, Bishop Hood's sacred history parts company with European American narratives by asserting "the ancient greatness of the Negro race." The Zion leader accused "modern historians of the Caucasian race" of trying to "rob" the Negro of a "history to which he can point with pride." Against this treachery, he proclaimed that "the Holy Bible has stood as an everlasting rock in the black man's defense." Employing the Bible and the work of selected white historians to buttress his case, the Zion leader argued that "Ethiopia and Egypt were the first among the early monarchies and these countries were peopled by the descendants of Ham, through Cush and Mizraim, and were governed by the same for hundreds of years." More than simply identifying African people in a white narrative, Hood's history celebrated the contributions of particular African cities and heroes to ancient culture: "Caucasian civilization can point to nothing that exceeds" the "gallantry" and "generosity" of the black city of Carthage or the "persons of St. Augustine and St. Cyprian. . . two of the ablest ministers of which the Christian Church can boast."[47] In this way, the Zion bishop refuted white beliefs that Africans were an inferior race.

Although Bishop Hood argued that white people had misrepresented the past by portraying Africans as a degraded race, he did not advise abandoning Christianity because of its contamination by this prejudice. Rather, he outlined what he saw as God's true plan. While realizing the original greatness of the race of Ham, Hood also recognized that Ham's son Nimrod "forsook God and took the world for his portion." In retaliation, God "confounded" the language of Ham's people at Babel and "scattered them abroad from thence upon the face of all the earth." Hood's narrative then moves to America, ignores the era of slavery, and asserts the special destiny of the black church. Though God punished the sons of Ham for their idolatry, he also gave them a "promise," Hood told his followers, that they "shall cast aside idolatry and return unto the Lord." The African American church was leading the way in this redemption. "That this promise is now in the course of fulfillment," Hood proclaimed, "the Negro Church stands forth as unquestionable evidence." The black church, in sum, was "the morning star which precedes the rising sun," leading all Christians toward the "millennial glory."[48]

Bishop Hood's race history must not be read as the product of an uneducated man. Though he was largely self-taught, his writings reflect a lifetime of intelligent reading. Consistent with his faith in its literal truth, the Zion bishop interpreted Scripture in a manner that encouraged his people. This was also a response to the inroads that the new intellectual currents of scientific and biblical criticism were making into religious authority, the black orthodox response to which was rooted in racial and religious concerns. The reality that most scholars gave black history insufficient attention additionally burdened black religious leaders and other learned African Americans like Hood. Some feared that the Darwinian theory and biblical criticism employed in the liberal assault on Scripture and traditional Christianity would be used to deny the humanity and rights of the black race.[49] In the face of these difficulties, Hood and his fellow denominational leaders turned to the Bible, where they found a more complete and compassionate presentation of the history and humanity of black people. Beyond the Bible, the bishop especially relied on the race histories of his fellow black churchmen to support his beliefs. He endorsed the most famous of these, the Baptist Rufus L. Perry's *The Cushites, or The Descendants of Ham*, as essential reading, a work of "profound learning" "respecting the ancient greatness of the descendants of Ham, the ancestors of the American Negro."[50]

The sacred history of the Prince Hall Masons provided further support for the Bible-inspired "truth" of the African American past. Although Grand Master Hood left no Masonic race history of his own, orations on the lore of the lodge likely acquainted him with the history that Martin Delaney wrote. This asserts that Africans created the institution of Masonry, which was "handed down only through the priesthood" in the earliest period of the Egyptian and Ethiopian dynasties, "anterior to the Bible record." These early Egyptians, Delaney continued, adduced and believed in a trinity of the Godhead, which later became "the Christian doctrine of three persons in one—Father, Son, and Holy Ghost." Moses, "the recorder of the Bible," Delaney states, "learned all of his wisdom and ability from Egypt." "Africans," therefore, "were the authors of this mysterious and beautiful Order" and "did much to bring it to perfection" prior to the writing of the Bible.[51]

Though Bishop Hood never addressed the question of Masonry's African origins in his public writings, he did import elements of the Masonic tradition into his Christian race history. Certain turns of phrase, such as the above "morning star" and "rising sun," also held such symbolic significance in Masonic beliefs that the grand master used them as names for his first North Carolina lodges. The bishop's essay "God's Purpose in the Negro Church as Seen in the History of the Movement," moreover, refers to the "ancient and honorable" Prince Hall fraternity's maintenance of its "rites and benefits" as part of the larger effort of black people to respond to "Jehovah's plan for the Negro's development."[52] Aside from these and other occasional mentions of the Masonic fraternity, its catchwords, and its ideas, the Zion leader's public writings remain silent on the relationship between his Christian and Masonic beliefs.

In the protected space of the lodge, however, Hood provided more insight. In his 1880 annual address to the North Carolina Grand Lodge, the "most worshipful" grand master instructed the gathered brethren on the relationship between the beliefs and ceremonies of Masonry and what he considered a faith.

> Most Masonic writers admit that Masonry does not claim to be a religion. I admit that it is not a religious sect, yet I am fully persuaded that it is the offspring of the only genuine religion known to man in the early history of the world. This I gather from tradition. . . . For hundreds of years tradition was the only channel through which the knowledge of events was handed down from generation to generation. . . . Oral instruction was the universal mode in ancient times. Masonry is the only Order that retains and adheres strictly to the ancient mode.[53]

Masonry, then, is heir to an oral transmission of knowledge that originated at the beginning of the world. It was not a religion but the "offspring of the only genuine religion" available to the first people. Since nowhere in either his Christian or his Masonic writings does Hood speak of a conflict between Christianity and Masonry, he appears to have believed that the orally transmitted, ancient knowledge passed through Masonry both predated and complemented Christian teachings. As the content of this knowledge constitutes what is most secret in Masonry, Hood did not divulge it. Yet he did explain the process of its transmission.

According to the inherited rituals and legends of Masonry, Grand Master Hood proceeded, the Masonic lodge represents King Solomon's Temple.

> There are many symbols which identify the Freemason's Lodge with the city and Temple at Jerusalem. (1)—The city was built on the high hills of Zoria and Moria, and near the Valley of Jehosaphat. Our lodge is symbolically situated upon the highest hills and lowest valleys. (2)—The Temple was built due east and west. So is our Lodge. (3)—The Temple was an oblong square, and its

ground was holy. Such is the form and ground of our Lodge. . . . Like the Temple, our Lodge is founded on the mercies of Jehovah: consecrated in His name, dedicated to His honor; and from the foundation to the cap-stone it proclaims "Glory to God in the highest, peace on earth and good will to man."[54]

The lodge's replication of the Temple in Jerusalem, therefore, symbolically represented Masonic wisdom. Participation in the rituals of initiation instilled an understanding of these symbols, which in turn gave access to this knowledge.

Though Hood did not believe that Masonry was either a religion or opposed to Christianity, he did think that "Masonic symbolism, from beginning to end, was capable of instructing us in the truths of evangelical religion." For example, as he explained it, when the "candidate was initiated into the ancient mysteries," he was "invested with a white apron in token of his newly attained purity." The grand master interpreted this article of lambskin through biblical references. "From the Book Divine we learn that it was the most ancient piece of apparel ever worn. It was worn by Adam and Eve before they were turned out of the Garden. . . . The apron, or girdle, was universally received as an emblem of truth among the ancients. Paul so styles it. 'Having your loins girded with truth.' . . . He, therefore, who wears the white apron as a badge of a Mason, is continually reminded of that innocence and purity which ought to be the distinguishing characteristic of every Mason." "The peculiar circumstances in which he receives it" dictates how each brother comes to understand the apron's symbolic meaning, according to Hood. Here he appears to be saying that the Christian idea of innocence and purity is most deeply apprehended through the Masonic ritual of initiation. However, the apron is a sign not of the initiate's entrance into the Christian community but rather of "his relationship to the fraternity."[55] Whether Masonic rituals deepened the candidate's understanding of Christian truths, as Hood stated, or of Masonic fellowship, as his remarks might be interpreted to mean, they clearly set the brotherhood apart from the practices of Christian congregations.

As we have seen, all American Masonic lodges, white and black, had three basic initiatory rituals, through which the candidate learned that the Mason must be obedient to God but whose major thrust was to teach the Masonic tenets. As the Methodist minister and Prince Hall deputy grand master William Spencer Carpenter explained in a Masonic sermon, "The traveling as a Master Mason is symbolic of the journey through life to that Celestial Lodge eternal in the Heavens, where God is the Worshipful Master, Jesus Christ is the Senior Warden, and where the Holy Ghost is the Junior Warden, whose duty it is to . . . call the craft [the assembled Masons] from labor to refreshment and from refreshment to labor again at the will and pleasure of the Master."[56] Like Grand Master Hood's explanation of the Mason's apron, Carpenter's sermon is not entirely clear on whether Christianity or Masonry has the upper hand.

In addition to these private rituals, Prince Hall Masons, like their white counterparts, conducted public parades that proclaimed the identity and dignity of the order. As elsewhere, these processions were the highlight of the North Carolina Grand Lodge's annual meetings. Preceded by a brass band, the members of the fraternity, dressed in their regalia, marched through the town's "principal" streets, usually to a Zion Methodist church. There a minister offered prayers, a Masonic anthem was sung, the grand master addressed "the Craft," the band played some music, all sang a Masonic ode, and a minister offered a benediction. After these "usual ceremonies," the "procession again was formed" and returned to the lodge.[57] Prince Hall parades had their origins in the practices of European American Masons yet had particular meaning in the African American community. As a form of public theater, complete with ornamented clothing and polished gestures, this performance of fraternal life enacted racial dignity and pride while challenging white control of public space. Louis Armstrong captured the heart of this positive function when he remembered watching his father march by as the grand marshal of the New Orleans Odd Fellows parade: "I was very proud to see him in his uniform and his high hat with the beautiful streamer hanging down. . . . Yes, he was a fine figure of a man, my dad. Or at least that is the way he seemed to me as a kid when he strutted by like a peacock at the head of the Odd Fellows parade."[58] Wearing an apron or a sash and making a "show in a procession" was admittedly one of the attractions of fraternal orders, but as Virginia's grand master Harrison Harris remarked, "We do not want a Masonry that makes a man anxious to shine in a procession" but rather a "Masonry that goes into the family and makes a man a better husband, a kinder father, a more devoted patriot and . . . a more liberal and devoted Christian."[59] It was this understanding of Masonry that attracted Hood.

COMPLEMENT AND CONFLICT

We cannot say for certain what the significance of Masonic beliefs and rituals was for Bishop Hood. We do know that he spent considerable time attending to the fraternity's affairs and presiding over its ritual life throughout his career. Following thirteen years as grand master, he continued to serve in such capacities as grand orator and supervisor of Masonic jurisprudence, guiding the brotherhood's beliefs and practices. Late in life, when he was too feeble to attend the annual Grand Lodge meetings, the past grand master Hood wrote letters to the assembled brethren that appeared prominently in their printed proceedings. Yet despite his annual unanimous reelection, Hood chose to step down from the position of grand master because of his more pressing "ecclesial labors."[60] In fact, any time, effort, or output comparison of Hood's work for the church and for the lodge would show that the former was more important.

It is also clear that Bishop Hood appropriated beliefs from Masonry that complemented his missionary efforts. Given his Christian conservatism, it is unlikely that the liberal Masonic ideals of interreligious brotherhood or scientific progress would have attracted the Zion leader. In addition to his biblical literalism, Hood remained opposed to non-Christian paths to salvation. He viewed Islam, for example, as a "corrupting influence" operating "against the Christian Church."[61] Instead, his Masonic teachings emphasized universal values such as "purity of heart" and "rectitude of conduct." The Mason was an honest, upright man, a good citizen and responsible member of the community. Moreover, as another Mason put it, the fraternity, "having fewer doctrines, can reach some that Christianity cannot reach, and not until Christianity shall cover the earth . . . will the demand for Masonry cease."[62] The best lodges, Hood believed, are those in which "all its members are professors of Christianity, and are men whose lives accord with their profession."[63] Further revealing Hood's evangelical Christian ideals, his Grand Lodge forbade alcohol, tobacco, and any illegal behavior. The Zion leader also spoke to his brothers of the need to "soften our hearts" by loving Jesus. At 1885 and subsequent North Carolina Grand Lodge gatherings, Hood's Masonic hymn "The Feast of Belshazzar" was sung—and ended with the following chorus:

See our deeds are all recorded,
There is a Hand that's writing now:
Sinners give your hearts to Jesus—
At His royal mandate bow;
For the day is fast approaching—
It must come to one and all,—
When the sinner's condemnation,
Shall be written upon the wall.[64]

In this way, Grand Master Hood emphasized the Christian teachings in Masonic beliefs. Moreover, though he did not share in the Masonic embrace of non-Christian religions, the Prince Hall leader did see the lodge as a vehicle for building Christian unity across black denominational lines. "It was my purpose," he reflected near the end of his life, "to invite the best men in all the Churches in this State into the Masonic Fraternity. In this our success has been all that could have been expected. Every denomination having a considerable membership has been represented in this Grand Lodge. Nearly all have been represented in the office of Grand Officers."[65] His appropriation of Masonic beliefs complemented his Christian efforts to uplift and unite his people.

An emphasis on discipline and respectability was central to both Masonry and Christianity. As we have seen, Hood and his fellow Northern missionaries who established most Southern black churches brought a formal organization, governed by published rules that stipulated adherence to standards of moral conduct and outlined punishments for those who transgressed. Duty bound to teach the values of religion, education, and hard work, these "respectable" people equated restrained public behavior with individual self-respect and the advancement of the race. Prince Hall emissaries, again often the same people, imposed a similar organizational structure and had similar behavioral expectations. Admissions committees looked for intelligent, clean-living, sober, and industrious young men, preferably married and able to provide for their households. In both organizations, expectations of respectable deportment and threats of expulsion conditioned behavior that encouraged racial "uplift."[66] But in these efforts, fraternal members claimed, "Masonry does not aspire to the office of Christianity. It provides no atonement, and consequently cannot save the soul; but it seeks to elevate man, to beautify and adorn his character with domestic virtues. It teaches him the lessons of sobriety, and industry, and integrity. But Christianity teaches him to prepare for a higher life, a future state, and a brighter world."[67]

Prince Hall lodges and Christian churches were central to the Southern institution building that freedom demanded. Following emancipation, African Americans quickly adapted the voluntary associational conventions of American life to suit their specific needs. Both Hood's Masonic fraternity and his AMEZ denomination continued to follow the doctrines and practices of their white counterparts yet shaped their respective histories to remove the stigma of slavery and endow the past and the future with a meaningful spiritual and moral purpose. Moreover, as part of an institution that a Northern AMEZ missionary carried to the South, Hood's North Carolina lodges shared with his churches a desire to bring discipline and respectability to the newly freed slaves. Broadly interdenominational in membership, the North Carolina lodges supported the major churches in this common effort to "purify" the beliefs and "uplift" the practices of blacks in the post-Reconstruction South. Though there is little evidence of regional consciousness in Hood's behavior or writings or of tensions between the North Carolina lodges and their Northern elders, further studies of Southern fraternalism may reveal regional distinctiveness and perhaps, as with the churches, disputes over resources and relative power in institutional structures that straddled the regions. Further, studies of other black Southern Masonic leaders may suggest a greater willingness on their part to follow liberal Masonic traditions, though not at the expense of the church, given the critical role it played in the post-1865 black world.

Certainly this marriage of church and lodge was not without conflicts. By the 1890s, leaders of the new Holiness movement, which emerged in the Mississippi Delta, were speaking out against the black church's involvement with fraternal orders.[68] Responding to the social estrangement that some African Americans experienced, Holiness leaders attacked "worldly" Baptists and Methodists for their fashionable standards of consumption and their allegiance to fraternal orders, calling them back to the simplicity of the early Christian church. Charles Price Jones encouraged the followers of his new Church of Christ, for example, to mark their spiritual birth as sanctified Christians by "pitching their secret order pins . . . out the church windows."[69] Though Hood participated in the Holiness movement, he did not address its attack on fraternal orders in print but, as we have seen, his Prince Hall lodges followed stringent rules of ethical conduct. At the same time, the Zion bishop resisted a growing worldliness in black Methodism by retaining earlier emphases on a holy ministry, morally pure and free of scandal. As participants in the Holiness movement, Hood and his contemporaries insisted that freedom from sin was attainable in this life, that every Christian should strive for this sanctification, and that their candidates for ministry must adhere to this teaching.[70] Though the rapid growth of the Holiness movement likely decreased Prince Hall membership elsewhere, Hood's emphasis on high ethical conduct and striving for sanctification may have worked against both lodge and church defections in North Carolina.

In addition to these attacks from outside the church-lodge nexus, there is also scattered evidence of tensions in the black church between fraternal members and church leaders. In the *Indianapolis Freeman* in 1891, a Baptist minister complained that fraternal "members took more interest in their societies than their church."[71] The Methodist H. T. Keating echoed in the *Christian Recorder* that "in order to be regular in their attendance upon lodge meetings," fraternal members "neglect their duties" to the church. These complaints were often couched in conciliatory language that recognized the power of the orders in the church. "It will be observed that we do not enter into a discussion of whether secret societies are right and good in principle," Keating continued, "but simply protest against the neglect of the church in the slightest degree for these societies. Assuming both church and society right, which is most right and worthy of support?"[72] In response, the Mason and AME minister S. H. Coleman, writing in the *AME Church Review*, defended the lodge as "not a substitute for the church but an handmaid of religion." The teachings of the order, he claimed, supplement rather than replace the truths of the Bible by showing "us our social and political duties."[73] Other Prince Hall members pointedly rebuked the church for its criticisms. Professor G. L. Knox specifically warned that "did it so desire, [the lodge] could destroy the power of the pulpit." He then added, "But such is not its mission. . . . Instead of being in antagonism with the church, it is content to draw its inspiration from God's holy house, and as an humble handmaiden, to do its Master's work, as it shall see it and understand it."[74] Though this evidence suggests some power struggles in the black church between lodge members and church leaders, they hardly compare with the successful evangelical Anti-Masonic campaign of the 1820s or the radical evangelical white churches' excommunication threats against members who dared join fraternal orders in the late nineteenth century.[75] While white Masons were less likely than black Masons to be church members, the black fraternal orders and the black church were deeply interwoven social institutions.

Gender tensions between black lodge members and women were another potential area of conflict, but here again, compared to white Masonry, there is less evidence of strife. Not only did the rituals of the Prince Hall Masons set them apart from the African American church, but their organization's exclusive male membership separated them from black women. In his study of the late nineteenth-century black Odd Fellow Amos Webber, Nick Salvatore remarks on Webber's relationship with his wife: "It was not that Amos thought Lizzie unimportant or that, after thirty years of marriage, he did not care for her. Rather his formal distancing from her suggested the overwhelming maleness of the world he inhabited."[76] Under the "powerful influence" of nineteenth-century gender roles, black fraternal members inhabited a distinctly male sphere. Fraternal rituals, unlike those of the Protestant churches, celebrated a man's bonds with his brothers while neglecting the event of his marriage. Even in the predominantly female churches, these distinctions continued, with men controlling the visible, public positions of authority and women providing for the social activities of Sunday school, prayer meetings, missionary work, social events, and care for the needy.[77] Yet underlying both the lodge and the church was a tangled thicket of male-female relations—including kinship ties between sisters and brothers, wives and husbands—that formed a common social framework for community activities. In the church, accepting male religious leadership did not prevent women from creating their own influential networks, while in the lodge, women's auxiliaries participated in social activities and found meaning in the order's larger purposes.[78]

Hood was instrumental in including women in both lodge and church activities. Shortly after founding the North Carolina Grand Lodge, he encouraged the establishment of a black version of the white ladies' auxiliary—the Order of the Eastern Star—which became involved in the maintenance and support of the order.[79] He also supported the full ministerial rights of women in the AMEZ denomination. He acted on this conviction first by ordaining Mrs. Julia A. J. Foote as a deacon at the New York Annual Conference in 1894 and then, in the ultimately successful struggle for women's ordination that engulfed the denomination at the turn of the century, leading those who supported full equality for women in all aspects of church life.[80] All of this is not to deny the gender tensions in an African American community where the male was dominant.[81] Doubtless there were conflicts as well between some black women and Prince Hall Masons. Yet in contrast, white Masons frequently were not members of their wives' churches, and most discouraged the creation of ladies' auxiliaries. There was substantially more interaction between the world of Prince Hall men and the activities of black women than between the male lodge and the female church of middle-class white Protestants.

. . .

James Walker Hood believed that his labors for Prince Hall Masonry complemented his work for the AMEZ denomination: Both provided encouragement and hope to black Southerners facing debilitating circumstances. In Bishop Hood's view, the church was more than a means of spiritual renewal—it was a providential movement to uplift the black race. Acting as part of this movement of God, the Zion leader appropriated beliefs and practices from Masonry that aided his missionary efforts. Membership in the Prince Hall lodges gave responsible and industrious men public recognition, moral authority, and an alternative history with which to buffer and respond to potentially disabling images of black people. Denied all but the most menial jobs and pushed to the margins of white society, black Masons found that the fraternity recognized each man's dignity and nurtured his growth by providing outlets for leadership and avenues for gaining status. At the same time, rituals of initiation secured a lasting, meaningful bond with other men, while the fraternity's eclectic ideology included a framework for a moral commitment that broadly drew on the spiritual values of the Judeo-Christian tradition. As responses to the indignities and racial violence that formed the fabric of African Americans' everyday life, the fraternity and the church helped to create a black counterpublic that challenged the racism of the white public sphere. Though largely unknown to white Americans, the Prince Hall lodges flourished alongside the black church after the Civil War, supplying African Americans with additional symbolic, ideological, and organizational resources that reinforced a collective sense of identity and pride.

CHAPTER 7

Freemasonry and Native Americans, 1776–1920

The story of Freemasonry and Native Americans begins in 1776, when the Mohawk leader Joseph Brant joined an English Masonic lodge.[1] As an Indian leader and Loyalist ally, Brant traveled several times to England, where he discussed the role of the Iroquois in the Revolutionary War. While in London, he was entertained by the Prince of Wales, had his portrait painted, and joined a Masonic lodge. In his lifetime, the Mohawk chief learned English, gained a Western education, joined the Anglican Church, and translated the Bible into his native language. At the same time, he was a member of the Iroquois Grand Council and a leader of the Indians who fought alongside the British against the Revolution. Following the war, the British provided him with a pension and a land grant along the Grand River in Upper Canada, where he settled in a Mohawk village and joined the local lodge.[2] Mediating between Indian and white worlds, Brant and the Native Masons who followed him worked to advance the interests of their people.

In the nineteenth century, as the American population moved westward into lands that the federal authorities had assigned to Indians, more Native Americans joined Masonic lodges. The majority of the Native American leaders in Indian Territory were Freemasons. The Cherokee leader John Ross and his Princeton-educated nephew William contributed to the 1849 founding of their tribe's first lodge. The Cherokee publisher and politician Elias Boudinot, the Cherokee Confederate general Stand Watie, and the Choctaw leader Peter Pitchlyn were all lodge notables. Farther north, the Seneca chief and Masonic lodge founder Ely S. Parker worked as an engineer, served as an adjutant to General U.S. Grant, and was appointed the first commissioner of the Bureau of Indian Affairs. In the early twentieth century, his grandnephew Arthur C. Parker directed the New York State Museum and held various positions in Freemasonry. Other well-known Indian Masons include the physician and author Charles Eastman, the Indian spokesman Carlos Montezuma, and the comedian Will Rogers.[3]

Freemasonry among Native Americans can be interpreted in the context of contact historiography. The history of Indian-white relations was once told as a story of conquest. The expansion of a growing European American population into the Indian country of North America was believed to be inevitable. In this framework, historians saw Freemasonry, when mentioned at all, much as the earlier triumphalists saw Christianity, as part of a large "civilizing" process. Since the 1970s, historians have emphasized Native American resistance to European American expansion. Newer studies have focused on Indian revitalization movements. Recently, scholars such as Rachel Wheeler "have explored the ways various Indian communities have engaged Christianity in a dialogue with native traditions as a means of preserving native identity and securing new spiritual resources with which to confront the challenges of colonialism."[4] This chapter considers the ways in which Indian leaders similarly engaged Freemasonry to both resist and adapt to European American society.

On the Atlantic frontier throughout most of the eighteenth century, Freemasonry was part of a cultural milieu peopled by Indians, Africans, and Europeans, and their various religious beliefs and practices. In their contact and interactions, Indian and white peoples attempted to grasp the ways of the other's culture and employ them for their own ends. By the early nineteenth century, the encroachment of European American settlers on Native American lands led to the end of relatively equal power relations and the removal of the southeastern Indians to the Indian Territory of present-day Oklahoma. The "civilization" program that began under George Washington and continued throughout the following five administrations held out the promise of acceptance once Indians had assimilated the values and practices of white society. Freemasonry was part of this process. At the same time, this chapter argues, Indians appropriated Masonic beliefs and practices in an effort to preserve Native identity and confront the challenges of accommodation to American society with new spiritual resources. In the late nineteenth and early twentieth centuries, while growing numbers of fraternal men were attracted to Native American wisdom in their quest for a primal American identity, modernizing Indians worked within Masonic discourse to navigate their place in American society.

FREEMASONRY IN INDIAN TERRITORY

Freemasonry became established in Indian Territory following the forced resettlement there of the Cherokee, Chickasaw, Choctaw, Creek, and Seminole Nations from their southeastern homelands. What became known as the Trail of Tears resulted from a change in Indian policy. Following the revolution, Thomas Jefferson reflected the then-prevailing view when he proclaimed that "the Indian" was "in body and mind equal to the white man."[5] By the 1830s, however, and despite Cherokee efforts to adapt to white society, this Enlightenment embrace of racial parity gave way to new "scientific" thinking that saw Indians merely as "savages" incapable of becoming civilized.[6] In 1833, Andrew Jackson told Congress that Indians "have neither the intelligence, the industry, the moral habits nor the desire for improvement." If not removed beyond the reach of European Americans, they "must necessarily yield to the force of circumstance and ere long disappear."[7]

In the nineteenth century, Cherokee leaders employed Freemasonry to resist this sentiment and assert their racial equality and political rights. Arriving in Indian Territory, the leaders of the different tribes began to band together in lodge meetings. The first lodge was built there in 1852 and led by John Ross, the principal chief of the Cherokee Nation.[8] From there, the brotherhood radiated throughout Indian Territory, creating as many as eight lodges before organizing the Grand Lodge of Indian Territory, in 1874.[9] This was a time when white settlers were forbidden on this designated Indian land. Until the late nineteenth century, each of what were known as the Five Civilized Tribes—because of their adaptations to white ways—had sovereignty over their land.[10] Control of the local government, judiciary, and educational system was in the hands of the Indians. Freemasonry in Indian Territory was also largely an Indian affair.

The Native Americans who created the first Indian Masonic lodge were attracted to elements of Masonry similar to those of the Indians' traditional world view, including commitments to brotherly love, ethical conduct, and concern for others. "During the many years of the existence of the Masonic Lodge at this place," one observer of the original

Cherokee lodge noted, "there have been quite a number of full blood Cherokee members [with] . . . more than ordinary interest in the mysteries of the Masonic order. Although there have been occasions where the services of interpreters were necessary in order that the instructions might be made clear, the full-blood initiates became proficient and worthy members of the ancient Order."[11] Also, like the first modern European lodges that emerged among a mobile elite in new urban centers, the earliest Indian Masonic lodges—scattered across the nascent settlements of the contiguous lands of the Five Civilized Tribes—provided a kinship that ideally transcended barriers of religion and politics, albeit within particular tribes. Names such as Cherokee Lodge and Choctaw Lodge suggest tribal allegiances, and indeed each was on the land of its named tribe. Cherokee Lodge at its beginning was almost entirely Cherokee. This composition changed, however, as the individual lodges moved toward the creation of the transtribal Grand Lodge of Indian Territory. Among Native American women, this movement toward transtribal identity was apparent in the names of their Eastern Star lodges, which began to appear in 1879. The first was called Ohoyoma (Red woman). The second was named Antek-homa (Red sisters).[12]

More significant than the tribal composition of the Native American lodges was their elite membership. Among the twenty-four members of Cherokee Lodge in 1850, for example, were a future chief of the nation, the editor of its newspaper, its superintendent of education, a leading cattleman, and several men who had led their people along the Trail of Tears.[13] One Indian Masonic leader said, "There were no second class men among us."[14] Indeed, the great majority of the nine hundred Indians in Indian Territory who had become Masons by 1884 were prominent tribal members.[15] Masonic membership provided them with the opportunity to shape Masonic understandings of Native Americans from a position of privilege. Annually from 1874, the *Proceedings of the Most Worshipful Grand Lodge of Indian Territory* took careful note of the many official comments from other state Grand Lodges that celebrated Indians' "warm and fraternal welcome into the Grand Masonic family."[16] At the same time, the *Proceedings* authors castigated those less frequent comments that depicted them as primitive "aborigines."[17] In like manner, the Grand Lodge of Indian Territory recognized that "owing to our anomalous political condition, Masonry cannot be expected to progress in this Territory at the same rate it does in other jurisdictions," yet "in due time . . . the Grand Lodge of the Indian Territory will take her stand in the Masonic family, first among her equals."[18]

This claim to equality extended to Indian Masons' political defense of Indian land rights. In 1878, the *Indian Journal*, published at Eufaula, Creek Nation, Indian Territory, reported on a public gathering of "Creek, Cherokee, and Choctaw" to witness the Masonic celebration of Saint John's Day. Following a procession of lodge members "to the beautiful grove where perhaps six hundred people had gathered," those present "listened to a practical and suggestive speech from Col. D. N. McIntosh on the present condition of the Territory, the dangers that threaten its perpetuity and the necessity of a united interest among the different nations to secure a just recognition of their rights and privileges under the treaties." McIntosh was the son of a Creek Indian chief, an ordained Baptist minister, a Confederate colonel in the Civil War, and, the journal said, "a great patriot who had served his people long and faithfully as well as his Masonic Lodge." The position he took in defense of Indian sovereignty, it pointed out, "may seem to the Mason of today . . . of a political nature: however, that is not the case for it was inspired by the highest sense of duty to his people and race."[19] Through Freemasonry, this Indian leader argued for his people's political rights.

Christianity provided complementary resources for Indian revitalization. As the example of the Creek Methodist Mason McIntosh suggests, ministers and Masons were interwoven into the social fabric of Indian Territory tribes. One of the few non-Indian members of the first Cherokee lodge was the Methodist minister Thomas Bertholf, who had married the daughter of a prominent Cherokee leader.[20] Bertholf worked at the same mission as the Creek Samuel Checote, a local preacher who was chosen by his Methodist conference to be the presiding elder to the Creek Nation, helped found the first Masonic Lodge in the Creek Nation, and, at the end of his life, was chosen to be the Creek Nation's principal chief.[21] He was one of a number of Indian Methodist and Baptist local preachers who participated in the creation of both Native Christian churches and Indian Masonic lodges.[22] The Methodist missionary C. M. Slover believed his Masonic work to be so important that in 1860 his presiding elder admonished him for attending a Masonic meeting rather than the annual conference of his denomination.[23] The Baptist missionary and Indian Territory grand master "Father" Joseph Murrow, often referred to as the Father of Oklahoma Masonry, was a prime mover in "drilling" his Indian brethren in the "sacred" practices and obligations of Freemasonry.[24] Most significantly, the Baptist minister John Buttrick Jones, who spent his entire life alongside his father,

Evan Jones, in missionary work among the Cherokee, was a founding member and a master of his local lodge. In 1875, John Jones was the grand lecturer for the Indian Territory Grand Lodge, responsible for instructing all of the lodges in correct Masonic practices.[25] In 1858, he and his father sparked the creation of what became the Keetoowah Society, which drew from traditional understandings of Cherokee identity, Christianity, and Freemasonry to become a "potent factor in the political affairs of the Cherokee Nation for many years."[26]

Most Cherokees created their own form of Christianity rather than conform to the white man's version. As William G. McLoughlin has noted, the first missionaries sent to these Indians were Moravians and American Board Presbyterian and Congregational ministers, who had little success in demanding strict observance of their denominational beliefs and practices and the renunciation of all "polluting pagan customs." By the mid-1820s, they were joined by the more successful Baptists and Methodists, who were less insistent on conformity to white Christian standards of behavior. The missionary most successful in gaining the respect of the Cherokees and converts for his denomination was the Reverend Evan Jones. In his years of service to the Cherokees for the Northern Baptists, from 1821 until his death in 1872, Jones learned their language, lived in their cabins, got to know their problems, and sided with them in disputes with the federal government. The Baptist missionary vehemently opposed the removal of Indians from the Southeast, marched with them on the Trail of Tears, and—once in Indian Territory—opposed white expansionism. For his efforts, the Cherokee Council adopted him, his son John B. Jones, and their families as full citizens of the nation in 1865. These were the only missionaries to whom the Cherokees extended this honor. Most important, Jones sought to rebuild Cherokee culture by finding connections between the "old ways" and what he saw as the best of Christianity.[27]

Jones's goal was Cherokee revitalization, not adoption of white culture. Key to this effort was establishing a native ministry that supported the Cherokee people's traditional values and quest for sovereignty. They embraced the redemption of the community rather than the individual salvation emphasized by evangelicals. Jones, his son John, and the native preachers they trained realized that a Christianity devoted to helping the individual rather than building community solidarity threatened the social harmony at the core of the Cherokee cultural framework. To counter this, they spoke of the ideal of Christian brotherhood and sisterhood while deemphasizing the Protestant ethic of self-reliance.[28] One result of such efforts was a steady growth in the Baptist and Methodist denominations from 1840 to 1860 while the American Board missions remained stagnant. Though no more than 12 to 15 percent of the Cherokees were formally members of Christian churches by 1860, McLoughlin argues that the new syncretic world view sufficiently bridged the gap between Christianity and the old ways to sustain the belief that the Cherokees were equal as a people and a nation to the United States. Consistent with the old myths, Cherokee Christianity moved evangelical theology closer to Native American understandings.[29]

Indian Freemasonry further strengthened Cherokee revitalization. What became the Keetoowah Society began with the efforts of Evan and John B. Jones to encourage Cherokee preachers to create a counter-organization to the proslavery, Masonic-influenced Knights of the Golden Circle, which emerged in nearby Arkansas in the 1850s. Under the leadership of these local preachers, Cherokee Baptists and Masons held a series of secret meetings in the Baptist Church that the Cherokee local preacher Jesse Bushyhead had founded. At these meetings, the opposition to slavery shifted to Cherokee nationalism. The movement particularly opposed a wealthy, mixed-blood elite who happened to own slaves and who no longer embodied the spirit of the Cherokee people. *Keetoowah* was said to be the name of the first southeastern town settled by the Cherokees, the sacred site of tribal origin. At the core of the movement were the ancient teachings of harmony and reconciliation, deeply woven networks of blood kinship, and the connective glue of community-wide ceremonies.

While the Joneses' participation and the leadership of dedicated Cherokee Baptists indicates the society's pro-Christian stance, it did nothing that would alienate adherents of the old ways.[30] Subsequent meetings were held at the *gatiyo*, or stomp grounds, and surrounded a sacred fire that the Cherokees were said to have brought from the East and kept constantly burning. These were ritual occasions that included opening pipe rites, offerings to the sacred fire, and the recitation of sacred myths, along with Christian hymns and prayers. The emphasis was on Cherokee brotherhood, the protection of the national welfare, and consensus decision making. Religious adherence was secondary to tribal loyalty. At the same time, suggesting the practices of the society's Masonic members, men joined the society in "a highly secret ritual" in which they vowed "to assist each other always and to work constantly for the aims of the organization."[31] Moreover, Patrick Minges has noted that the society's laws describe its meeting room as a "lodge," its initiation ceremony involved a "door to the temple" that was "guarded in the East," and a provision in the society's constitution states that on the death of a member, "all brother Keetoowahs shall march in line to the grave following the dead. And each shall take a shovel full of dirt and put it in the grave."[32] This was similar to the Masonic funeral, at which each lodge member cast dirt on their brother's grave. This mixing of the old ways, Christianity, and Freemasonry resulted in a syncretic revitalization movement that sought to redefine what it meant to be a Cherokee.

As the Keetoowah Society emerged from secrecy in the early 1860s, it came to include Cherokees, Masons, and Christians on both sides of the Civil War. In this fratricidal conflict, the rift that divided ethnic groups, Christians, and the Masonic brotherhood throughout the larger United States also entered Indian Territory. The Cherokee Grand Council, including members of the same Masonic lodges, divided between North and South affiliation. The members of the Joneses' Northern Baptist churches were similarly in conflict. As the war progressed, not only Confederate and Union forces but also warring factions in these groups alternately raided and sacked settlements throughout the territory. In 1863, the Keetoowah boldly declared that slavery should end. With the rise of Lewis Downing to principal chief of the Cherokee Nation in the mid-1860s, the society became a force for national reconciliation. Downing, an ordained Baptist minister, was one of the founding members of the Keetoowah Society and a veteran of both the Confederate and federal armies. Subsequent Masons and principal chiefs of the Cherokees included Downing's Baptist colleague Oochalata (Charles Thompson) and Downing's successor Dennis Bushyhead, Jesse's son, who served until 1887. These elected leaders, all early Keetoowah Society members, proclaimed a message of national reconciliation and affirmation of the old ways that provided a unifying sense of identity and purpose in the reconstruction of the Cherokee Nation after the war and prior to the opening of Indian Territory to white settlers in the 1890s.[33]

FREEMASONRY AND NATIVE AMERICAN IDENTITY

While leading Native Americans were adopting the "civilized" dress and behavior of white men and joining Masonic lodges, European Americans were dressing up like Indians and creating their own versions of Native American rituals and organizations. In *Playing Indian*, Philip J. Deloria argues that since the late eighteenth century, European

Americans have dressed up and acted like Indians as part of various efforts to resolve questions of authenticity and identity.[34] Costumed as Indians, the colonial English members of the Boston Tea Party sought identification with the land's original inhabitants. As the revolution gave way to the republic, members of the New York Tammany Society connected themselves to a larger American identity through face paint and costumes. In the 1820s, the Independent Order of Red Men claimed the same primal Indian identity for the new American society and performed secret "Indian" rituals of initiation, reminiscent of the enduring Masonic quest for ancient wisdom. Though the Masons did not go so far as to don native dress, they shared the attraction to Native American wisdom. Ironically, Indian play provided citizens of the early republic with an identification with their newly claimed land just as Western expansion was destroying native peoples and cultures. By the 1830s, the newly ascendant vanishing-Indian ideology resolved this dilemma by arguing that primitive societies naturally disappear with the emergence of more advanced civilizations. As the century progressed, evolutionary theories informed by social Darwinism and industrialization affirmed European American ascendance. Yet at the same time, anxieties created by rapid modernization contributed to a longing for escape to an ancient world of enduring truth.[35] For some modernizing European American men, "going native" became an avenue for responding to the disorientations of the newly emerging American social order and an antidote to misgivings about the annihilation of the Indians.

The literature on European American appropriations of Native American dress and behavior speaks engagingly about how white people employed Indian history and culture yet says little about the native appropriation of Freemasonry, though the two are intertwined.[36] For the Cherokee who joined lodges in Indian Territory, the Masonic ideals of brotherly love, ethical conduct, and concern for others reinforced their traditional worldview while providing a basis for kinship that transcended tribal boundaries. Membership was also an avenue for asserting political rights, as a common Indian Masonic voice affirmed their right to equal status in the fraternity and defended Indian land ownership. Moreover, the inclusion of Masonic elements in the organizational structure and practices of the Keetoowah Society contributed to the syncretic movement for the revitalization of traditional Cherokee society. This cultural borrowing continued in the late nineteenth and early twentieth centuries as European Americans sought a more primal American identity through Native American appropriations and Native

Americans employed Freemasonry to navigate their place in modern American society.

One origin point for this ongoing cultural exchange was the chance encounter of Lewis Henry Morgan with Ely S. Parker in an Albany, New York, bookstore in 1844. Through his later research on the Iroquois, Morgan developed a widely adopted social evolutionary theory that describes unified human progress through stages of savagery and barbarism to civilization. In 1844, however, he was a young lawyer still living in his hometown of Aurora, New York, and obsessed with creating a fraternal order whose "Indian" rituals would tie him and his friends to an American self-image that would stand up to derogatory European commentaries on their upstart new nation's lack of an ancient cultural heritage. Unlike the founders of previous societies that had been content to enact rituals based on fanciful imaginings of ancient Indians, Morgan turned from romanticism toward the empirical study of actual Indians in his quest for more inspirational rituals for his New Confederacy of the Iroquois. Significant in this shift was his encounter with Parker, a real Indian. Parker was a leading Seneca tribesman who was soon to be chosen the grand sachem, or leader, of the Six Nations of the Iroquois Confederacy. Later, in the Civil War, he served under Ulysses S. Grant, who subsequently made the Seneca chief the first Indian commissioner of the Bureau of Indian Affairs. In 1844, the young Parker had come to Albany as a translator for his tribal leaders, who were demanding changes in a treaty that had been imposed on them and stipulated that they were to leave their homeland by 1846. Through Parker, Morgan gained access to Iroquois society and ceremonial practices. His research resulted in his major ethnographic work, *The League of the Ho-de-no-sau-nee or Iroquois*, published in 1851 and dedicated to Parker. At the same time, Parker made use of Morgan and his society. The members of the short-lived New Confederacy not only funded Parker's continuing education at Morgan's alma mater, the Cayuga Lake Academy, but, at Parker's prompting, protested against the coming forced removal of the Seneca from their land. Standing at the borders of Iroquois and white American cultures, Morgan and Parker sought to understand enough of the other's culture to use it for their own purposes.[37]

As a transitional figure between the European American romantic appropriation of Indian identities for the purposes of patriotic nationalism and the development of ethnographic research, Morgan provoked fresh questions about the place of Indians in the emerging American society with his Iroquois investigations. For his part, he was loath to admit the "secret society" origins of his later "objective" scholarship, for fear not only of not being taken seriously but also of becoming a target of the Anti-Masonic crusades that had recently enveloped the area.[38] His New Confederacy often met in the abandoned Aurora Masonic Lodge, which his father had helped to build.[39] Ethnographic research like Morgan's made it difficult for white America to idealize the "long departed" American aborigines. European American cultural imaginings of the noble savage who embodied a natural American identity increasingly confronted the reality of Indians who were not disappearing but living in places such as upstate New York. Morgan resolved this problem with his theory of social evolution, which recognized the existence of real Indians yet cast them as representatives of the lowest, "savage" stage of human development. By the late nineteenth century, federal Indian policy reflected his view that the Indians "could" rise to a higher level of "civilization" and explained away removals and reservations as necessary to the greater goal of human progress.[40]

Parker, in turn, employed the resources of Freemasonry in crossing the borders between Indian and white culture. The Seneca tribesman was raised among the traditional ceremonial leaders of the Tonawanda Reservation and took over tribal duties as he grew to manhood. According to his grandnephew, biographer, and fellow Mason Arthur Parker, Ely was committed throughout his life to securing the "blessings of civilization and the justice of its courts" for his people. Educated at a Baptist mission school and serving as an interpreter for tribal leaders when he met Morgan, Parker later studied law out of an awareness of the "despondency of his people" but was denied admission to the bar because he was "not an American citizen." Turning to engineering, he achieved greater success working for the federal government on projects as far away as Illinois, yet when he offered his services to the War Department on the eve of the Civil War, Secretary William H. Seward told him to "go home," for "the fight must be settled by white men alone." Angered by these rejections, Parker decided that although he "could not immediately serve his country . . . he could serve Masonry." In 1847, Brother Parker became a Freemason in Batavia, New York. When his engineering work took him to Galena, Illinois, he helped to create the first lodge there and served as its worshipful master. Rising in the ranks of Masonry in Illinois and New York, he served as a high priest of Royal Arch chapters and several times as a master of a lodge, received orders for knighthood from the Knights Templar, was appointed the grand orator of the Grand Lodge of Illinois, and had an Illinois lodge named after him for his organizational efforts. In the Civil War, Parker received an officer's commission through the intervention of General J. E. Smith, whom he had earlier "raised" to master mason in the Galena lodge.[41]

Masonic membership provided Parker with both a refuge in American society and the opportunity to influence the opinion of both the public and the leading Americans who were his Masonic brothers. In his Masonic addresses, he argued for Indians' social equality. At an 1859 Knights Templar convention in Chicago, for instance, Brother Parker worked within the vanishing-Indian ideology of the day to both acknowledge fraternal empathy for his "dying" race and affirm the brotherhood's inclusion of Native Americans as equal members.[42]

> Where shall I go when the last of my race shall have gone forever? Where shall I find a home and sympathy when our last council-fire is extinguished? I said, I will knock at the door of MASONRY, and see if the white race will recognize me, as they had my ancestors, when we were strong and the white men weak. I knocked at the door of the *Blue Lodge*, and found brotherhood around the altar. I knelt before the Great Light in the Chapter, and found companionship beneath the Royal Arch. I entered the Encampment, and found valiant Sir Knights willing to shield me there without regard to race or nation.[43]

In speaking to European Americans, Parker adopted the only idiom available to him—that of Native American extinction. Though the educational and social success of his family suggest otherwise, Parker had to accept the inevitable demise of his race in order for white society to accept him.[44] Seen in this light, he was speaking neither as an "authentic" Indian nor as one wholly assimilated to white society. Rather, he was responding to one particular moment in the Native American experience of involvement with European Americans. Moreover, in framing his address as he did, Joy Porter has pointed out, Parker allowed future Native Americans to have access to the resources of Freemasonry by turning his fellow Masons toward a greater respect for and understanding of his people.[45] In the early twentieth century, his grandnephew Arthur went further, arguing that Native Americans were "natural" Masons.

Born in 1881, Arthur Parker was part of the first generation of Indians who entered American life after the closing of the frontier, when the American public was coming to grips with Indians as a new minority.[46] Despite enduring ambivalence toward Native Americans, in the 1880s there was widespread interest among whites in transforming Indians through universal education and the protection of Indian resources. The Dawes Act of 1887 reflected this approach in its efforts to rapidly "civilize" Indians into productive citizenship.[47] Parker's family had pursued the assimilationist model for generations, with mixed success. His grandfather Nicholas was a successful reservation farmer and U.S. Indian interpreter. Nicholas met his white wife, Martha, at the local Congregational mission where he was being paid to translate the Bible. Parker's father, Frederick, was a teacher in the local public schools, where he met his white fellow teacher Geneva Griswold of Saybrook, Connecticut, whom he married. Arthur spent his early years until the age of eleven on the Cattaraugus Reservation before his father took a position as a clerk with the New York Central Railroad and the family moved to White Plains. Arthur subsequently attended public schools in White Plains and summered back at the reservation.[48] Until his adoption into the Seneca Bear Clan, in 1903, he felt his in-between status acutely, treated as an outsider both by the matrilineal Seneca Iroquois Indian Nation because his mother was white and by the dominant culture, which measured descent through the father's line and was prejudiced against his physical appearance and reservation residence. Even more than his full-blood granduncle Ely, Arthur Parker lived in a liminal area between Indian and European American society. Given these circumstances, as he entered adulthood, his strategy was to subscribe to Morgan's social evolutionary theory and so think of assimilated Indians such as himself as evolving toward the white ideal of civilization.[49]

In 1904, Parker secured a position at the New York State Museum in Albany, which was founded fifty years earlier with the Native articles that Morgan collected. Parker was tasked with visiting Native tribes and getting from them all the information and material objects that he could. Beginning in 1905, he produced a number of widely noticed monographs and papers on all aspects of Iroquois life, which drew attention to the new ethnology under way at the State Museum.[50] The thrust of his work was closely connecting the Indian past with contemporary American society. According to one biographer, "He used anthropology to present the Iroquois as a people whose history made them acceptable Americans, worthy of assimilation." Most transparent was *The Constitution of the Five Nations*, published in 1916, which presents the Iroquois governing structure as closely resembling the American model. Reviews exposed the author's subjective intent, effectively ending his career as an ethnologist.[51]

Accompanying this setback was the advent of a new phase in American Indian policy, which continued to work for the incorporation of Native Americans into the majority society but no longer sought to transform them or to guarantee their equality. Contributing to this turn was the work of the anthropologist Franz Boas, which, while acknowledging the integrity of Native American culture, offered little hope that Indians could evolve beyond their "primitive" status.[52] By 1920, Indians were labeled a minority group, destined to live on the margins of white society.[53] Though Parker continued to believe in the Morgan agenda of Indian assimilation, like his granduncle Ely, he now turned increasingly to Freemasonry for acceptance and the opportunity to influence thinking about the place of Indians in American society.

Parker's deepening attraction to Freemasonry coincided with his growing disbelief in the possibility of full assimilation into white American society.[54] Though he became a Mason in 1907 at the age of twenty-six, he did not choose to progress to the second degree, Fellow Craft, until 1918. By 1924, however, he had completed the additional thirty degrees beyond the Blue Lodge to reach the apex of Scottish Rite Masonry.[55] Masonic membership allowed him to associate on an equal footing with the white middle-class professionals he considered his peers. To be sure, despite its claim to universal membership—transcending race, religion, and nationality—the fraternity had always excluded African Americans and, by the early twentieth century, embraced nativist alarm over the immigration of Jews and Catholics.[56] Ironically, it was probably less Freemasonry's stated commitment to universality than its embrace of an ancient past that permitted Parker to join this largely old-stock white Protestant society—*because* he was an Indian.

Part of the attraction of turn-of-the-century Freemasonry was its claimed knowledge of universal truth, a feature of its alleged primeval and mystical origins. As we have seen, ancient and mystical wisdom and biblical stories surrounding the building of Solomon's Temple were part of this mix, which connected the brotherhood to the dawn of history. As the historian T. J. Jackson Lears has argued, modern men engaged in the rapid development of a new industrial order that was increasingly devoid of emotional sustenance and intellectual meaning were attracted to an "alternative past" that allowed them to create and participate in an antimodern world of what they thought to be enduring, universal beliefs and practices.[57] As part of this quest for the primeval, as early as the mid-nineteenth century, Indians had come to be seen as another ancient origin of the order.

Though Masons, unlike some fraternal orders, did not dress up like Indians or engage in "Indian-like" ritual activities, they did pursue identification with the Native American past. In 1850, B.T. Kavanaugh, the first grand master of Wisconsin, asserted that "Indians have, unquestionably, a knowledge of the universal language of Masonry," which they must have received "before they left their Asiatic ancestors . . . about the time of the Babel dispersion."[58] Later Masons who encountered Indians emphasized their "natural" Masonic attributes, which were thought to be inherent in Indian society.[59] Burial mounds marked by signs of geometry and astrology, secret male societies, ceremonies of initiation, tribal signs, and secret words all suggested a correspondence with Masonic ways.

Parker's deepening involvement in the fraternity accelerated the effort to provide American Freemasonry with a Native American past. Because American Masons sought identification with America's original inhabitants, moreover, he was able to use his Indian descent and ethnographic research to advance the standing of Indians in the fraternity. Between his completion of the entry-level degrees in 1918 and his elevation to thirty-third degree Scottish Rite Masonry in 1924, Parker wrote a series of articles for Masonic publications, seeking to elevate the Indian to middle-class status. He did this by identifying correspondences between Masonic beliefs and practices and Indian religious life.

Brother Parker argued that American Indians were "natural Masons." Though Native peoples did not hold lodge "charters or dispensations from some Grand Body of competent Masonic jurisdiction," there was an "inherent capacity" in the "higher members of the various tribes to receive the teachings of Masonry."[60] Like operative Masons, the "Indians in some instances drew moral lessons from the art of building their long houses and other dwellings, but for the most part their symbolism was drawn from the Study of the Temple of Nature."[61] Implicit in the Native world view were the "unwritten gospels" of Masonic teachings, which the "wise" among them were able to discern. Drawing from his ethnographic research, Parker described the existence of secret societies in his own Seneca Nation, whose members swore one another to keep their ritual words from outsiders. Even more explicitly Masonic was his description of the rite of the Iroquois Little Water Society. Like the third degree ritual of Freemasonry, the Indian ceremony took place in a "lodge" and enacted the candidate's resistance to three ruffians, who demanded the secret of his power; his resulting death; and his final resurrection.[62]

In these writings, Parker worked to provide early twentieth-century Masons with an ancient Indian heritage; in exchange, Freemasonry gave him a platform from which to argue for the recognition of Indians as middle-class Americans. If Masons were respectable American citizens and Indians were natural Masons, he pointed out, then Indians should be accepted as equal members of middle-class American society. Drawing the Masonic gaze from the primordial past, Parker reminded his brethren that Indian Masons were very much a part of the Masonic present. "One can scarcely travel in Oklahoma, Nebraska, Kansas or the Dakotas," he observed, "without meeting Indians who belong to the ancient fraternity. Many of the most influential Indians of the Dakotas and especially of Oklahoma have full knowledge of the mysteries of Masonry."[63]

An emphasis on the Indian past to draw attention to the Native American present characterized Parker's generation of progressive Indian leaders. In the early twentieth century, educated Indians employed the attractions of antimodernity to publicly critique the Indian's treatment by American society. Literary figures such as Mourning Dove—one of the first Native American women to publish a novel—belittled the modern American understanding of progress by celebrating the noble life of their tribal past. Most famously, the Santee Sioux physician Charles Eastman wrote the memoir *Indian Boyhood*, which promoted a positive, antimodernist understanding of Indian culture that challenged negative public stereotypes of their "savagery." The Boy Scouts adopted his belief that an Indian upbringing provides the best moral training and incorporated some of his material into their efforts to create "all-American" boys. Mourning Dove, Eastman, and other Indian intellectuals of Parker's generation appeared at a cultural moment when many Americans had become disenchanted with modern society. These early Indian writers appealed to their white readers in depicting an idyllic world untouched by the acids of modernity.[64] At the same time, they began to create a counterpublic that defended Native cultures and criticized emerging industrialization in order to claim a place for Indians in a more democratic and inclusive American society.[65]

Fraternal orders provided Indian and white Americans with common ground for creating new identities. When European American men dressed in feathers and Indian tribesmen put on suits, they played with the boundaries of their identities. Yet as Philip Deloria has argued, "It would be wrong to make the two acts equivalent." Lewis Henry Morgan and his fellow nineteenth-century fraternalists "did not have to" imagine themselves as Indians, but Ely S. Parker and his Indian people's survival depended on their skill in finding a place in the new American nation.[66] In the early twentieth century, Parker's grandnephew Arthur continued to shape the discourse of Freemasonry on Native Americans. Though his efforts could never adequately redress the subordinate position of Indians in American society, Arthur Parker influenced the American debate on the proper social order. Moreover, by making his ideas known, he, alongside the other leading Indians of his generation, helped to establish an early public framework for the activism of today's Native American community.[67]

CHAPTER 8

Jews and Catholics, 1723–1920

Jews and Catholics have long been members of the Masonic brotherhood. Jews were first admitted shortly after the publication of the modern fraternity's 1723 constitution, which stipulates that membership
cannot be denied on the basis of religious affiliation. Subsequent Jewish
involvement in Freemasonry corresponds with the history of Jewish
participation in European and American society. In America, the first
Jewish Masons were prominent members of their colonial coastal settlements. After the Revolution, Jews rose to leadership in the fraternity,
though their presence was at times unsettling. Some founded "Jewish
lodges" in greater conformity with Jewish religious practices. Others
borrowed Freemasonry's organizational structure to create associations, such as B'nai B'rith, that responded to the need to unify and
"elevate" all Jewish immigrants. At the height of their late nineteenth-
and early twentieth-century migration to America, Jews started myriad
fraternal orders and hometown societies (or landsmanshaftn) to foster
an American commitment to Jewishness that both included and transcended Old World ties.

In contrast to Jews, who were first admitted to the eighteenth-
century speculative fraternity's gatherings of aspiring noblemen and
gentry, all of Freemasonry's original members were part of a medieval
Catholic confraternity of practicing stoneworkers. Following the creation of the modern fraternity, Catholics remained prominent in its
membership. In the early nineteenth century, though, papal letters

threatened excommunication for Catholic Masons. The fraternity's perceived involvement in European political conspiracies prompted the church's early warnings, resulting in the punishment of Catholic Masons on the continent. In Ireland, England, and America, however, some time passed before the local hierarchy gave the church's condemnations serious attention. In the early nineteenth century, America's affluent Catholics were welcomed into the lodges. But American Freemasonry's attitude toward the Catholic Church began to change by midcentury, with the arrival of large waves of Irish, then German and Italian Catholic immigrants and the more widespread enforcement of papal condemnations of the order. While lodge members largely supported their Catholic brothers, attitudes toward the institutional church ranged from tolerance to a rabid anti-Catholicism, by the late nineteenth century the fraternity as a whole did not look favorably on the Roman Church. In 1882, Irish Catholics created a brotherhood intended to unite all practicing American Catholics regardless of nationality. A response to both the papal condemnations of Freemasonry and their desire for a society that addressed their particular needs, the Knights of Columbus emphasized loyalty to the new American nation. By embracing Christopher Columbus as their patron, the Knights claimed America's discovery as a Catholic event, to be celebrated by all Catholic immigrants to America.

In founding B'nai B'rith and the Knights of Columbus, this chapter argues, immigrant Jews and Catholics used the Masonic framework to create fraternities to meet their needs of both assimilating into American society and retaining their Old World identities. Both built on the Masonic emphases on universalism, democracy, and opportunities for advancement in the order. Different from Masonic religious tolerance and B'nai B'rith's acceptance of all Jews were the Knights of Columbus's restriction of membership to practicing Catholics and submission to the church. Where the rites of Masonry bound initiates to the brotherhood and the ceremonies of B'nai B'rith sanctified Jewish American identity, the rituals of the Knights of Columbus cemented allegiance to the American Catholic Church. Though the most Americanized of their communities, the members of the Jewish B'nai B'rith and the Catholic Knights of Columbus were more closely bound to their synagogues and parishes, respectively, than native-born Masons to their churches. In their respective ethnic enclaves, moreover, cultural patterns from their countries of origin influenced gender relations.

JEWS AND FREEMASONRY

The Jewish encounter with Freemasonry began in 1732. In the modern fraternity's 1723 constitution, the Presbyterian clergyman James Anderson declares that no member can be discriminated against because of his religion.[1] This universalist principle, while excluding atheists, requires obedience only to "the moral Law." It is not likely, however, that Anderson's eighteenth-century interest in sidestepping religious controversies extended beyond wishing to avoid Christian denominational differences.[2] At that time, Jews lived on the margins of a largely Christian European society. It is doubtful that Anderson meant to include them in the membership of the modern fraternity. Nevertheless, his statement "Concerning God and Religion" provides support for their inclusion.[3]

The first Jewish Masons came from London's small Sephardic community of Spanish and Portuguese merchants and financiers. Following the devastation of the seventeenth-century English Civil Wars, Oliver Cromwell invited the Jews, whom England had expelled in 1290, to resettle in the country and help rebuild its economy.[4] In 1732, a Jew named Edward Rose was admitted to the London fraternity, creating some excitement. Debates ensued over the legitimacy of Jewish membership. The number of Jewish names on lodge membership lists by 1740, some in leadership positions, suggests their acceptance. In 1759, more than half of the twenty-three men who petitioned the London Grand Lodge to form a new lodge were Jewish.[5] By the late eighteenth century, growing numbers of Anglicizing Jews were joining the fraternity.

The admission of Jews to Masonic lodges was a product of the large social changes that had led to the creation of the modern fraternity. As chapter 1 discusses, beginning in the late seventeenth century, traditional patterns of community life dissolved in England and subsequently all of western Europe, leading to new economies, new forms of governance, and diminished religious authority. In the early eighteenth century, London experienced a threefold increase in population and growing social diversity. In this new social environment, nobles, gentry, craftsmen, and strangers moved about without the kinship or communal bonds of earlier village life. New ideas that proclaimed a natural harmony among the members of this redefined social world aided this easy mixing of a diverse population. Modern Freemasonry was an expression of this new social vision. It attracted members from the expanding middling ranks of men who had separated themselves from the rest of society through their professional training, education, or greater wealth yet were usually not among the landed gentry or nobility.

At about the same time, a new kind of Jew appeared in European society and sought admission to Masonic lodges. This "modern" Jew rapidly adjusted to the attitudes and behaviors of Gentiles. Previously, restrictive laws had prevented Jews from participating in most aspects of European social life, while their traditional practices had little affinity with the universalism of modern Freemasonry. The history of Jewish participation in European society corresponds with the history of their involvement with the modern fraternity. As Jews gained civil emancipation, they pursued the badge of social respectability that Masonic membership conferred. At the origins of the modern fraternity, only a few tried to breach the lodge's social barrier. After the 1780s, however, acculturated Jews became established participants in European social life and the Masonic brotherhood.[6]

A key attraction of Freemasonry to Jews was that it sought to provide a neutral ground for people of different religious and social backgrounds to interact while not violating their particular religious values. Moreover, the Jew entering a Masonic lodge discovered aspects of his religious heritage. The society's central origin story identifies its modern members as descendants of the Jewish builders who constructed a temple to God in the reign of King Solomon. Abraham, Noah, David, and other biblical heroes are significant figures in this mythical history. Moreover, as Bill Williams has written about eighteenth-century Manchester, "Freemasonry was perhaps the only organised body of public opinion in Manchester which favoured the integration of foreigners (including Jews) into local society and sought to influence public attitudes towards them."[7] Such acceptance was not always the case. As early as 1752, individual lodges tried to exclude Jews on the grounds that the fraternity was a Christian institution.[8] Indeed, Christian saints stand alongside Jewish heroes in the fraternity's heritage. Most notably, Masons claim John the Baptist and John the Evangelist as patron saints and celebrate their feast days annually, on June 24 and December 27 respectively.[9]

Jewish discomfort with Freemasonry's Christianity led to the occasional creation of what became known as Jewish lodges. The 1756 appearance of an anthology of Masonic prayers, that sought to replace Christian prayers to the Father, the Son, and the Holy Ghost with Jewish prayers that invoke Moses as the master of a lodge who taught the Torah to his followers, foreshadowed this development. The title page states that the prayers are to be used in "Jewish Lodges."[10] Masonic researchers have established the London Lodge of Israel No. 205, founded in 1793, as the oldest extant Jewish lodge. Its founders and members were largely tradesmen from the East End. Such lodges characteristically abided by Jewish dietary laws, avoided meeting on the Jewish Sabbath or festivals, displayed the Old Testament, and employed Hebrew prayers.[11] Additionally, they provided the significant benefit of a meeting place for Jews of different nationalities and backgrounds. Although Jewish names in lists of lodge members prove that for some, neither anti-Semitic resolutions nor Christian symbols overcame the tangible benefits of joining a group composed of prominent members of society, the presence of Jews in Masonic lodges in this period can best be understood as the outcome of compromises on both sides. This suggests that boundaries between Jews and Christians were weakening as the eighteenth century progressed.

The story of Jewish Freemasonry in the United States begins about the time when Sephardic Jews from Spain and Portugal were gaining acceptance in the new Masonic lodges of England and Holland. By the early eighteenth century, the Jewish Atlantic Diaspora from Sephardic centers in Portugal, Spain, Holland, and England had established settlements in Brazil and the West Indies. The first Jewish Freemasons in North America came across the Atlantic from Europe's Sephardic communities or north from the new Caribbean and South American settlements. In the mixed urban populations of New York; Savannah, Georgia; Charleston, South Carolina; Philadelphia; and Newport, Rhode Island, newly arriving Jews found economic opportunities and a religiously tolerant environment. By 1790, there were an estimated fewer than fifteen hundred Jews in North America, with no more than a few hundred in any one of these settlements.[12] Drawing on Sephardic communal patterns from the Iberian Peninsula, the new American synagogue-communities promoted group solidarity and Jewish identity. Unlike the Sephardic Old World, however, they welcomed Jews of diverse origins, including a growing number of Ashkenazim from central and eastern Europe. And different from medieval synagogues, which controlled all aspects of Jewish life, the developing synagogue-communities of colonial America confined their activities to the religious sphere, apart from the larger social world.[13]

The first Jewish Masons in North America were prominent members of these colonial settlements. In Newport, an influx of Jewish immigrants beginning in 1740 resulted in the formation of Saint John's Lodge No. 1

in 1749, less than twenty years after the admission of the first Jew to a London lodge. Its original members included Aaron Lopez, Jacob Rodrigues Rivera, Moses Levy, Isaac Hart, and Isaac Pollock, representing five of the city's most important and commercially successful Jewish families. One historian has estimated that between two-thirds and five-sixths of the late eighteenth-century Newport Jewish adult male community belonged to the Masonic fraternity.[14]

Moses Seixas, a prominent banker, was both the president of the local Yeshuat Israel congregation and the master of Saint John's Lodge. He was a grandson of the Sephardic London broker Abraham Mendes Seixas and a son of Isaac Mendes Seixas, who came to New York in 1720 and married into the wealthy, Ashkenazic Levy family. His brother Gershom Mendes Seixas was the religious leader of New York's Congregation Sheraith Israel and a leading advocate of the American Revolution.[15] Following the war, Moses was instrumental in forming the Grand Lodge of Rhode Island and served as its grand master from 1802 to 1807. He is best known for authoring two letters of welcome on the occasion of George Washington's visit to Rhode Island in 1790, one from the Masons and the other from his synagogue.[16] Washington's response to the synagogue letter endorses Seixas's line "To bigotry no sanction, to persecution no assistance," which became a founding statement of American religious liberty.[17]

A pattern of prominent immigrants participating in or creating both synagogues and Masonic lodges while moving into the new American society characterized early Jewish America. Seventeen of the original fifty-six members, and most of the leadership, of Philadelphia's Sublime Lodge of Perfection (est. 1781) were also founding members of that city's Mikve Israel Synagogue (1782).[18] These included Mordecai M. Mordecai, who, reflecting American impulses, on several occasions challenged his congregation's leaders by claiming to interpret God's laws as he understood them;[19] Lieutenant Colonel Solomon Bush, the highest-ranking Jewish officer in the Continental Army;[20] and Solomon Etting, the first Jew elected to office in the state of Maryland.[21] To take another example, the 1793 laying of the cornerstone of the new building of Charleston's synagogue Beth Elohim "was conducted by the rules and regulations of the ancient and honorable fraternity of Freemasons." The committee of arrangements included Moses C. Levy, the congregation's president and a Freemason.[22] When the Beth Elohim congregation was first organized, in 1750, it elected Isaac Da Costa as reader. He was educated for the rabbinate in London before coming to Charleston in

1749. A member of an illustrious Sephardic family that played an important role in English Jewry, he had joined Charleston's King Solomon's Lodge by 1753, and his fellow English gentlemen elected him its treasurer in 1758. A prosperous merchant, Da Costa formed a business partnership with a non-Jewish Masonic brother in 1779. During the British occupation of Charleston, he refused to take the British oath of allegiance, lost his property, and fled to Philadelphia, where he joined the Mikve Israel congregation and the Scottish Rite's Sublime Lodge of Perfection.[23]

The early identification of American Jews with what became the Scottish Rite sequence of higher Masonic degrees can be traced to the influence of the Sephardic Jew Moses Michael Hays. After coming to America from Europe, he organized King David's Lodge in New York in 1769 and then transferred it to Newport, where he served as its master from 1780 to 1782. In 1788, he was elected the grand master of the Massachusetts Grand Lodge, with the Revolutionary War patriot Paul Revere serving under him as the deputy grand master. Hays' connection with Masonry probably began about 1768, when Henry Andrew Francken, who claimed the title "Deputy Inspector General over all Lodges, Chapters, Councils and Grand Councils of the Superior degrees of Ancient and Modern Free Masonry over the Surface of the Two Hemispheres," appointed him one of several deputy inspectors general for North America. These appointments were made with a view toward establishing the Order of the Royal Secret (later the Scottish Rite) in America, and the deputies had the authority to appoint others with like powers. Recall that the Scotsman Andrew Michael Ramsay, who became the grand orator of the Grand Lodge of France in 1740, inspired these degrees (see chapter 3). Chevalier Ramsay rejected the operative origins of Freemasonry and instead traced its birth to Palestine at the time of the Crusades. In 1781, Hays appointed several Jewish deputy inspectors general, including Bush and Da Costa, to superintend the Order of the Royal Secret in various jurisdictions.[24] In 1801, the Supreme Council of Scottish Rite Masonry, built on the Order of the Royal Secret, was founded in Charleston, with Jews accounting for four of the nine original members.[25] The appointment of Hays and others to such high honors in America when Jews were being persecuted and expelled throughout Europe is another indication of the significance of Freemasonry for colonial Jews. Moreover, in what became known as the Southern Jurisdiction of the Scottish Rite in America, Jews influenced Freemasonry by modifying the Christian content of some rites so they could participate, according to the editors of the Supreme Council's bulletin, "without sacrifice of conscience."[26]

After the Revolution, American Judaism was transformed. The new country's republican and democratic ethos undermined the traditional hierarchical synagogue-community while expanding the boundaries of religious liberty. A new emphasis on individual freedom pervaded the republic. In both Jewish and Christian communities, tensions between traditional religious values and those of the new American society resulted in a tumultuous remapping of the religious landscape. Though there were but three to six thousand Jews in America by the 1820s, many were native born, and growing numbers of immigrants from western and central Europe joined them. New fault lines appeared between young and old, innovators and traditionalists, Ashkenazim and Sephardim. These developments took place in the midst of the Second Great Awakening, a time of western population movement, growing merchant capitalism, democratization, evangelical revivals, and some misgivings about religious pluralism and modernity. By the 1830s, American synagogues encompassed a range of practices and constituencies that now competed with one another and so rendered obsolete the traditional weaving together of synagogue and community.[27] How these forces played out in the life of Mordecai Noah, among the most prominent American Jews of the early nineteenth century, suggests the pull of ethnic identity to restore Judaism and the conflicting desire to adapt to modern society that American Jews of his generation experienced.

RESTORATION

On the morning of September 15, 1825, a loud cannon blast booming from the front of the courthouse and reverberating across the lake surrounding Grand Island startled the inhabitants of the frontier village of Buffalo, New York, from their slumber. At eleven o'clock, Mordecai Noah, resplendent in black Richard III robes and assuming the role of "Judge of Israel," emerged from the Masonic lodge and, accompanied by a military band, led a grand parade of political dignitaries, clergy, other prominent citizens, and hundreds of Masons through the streets to Saint Paul's Episcopal Church. Throngs of people, many of whom had streamed into town in the past few days from the general direction of New York City, gathered to watch Noah's performance. The aged Seneca chief Red Jacket, whose people had lived on Grand Island, came ashore. In the church, the Episcopal priest and Mason Addison Searle conducted an ecumenical service replete with the choir's rendition of "Before Jehovah's Awful Throne" and the singing of a Hebrew psalm. On the communion table lay a cornerstone, crowned with silver cups of Masonic corn, oil, and wine and bearing this inscription:

> Hear O' Israel, the Lord our God, the Lord is one
> ARARAT
> A City of Refuge for the Jews
> *Founded by* Mordecai Manuel Noah *in the month of* Tzri 5586,
> *Sept.* 1825 & *in the 50th Year of* American Independence

Against the background of this kaleidoscopic mixture of Christian and Hebrew symbols in a Masonic ritual framework, the self-declared Judge of Israel ascended to the high pulpit and declaimed in booming prose his "Jewish Declaration of Independence."[28]

The speech that Noah delivered that morning was a version of his "Proclamation to the Jews," which he had earlier sent out to world Jewry.[29] His purpose was to announce the planned creation of a "temporary and provisionary" new homeland for the Jews, on nearby Grand Island. Ararat was to be a "city of refuge" where Jews could establish an independent republic "under the auspices and protection of the constitution and laws of the United States of America." After briefly chronicling the long history of Jewish persecution, Noah argued that "the time has emphatically arrived to do something calculated to benefit our own condition": reviving the ancient Jewish government in a "refuge" within "a country free from ignoble prejudices and legal disqualifications." Deeming "it expedient to reorganize the nation under the direction of the Judges," Noah proclaimed himself the Judge of Israel and noted that "he who assumes this power . . . will always be sustained by public opinion. . . . By this test I wish to be judged." The Jewish leader then proposed that a census and registration of the world's Jews be conducted and a tax paid by each in support of the Ararat enterprise. He encouraged young Jews from throughout the world to emigrate to this "asylum," which would combine their many social and cultural differences into an American Jewish identity that would prepare them for a hoped-for return "to the land of the Patriarchs." Noah's Ararat would be a progressive place where merchants, industrialists, and financiers would create a bustling commercial metropolis. Anticipating the changes to Jewish religious beliefs and practices of the coming Reform movement, he proclaimed that there would be greater use of the vernacular in Ararat, "together with such reforms, which, without departing from the ancient faith, may add greater solemnity to our worship." Striking a more restorationist note, he said that the rich soil of the area would allow the Jews to once again become an agricultural people, now cultivating their land free from "feudal lords." Moreover, reflecting a current of early nineteenth-century thought, he presumed that the neighboring Indians were "in all probability the descendants of the lost ten tribes of Israel." Through relations between the Ararat settlers and the surrounding Indians, the Judge of Israel hoped that "the tribes could be brought together, could be made sensible of their origin, could be civilized, and restored to their long lost brethren." He concluded his remarks by appointing, without their consent, many of the world's Jewish leaders to help him carry out his plan.[30]

Noah was a fourth-generation product of the energetic young republic. His Portuguese ancestor Dr. Samuel Nunez had escaped from Lisbon to London in 1726 and then embarked for America with a party of settlers in 1733, landing in Savannah, Georgia, and joining the local Masonic lodge. Noah's grandfather Jonas Phillips was a Mason and one of the founders of Philadelphia's Mikve Israel congregation, in 1782.[31] His father, Manuel, was a member of Charleston's Beth Elohim synagogue and the city's Masonic lodge before joining General Francis "Swamp Fox" Marion to fight against the British and later moving to Philadelphia. Born in Philadelphia in 1785, Noah was an observant member of the Mikve Israel synagogue, a Freemason, the editor of several political journals, a Jewish community activist, and an influential member of the Democratic-Republican Party in the early years of the republic.[32] Acting "somewhat like a professional court Jew," he appealed to the Jeffersonian party's hierarchy on behalf of his coreligionists while promising their electoral loyalty to James Madison.[33] As a reward for his political support, Noah received several patronage appointments, including major in the Pennsylvania militia, American consul to Tunis, and sheriff of New York. In 1817, in recognition of his prominence in party politics, Major Noah was chosen to address a New York City Fourth of July gathering of the "Tammany Society of Columbian Order, Hibernian Provident Society, Columbian Society, Union Society of Shipwrights, and Caulkers, Tailors', House Carpenters' and Masons' Benevolent Societies." Before this heterogeneous assembly, the political leader went out of his way to praise the "comfort and consolation" of America's "republican institutions," which protected the rights and privileges of its citizens.[34] One year later, Noah's central role in the New York Jewish community was recognized in his selection as the speaker at the consecration of New York City's Kahal Kadosh Shearith Israel synagogue. In this address, he held up America as the very best place in the world for

Jews at the time. "Until the Jews can recover their ancient rights and dominions, and take their rank among the governments of the earth, this is their chosen country."[35] As a patriotic citizen and an influential politician, Noah promoted the young republic's ideals of freedom, democracy, and tolerance. As an observant Jew, in contrast, he called for a refuge that was both sectarian and ruled by Hebrew judges. He never resolved this paradox. As his biographer Jonathan Sarna has concluded, Noah "embodied but could not resolve the tension faced by all minority groups: the simultaneous search for benefits of wholehearted assimilation and the security of ethnic-roots identification."[36]

Utopian visions were common in early nineteenth-century America. Ever since the Puritans, European immigrants had sought to create ideal societies in their new country based on religious or ethnic identities. Amid the pluralism of the early nineteenth century, a growing number of plans were hatched to create insulated ethnic homelands as well as Mormon, Shaker, and similar theocracies.[37] Noah's Ararat, moreover, followed a number of American Jewish colonial experiments, real and imagined, that dated back to the establishment of a Jewish colony in Georgia in 1733 by his ancestor Samuel Nunez and Nunez's fellow immigrants from England. As recently as 1816, Moses Elias Levy had spoken of using the land he owned in Florida for a Jewish colony.[38] In 1819, riots and attacks on Jews in Germany heightened interest in Jewish colonization. Like all of these utopians, Noah planned a homogenous community for European immigrants. His imagined colony was also a response to the use of exclusion and conversion to shape American society. The desire to separate those who did not fit in with the white majority was behind, for example, the 1819 creation of the American Colonization Society, whose goal was to buy slaves and send them back to Africa. Of greater concern to Noah were the efforts of the American Society for Ameliorating the Conditions of the Jews, which was trying to establish a Jewish-Christian colony in nearby Harrison, New York, and intended to improve the conditions of the Jews by converting them to Christianity. Ararat, Noah argued in response, would defend and strengthen the Jews through the restoration of their religion.[39]

Ararat's design embodied the tensions that Noah experienced between an idealized past and an uncertain future. In seeking to restore the ancient government of the judges, he looked to a primordial past for guidance. This impulse resembled that of contemporary Masonic ritualists, Christian primitivists, African American race historians, and Native American members of the Keetoowah Society, who all sought an anchoring in ancient wisdom amid the rapidly changing present. Moreover, like Joseph Smith's restorationist vision for the Latter-Day Saints, Noah's plan called for the gathering of religiously minded settlers from throughout the world in a theocratic refuge governed by Scripture and the contemporary embodiments of biblical leaders. Both men also called for people of Israelite descent, including tribes of American Indians, to populate the new colonies.

For Jews and Christians who believed that the Flood had left only Noah and his family, the discovery of Native Americans raised a theological problem, which some resolved by asserting that the Indians were descendants of the Hebrews.[40] For Smith, the Indians were descendants of the lost ten tribes of Israel and had come to America before the birth of Christ.[41] Noah identified them as descendants of the Jewish Diaspora and thought that they had spread into China and over the Bering Strait to America many thousands of years ago.[42] Though the need to establish the Native Americans' biblical roots had been a concern ever since the first European encounters with them, some attributed Smith's understanding to Noah's explanation.[43]

Despite Noah's Jewish restorationist vision, Ararat remained oddly suspended between past and present. How could Noah both celebrate the separation of church and state and advocate a Jewish theocracy? How could the authority of the judges work with American laws? Adding to these difficulties was the public response. Following the Buffalo ceremony, the widely read and influential *Niles' Weekly Register* concluded that the "cornerstone of the project" was to "fill the pockets of Mr. Noah and his associates."[44] More important, Jewish leaders branded Noah as impious. Protesting the Ararat project, Grand Rabbi De Cologne declared that "God alone knows the epoch of the Israel restoration; and he alone will make it known to the whole universe."[45] A few months after Noah's 1825 address, the Ararat project was dead. In his later years, Noah moved away from such plans for an American colony and instead became a forceful advocate for the restoration of the world's Jews to Israel. "Every attempt to colonize the Jews in other countries has failed," he observed in an 1844 address. "Their eye has steadily rested on their own beloved Jerusalem."[46]

REFORM

As Noah's prescient Zionism moved from Ararat to Israel, his embrace of assimilation expanded to include changes in liturgical practices. In

1834, he announced the need for a series of "improvements" in congregational worship. These included dispensing with "burdensome ceremonies" that lacked biblical precedents, inviting public discussion of previously unquestioned beliefs and practices, adopting vernacular prayers, enjoying the uplifting benefits of instrumental music, and other German innovations. For Noah and other leading Jews of his generation, Reform Judaism meant emancipation from the inessential restrictions of their traditional religion and liturgical advances that would mesh easily with the ways of middle-class Protestantism. Moreover, the new movement's emphasis on rational ethical teachings pointed toward the Masonic universalist ideal.[47]

In 1856, Charles W. Moore, the editor of the *Freemason's Monthly Magazine*, remarked that "we have understood that [Dr. Noah] was a Mason. . . . With his liberal views, there is certainly nothing in Masonry to which he could have taken exception. . . . Many of the most eminent and talented of his Jewish Brethren were in his day filling high and honorable places in the fraternity." These "were gentlemen and Masons," he continued, "of enlarged views and liberal minds; and by the exercise of a tolerant spirit, and a courteous bearing towards those who differed from them in matters of conscience, endeared themselves to their Christian Brethren, and contributed largely to elevate the social position of those to whom they were allied by ties of kindred blood."[48]

One year earlier, the rabbi and Mason Isaac M. Wise, the leader of Reform Judaism in America, had remarked that the "beauty and pride of Masonry was its universal character, its tendency to fraternize mankind, and its being free from the elements which have been ever the efficient causes of hatred, persecution, fraud, and rude barbarism."[49] In his study of Freemasonry in Gilded Age San Francisco, Anthony D. Fels discovered that 13 percent of San Francisco's Freemasons were Jewish and that of the 36 percent of these who were also members of synagogues, nearly all were in Reform or Reform-leaning congregations.[50] These most forward-looking Jews performed bonding rituals with non-Jews and committed themselves to universal brotherhood and bourgeois values, furthering their assimilation into American society. By 1910, their acceptance in Masonry had resulted in the election of twenty-four Jewish grand masters in states throughout the country.[51]

The admission of Jews into American Freemasonry was not without controversy. By the 1850s, the growing number of "undesirable" immigrants had led to calls for the fraternity to join the nativist Know-Nothing political party and assert Freemasonry as a "Protestant institution." In the *Boston Daily Times*, a Massachusetts Mason decried "universal Masonry" in favor of a "Christian Masonry" that "wished that the ships that brought the foreigners across the Atlantic had sunk ere they landed upon our shores."[52] Responding to this attack in Cincinnati's Reform newspaper, the *Israelite*, Wise declared that "what the people of Massachusetts call Masonry actually is nothing else than the excrescence of puritan bigotry and damnable fanaticism." In contrast to this nativist aberration, he wrote, true Freemasonry makes no distinctions between "Jew and Gentile, Native and Foreigner, Protestant and Catholic." If anything, Wise assured his Jewish readers, "Masonry is a Jewish institution whose history, degrees, charges, passwords and explanations are Jewish from the beginning to the end."[53] Although scattered instances of such tensions crop up in American Masonic documents, they should not detract from the fact that throughout the nineteenth century, Jews played a significant role in the life of the fraternity.

B'NAI B'RITH

Despite Freemasonry's apparent acceptance of Jews, in 1843, twelve German-speaking Jews, several of whom were Masons or Odd Fellows, created from the organizational structure of fraternalism an exclusively Jewish brotherhood dedicated to both the universalism of Freemasonry and the desire to unify and elevate a burgeoning Jewish community increasingly marked by class, religious, and nationalistic conflicts. Although a Jewish organization, the new Independent Order of B'nai B'rith (Sons of the Covenant) was dedicated to the promotion of the bonds of ethnic and communal peoplehood rather than a shared faith. Its original constitution avoids mention of God, Torah, or ritual obligations while emphasizing Jewish unity. In place of the Masonic ritual trappings, the new fraternity used the menorah and other Jewish symbols in a hierarchy of six degree rituals replete with regalia and secret passwords. The Hebrew names of the officers, grand nasi abh (president), grand aleph (vice president), and grand sopher (secretary), similarly maintained fraternalism's penchant for grand titles. The new fraternity responded to the need of a growing number of German Jewish immigrants for an organization that would preserve Jewish life by uniting all Israelites in a common effort of promoting both their own and humanity's best interests.[54]

B'nai B'rith's Judaic version of Masonic universalism helped to create a more secular Jewish culture. While some experienced growing alienation as a result of the increasingly rancorous divisions of synagogue life, the new fraternity argued that only through the ties of their common covenant (b'rith) could Jews achieve unity. For some members, this meant that the center of Jewish identity moved from the synagogue to the fraternal framework. Deborah Dash Moore has called B'nai Brith "a secular synagogue."[55] Other members, however, remained active in synagogue life while supporting the fraternity's work of strengthening the "peoplehood" of the Jews. Despite these different responses, Moore concludes that B'nai B'rith's "lodge rituals" and "opportunities for self-improvement" helped to "bridge the gap from immigrant standing to American status."[56] Spearheading this effort were the fraternity's leaders, each of whom, the chair of its executive committee declared, had "a double duty to perform. As a gentleman he owes his co-operation to gentle society; as a Jew he owes the benefit of his example and association to his people."[57] Though B'nai B'rith spoke of uniting all Jews, like Freemasonry, it fell short of its universal ideal. By the end of the century, the organization consisted largely of successful German immigrants and their American-born children who had effectively assimilated into American society.[58]

LANDSMANSHAFTN

More than two million eastern European Jews flooded into America at the turn of the century, and new organizations sprang up to join B'nai B'rith in responding to their needs. By the 1880s, B'nai B'rith had twenty-five thousand members, followed by the twelve thousand of the Independent Order Free Sons of Israel, the nine thousand of Keshar shel Barzel (Bond of Iron), the thirty-three hundred of the Improved Order Free Sons of Israel, and the smaller numbers of many other groups.[59] In the early twentieth century, myriad Jewish hometown societies, or landsmanshaftn, appeared, with an estimated total membership of nearly one-quarter of New York's eastern European Jews. In the 1930s, the Yiddish Writers' Group, funded by the Works Progress Administration, undertook the first large-scale study of this phenomenon.[60] It found that the life-span of these organizations was three generations, characterized by a transition from immigrant to American identity. Gradually their membership expanded to include nontownsmen. The exclusive use of Yiddish in the first generation yielded to a predominance of English in the third. In the first generation, poor immigrants of nondescript backgrounds were attracted to the recognition and honor of ceremonies and leadership positions, which for many replaced the need for a synagogue. As the report said, "In the old country a poor Jew dared not dream of becoming even a beadle in a synagogue; here he might become president of a society." By the third generation, the emphasis on ritual and status gave way to a businesslike focus on benevolence in a more democratic organization. Beyond "instructing its members in the issues of Americanism, the lodge also brought home to them a clearer understanding of broad Jewish interests." Though some of the landsmanshaftn's most "Americanized Jews" joined the "Masons, . . . perhaps actuated by a desire to round out their process of Americanization," most of these Jewish Masons did not neglect "their social obligations as Jews" while maintaining "membership in both organizations."[61]

Like B'nai B'rith, all of these new immigrant orders merged Jewish and American symbols in a fraternal framework. Though widely varying in ethnic elements and ritual actions, their rites characteristically shared a content of biblical stories, a menorah, Hebrew heroes and the intent of endowing the newcomer with, as some orders' names suggest, "independent" and "improved" American status.[62] Landsmanshaftn "made [it] possible," *The Jewish Communal Register of New York City* declared, "for men from the same country and often from the same town, to meet together quite often, and created the opportunity of keeping up old friendships and of facilitating the creation of new valuable relations."[63] In the process, these societies helped to produce an American commitment to Jewishness that both included and transcended loyalties to country of origin, language, and religion.

Fraternal rituals responded to different needs and desires for America's Jewish immigrants than for native-born Masons.[64] Newcomers arriving from distant lands were confronted with finding a way to both maintain their Old World loyalties and adapt to American society. The initiation rites of the immigrant orders in particular worked to create new understandings of ethnic and religious identities that would aid this pursuit. In one respect, the attraction of Jews to fraternal orders represented their desire to acculturate to their American surroundings. Participation in the ritual life of the orders marked a change in status from foreign immigrant to equal citizen in the newly formed community of Jewish Americans. As the Yiddish Writers' Group reported, "To a vast number of Jews the lodge symbolized some higher conception, and joining one was considered a step forward in the direction of true Americanism. It taught its members English and parliamentary tactics of which they previously had no idea."[65] Yet in another respect, the immigrant orders allowed newcomers to resist the pressures of assimilation by retaining their language and particular culture. Rather than native-born members inducting immigrants into the American values of fraternal life, a common European American Masonic experience, their countrymen conducted immigrants' rituals of initiation in the ethnic orders. Surrounded by friends from the old country and speaking in their native tongue, "immigrants reassured themselves that they could remain faithful to received ethnic and religious traditions and, at the same time, take part in a distinctively American cultural form."[66]

That the primary purpose of immigrant fraternal initiation rites was to provide a bridge to American status is underscored by their decline after the first generation had settled into American society. Within twenty years of the founding of B'nai B'rith, discussions commenced concerning the length and dramatic tone of its rites that resulted in the elimination of successive degrees and most of the costumes and theatricality by the 1890s. The order's affluent, assimilated German Jewish members no longer needed the involved rites of passage for which the original ceremonies were intended. The flamboyant rituals of most Jewish orders were obsolete by the 1930s. The settlements of eastern European Jews in America were beyond the first generation by then and, following World War I and the passage of new restrictive laws on immigration, the waves of newcomers seeking assistance in their transition into American society dramatically diminished. "Not that all the dualities inherent in ethnic identity had been reconciled," Daniel Soyer notes, "but the former immigrants no longer faced quite the same crisis of identity as they had earlier."[67]

CATHOLICS AND FREEMASONRY

In contrast to Jews, who first entered the fraternity in its modern incarnation, often in the face of opposition, all of the original members of operative Freemasonry were Catholics. It began as a medieval craft guild of practicing stoneworkers who annually celebrated a mass on the Feast of the Four Crowned Martyrs. This day commemorated the courage of four Roman stoneworkers whom Diocletian sentenced to death for refusing to repudiate Christianity.[68] One of the confraternity's earliest charges read, "That you shall bee true to man to God and holy church, and that you use no heresie or error by your understanding or by teachings of indiscreet men."[69] Following the creation of the speculative fraternity, Catholics remained prominent among its membership.

Within two decades of the 1717 establishment of the modern fraternity, men of Catholic backgrounds founded lodges in France (1721), Ireland (1725), and Italy (1733). As recently as 1772, Lord Petrie, regarded as the leader of the Roman Catholic community in England, was chosen as the grand master of the premier London Grand Lodge.[70]

Beginning with Pope Clement XII's 1738 encyclical *In Eminenti*, however, and extending through 1902, the Catholic Church issued more than a dozen warnings that threatened Catholic Freemasons who did not renounce the fraternity with excommunication. European political factors figured prominently in their motivation. The first two, those of Clement XII and Benedict XIV (1751), saw the order's secret oaths as binding the brotherhood to conspiratorial activity that threatened the overthrow of both civil government and the church. Benedict, moreover, warned that the apparent universalism of such societies caused "great injury" to the "sole verity" of Catholicism. Bishops and other prelates were directed to pursue and investigate these transgressors "as being most suspect of heresy." In Italy, many suspected of being Freemasons were arrested and placed in dungeons. Similar efforts to destroy the fraternity were implemented in Spain and Portugal. In 1745, Masonic assemblies were prohibited throughout Switzerland.[71]

In Ireland, England, and America, in contrast, some time passed before the papal warnings were enforced. In Ireland, nothing was published until after the suppression of the 1798 rebellion against British rule. Even then, papal condemnation of Freemasonry moved slowly through the dioceses, with more affluent Catholics persisting in their lodge adherence. One of the attractions of Freemasonry to Irish Catholics was that it provided refuge from the country's penal laws, which forbade equal relations between Catholics and Protestant. As recently as the mid-nineteenth century, one Irish Mason recalled, "there was hardly a Lodge in Dublin which had not an admixture of Roman Catholics."[72] In England, which had far fewer Catholics, the fraternity was aware of the church's potential condemnations, but there were no known reprisals.[73]

Following the American Revolution, the small, relatively wealthy American Catholic community of primarily English, Irish, and French immigrants moved rather freely in Anglo-American society and the Masonic lodges.[74] Bishop John Carroll of Baltimore was the only American bishop. His diocese covered the whole of the country and encompassed about thirty-five thousand Catholics. His brother Daniel was an active Mason, and Bishop Carroll apparently did not enforce the papal ban for some time after 1800. In 1794, he discussed the papal letters on

Freemasonry with a layman, ending with this statement: "I do not pretend that these decrees are received generally by the Church, or have full authority in this diocese."[75] When the bishop's Americanizing church inaugurated the election of parish boards, Saint Mary's Church in Albany, New York chose its most prominent laymen to serve, all of whom were members of the local Masonic lodge. When the new Saint Mary's Church was built in 1797, these men participated in the Masonic ceremony of laying its cornerstone.[76]

The relationship between the American Catholic Church and Freemasonry changed in the following century. Beginning in the 1820s and peaking in the 1840s, a rush of more than a million poor and unskilled Irish Catholics arrived in the seaboard cities of the East Coast. Along with subsequent waves of German and Italian Catholics, they transformed the character of American Catholicism while facing the economic, social, and cultural difficulties of assimilation into American society. With its hierarchical governance, obedience to Rome, and identification with millions of strange immigrants, the Catholic Church was at odds with the new cultural ideals of popular democracy and individual autonomy that nineteenth-century Protestant America embraced. Though also accused, during the Morgan affair, of autocratic control and group coercion, by the 1840s a chastened Freemasonry was willing to align itself with Protestant efforts to target the American Catholic Church as a threat to the emerging society. Moreover, beginning in 1821, a new and more widely enforced series of papal attacks on the brotherhood helped to turn the tide of fraternal sentiment against the authoritarian hand of the church hierarchy and its attendant "Jesuitical" orders. In 1831, Bishop Francis Kenrick of Philadelphia angered the fraternity by refusing to admit a procession of Masons to their brother's Catholic funeral.[77] In the 1850s, American Catholic Masons reported being excommunicated by their "blindly superstitious Catholic brethren."[78]

Within the larger anti-Catholic, nativist impulses of the nineteenth century, Freemasonry's opposition to papal attacks struggled with its commitment to universalism. Though its universalism discouraged the fraternity from excluding Catholics, Masons joined with others in forming nativist societies, such as the American Protective Association, to attack Rome and its immigrants.[79] Moreover, the brotherhood had an unknown number of baptized but no longer practicing Catholics, for whom excommunication was "of little consequence." One said, "If I do right and live as a true and faithful Mason should do, I am sure all will be well in the end, and I shall finally receive the approbation of the great

Master in heaven." While damning the "intolerance of the Roman church," some in the fraternity applauded these "sincere and honest-hearted" Catholic brothers for withstanding papal censure.[80] Others complained that "bigoted" Jesuit priests preyed on Catholic Masons, extracting renunciations of Freemasonry from them at the moment of their death. This led some in the fraternity to conclude that "however honest and sincere in his present intentions," the Catholic Mason "is not a free agent. He belongs to the priests."[81] While both tolerant universalists and staunch anti-Catholics could be found in the American fraternity, and most brothers were willing to stand up for their own, American Masonry as a whole could be characterized as having a negative view of the institutional Catholic Church by the late nineteenth century.[82]

This situation worsened in 1884 with the publication of Pope Leo XIII's encyclical *Humanum Genus*. Whereas earlier papal letters were directed against European Masons' involvement with such political conspirators as the French Illuminati and the Italian Carbonari, *Humanum Genus* also addressed the failings of the worldwide brotherhood, the majority of whom were American. Leo especially singled out for criticism Freemasonry's belief that all true religions could be understood by "human intelligence" alone, from which the fraternity had decided, along with nearly all Americans, that "states ought to be constituted without any regard to the laws and precepts of the Church." In support of this central accusation, the pope adduced and attacked the "naturalist" view of marriage as a civil contract, education without Catholic religious instruction, and the freedom to choose "whatever [beliefs one] may prefer."[83]

Infuriated by these charges, Albert Pike, the sovereign grand commander of the Scottish Rite's Southern Jurisdiction, publicly replied that "under the guise of the condemnation of Freemasonry," the pope's letter was nothing less than a "declaration of war . . . against the separation of Church and State."[84] He had a point. Aside from resurrecting the older attack on Freemasonry for harboring a conspiracy against the church and civil society, *Humanum Genus* blamed the order for widely accepted American beliefs and practices. Though the reasons for Leo's attack had more to do with his views on the evils of modern society (his recent papal letters had denounced communism, civil marriage, and secular government) than the particular transgressions of Freemasonry, its effect was to further alienate the American fraternity from the Catholic Church. The statements and actions of American bishops further exacerbated the situation. In the year the bull was issued, for example, the Richmond, Virginia, bishop John McGill attacked the purportedly clandestine business practices of lodge members for effectively placing a "sword at the entrance of all avenues of trade."[85] Within a decade, on Rome's authority, the archbishop of Cincinnati proclaimed that members of secret societies "must not be admitted to the Sacraments."[86]

Despite the papal ban, the fraternal organizational culture of the late nineteenth century attracted Catholics no less than others. Irish, German, Italian, and other ethnic Catholics could be found among the Masons, the Odd Fellows, the Knights of Pythias, and other mainstream orders. More made their way into a variety of trade unions with secret ceremonies. One of the most significant of these, the Knights of Labor, was led by Grand Master Workman Terrance Powderly, himself a Catholic, who sought to modify the Knights' ritual to make it more acceptable to Catholic sensibilities.[87] Some ethnic orders used the ceremonial medium to affirm their ethnicity and purpose, such as the Clan na Gael's dedication to liberating Ireland from English rule. Many more newcomers organized ethnic and hometown mutual aid societies that adopted the trappings of fraternal rites while maintaining their loyalty to the Catholic Church.

THE KNIGHTS OF COLUMBUS

Partly in response to papal condemnations of Freemasonry and partly as an act of self-determination, in 1882 a young Irish priest named Michael McGivney convened a group in New Haven, Connecticut, that later became the Knights of Columbus. By the 1880s, the city's Irish residents had formed a gaggle of ethnic mutual benefit societies to provide some communal and economic security to recent immigrants. Many of the upwardly mobile young Irish were members of the Red Knights, formed in 1874 and believed to be an avenue for social and economic advancement. Most of the founding members of the Knights of Columbus had been members of the Red Knights. That organization had failed, however, for lack of a strong insurance program. The Knights of Columbus not only remedied this economic flaw but, more importantly, emphasized loyalty to the new American society rather than ties to home countries.[88]

The Knights' embrace of Christopher Columbus affirmed the discovery of America as a Catholic event, appealing to immigrant Catholic men of all nationalities. Moreover, they promoted the church's ethnic pluralism and American Catholic culture as means of overcoming Old World antagonisms in their belief that "the American Catholic experience had a transforming effect upon Catholicism and upon American society."[89] As Knights inducted into the coveted Fourth Degree declared, "Proud in the olden days was the boast, 'I am a Roman Catholic'; prouder yet today is the boast, 'I am an American citizen'; but the proudest boast of all times is ours to make, 'I am an American Catholic citizen.'"[90] Nonetheless, the order faced opposition from some Catholic clergy and lay leaders: for instance, one prominent bishop charged that it merely imitated "all the forms and tomfoolery of the Masons and Odd Fellows." Instead, the Knights saw their movement as providing an alternative to the condemned secret societies in a battle for the allegiance of young Catholic men. Over the next century, their assertion of the social legitimacy and patriotic loyalty of Catholic immigrants contributed to the Knights' becoming the largest American Catholic fraternal order.[91]

The creation of the Knights of Columbus was yet another adaptation of the fraternal model to the needs of late nineteenth-century American men. Like the founders of B'nai B'rith, who took Freemasonry's universalism, democratic structure, and opportunities for internal advancement and employed them to form a pan-Jewish organization for the assimilation of Jews into American society, the Knights of Columbus appropriated the fraternal framework to foster ethnic pluralism and American ideals among Catholic immigrants. Each group, moreover, sought to retain and defend its particular identity in American society. Both eventually formed antidefamation organizations to defend themselves against prejudice. But whereas Freemasonry's rites bound its members to the fraternity and B'nai B'rith's ceremonials reinforced American Jewish identity, the Knights' rituals fostered an allegiance to the American Catholic Church. The order admitted only practicing Catholics to a society that was under the church's authority through the membership of a priest who served as its supreme chaplain.

Columbian manhood located men squarely in their parishes as supporters and defenders of their family, church, and community. In contrast to the mainstream American Masonic model, in which men stood somewhat apart from the contagious femininity of church and family, the Columbian ideal equated American manhood with a virtuous, virile faith that extended to family obligations. The Knights were to be chivalrous men who militantly opposed the strong anti-Catholicism of American society while sacrificing themselves for the greater social welfare of their coreligionists, a sacrifice that included having only modest economic ambitions, so as not to disrupt their familial or church obligations.[92] The

Knights of Columbus ideal of manhood thus brought together immigrant men's obligations as Catholics with the manliness expectations of Victorian society. Through this Columbian adaptation of the fraternal model, Amy Koehlinger has argued, "Catholic men could claim a manhood of middle-class American respectability without forfeiting their preexisting ethnic and religious identities."[93]

CHANGING GENDER RELATIONS

The Masons, B'nai B'rith, and the Knights of Columbus socialized all of their late nineteenth-century members to a middle-class Victorian world that encouraged the separation of men and women into male and female spheres, yet all of these men were embedded in webs of relationships that limited the time they spent with other men. Most fraternal members were husbands, fathers, and sons with extended connections of family and kin. Their ethnic backgrounds and denominational commitments also joined them to women. Together, these obligations and identities worked to shape their social experience. Moreover, by the turn of the century, men's and women's experiences were becoming more closely entwined.

At the end of the nineteenth century, changing social and economic conditions among the middle class provided the basis for new patterns of relationship between men and women. The rise of the corporation provided greater job security than mid-nineteenth-century entrepreneurs and independent professionals had experienced, allowing husbands to devote more attention to their families than had been expected of their fathers. At the same time, women increasingly left the home to go shopping, participate in clubs and reform activities, and pursue higher education. John Higham has argued that a "new woman," more assertive in social life and "masculine" in her pursuit of political power, made her appearance in the 1890s.[94] This growing incursion of women and men into each other's spheres encouraged a more companionate ideal of marriage. Rather than go out in the evenings with his buddies, a married man would now more frequently make his wife his evening companion. To a greater extent than their parents or grandparents had, men and women of this generation spent time with each other. Movement into the suburbs, where people founded and frequented various mixed athletic and social clubs that welcomed the whole family, also encouraged the greater participation of men in the lives of their wives and children. More open home designs in the suburbs, moreover, encouraged greater family interaction by replacing the upper-class Victorian study, parlor, and sitting room combination, which served to separate family members, with single living rooms, which brought them together. Though these changes had little immediate effect on most people's lives, they indicate the emergence of a new model for male and female interaction.[95]

Evidence of closer interactions of fraternal men with women can be seen in the emergence of women's auxiliaries, the invitation of women to lodge lectures and social occasions, and the appearance of family-oriented fraternal magazines. Like the women of the Masonic Order of the Eastern Star, the female relations of B'nai B'rith members sought to become more involved with the fraternity throughout the late nineteenth century, finally settling for an independent organization, B'nai B'rith Women, in 1897.[96] The Daughters of Isabella, the ladies' auxiliary of the Knights of Columbus, was also established in 1897 to participate in and support the mission of its male counterpart.[97] Though none of these auxiliaries was absorbed into its fraternal counterpart, all were active in the social life of the local male chapters.[98] As women joined fraternal life, fraternal men showed a new interest in family and home. In 1870, the Masons who published the *Voice of Masonry* periodical changed its name to the *Voice of Masonry and Family Magazine*. Beginning in the 1880s, B'nai B'rith's the *Menorah* occasionally added the subtitle *A Monthly for the Jewish Home*, while the *Columbiad*, published by the Knights of Columbus beginning in 1903, offered stories and articles that reflected family life.

Although the largely German, Reform-minded Jewish men of B'nai B'rith and the predominantly Irish, upwardly mobile Catholic men of the Knights of Columbus were the leading Americanizing edge of their ethnic communities, both groups were more closely identified with synagogues and parishes, respectively, than were native-born Masons with churches. Anthony D. Fels has found that in late nineteenth-century San Francisco the proportion of Jewish synagogue members among all Jews who joined the Masons (36 percent) was considerably higher than that of native-born Masons who joined Protestant churches (14 percent).[99] The emergence of the pan-Jewish B'nai B'rith and myriad hometown mutual benefit societies reinforced Jewish ethnic and religious separatism. Similarly, immigrant Catholics sought close ties to their countrymen in an effort to retain their ethnic and religious identities and respond to nativist attacks.

Thus it was that as the worlds of middle-class American fraternal men and their female relations became more closely entwined, gender relations among Jews and Catholics were more static, although more egalitarian in some ways, influenced by their outsider statuses in a culturally Protestant America and their respective immigrant cultures. Among Jewish immigrants, men identified with the fraternal organizations they formed, while women were engaged in the creation and nurturance of relations in the neighborhood, although less formally. The large waves of Jews who came to America in the early twentieth century brought clearly defined gender roles from the older, eastern European cultures of their origin. Men held positions of leadership in the family, synagogue, and community, and women maintained the home. On the other hand, "although their status was clearly inferior to men's," Paula E. Hyman has argued, "within the secular sphere women were given a great deal of autonomy in order to support their families and to provide social welfare through their own charitable associations."[100] Jewish women also maintained more of a presence than Protestant women in the predominantly male lodges, at times attending meetings, and some Jewish fraternal organizations, such as the Independent Order of B'rith Abraham, counted women as members. Further, Daniel Soyer has found that in 1917, a few (9 of 462) Jewish lodges had female presidents. While men were centrally involved in securing the insurance benefits of these societies for their families, women "contributed to the cultural and social lives of the individual landsmanshaftn and represented their members' interests to the men's societies."[101] The Americanization of these eastern European patterns can be seen among the most affluent Jewish women, who formed B'nai B'rith Women and synagogue sisterhoods by the end of the nineteenth century. These sisterhoods gave women greater access to synagogue life—and did not threaten male prerogatives—by allowing them to make such domestic contributions as providing meals.[102]

Among Irish Catholics, the ideal Knight of Columbus, who helped his wife at home, dedicated himself to church participation and defense, and refrained from obsessing over work so as not to interfere with his obligations to others, was complemented by the virtuous Catholic woman who accepted the Protestant cult of domesticity but centered her religious activities in the church and its many female devotional societies rather than the home.[103] Irish immigrants brought the effects of the late nineteenth-century "devotional revolution," which encouraged the development of parish-centered activities and held the married state as secondary to that of the priest or the nun, to America.[104] Like the separate religious sphere of middle-class Protestant women, devotionalism gave

Irish Catholic women a religious universe that endowed their role in the family with new meaning and authority. Unlike Protestant women's moral reform societies, however, those of Catholic women did not have an institutional base outside the church. While church-based fraternal orders such as the Knights of Columbus were providing growing numbers of men with the opportunity to assert their role as promoters and defenders of their faith, women's devotional societies encouraged a peculiarly Catholic affective bonding between believers and supernatural patrons (such as devotion to Mary and the saints) that remained within the confines of the church and under the supervision of its hierarchy.[105] In contrast with the Protestant separation of female churches from male lodges, Catholic men and women were divided within the arena of the church. As they moved into the middle class, moreover, the church hierarchy remanded Catholic women to the moral nurture of the family while asserting their moral superiority to improve the social world—much like the message conveyed to most Protestant women. Apparently, as Paula Kane has argued, the fear that Catholic women would be harmed by going into the world militated "against the development of a Catholic feminist awareness, and forestalled Catholic support for out-of-home careers for women."[106]

. . .

For Jewish and Catholic immigrants to America, the beliefs and ritualized initiatory practices of Freemasonry provided a means of assimilation into American society while allowing for the retention of their respective ethnic and religious identities. Through membership in the colonial brotherhood, prominent Jewish immigrants developed relationships that fostered their movement into American society. By the end of the nineteenth century, Reform-minded community leaders had risen to prominent positions throughout the American fraternity. Following the Revolution, members of America's small Catholic community were similarly accepted into the brotherhood, only to find their Masonic involvement challenged by a series of papal bans. Responding to the needs of their fellow immigrant countrymen, both Jews and Catholics created fraternal orders out of the Masonic framework. Like mainstream Freemasonry, the Americanizing Jewish order of B'nai B'rith and the Catholic Knights of Columbus sought to transcend boundaries. B'nai B'rith was the first American Jewish organization formed on the basis of a common Jewish ethnic identity. The Knights of Columbus was the first American Catholic organization founded on the basis of a common Catholic religious identity. Participation in their ritual life represented a change in status from foreign immigrant to American citizen. Yet by enabling the retention of ethnic (B'nai) or religious (Knights) identities, the new orders gave their members a basis for resisting the pressures of assimilation into native-born, Protestant America. By the early twentieth century, moreover, for better or worse, European practices in these minority communities moderated the effects on their members of changing gender relations in American society.

Epilogue

Like many American voluntary societies, Freemasonry expanded and then contracted in the twentieth century. Between 1900 and 1930, Masonic membership grew from about 850,000 to 3.3 million.[1] The fraternity's new emphases on efficient business practices, community service, social auxiliaries, and a patriotic, middle-class Anglo-Saxon identity attracted many young men. In the Great Depression, however, membership plummeted by 25 percent. Between 1927, the membership peak, and 1997, it decreased 71 percent. This was part of a larger decline in chapter-based associations. Robert D. Putnam has demonstrated that between 1951 and 1997, the membership rate in thirty-two such national organizations dropped by 58 percent. Included in his sample are the Masons and other major fraternal orders, such as B'nai B'rith and the Knights of Columbus, as well as the Lions, the Kiwanis, the Rotary, and other major service clubs. Putnam convincingly interprets the overall decline in civic associations as a loss of vital "social capital" networks that hold society together and facilitate social interactions.[2] Long gone are the days when Americans regularly attended Parent-Teacher Association meetings and joined all manner of social and service organizations. We now live in a world where people are less involved in school and social organizations, distrust the government, and spend long, solitary hours before televisions and computers. Scholars who argue that the stability and vigor of democratic political institutions depend on voluntary associations have affirmed Putnam's findings.[3] Jürgen Habermas has described this decline as a "refeudalization" of the public sphere, where media manipulations controlled by elites have taken the place of citizens engaged in critical debates over the direction of their society.[4]

EXPANSION

In the early twentieth century, white middle-class Freemasonry grew rapidly by taking on the attributes of a modern service club. As an affable younger generation took over its leadership, they replaced an older elite who, in the nineteenth century, had created an intimate world of brotherhood in the fraternity, apart from the realms of work and feminine domesticity. Earlier in that century, lodges had met in public houses and counted no more than an average of forty members. By 1900, membership averaged as many as two hundred men, many of whom met in richly appointed buildings at the center of urban affairs.[5] This rapid membership growth and the development of larger, more impersonal lodges worked against the fulfillment of the brotherhood's communal aims. At the same time, the new, outward-looking fraternal leaders began to transform the society from a sacred asylum into a secular, modern organization. New life insurance initiatives encouraged modern business practices, new social auxiliaries challenged the fraternity's sense of honor and noble purpose, and self-improvement through ritual drama gave way to a "progressive" interest in community projects.

The new emphasis on life insurance responded to the economic insecurity that middle-class men experienced as a result of the industrialization of the late nineteenth century. Traditionally, Masonic benevolence was understood as encouraging members' love for one another rather than promising financial security. Though lodge officers occasionally gave monetary assistance to those in need, Masonic membership was not intended as a financial safety net. This perspective began to change with the midcentury Independent Order of Odd Fellows' legal agreement to financially support disadvantaged members. Affluent Masons saw this incentive for membership as undercutting the benevolent nature of brotherly love. Less affluent members, needing protection for their families, viewed the matter differently. When the Masons refused to guarantee such benefits, some members sought or created them elsewhere. The railroad mechanic and Mason John Jordan Upchurch, for example, founded the first major national mutual benefit society in 1868, the Ancient Order of United Workmen (AOUW), by including in its charter a life insurance plan with a death benefit of one thousand dollars, funded through a monthly assessment of one dollar per member.[6] Soon thereafter, other national life insurance fraternities sprang up, and older brotherhoods instituted new plans. Recruiting policyholders throughout the country, the salesmen for the insurance orders came to be known as fraternalists. Their success relied on denying fraternal membership to those in high-risk occupations, the aged, and the infirm, for fear that these men's policies would increase the cost of premiums for everyone in the order. By 1895, such mutual benefit fraternities provided half the total value of the nation's life insurance policies.[7] Though the Masons resisted this trend, as many as twenty local, state, and national organizations offering some form of unofficial "Masonic" insurance had grown up around the order by 1896.[8]

While modern business practices were taking hold in the fraternity, the young men now joining it were more interested in good times than somber rituals. One sign of this new focus was the acceptance of flamboyant social organizations with a Masonic structure. The Ancient Arabic Order of the Nobles of the Mystic Shrine (est. 1872), later known as the Shriners, saw recreational fun as its primary objective. The Shrine was popularly known as "the playground of the Masons," and its members created chorale groups, paraded on camels while dressed as "Arabs," went fishing and hunting together, and developed entertaining rituals laced with burlesque humor. Though these men were Masons who had completed either the York or the Scottish Rite degree sequence, the Shrine did not believe itself to be a Masonic society and so did not feel bound to embody Freemasonry's commitment to self-improvement and sober introspection. Its popularity prompted imitations, such as the Odd Fellows' Improved Order of Muscovites, which formed in 1894. Several other independent social organizations also sprang up. These included the Elks (est. 1867), the Moose (1888), the Eagles (1898), the Owls (1904), and the Orioles (1910), as well as the African American Improved Order of the Elks (1898), Improved Order of Owls (1911), and Improved Benevolent and Protective Order of Moose (1922).[9] The new emphasis on fun and games was in stark contrast to Gilded Age Masonry's solemn embrace of rituals and symbols and ushered in an outward-facing, glad-handing social style that came to characterize the twentieth-century fraternity.

A new, progressive focus on social reform also undercut Freemasonry's self-improvement mission. In the early 1900s, good citizenship became the measure of respectability. Instead of the individual Mason's possession of moral virtues, lodges now stressed an ethic of service, marked by practical community involvement. Despite this shift in emphasis, new organizations, built to express the new ideals of efficiency, altruism, and social improvement, emerged and grew rapidly, eclipsing the Masons as the century progressed. Foregrounding business instead of recreation, the Lions, the Kiwanis, the Rotary, and other new service clubs aspired to make practical social improvements. Instead of secrecy, they offered businessmen and professionals presentations on important issues, business contacts, and opportunities for altruism. Their members met in public hotels and restaurants rather than private lodges, wore business suits rather than fraternal costumes, and participated in comedy skits and choruses rather than solemn rituals. Meeting for luncheons, they left the evenings free for social time with their wives and other couples.

Emphasizing civic progress over self-improvement, these service clubs saw themselves as progressing beyond the Victorian ritualism of the Masonic lodges. Critics within Freemasonry also questioned its disregard for the new interest in social activities and the need for lengthy rituals that dwelled on eternal moral truths. By the early twentieth century, the fraternity's celebrated lectures on the arts and sciences seemed out of place in a modern, scientific era populated by college- and university-educated men and women. At the same time, the theater and motion pictures had eclipsed the lodge as purveyors of dramatic entertainment.[10] Modern young men and women interacted much more than those of their parents' generation, in the new social settings of dance halls, nightclubs, and sporting events. Some Masons complained that the order's cavernous, gender-segregated urban lodges, repetitive, boring rituals, peculiar costumes, and time-consuming meetings were making it obsolete. By the late 1920s, the new service clubs were in ascendance, while those fraternities for which ritualism remained an integral component were in decline.[11]

Amid these changes, large-scale European immigration resulted in a more forceful assertion of the brotherhood's Anglo-Saxon American identity against what many members tacitly believed were lesser minorities. In the First World War, Masonic lodges encouraged a fervid faith in America (understood as middle-class Anglo-Saxon Protestant America) with patriotic parades, military clubs for Masonic servicemen, and fund raising to support the war effort. American flags appeared in lodge rooms. Following the war, lodge efforts advocating "100 percent Americanism" coalesced around support for a public education system that would mold the "lower reaches" of humanity, especially blacks, Jews, and Catholics, into embodiments of the moral character and patriotism of the Protestant middle class. Though racism, anti-Semitism, and anti-Catholicism were not written into Masonic policy, membership became more exclusively Anglo-Saxon in the 1920s. While the fraternity continued to embrace the ideal of universal brotherhood, a growing body of evidence was witness to some brothers' prejudices.[12]

Although lodge leaders forcefully denounced the violent racism and anti-Catholicism of the Ku Klux Klan, a substantial number of rank and file Masons appear to have joined it. The movement's founder, William Joseph Simmons, was a member of several fraternal groups, including the Masons.[13] Klan advertisements for members included the statement "Masons preferred." In the early 1920s, a reporter for the Minneapolis *Daily Star* stated that most of the Klansmen in that city were Masons.[14] One Klansman claimed that more than half of Oregon's Klansmen were Masons.[15] New York's Grand Lodge master bitterly denied the claim of one Mason and Klan recruiter that 75 percent of his state's Klansmen were Masons.[16] Though the number of Masons who joined the Ku Klux Klan is not known and their influence on local lodges varied by region, the fact that several grand masters spoke out against this racist organization suggests that its infiltration of the fraternity was a matter of considerable concern. The order's support of Americanism fell far short of the Klan's hatred of—not to mention violence against—minorities, but Lynn Dumenil has pointed out that "in the 1920s both organizations shared some of the same goals."[17] Both called for a return to a homogeneous America where everyone conformed to the values of the native-born Anglo-Saxon Protestant middle class.

Prince Hall Masons faced the deteriorating racial situation in the early twentieth century from a different angle. During Reconstruction, members of this African American fraternity were active in the Freedmen's Bureau and the National Colored Labor Union.[18] After Reconstruction, a flowering of its lodges in Northern cities accompanied the black migration from the South toward factory work in such places as Chicago, Detroit, Pittsburgh, and New York. Between 1904 and 1955, membership in Prince Hall Freemasonry increased from forty-six thousand to well over three hundred thousand men.[19] Racial tensions also heightened in this period. Prince Hall Grand Lodges and members responded with key support for the creation, in 1909, of the National Association for the Advancement of Colored People and for federal antilynching laws. Faced with violent, political racism, especially in the South, black Masonic lodges joined African American churches and

NAACP chapters in voting rights campaigns. In the early 1950s, the Prince Hall Masons Legal Research Fund was established in the NAACP. In 1958, Thurgood Marshall, the lead attorney for the NAACP and a Freemason, proclaimed that "whenever and wherever I needed money and did not know any place to get it, Prince Hall Masons never let me down."[20] The story of the Prince Hall Masons in the civil rights movement has yet to be told.

Despite these efforts, Prince Hall Freemasonry declined relative to America's black population as the twentieth century progressed. During Reconstruction, the lodge and the church stood together as the two most prominent social institutions in the ongoing organization of African American life. As the black population grew and expanded to Northern cities, the number of civic groups, professional societies, charities, and social clubs mushroomed in the black community, diminishing the fraternity's influence. Despite its lessening attraction, Prince Hall Freemasonry included the famed social reformers Booker T. Washington and W.E.B. DuBois at the end of the nineteenth century and later provided a retreat for Duke Ellington, Count Basie, and other cultural pioneers. After the Second World War, prominent members of the black community joined the fraternity, including the civil rights leaders Medgar Evers, Benjamin Hooks, and Andrew Young and the politicians Tom Bradley, Charles Rangel, and Carl Stokes. In 1989, amid the continuing membership losses of both white and black Masonry, the Grand Lodge of Connecticut and the Prince Hall Grand Lodge of Connecticut recognized each other, reversing the long-standing refusal of white lodges to accept the legitimacy of the Prince Hall Masons. Despite its reduced status, the black fraternity continues to be involved in community and mutual aid projects and the promotion of positive images of African Americans.[21]

Like the Prince Hall Masons, the Jewish B'nai B'rith and the Catholic Knights of Columbus responded to the heated prejudice of this period according to their circumstances. Both formed antidefamation societies in the second decade of the twentieth century while continuing to assert their American identities. In 1913, the Anti-Defamation League was founded to defend Jews against anti-Semitism and unify their claims to their full rights as American citizens.[22] The Knights of Columbus formed its Commission on Religious Prejudices in 1914 to combat accusations that bigoted, superstitious, Rome-directed Catholics were taking over city governments, subverting public education, and threatening American democracy.[23] Matters became more complicated in 1919 with the

appearance of "The Protocols of the Elders of Zion." This widely circulated forgery accused the fictitious title group of controlling and manip-
ulating Freemasonry, the Catholic Church, and communism toward
evil ends.[24] Around the same time, another forgery, a spurious fourth
degree oath that pledged the Knights of Columbus's loyalty to Rome,
contributed to the general paranoia about immigrant groups.[25] In both
instances, the Jewish and Catholic brotherhoods defended themselves
while Protestant Masons asserted their patriotism by publishing books
and pamphlets that ignored these conflicts and instead celebrated
George Washington and other American Masonic heroes.

DECLINE

Though aware of their falling numbers, Freemasons exacerbated the
situation by ignoring the divisive social tumult of the 1960s, the failures
of Vietnam, the impeachment of President Richard Nixon, and other
troubles. If Masonic publications are any measure of what has been on
the brotherhood's mind, then they are most interested in the celebration
of George Washington and other famous Masons from revolutionary
days, when the fraternity's symbols and reach across ethnic and denominational lines helped a nascent United States create a national identity.
Beyond these patriotic interests, Masonic periodicals devote their pages
to lodge celebrations, charitable activities, and the many meanings of
the craft's symbolism and history. Dominated by internal interests, they
rarely offer commentary on contemporary affairs.

Counter to Masonic tradition, the fraternity aggressively marketed
itself in an effort to attract new members in the 1980s. Nevertheless, by
2000, its aging, dwindling membership was apparent in its now ill-kept
and largely vacant buildings yet standing near the centers of towns and
cities. The old guard still came to the lodge and supported Masonic
charities, but their sons stayed away. Today, aside from the occasional
flare-up resulting from a mystery best-seller or a loose-cannon attack by
religious antagonists, the fraternity has faded from public view. "Most
Americans," the Masonic historian Mark Tabbert observes, "have little
knowledge of Freemasonry, and some consider it nothing more than a
quaint family tradition."[26]

Yet in the midst of this decline, there are some signs of revival. In
recent years, a new generation of Internet-savvy young men has joined
the fraternity. Attracted by effective websites that encourage curiosity
about the brotherhood, these "millennial Masons" share with their

older brothers a desire to be part of something larger than themselves. In California in particular, amid an average annual membership decline of 3.5 percent between 2002 and 2011,[27] the average Masonic age has dropped from seventy-one to sixty-five and new lodges have formed. The average age of the active brothers at the fastest-growing of these, Santa Monica–Palisades Lodge No. 307, is thirty-three. One journalist reported the professions of its members as ranging from lawyer and judge to scrap iron shop owner, proprietor of a hip clothing boutique, and Hollywood actor. The incoming master, Zulu, a thirty-nine-year-old African American tattoo artist, said that he became aware of the lodge after inscribing Masonic symbols on several young men and decided to join "because I was looking for people to hang with that were like-minded but also hip and cool." "'Star Trek' without the chicks" is how Jim Warren, the lodge's senior deacon, describes its diversity. "We have every possible national origin, ethnicity and religious denomination you could imagine."[28] Another new lodge, Panamericana Lodge No. 849 in Granada Hills, appeals especially to young men who "come from foreign countries" in Latin America. The Internet has spurred growth in both. Zulu reports that he receives as many as four e-mail inquiries a week. Allan Benavides of Panamericana says that "without the Web site, I would not have joined." The California Grand Lodge has also embraced new technology. Lodge leaders now have access to a monthly e-newsletter, and members can participate in monthly informational webinars. Freemasons.org, a California product, recently received a national award for design excellence. In 2009, as the Internet entered more deeply into lodge life, California Masons reported that their annual number of degrees conferred was the greatest since 1978, their annual fund contributions were the highest since 1987, and the Grand Lodge's online magazine, the *California Mason*, had increased production from four to six issues annually.[29] Observing these trends, the respected historian of Freemasonry Margaret C. Jacob has suggested that the order "may be making a comeback."[30]

Since 2001, the Masonic Restoration Foundation has facilitated this growth. Working within existing Masonic structures, it is alert to the needs of young men who "perceive Freemasonry as a venue for truth-seeking, a vehicle for self-improvement and spiritual development, a quest for maturity in masculinity, and the discovery of one's inner potential." In contrast to late twentieth-century trends that resulted in laxness in Masonic practices, the MRF has proposed downsizing lodge membership, raising standards, and paying greater attention to ritual. Lodges that comply with this restoration of traditional practices are designated Traditional Observance Lodges. They are to be small enough so that members can "closely know each other." Brothers are expected to grow intellectually and spiritually. Ceremonies are to be "conducted with the utmost reverence and solemnity." "Sufficient time" is to be set aside between degree rituals for a candidate to "enhance his self-transformation" through contemplation and study. Lodge officers must be elected "solely on their merit" and be well versed in lodge traditions and teachings.[31] In contrast to recent practices, "the 'work' of a Traditional Observance lodge is not to review minutes or bills, or plan social or philanthropic activities, but rather to create an atmosphere where the members can learn the lessons of Freemasonry and how they can be inculcated into their daily lives."[32] In 2012, there were more than forty-five Traditional Observance Lodges in states throughout the country, with the largest numbers of new brothers in California, Colorado, and Virginia.[33]

Whether or not this revival is successful, it underscores the fraternity's ability to reinvent itself throughout American history. Born in London amid a new social and religious order, the English Freemasonry that came to America in the mid-1700s carried a variety of cultural elements that were employed, augmented, and transformed in its journey through American culture. As a widely available resource for organizing collective ideology and social relations, the history of Freemasonry in American culture helps us to better understand the American religious past.

Notes

INTRODUCTION

1. Anthony Ashley Cooper, third Earl of Shaftesbury, treatise 2, "*Sensus communis:* An Essay on the Freedom of Wit and Humour—in a Letter to a Friend," in his *Characteristics of Men, Manners, Opinions, Times* (London, 1711), 64–122.

2. Anthony Ashley Cooper, third Earl of Shaftesbury, "Inquiry Concerning Virtue," in *British Moralists, 1650–1800*, vol. 1, ed. D.D. Raphael (Indianapolis: Hackett, 1991), 6–63.

3. James Anderson, *The Constitutions of the Free-Masons* (1723), reprint of Anderson's book by Benjamin Franklin (1734; repr., Bloomington, IL: Masonic Book Club, 1971), 54. Hereafter cited as *Constitutions*.

4. *Constitutions*, 48.

5. On the uses of secrecy, see Margaret C. Jacob, *The Radical Enlightenment: Pantheists, Freemasons, and Republicans* (London: Allen and Unwin, 1981).

6. *Constitutions*, 48.

7. Sydney Ahlstrom, *A Religious History of the American People*, 2 vols. (New Haven, CT: Yale University Press, 1972), 1:669 n. 1.

8. Jonathan Z. Smith, "Religion, Religions, Religious," in *Critical Terms for Religious Studies*, ed. Mark C. Taylor (Chicago: University of Chicago Press, 1998), 281–82.

9. See Tisa Wenger, *We Have a Religion: The 1920s Pueblo Dance Controversy and American Religious Freedom* (Chapel Hill: University of North Carolina Press, 2009); Richard King, *Orientalism and Religion: Postcolonial Theory, India and "the Mystic East"* (New York: Routledge, 1999); Donald S. Lopez, *Prisoners of Shangri-La: Tibetan Buddhism and the West* (Chicago: University of Chicago Press, 1998); David Chidester, *Savage Systems: Colonialism*

and Comparative Religion in Southern Africa (Charlottesville: University Press of Virginia, 1996).

10. On what is at stake in definitions of *religion*, see especially Timothy Fitzgerald, *The Ideology of Religious Studies* (Oxford: Oxford University, 2000); Russell T. McCutcheon, *Manufacturing Religion: The Discourse on Sui Generis Religion and the Politics of Nostalgia* (New York: Oxford University Press, 1997); Talal Asad, *Genealogies of Religion: Discipline and Reasons of Power in Christianity and Islam* (Baltimore: Johns Hopkins University Press, 1993).

11. This definition originates in Emile Durkheim's understanding of religion as adapted and applied by Robert N. Bellah, Clifford Geertz, David Chidester, and many others. See Durkheim, *The Elementary Forms of Religious Life* (London: George Allen and Unwin, 1915); Bellah, *Beyond Belief: Essays on Religion in a Post-traditional World* (San Francisco: Harper and Row, 1970); Geertz, *The Interpretation of Cultures* (New York: Basic Books, 1973); Chidester, *Authentic Fakes: Religion and American Popular Culture* (Berkeley: University of California Press, 2005).

12. See David D. Hall, *Worlds of Wonder, Days of Judgment: Popular Religious Belief in Early New England* (New York: Knopf, 1989); Jon Butler, *Awash in a Sea of Faith: Christianizing the American People* (Cambridge, MA: Harvard University Press, 1990), 67–97.

13. W. Clark Gilpin, "Recent Studies of American Protestant Primitivism," *Religious Studies Review* 19, no. 3 (July 1993): 231–35.

14. John L. Brooke, *The Refiner's Fire: The Making of Mormon Cosmology, 1644–1844* (Cambridge: Cambridge University Press, 1994).

15. See Laurie Maffly-Kipp, *Setting Down the Sacred Past: African-American Race Histories* (Cambridge, MA: Harvard University Press, 2010); Patrick N. Minges, *Slavery in the Cherokee Nation: The Keetoowah Society and the Defining of a People, 1855–1867* (New York: Routledge, 2003); Jonathan D. Sarna, *Jacksonian Jew: The Two Worlds of Mordecai Noah* (New York: Holmes and Meier, 1981); T. J. Jackson Lears, *No Place of Grace: Antimodernism and the Transformation of American Culture, 1880–1920* (Chicago: University of Chicago Press, 1981).

16. On Protestantism and the early republic, see Nathan O. Hatch, *The Democratization of Christianity* (New Haven, CT: Yale University Press, 1989); Butler, *Awash in a Sea of Faith*, 194–288.

17. For a discussion of this scholarship, see Linda K. Kerber, Nancy F. Cott, Robert Gross, Lynn Hunt, Carroll Smith-Rosenberg, and Christine Stansell, "Beyond Roles, Beyond Spheres: Thinking about Gender in the Early Republic," *William and Mary Quarterly* 46 (July 1989): 565–85.

18. Mark C. Carnes, *Secret Ritual and Manhood in Victorian America* (New Haven, CT: Yale University Press, 1989).

19. On African Americans and class, see William A. Muraskin, *Middle-Class Blacks in a White Society* (Berkeley: University of California Press, 1975); Loretta J. Williams, *Black Freemasonry and Middle-Class Realities* (Columbia: University of Missouri Press, 1980). On black masculinity, see Martin Summers, *Masculinity and Its Discontents: The Black Middle Class and the Transformation of Masculinity, 1900–1930* (Chapel Hill: University of North

Carolina Press, 2004); Maurice Wallace, *Constructing the Black Masculine: Identity and Ideality in African American Men's Literature, 1775–1995* (Durham, NC: Duke University Press, 2002). On civil society, see Corey D.B. Walker, *A Noble Fight: African American Freemasonry and the Struggle for Democracy in America* (Urbana: University of Illinois Press, 2008); Stephen Kantrowitz, "'Intended for the Better Government of Man': The Political History of African American Freemasonry in the Era of Emancipation," *Journal of American History* 96, no. 4 (March 2010): 1001–26.

20. For a discussion of this approach, see Rachel Wheeler, *To Live upon Hope: Mohicans and Missionaries in the Eighteenth-Century Northeast* (Ithaca, NY: Cornell University Press, 2008), 10.

21. Jürgen Habermas, *The Structural Transformation of the Public Sphere: An Inquiry into a Category of Bourgeois Society*, trans. Thomas Burger, with the assistance of Frederick Lawrence, from the 1962 German original (Cambridge, MA: MIT Press, 1989), 14–67. See also Craig Calhoun, "Reflections on the Public Sphere," in *Habermas and the Public Sphere*, ed. Calhoun (Cambridge, MA: MIT Press, 1992), 1–42.

22. David Shields, *Civil Tongues and Polite Letters in British America* (Chapel Hill: University of North Carolina Press, 1997), xix–xx.

23. Since the introduction of Habermas's "public sphere" in German in 1962, and especially since its translation into English in 1989, the formulation has undergone considerable refinement as a result of its interaction with the historical realities of American society. Some historians have argued that forms of discourse other than rational debate, such as satire, poetry, and plays, or the visual vocabulary of parades, festivals, and protests shaped the ideologies of the public sphere. Others have pointed to the political motives of a coalescing white male upper class while convincingly arguing for the presence of growing female, African American, underclass, and other groups in an expanded arena that contended with and complemented Habermas's decidedly male and elite public sphere. Moreover, where Habermas saw a decline of the public sphere in the mid-to-late nineteenth century, some have seen the vibrant emergence of multiple alternative race, class, and gender "counterpublics" that challenged the authority of affluent gentlemen. Significant scholarship in this expanding literature includes Nancy Fraser, "Rethinking the Public Sphere: A Contribution to the Critique of Actually Existing Democracy," Mary Ryan, "Gender and Public Access: Women's Politics in Nineteenth-Century America," and Geoff Eley, "Nations, Publics, and Political Cultures: Placing Habermas in the Nineteenth Century," in Calhoun, *Habermas and the Public Sphere*, 109–142, 259–339; Shields, *Civil Tongues and Polite Letters*; David Waldstreicher, *In the Midst of Perpetual Fetes: The Making of American Nationalism, 1776–1820* (Chapel Hill: University of North Carolina Press, 1997); Joanna Brooks, "The Early American Public Sphere and the Emergence of a Black Print Counterpublic," *William and Mary Quarterly*, 3rd ser., 62, no. 1 (January 2005): 67–92. Habermas has acknowledged these understandings of the public sphere, expanded beyond the narrow parameters of rational communication and the privileged participation of affluent gentlemen, while arguing that since the formal structures of communicative action do not change, deliberative politics still provides

232 I Notes to Pages 9–10

a dependable framework for authentically plural democracy. See his "Further Reflections on the Public Sphere," in Calhoun, *Habermas and the Public Sphere*, 421–61; *Between Facts and Norms: Contributions to a Discourse Theory of Law and Democracy*, trans. William Rehg (Cambridge, MA: Harvard University Press, 1996). For a discussion, see John L. Brooke, "On the Edges of the Public Sphere," *William and Mary Quarterly*, 3rd ser., 62, no. 1 (January 2005): 93–98.

24. For the interpretation of Anti-Masonry as paranoia, see David B. Davis, "Some Themes of Counter-Subversion: An Analysis of Anti-Masonic, Anti-Catholic and Anti-Mormon Literature," *Mississippi Valley Historical Review* 47 (1960): 205–24; Richard Hofstadter, *The Paranoid Style in American Politics* (New York: Knopf, 1965), 6; Seymour Martin Lipset and Earl Raab, *The Politics of Unreason: Right-Wing Extremism in America, 1790–1970* (New York: Harper and Row, 1970), 39–49.

25. For early social scientific explanations, see, among others, Rowland Berthoff, *An Unsettled People: Social Order and Disorder in American Society* (New York: Harper and Row, 1971), 272–74, 445, 447; Don H. Doyle, *The Social Order of a Frontier Community: Jacksonville, Illinois, 1825–70* (Urbana: University of Illinois Press, 1978), 178–93.

26. Albert Gallatin Mackey, *The History of Freemasonry in South Carolina, from Its Origins in the Year 1736 to the Present Time . . .* (Columbia: South Carolinian Steam Power Press, 1861; repr., Columbia: Walker, Evans and Cogswell, 1936); Mackey, Robert Ingham Clegg, and H. L. Haywood, *Encyclopedia of Freemasonry*, rev. ed. (London: Kessinger, 1946; first published 1905); Mackey, Clegg, and William James Hughan, *Mackey's History of Freemasonry* (New York: Masonic History, 1921); Edward T. Schultz, *History of Freemasonry in Maryland . . .* (Baltimore: J. H. Medairy, 1884); Charles T. McClenachan, *History of the Most Ancient and Honorable Fraternity of Free and Accepted Masons in New York . . .* (New York: Grand Lodge, 1888–94); Norris S. Barratt and Julius F. Sachse, *Freemasonry in Pennsylvania, 1727–1907* (Philadelphia: Grand Lodge of Pennsylvania, 1908); Sachse, *Old Masonic Lodges of Pennsylvania* (Philadelphia: Grand Lodge of Pennsylvania, 1912); Melvin Maynard Johnson, *The Beginnings of Freemasonry in America* (New York: George H. Doran, 1924); Jacob Hugo Tatsch, *Freemasonry in the Thirteen Colonies* (New York: Macoy Publishing and Masonic Supply, 1929).

27. Dudley Wright, ed., *Gould's History of Freemasonry throughout the World*, 6 vols. (New York: Charles Scribner's Sons, 1936); Douglas Knoop and G. P. Jones, *A Short History of Freemasonry to 1730* (Manchester, U.K.: Manchester University Press, 1940), *The Early Masonic Catechisms* (Manchester, U.K.: Manchester University Press, 1943), and *The Genesis of Freemasonry: An Account of the Rise and Development of Freemasonry in Its Operative, Accepted, and Early Speculative Phases* (Manchester, U.K.: Manchester University Press, 1947); David Stevenson, *The Origins of Freemasonry: Scotland's Century, 1590–1710* (Cambridge: Cambridge University Press, 1988).

28. Wayne A. Huss, *The Master Builders: A History of the Grand Lodge of Free and Accepted Masons of Pennsylvania* (Philadelphia: Grand Lodge, 1986);

Mark A. Tabbert, *American Freemasons: Three Centuries of Building Communities* (Lexington, MA: National Heritage Museum, 2005); R. William Weisberger, Wallace McLeod, and S. Brent Morris, eds., *Freemasonry on Both Sides of the Atlantic: Essays Concerning the Craft in the British Isles, Europe, the United States, and Mexico* (Boulder, CO: East European Monographs; New York: Columbia University Press, 2002); Arturo de Hoyos and Morris, eds., *Freemasonry in Context: History, Ritual and Controversy* (Lanham, MD: Lexington Books, 2004).

29. For further information, see the conference's website, http://ichfonline .org/.

30. Dorothy Anne Lipson, *Freemasonry in Federalist Connecticut, 1789–1835* (Princeton, NJ: Princeton University Press, 1977); Lynn Dumenil, *Freemasonry and American Culture, 1880–1930* (Princeton, NJ: Princeton University Press, 1984); Anthony D. Fels, "The Square and the Compass: San Francisco's Freemasons and American Religion, 1870–1900," (PhD diss., Stanford University, 1987); Mary Ann Clawson, *Constructing Brotherhood: Class, Gender, and Fraternalism* (Princeton, NJ: Princeton University Press, 1989); Mark C. Carnes, *Secret Ritual and Manhood in Victorian America* (New Haven, CT: Yale University Press, 1989).

31. Steven C. Bullock, *Revolutionary Brotherhood: Freemasonry and the Transformation of the American Social Order, 1730–1840* (Chapel Hill: University of North Carolina Press, 1996).

32. Theda Skocpol and Jennifer Lynn Oser, "Organization Despite Diversity: The Origins and Development of African American Fraternal Associations," *Social Science History* 28, no. 3 (Fall 2004): 367–437.

33. Nick Salvatore, *We All Got History: The Memory Books of Amos Webber* (New York: Times Books, 1996); Joanna Brooks, *American Lazarus: Religion and the Rise of African American and Native American Literatures* (New York: Oxford University Press, 2003), 115–50; Corey D.B. Walker, *A Noble Fight: African American Freemasonry and the Struggle for Democracy in America* (Urbana: University of Illinois Press, 2008); Stephen Kantrowitz, "'Intended for the Better Government of Man': The Political History of African American Freemasonry in the Era of Emancipation," *Journal of American History* 96, no. 4 (March 2010): 1001–26. See also Peter P. Hinks and Kantrowitz, eds., *All Men Free and Brethren: Essays on the History of African American Freemasonry* (Ithaca, NY: Cornell University Press, 2013).

34. Philip J. Deloria, *Playing Indian* (New Haven, CT: Yale University Press, 1998), 46–73; Joy Porter, *To Be Indian: The Life of Iroquois-Seneca Arthur Caswell Parker* (Norman: University of Oklahoma Press, 2001), 143–64; Porter, *Native American Freemasonry* (Lincoln: University of Nebraska Press, 2011); Minges, *Slavery in the Cherokee Nation*.

35. Daniel Soyer, *Jewish Associations and American Identity in New York, 1880–1939* (Cambridge, MA: Harvard University Press, 1997); Christopher J. Kauffman, *Faith and Fraternalism: The History of the Knights of Columbus*, rev. ed. (New York: Simon and Schuster, 1992).

36. See Robert D. Putnam, *Bowling Alone: The Collapse and Revival of American Community* (New York: Simon and Schuster, 2000).

1. COLONIAL FREEMASONRY AND POLITE SOCIETY, 1733–1776

1. *South Carolina Gazette*, December 28, 1738, reproduced in Albert Gallatin Mackey, *The History of Freemasonry in South Carolina, from Its Origins in the Year 1736 to the Present Time* ... (Columbia: South Carolinian Steam Power Press, 1861 ; repr., Columbia, Walter, Evans, and Cogswell, 1936), 15.

2. *New York Mercury*, December 31, 1753, reproduced in Jacob Hugo Tatsch, *Freemasonry in the Thirteen Colonies* (New York: Macoy Publishing and Masonic Supply, 1929), 66–67.

3. *Pennsylvania Gazette* (Philadelphia), June 20, 1755, reproduced in Grand Lodge of Pennsylvania, *Bi-centenary of the Birth of Right Worshipful Past Grand Master Brother Benjamin Franklin* (Philadelphia: Grand Lodge of Pennsylvania, 1906), 141–46. Descriptions of similar eighteenth-century Masonic processions can be found in the early lodge histories. See, for example, Edward T. Schultz, *History of Freemasonry in Maryland* ..., vol. 1 (Baltimore: J.H. Medairy, 1884); Mackey, *History of Freemasonry in South Carolina;* Melvin Maynard Johnson, *The Beginnings of Freemasonry in America* (New York: George H. Doran, 1924).

4. *South Carolina Gazette*, quoted in Tatsch, *Freemasonry in the Thirteen Colonies*, 86 (December 29, 1737), 89 (December 28, 1738). The latter also appears in Mackey, *History of Freemasonry in South Carolina*, 15.

5. James Anderson, *The Constitutions of the Free-Masons* (1723), reprint of Anderson's book by Benjamin Franklin (1734; repr., Bloomington, IL: Masonic Book Club, 1971), 68. Hereafter cited as *Constitutions* (1723).

6. T.O. Haunch, "The Formation, 1717–1751," in *Grand Lodge, 1717–1967*, (Oxford: United Grand Lodge of England, 1967), 80.

7. Peter Clark and Paul Slack, *English Towns in Transition, 1500–1700* (London: Oxford University Press, 1976), 131; E.P. Thompson, "Patrician Society, Plebeian Culture," *Journal of Social History* 7 (1973–74): 389. See also Steven C. Bullock, *Revolutionary Brotherhood: Freemasonry and the Transformation of the American Social Order, 1730–1840* (Chapel Hill: University of North Carolina Press, 1996), 55.

8. Gary Nash, "Social Development," in *Colonial British America: Essays in the New History of the Early Modern Era*, ed. Jack P. Greene and J.R. Pole (Baltimore: Johns Hopkins University Press, 1984), 247.

9. Jack P. Greene, *Pursuits of Happiness: The Social Development of Early Modern British Colonies and the Formation of American Culture* (Chapel Hill: University of North Carolina Press, 1988), 170–206. See also T.H. Breen, "'Baubles of Britain': The American and Consumer Revolutions of the Eighteenth Century," in *Of Consuming Interests: The Style of Life in the Eighteenth Century*, ed. Cary Carson, Ronald Hoffman, and Peter J. Albert (Charlottesville: University Press of Virginia, 1994), 444–82; Breen, "An Empire of Goods: The Anglicization of Colonial America, 1690–1776," *Journal of British Studies* 25, no. 4 (October 1986): 467–99; Breen, *The Marketplace of Revolution: How Consumer Politics Shaped American Independence* (New York: Oxford University Press, 2004).

10. John M. Murrin first investigated the concept of Anglicization in his dissertation's description of eighteenth-century institutional changes in Massa-

chusetts: "Anglicizing an American Colony: The Transformation of Provincial Massachusetts" (PhD diss., Yale University, 1966).

11. John Lane, *Masonic Records 1717–1894: Being the Lists of All the Lodges at Home and Abroad Warranted by the Four Grand Lodges and the United Grand Lodge of England*, 2nd ed. (London: Freemasons' Hall, 1895). Although this book focuses on the United States, Freemasonry was part of a larger world of cultural exchange between and among peoples connected by the Atlantic Ocean. As Jessica Harland-Jacobs has demonstrated, the fraternity's global network facilitated the growth and cohesion of the British Empire. Harland-Jacobs, *Builders of Empire: Freemasonry and British Imperialism, 1717–1927* (Chapel Hill: University of North Carolina Press, 2007).

12. This estimate is based on Martin Huss's statistics that show fifty as the average number of members in Pennsylvania's nineteen colonial lodges. Huss, *The Master Builders: A History of the Grand Lodge of Free and Accepted Masons of Pennsylvania*, vol. 1 (Philadelphia: Grand Lodge, 1986), 286, 291. In 1783, Saint John's Lodge in Boston suggested that the membership of a lodge not exceed forty, officers included. *History of St. John's Lodge of Boston* (Boston: privately printed, 1917), 69. The colonies had 1,462 churches in 1750. Edwin Scott Gaustad and Philip L. Barlow, *New Historical Atlas of Religion in America* (New York: Oxford University Press, 2001), 399. So in 1770 there was likely no more than one lodge for every fifteen churches.

13. Steven C. Bullock, "The Revolutionary Transformation of American Freemasonry, 1752–1792," *William and Mary Quarterly*, 3rd ser., 47, no. 3 (July 1990): 355–57. See also Bullock, *Revolutionary Brotherhood*, 59–63.

14. Richard Bushman, *The Refinement of America: Persons, Houses, Cities* (New York: Random House, 1992), 3–203.

15. David S. Shields, *Civil Tongues and Polite Letters in British America* (Chapel Hill: University of North Carolina Press, 1997), xiv–xxxi.

16. Douglas Knoop and G.P. Jones, *A Short History of Freemasonry to 1730* (Manchester, U.K.: Manchester University Press, 1940), 61–73.

17. Dudley Wright, ed., *Gould's History of Freemasonry throughout the World*, 6 vols. (New York: Charles Scribner's Sons, 1936), 1:262. *Enlightenment* meant different things to different people in England, from those most sympathetic to traditional religion to those who took a more rational, scientific approach. Beyond the "scientific" members of the Royal Society, English Freemasons had a variety of religious perspectives. For a discussion of religion and the English Enlightenment, see Peter Harrison, *"Religion" and the Religions in the English Enlightenment* (Cambridge: Cambridge University Press, 1990).

18. In their history of early Freemasonry in England, Knoop and Jones observe that the first mention of a mason's lodge occurs in a 1278 record of Vale Royal Abbey. Lodges probably existed much earlier, "for without them it is difficult to see how a church, abbey, castle of any size and pretension to ornament could have been erected" (*Short History*, 11–12).

19. The several possible meanings of *free* for Masons include references to freestone, a building material found in Scotland, and freedom from feudal serfdom. The term might also have referred to liberality (as in the seven liberal arts). See Wright, *Gould's History*, 1:249–58; David Stevenson, *The Origins of*

Freemasonry: Scotland's Century, 1590–1710 (Cambridge: Cambridge University Press, 1988), 11; Douglas Knoop and G. P. Jones, *The Genesis of Freemasonry: An Account of the Rise and Development of Freemasonry in Its Operative, Accepted, and Early Speculative Phases* (Manchester, U.K.: Manchester University Press, 1947), 10–15. For changing meanings of the term in later Freemasonry, see Bernard E. Jones, "'Free' in 'Freemason' and the Idea of Freedom through Six Centuries," in *The Collected Prestonian Lectures, 1925–1960*, ed. Harry Carr, vol. 1 (London: Lewis Masonic, 1983), 363–76.

20. Knoop and Jones, *Short History*, 23–26; Wright, *Gould's History*, 1:221–58. See also Henry Wilson Coil, *Freemasonry through Six Centuries*, vol. 1 (Richmond, VA: Macoy, 1967), 17–118.

21. Stevenson, *Origins of Freemasonry*, 43; Thomas Paine, "Origin of Freemasonry," in *The Life and Works of Thomas Paine*, ed. William M. Van der Weyde, 10 vols. (New Rochelle, NY: Thomas Paine National Historical Association, 1925), 9:179; Alex Horne, "The Saints John in the Masonic Tradition," *Ars Quatuor Coronatorum* 75 (1962): 76–123; Jacob Norton, "The Two Saints John Legends," *Ars Quatuor Coronatorum* 8 (1894): 135–36.

22. Knoop and Jones, *Short History*, 37.

23. Ibid., 2–38. Dating from the fifteen through the seventeenth centuries, more than one hundred of these Old Charges or Old Constitutions are known to exist. Though no two are alike, there is substantial agreement among them. Knoop and Jones review and compare their contents in *Genesis of Freemasonry*, 8–9, 62–86. See also "The Old Charges of British Freemasons," in Wright, *Gould's History*, 1:24–63.

24. This synopsis is taken from the seventeenth-century Buchanan MS. See Wright, *Gould's History*, 1:55–60. See also Stevenson, *Origins of Freemasonry*, 19–21.

25. See Harry Carr, "600 Years of Craft Ritual," *Ars Quatuor Coronatorum* 81 (1968): 153–205.

26. Stevenson, *Origins of Freemasonry*, 135–38; Douglas Knoop and G. P. Jones, *The Early Masonic Catechisms* (Manchester, U.K.: Manchester University Press, 1943).

27. For the derivation of the term *lodge*, see Knoop and Jones, *Genesis of Freemasonry*, 37–38.

28. Stevenson, *Origins of Freemasonry*, 149. See also Harry Carr, "An Examination of the Early Masonic Catechisms," series of articles in *Ars Quatuor Coronatorum* 83 (1970): 337–57; 84 (1971): 293–307; 85 (1972): 331–48.

29. Stevenson, *Origins of Freemasonry*, 136.

30. Ibid., 120. On the far-reaching religious effects of the Reformation, see Keith Thomas, *Religion and the Decline of Magic* (New York: Scribner, 1971), 88.

31. Stevenson, *Origins of Freemasonry*, 121–23. See also Michael Lynch, *Edinburgh and the Reformation* (Edinburgh: John Donald, 1981), 28–29; J. J. Scarisbrick, *The Reformation and the English People* (Oxford: Blackwell, 1984) 20–34; R. Lamond, "The Scottish Craft Guild as a Religious Fraternity," *Scottish Historical Review* 16 (1918–19): 191–211.

32. Secrecy itself may have been the motive, following Georg Simmel's belief that people value more the knowledge that is kept hidden. See Simmel, "The

Secret and the Secret Society," in *The Sociology of Georg Simmel*, ed. Kurt H. Wolff (New York: Free Press, 1950), 355–56.

33. John L. Brooke, *The Refiner's Fire: The Makings of Mormon Cosmology, 1644–1844* (New York: Cambridge University Press, 1994), 8–10, 18–19.

34. In the 1960s, Frances Yates, a historian of hermeticism and a biographer of Bruno, hypothesized the existence of this link between hermeticism and Freemasonry. Yates, *Giordano Bruno and the Hermetic Tradition* (Chicago: University of Chicago Press, 1964), 274. David Stevenson suggests this link came through Schaw's contact with Bruno. Stevenson, *Origins of Freemasonry*, 85.

35. Stevenson, *Origins of Freemasonry*, 22, 196–205.

36. Margaret C. Jacob, *The Radical Enlightenment: Pantheists, Freemasons, and Republicans* (London: Allen and Unwin, 1981), 116–17; Wright, *Gould's History*, 1:272, 334; Stevenson, *Origins of Freemasonry*, 219–23.

37. Knoop and Jones, *Genesis of Freemasonry*, 108–128.

38. Jacob, *Radical Enlightenment*, 114–15; Jacob, *The Origins of Freemasonry* (Philadelphia: University of Pennsylvania Press, 2006), 13–25.

39. Michael Spurr, "William Stukeley: Antiquarian and Freemason," *Ars Quatuor Coronatorum* 100 (1987): 113–30. Stukeley was one of the most important interpreters of Britain's Druidic heritage. See Stuart Piggott, *William Stukeley: An Eighteenth-Century Antiquary*, rev. ed. (New York: Thames and Hudson, 1985); Bullock, *Revolutionary Brotherhood*, 9–10, 18–19.

40. William Stukeley, *Memoirs of Sir Isaac Newton's Life*, ed. A. Hastings White (London: Taylor and Francis, 1936), viii, 4.

41. For discussions of Newton and ancient wisdom, see James Gleick, *Isaac Newton* (New York: Pantheon Books, 2003); John T. Young, "Isaac Newton's Alchemical Notes in the Royal Society," *Notes and Records of the Royal Society of London* 60, no. 1 (January 22, 2006): 25–34; Piyo Rattansi, "Newton and the Wisdom of the Ancients," in *Let Newton Be!*, ed. John Fauvel, Raymond Flood, Michael Shortland, and Robin Wilson (Oxford: Oxford University Press, 1988), 185–202.

42. Dan Edelstein, "Introduction to the Super-Enlightenment," and David Bates, "Super-epistemology," in *The Super-Enlightenment: Daring to Know Too Much*, ed. Edelstein (Oxford: Voltaire Foundation, 2010), 1–33, 53–74. On occult knowledge in the eighteenth century, see W.R. Ward, *Early Evangelicalism: A Global History, 1670–1789* (Cambridge: Cambridge University Press, 2006). On the persistence of occult practices within the American Enlightenment, see Herbert Leventhal, *In the Shadow of the Enlightenment: Occultism and Renaissance Science in Eighteenth-Century America* (New York: New York University Press, 1976). Investigating the broader arena from which Enlightenment thought emerged, Leigh Eric Schmidt has creatively explored how religious sounds and the controversies surrounding them were understood during and after the American Enlightenment. Schmidt, *Hearing Things: Religion, Illusion, and the American Enlightenment* (Cambridge, MA: Harvard University Press, 2000). Similarly, Ann Taves has insightfully described how modern thinkers came to understand involuntary religious experiences. Taves, *Fits, Trances, and Visions: Experiencing Religion and Explaining Experience from Wesley to James* (Princeton, NJ: Princeton University Press, 1999).

43. Samuel Smiles, *The Huguenots: Their Settlements, Churches, and Industries in England and Ireland* (London: Murray, 1867), 292–94; Jacob, *Radical Enlightenment*, 100–37.

44. Peter Clarke, *British Clubs and Societies 1580–1800: The Origins of an Associational World* (New York: Oxford University Press, 2000); Roy Porter, *English Society in the Eighteenth Century*, rev. ed. (New York: Penguin Books, 1990).

45. Thomas Hobbes, *Leviathan* (London: Andrew Cooke, 1651). For a discussion of these changes, see Keith Wrightson, *English Society, 1580–1680* (New Brunswick, NJ: Rutgers University Press, 1982).

46. David Zaret, *Origins of Democratic Culture: Printing, Petitions, and the Public Sphere in Early-Modern England* (Princeton, NJ: Princeton University Press, 2000).

47. Anthony Ashley Cooper, third Earl of Shaftesbury, *Characteristics of Men, Manners, Opinions, Times* (London, 1711). For a general discussion, see Stephen L. Darwall, *The British Moralists and the Internal "Ought," 1640–1740* (Cambridge: Cambridge University Press, 1995).

48. On ceremonial behavior in the royal court, see Norbert Elias, *The Court Society*, trans. Edmund Jephcott (Oxford: Blackwell, 1983).

49. Anthony Ashley Cooper, third Earl of Shaftesbury, treatise 2, "*Sensus communis:* An Essay on the Freedom of Wit and Humour—in a Letter to a Friend," in his *Characteristics of Men, Manners, Opinions, Times*, 64–76, 98, 122.

50. Peter Earle discusses the momentous changes that this social cohort experienced in his *The Making of the English Middle Class: Business, Society, and Family Life in London, 1660–1730* (Berkeley: University of California Press, 1989).

51. *Constitutions* (1723), 48, 49.

52. James Anderson, *The New Book of Constitutions of the Ancient and Honourable Fraternity of Free and Accepted Masons . . .* (London, 1738), 111. Hereafter *Constitutions* (1738).

53. *Constitutions* (1723), 59.

54. Ibid., 78, 25.

55. Ibid., 35–43.

56. Ibid., 48.

57. Latitudinarianism was a moderate political and religious tendency in the Church of England that employed Newton's writings to provide scientific validation for a model of religion and society midway between those advocated by Catholicism and religious indifference or atheism. Among many secondary treatments, see especially Martin I. J. Griffin, *Latitudinarianism in the Seventeenth Century Church of England* (Leiden, Netherlands: E. J. Brill, 1992).

58. David Stevenson's explanation for this apparent anomaly is that while working as a Mason, Anderson "was acting in his professional capacity" and so reflecting the position of his fellow Freemasons in putting his more personal "arguments aside." Stevenson, "James Anderson: Man and Mason," *Heredom* 10 (2002): 93–138. Per Jürgen Habermas's description of the formation of the public sphere, this is an instance of setting aside narrow positions to forge common ground. Habermas, *The Structural Transformation of the Public Sphere:*

An Inquiry into a Category of Bourgeois Society, trans. Thomas Burger, with the assistance of Frederick Lawrence, from the 1962 German original (Cambridge, MA: MIT Press, 1989), 36.

59. *Constitutions* (1723), 48.

60. Jacob Katz, *Jews and Freemasons in Europe, 1723–1939* (Cambridge, MA: Harvard University Press, 1970), 13–15, 198–99.

61. Buchanan MS. (1670), quoted in Wright, *Gould's History*, 1:59.

62. *Constitutions* (1723), 48.

63. For a discussion of the politics of this period, see Gary Stuart De Krey, *A Fractured Society: The Politics of London in the First Age of Party, 1688–1715* (Oxford: Clarendon Press, 1985).

64. Margaret C. Jacob, *Living the Enlightenment: Freemasonry and Politics in Eighteenth-Century Europe* (New York: Oxford University Press, 1991), 46.

65. For an insightful discussion of these private clubs and countercultural activities, see David S. Shields, "Anglo-American Clubs: Their Wit, Their Heterodoxy, Their Sedition," *William and Mary Quarterly*, 3rd ser., 51, no. 2 (April 1994): 293–304. See also Jacob, *Living the Enlightenment*, 23–51.

66. Wright, *Gould's History*, 4:279–374.

67. Shields, *Civil Tongues and Polite Letters*.

68. Michael Warner, *The Letters of the Republic: Publication and the Public Sphere in Eighteenth-Century America* (Cambridge: Harvard University Press, 1990); David W. Conroy, *In Public Houses: Drink and the Revolution of Authority in Colonial Massachusetts* (Chapel Hill: University of North Carolina Press, 1995); David S. Shields, *Civil Tongues and Polite Letters*. See also Shields, *Oracles of Empire: Poetry, Politics, and Commerce in British America, 1690–1750* (Chicago: University of Chicago Press, 1990).

69. As John L. Brooke has commented, "Whether this [i.e., public mingling of religious and secular ideas] constituted a coherent 'Habermasian public sphere' may be debated. But it did slowly construct the ground of a civil secular discourse running in parallel and intermingled with the religious." Brooke, "Consent, Civil Society, and the Public Sphere in the Age of Revolution and the Early American Republic," in *Beyond the Founders: New Approaches to the Political History of the Early American Republic*, ed. Jeffrey L. Pasley, Andrew W. Robertson, and David Waldstreicher (Chapel Hill: University of North Carolina Press, 2004), 231.

70. Even for seventeenth-century England, as David Zaret has pointed out, Habermas's formulation "glosses over the relevance of religion for the emergence of the public sphere in politics at a time when religious discourse was a, if not the, predominant means by which individuals defined and debated issues in this sphere." Zaret, "Religion, Science, and Printing in the Public Spheres in Seventeenth-Century England," in *Habermas and the Public Sphere*, ed. Craig Calhoun (Cambridge: MIT Press, 1992), 213. See also William J. Meyer, "Private Faith or Public Religion: An Assessment of Habermas's Changing View of Religion," *Journal of Religion*, 75, no. 3 (July 1995): 371–91. On Habermas and public theology, see Don S. Browning and Francis Schussler Fiorenza, eds., *Habermas, Modernity, and Public Theology* (New York: Crossroads, 1992); Nicholas Adams, *Habermas and Theology* (Cambridge: Cambridge University Press, 2006).

71. David Hall, "Religion and Society: Problems and Reconsiderations," in *Colonial British America: Essays in the New History of the Early Modern Era*, ed. Jack P. Greene and J.R. Pole (Baltimore: Johns Hopkins University Press, 1984), 327.

72. On the historiography of eighteenth-century religion, see Charles L. Cohen, "The Post-Puritan Paradigm of Early American Religious History," *William and Mary Quarterly*, 3rd ser., 54, no. 4 (October 1997): 695–722.

73. David D. Hall, introduction to *The Colonial Book in the Atlantic*, ed. Hugh Amory and Hall, vol. 1 of *A History of the Book in America* (Cambridge: Cambridge University Press, 2000), 10.

74. Timothy H. Breen, "Retrieving Common Sense: Rights, Liberties, and the Religious Public Sphere in Late Eighteenth Century America," in *To Secure the Blessings of Liberty: Rights in American History*, ed. Josephine E. Pacheno (Fairfax, VA: George Mason University Press, 1993), 60.

75. Frank Lambert, *Pedlar in Divinity: George Whitefield and the Transatlantic Revivals, 1737–1770* (Princeton, NJ: Princeton University Press, 1994).

76. On changing forms of religious communication, see Harry S. Stout, "Religion, Communications, and the Ideological Origins of the American Revolution," *William and Mary Quarterly*, 3d ser., 34, no. 2 (September 1977): 519–41.

77. John Caldwell, "The Nature, Folly, and Evil of Rash and Uncharitable Judging: A Sermon Preached at the French Meeting-House in Boston, New England, July the 11th, 1742," in *The Great Awakening: Documents on the Revival of Religion, 1740–1745*, ed. Richard L. Bushman (Chapel Hill: University of North Carolina Press, 1969), 160.

78. Timothy H. Breen and Timothy Hall, "Structuring Provincial Imagination: The Rhetoric and Experience of Social Change in Eighteenth-Century New England," *American Historical Review* 103 (1998): 1411–39.

79. Gary B. Nash, *The Urban Crucible: Social Change, Political Consciousness, and the Origins of the American Revolution* (Cambridge, MA: Harvard University Press, 1979), vii.

80. Shields, *Civil Tongues and Polite Letters*, xii–xxxii.

81. *History of St. John's Lodge*, 16. On upscale tavern life in colonial America, see Bushman, *Refinement of America*, 163–64. Steven Bullock's analysis has influenced my discussion of Freemasonry and elite colonial society. See Bullock, *Revolutionary Brotherhood*, 50–82.

82. Charge VI, "Concerning Masons' Behavior," *Constitutions* (1738). Instances of possible infractions are scattered through the Masonic records. See, for example, *History of St. John's Lodge*; Schultz, *History of Freemasonry in Maryland*; Charles T. McClenachan, *History of the Most Ancient and Honorable Fraternity of Free and Accepted Masons in New York . . .*, 4 vols. (New York: Grand Lodge, 1888–94). As an institution in polite society, the fraternity was concerned with individual behavior but even more so with the lodge's public reputation. Members were instructed to work out all squabbles between themselves within the brotherhood and to defend one another's character outside the lodge, "that we may shew to all the world the benign influence of Masonry." Charge VII, "Concerning Lawsuits," *Constitutions* (1738).

83. Darrett Rutman first proposed this vertical-horizontal distinction, in "The Social Web: A Prospectus for the Study of the Early American Community," in *Insights and Parallels: Problems and Issues of America Social History*, ed. William L. O'Neill (Minneapolis: Burgess, 1973), 57–88.

84. Anne Grant, *Memoirs of an American Lady: With Sketches of Manners and Scenes in America* (Albany, NY: Joel Munsell, 1876), 32.

85. Ibid. In the 1760s, Grant spent her adolescence with the Schuyler family, while her British officer father moved among colonial military forts. Forty years later, as an established Scottish author, she penned her memories of Albany. Though historians have frequently employed her memoir to describe the quaint ways of the colonists, its larger framework of lament for the lost innocence of colonial America has only recently been explored. See Pamela Ann Perkins, "Paradises Lost: Anne Grant and Late Eighteenth-Century Idealizations of America," *Early American Literature* 40, no. 2 (2005): 315–40. For a social history of colonial Albany, see David G. Hackett, *The Rude Hand of Innovation: Religion and Social Order in Albany, New York, 1652–1836* (New York: Oxford University Press, 1991), 3–55.

86. Grant, *Memoirs*, 49, 73–75, 45.

87. Hackett, *Rude Hand of Innovation*, 3–55.

88. Grant, *Memoirs*, 44.

89. Ibid., 47, 108, 47, 109, 134.

90. Ibid., 164, 174, 171, 175, 172.

91. Alexander Hamilton, *Gentleman's Progress: The Itinerarium of Dr. Alexander Hamilton, 1744*, ed. Carl Bridenbaugh (Chapel Hill: University of North Carolina Press, 1948), 63. On Hamilton's involvement in Freemasonry, see Robert Micklus, "The Secret Fall of Freemasonry in Dr. Alexander Hamilton's *The History of the Tuesday Club*," in *Deism, Masonry and the Enlightenment*, ed. J. A. Leo Lemay (Newark: University of Delaware Press, 1987), 127–36. A leading proponent of colonial polite society, Hamilton employed wit and candor in making fun of political and religious authorities in his *The History of the Ancient and Honorable Tuesday Club* (repr., ed. Robert Micklus, 3 vols. [Chapel Hill: University of North Carolina Press, 1990]).

92. Joseph F. Meany Jr., "Merchant and Redcoat: The Papers of John Gordon Macomb, April 1757–1760" (PhD diss., Fordham University, 1990), 49–150.

93. Grant, *Memoirs*, 192–200.

94. Hackett, *Rude Hand of Innovation*, 33.

95. McClenachan, *History of Masons in New York*, 1:151–83; "Manuscript Minutes of Master's Lodge, Albany 1768–1807," Albany Grand Lodge.

96. See "Masonic Lodge" and (s.v. "Biographies") "Cartwright, Richard," "Gansevoort, Leonard," and "Wendell, John W." at the Albany Social History project, www.nysm.nysed.gov/albany/pcalhindex.html.

97. "Constitution of the Sons of Liberty of Albany" (includes the names of its signers), *American Historian and Quarterly Genealogical Record* 1 (1875): 145–46.

98. See Hackett, *Rude Hand of Innovation*, 49–52; relevant entries on the Albany Social History project website, www.nysm.nysed.gov/albany/pcalhindex.html.

99. William Smith, *Ahiman Rezon . . . to Which Is Added a Sermon Preached in Christ-Church, Philadelphia . . .* (Philadelphia: Grand Lodge of Pennsylvania, 1778).

100. Evidence of the denominational allegiance of prominent Masons is scattered throughout the major proceedings and histories of the regional lodges. For an extended look at the membership of Philadelphia's original Saint John's Lodge, see Julius F. Sachse, *Old Masonic Lodges of Pennsylvania*, vol. 1 (Philadelphia: Grand Lodge of Pennsylvania, 1912), 29–49. As early as the 1730s, Jews were admitted to Freemasonry in both England and America. In Newport, Rhode Island, Jews from Portugal and the Caribbean formed a large portion of the membership. Bernard Kusinitz, "Masonry and the Colonial Jews of Newport," *Rhode Island Jewish Historical Notes* 9 (November 1984): 180–84. On Jews in colonial America, see Eli Faber, *A Time for Planting: The First Migration, 1654–1820* (Baltimore: Johns Hopkins University Press, 1992). For Jews in English Freemasonry, see John M. Shaftesley, "Jews in English Freemasonry in the 18th and 19th Centuries," *Ars Quatuor Coronatorum* 92 (1979): 25–63. For an extended discussion, see ch. 8.

101. *Constitutions* (1723), 48; Anthony Ashley Cooper, third Earl of Shaftesbury, "An Inquiry Concerning Virtue, or Merit," in *British Moralists, 1650–1800*, ed. D.D. Raphael, vol. 1 (Indianapolis: Hackett, 1991), 6–63.

102. John Locke, *Some Thoughts Concerning Education* (Cambridge: Cambridge University Press, 1902), 43.

103. Robert W. Prichard, *A History of the Episcopal Church* (Harrisburg, PA: Morehouse, 1991), 34–35.

104. John Frederick Woolverton, *Colonial Anglicanism in North America* (Detroit: Wayne State University Press, 1984), 13–35, 189–206.

105. Richardson Wright, "The American Masonic Sermon," *Transactions of the American Lodge of Research* 3 (1937): 214–15. This article discusses and provides a bibliography of printed Masonic sermons from 1750 to 1828.

106. Ibid., 209–15.

107. Charles Brockwell, *Brotherly Love Recommended: In a Sermon Preached before the Ancient and Honourable Society of Free and Accepted Masons, in Christ-Church, Boston . . .* (Boston: John Draper, 1750)

108. Ibid., 10–14.

109. Simeon Howard, *A Sermon on Brotherly Love: Preached at the Old Brick Meeting-House in Boston . . .* (Boston: Brother Thomas Fleet, 1779), 13.

110. Thomas Pollen, *Universal Love: A Sermon Preached in Trinity-Church, at Newport, in Rhode Island, before the Right Worshipful Lodge of Free and Accepted Masons . . .* (Boston: Green and Russell, 1758), 13. Margaret Jacob's analysis of Masonic European and American pocket diaries of the late eighteenth century similarly identifies this movement away from specific religious content and toward Enlightenment themes. Jacob, *Origins of Freemasonry*, 26–46.

111. Mackey, *History of Freemasonry in South Carolina*, 17; Tatsch, *Freemasonry in the Thirteen Colonies*, 68.

112. John Rodgers, *Holiness the Nature and Design of the Gospel of Christ: A Sermon Preached at Stockbridge . . . before the Lodge of Free and Accepted*

Masons . . . (Hartford, CT: Hudson and Goodwin, 1780), vi; Brockwell, *Brotherly Love Recommended*, 10; Pollen, *Universal Love*, 15.

113. Zabdiel Adams, *Brotherly Love and Compassion, Described and Recommended in a Sermon Preached before a Society of the Most Ancient and Honourable Free and Accepted Masons in Lancaster, New England* . . . (Worcester, MA: Isaiah Thomas, 1778), 24–25.

114. Schultz, *History of Freemasonry in Maryland*, 29.

115. Brockwell, *Brotherly Love Recommended*, 14; Pollen, *Universal Love*, 16.

116. Norbert Elias, *The History of Manners* (New York: Pantheon, 1978).

117. On courtesy books, see John Edward Mason, *Gentlefolk in the Making; Studies in the History of English Courtesy Literature and Related Topics from 1531 to 1774* (New York: Octagon, 1971).

118. Earl of Chesterfield, *Letters to His Son: On the Art of Becoming a Man of the World and a Gentleman*, vol. 1 (New York: Chesterfield, 1917), 2.

119. Richard Allestree, *The Whole Duty of Man: Laid Down in a Plain and Familiar Way for the Use of All, but Especially the Meanest Reader; Divided into Seventeen Chapters, One Whereof Being Read Every Lord's Day, the Whole May Be Read over Thrise in the Year* . . . (London: Griffith, Farran, Okeden, and Welsh, 1657).

120. Bushman, *Refinement of America*, 59–60.

121. Z. Adams, *Brotherly Love and Compassion*, 12, 27; Howard, *Sermon on Brotherly Love*, 17; Brockwell, *Brotherly Love Recommended*, 15–21.

122. Charles Brockwell to the Society for the Propagation of the Gospel, February 8, 1742, reproduced in *Historical Collections Relating to the American Colonial Church*, ed. William Stevens Perry, 5 vols. (New York: AMS Press, 1969) 3:353–57.

123. On the First Great Awakening see Thomas S. Kidd, *The Great Awakening: The Roots of Evangelical Christianity in Colonial America* (New Haven, CT: Yale University Press, 2007) and most recently Catherine A. Brekus, *Sarah Osborn's World: The Rise of Evangelical Christianity in Early America* (New Haven: Yale University Press, 2013).

124. Mackey, *History of Freemasonry in South Carolina*, 14.

125. In the ensuing months, Garden's supporters accused Whitefield of, e.g., "Pride and Insolence very unbecoming an unexperienced Youth to a wise Superior." "A Member of the Church of England," *South Carolina Gazette*, July 5, 1740.

126. *George Whitefield's Journals* (London: Banner of Truth Trust, 1960), 401; Alexander Garden, *Take Heed How Ye Hear* . . . (Charlestown, SC, 1741), 17–20.

127. Whitefield to Garden, March 13, 1739, in Alexander Garden, *Six Letters to the Rev. Mr. George Whitefield*, 2nd ed. (Boston: T. Fleet, 1740), 6–7.

128. Lambert, *Pedlar in Divinity*, 169–71.

129. Garden, *Six Letters*, 8, 33.

130. Letter from "Arminius," *South Carolina Gazette*, January 26, 1740; George Whitefield, *Eight Sermons . . . to Which Is Prefixed, Mr. Joseph* [sic for *Josiah*] *Smith's Sermon, on the Character, Preaching, etc., of the Reverend Mr. George Whitefield* (Glasgow: Paisley, 1741), 12. Turning the tables on White-

field's accusers, Smith reminded his readers that while Whitefield clearly affirmed the teachings of Scripture, others believed that "Faith is a Word of great Latitude, and has various Significations affix'd to it in Scripture and can be determin'd to no precise sense but from the Subject and Scope of the Writer." Smith, reply to "Arminius," *South Carolina Gazette*, February 23, 1740.

131. *Whitefield's Journals*, 97.

132. Frank Lambert, "Subscribing for Profits and Piety: The Friendship of Benjamin Franklin and George Whitefield," *William and Mary Quarterly*, 3rd ser., 50, no. 3 (July 1993): 529–54.

133. On Franklin's religious beliefs, see Carl Van Doren, *Benjamin Franklin* (New York: Viking, 1938), 777; Alfred Owen Aldridge, *Benjamin Franklin: Philosopher and Man* (Philadelphia: Lippincott, 1965), 44–54; Edwin Gaustad, *Benjamin Franklin* (New York: Oxford University Press, 2006), 24–26; Kerry S. Walters, *Benjamin Franklin and His Gods* (Urbana: University of Illinois Press, 1999).

134. Julius F. Sachse, "The Masonic Chronology of Benjamin Franklin," *Pennsylvania Magazine of History and Biography* 30, no. 2 (1906): 238–40.

135. R. William Weisberger, "Benjamin Franklin: A Masonic Enlightener in Paris," *Pennsylvania History* 53, no. 3 (July 1986): 165–80.

136. Van Doren, *Benjamin Franklin*, 135–36.

137. Lambert, "Subscribing for Profits," 529–54.

138. Johnson, *Beginnings of Freemasonry in America*, 121.

139. Isaiah Thomas, *History of Printing*, vol. 1 (Worcester, MA: Isaiah Thomas, 1810), 326–27.

140. Philo-Mathes, "To the Publisher of the Boston Gazette," *Boston Gazette*, February 2, 1739.

141. Johnson, *Beginnings of Freemasonry in America*, 343. Short biographies of these early Masons are scattered throughout.

142. Rodgers, *Holiness the Nature*, v–vi, 15.

143. Thomas Fessenden, *A Luminous Shining Character: Delimited and Recommended in a Sermon, Preached before the Most Ancient and Honorable Society of Free and Accepted Masons* . . . (Keene, NH: James D. Griffith, 1789), 9.

144. Z. Adams, *Brotherly Love and Compassion*, 22.

145. Charles Brockwell, "A Dissertation upon Masonry, Delivered to a Lodge in America, June 24, 1734," *Freemasons' Monthly Magazine* (Boston) 8, no. 10 (August 1, 1849): 289–93.

146. Masons most likely adopted this manner of measuring time from the writings of James Ussher (1581–1656), the archbishop of Armagh, primate of all Ireland, and vice-chancellor of Trinity College. Ussher's treatise on chronology, based on ancient histories and the Bible, gained widespread acceptance after it was incorporated into an authorized version of the Bible printed in 1701. G. Y. Craig and E. J. Jones, *A Geological Miscellany* (Princeton, NJ: Princeton University Press, 1982), 2–3.

147. Jacob, *Living the Enlightenment*. See also her "Exits from the Enlightenment: Masonic Routes," *Eighteenth Century Studies* 33, no. 2 (2000): 251–54.

148. David D. Hall, *Worlds of Wonder, Days of Judgment: Popular Religious Belief in Early New England* (New York: Knopf, 1989).

149. Jon Butler, *Awash in a Sea of Faith: Christianizing the American People* (Cambridge, MA: Harvard University Press, 1990), 96.

150. Patricia U. Bonomi, *Under the Cope of Heaven: Religion, Society and Politics in Colonial America* (New York: Oxford University Press, 1986), 37.

151. Edwin S. Gaustad and Philip L. Barlow, *New Historical Atlas of Religion in America* (New York: Oxford University Press, 2001), 7–8.

152. In America, Thomas Paine was among the first to develop the thesis, well known in England, that Masonry descends from the religion of the Druids. See his "Origin of Freemasonry," in Van der Weyde, *Life and Works of Thomas Paine*, 9:167–68.

153. Brooke, *Refiner's Fire*, 194–295.

154. Johnson, *Beginnings of Freemasonry in America*, 383.

155. Between 1739 and 1751, for example, 238 men joined Boston's First Lodge, of whom only eighty-four became Master Masons. Wright, *Gould's History*, 4:446.

156. McClenachan, *History of Masons in New York*, 1:444.

157. Grant, *Memoirs*, 309.

158. Grant, *Memoirs*, 205, 316, 332.

159. On the decline of colonial polite society in the 1760s, see Shields, *Civil Tongues and Polite Letters*, 308–28. On the growth of voluntary organizations just before the revolution, see, among others, Richard D. Brown, "The Emergence of Urban Society in Rural Massachusetts, 1760–1820," *Journal of American History* 61 (1974): 29–51. On the rise in the volume of print in the 1760s, see Warner, *Letters of the Republic*, 32.

160. Grant, *Memoirs*, 333; on Freemasonry and the growth of associations throughout American history, see Theda Skocpol, Marshall Ganz, and Ziad Munson, "A Nation of Organizers: The Institutional Origins of Civic Voluntarism in the United States," *American Political Science Review* 94, no. 3 (September 2000): 527–46.

2. REVOLUTIONARY MASONRY

1. Ruth H. Bloch, "Religion and Ideological Change in the American Revolution," in *Religion and American Politics: From the Colonial Period to the 1980s*, ed. Mark A. Noll (New York: Oxford University Press, 1990), 44–61. See also Bloch, *Visionary Republic: Millennial Themes in American Thought, 1756–1800* (New York: Cambridge University Press, 1985); Nathan O. Hatch, *The Sacred Cause of Liberty: Republican Thought and the Millennium in Revolutionary New England* (New Haven, CT: Yale University Press, 1977). Older literature on this period includes Alan Heimert, *Religion and the American Mind from the Great Awakening to the Revolution* (Cambridge, MA: Harvard University Press, 1966); Perry Miller, "From the Covenant to the Revival," in his *Nature's Nation* (Cambridge, MA: Harvard University Press, 1967); Edmund S. Morgan, "The Puritan Ethic and the American Revolution," *William and Mary Quarterly*, 3rd ser., 24, no. 2 (January 1967):3–43. The democratization theme is most prominent in Hatch, *The Democratization of Christianity* (New Haven, CT: Yale University Press, 1989). For demographics, see

Roger Finke and Rodney Starke, *The Churching of America, 1776–1990: Winners and Losers in Our Religious Economy* (New Brunswick, NJ: Rutgers University Press, 1992). For an overview of the scholarship on Christianity and republicanism, see James T. Kloppenberg, "The Virtues of Liberalism: Christianity, Republicanism, and Ethics in Early American Political Discourse," *Journal of American History* 74, no. 1 (June 1987): 9–33.

2. Alexis de Tocqueville, *Democracy in America*, ed. and trans. Harvey C. Mansfield and Delba Winthrop (Chicago: University of Chicago Press, 2000), 489–92.

3. In the 1830s, Tocqueville identified the voluntary organizations that emerged from these postwar institutions as providing the critical medium for creating a democratic society. He did not, however, recognize the elite white male composition of most of these groups. Contemporary neo-Tocquevillians, such as Robert D. Putnam have run into similar criticism. See Putnam, *Bowling Alone: The Collapse and Revival of American Community* (New York: Simon and Schuster, 2000). Putnam's argument for voluntary associations as critical to making democracy work has been countered by those who, following Antonio Gramsci, envision civil society as a site of contestation between the hegemony of the elite and the interests of subordinate groups. See, e.g., Bob Edwards, Michael W. Foley, and Mario Diani, eds., *Beyond Tocqueville: Civil Society and the Social Capital Debate in Comparative Perspective* (Hanover, NH: University Press of New England, 2001); Theda Skocpol, *Diminished Democracy: From Membership to Management in American Civic Life* (Norman: University of Oklahoma Press, 2003). This chapter presents postwar Freemasonry as it was widely understood at the time. Subsequent chapters will take up the gender, class, and race criticisms of the brotherhood.

4. Walker, quoted in David S. Shields, "Clio Mocks the Masons: Joseph Green's Anti-Masonic Satires," in *Deism, Masonry, and the Enlightenment: Essays Honoring Alfred Owen Aldridge*, ed. J. A. Leo Lemay (Newark: University of Delaware Press, 1987), 109.

5. T. O. Haunch, "The Formation, 1717–1751," pt. 1 of *Grand Lodge, 1717–1967* (Oxford: United Grand Lodge of England, 1967), 86–91.

6. J. R. Clarke, "The Formation, 1751 to 1813," pt. 2 of *Grand Lodge,* 92–105. See also Robert Freke Gould, *The History of Freemasonry: Its Antiquities, Symbols, Constitutions, Customs . . .*, vol. 3 (London: Yorston, 1906), 186–217. For a summary of the major differences between these two bodies, see Wayne A. Huss, *The Master Builders: A History of the Grand Lodge of Free and Accepted Masons of Philadelphia*, vol. 1 (Philadelphia: Grand Lodge of Pennsylvania, 1986), 12–14.

7. Laurence Dermott, *Ahiman Rezon: Or, A Help to All That Are or Would Be Free and Accepted Masons, Containing the Quintessence of All That Has Been Published on the Subject of Freemasonry . . .*, 2nd ed. (London: Robert Black, 1764; repr., Philadelphia: Leon Hyneman, 1855).

8. On Dermott, see William Matthew Bywater, *Notes on Laurence Dermott and His Work* (London: privately printed, 1884); Richard J. Reece, *Laurence Dermott: His Masonic Life and Work* (London: Grand Lodge, 1914); George M. Martin, "Laurence Dermott and the Grand Lodge of the 'Ancient' or 'Athol'

Masons, 1751–1813," in Martin, *British Masonic Miscellany* (Dundee, Scotland: David Winter and Son, 1832) 18, 99–106.

9. Dermott, *Ahiman Rezon*, 14; Clarke, "The Formation, 1751 to 1813," 92–105.

10. Henry Wilson Coil, *Freemasonry through Six Centuries*, 2 vols. (Richmond, VA: Macoy, 1967), 1:12.

11. Norris S. Barratt and Julius F. Sachse, *Freemasonry in Pennsylvania, 1727–1907* (Philadelphia: Grand Lodge of Pennsylvania, 1908), 13–64. See also Huss, *Master Builders*, 32–54. Bush was acting as a representative of the Philadelphia Grand Lodge. He later became the highest-ranking Jewish officer in the Continental Army. Samuel Oppenheim, "The Jews and Masonry in the United States before 1810," *Publications of the Jewish Historical Society* 19 (1910): 47. As ch. 8 argues, Jews were prominent members of the eighteenth- and nineteenth-century fraternity.

12. Charles E. Meyer, "Masonic Lodges in Pennsylvania from 1730 to 1880," in *Early History and Constitutions of the Grand Lodge of Pennsylvania* (Philadelphia: Grand Lodge of Pennsylvania, 1877), 1–15, xxviii–xl. Jessica Harland-Jacobs, *Builders of Empire: Freemasonry and British Imperialism, 1717–1927* (Chapel Hill: University of North Carolina Press, 2007), 26–31, 45–47, explains the decline of the Moderns and the rise of the Ancients in Great Britain; Steven C. Bullock, *Revolutionary Brotherhood: Freemasonry and the Transformation of the American Social Order, 1730–1840* (Chapel Hill: University of North Carolina Press, 1996), 85–108, extends the discussion to North America.

13. Coil, *Freemasonry through Six Centuries*, 2:11.

14. Dermott, *Ahiman Rezon*, 18.

15. Huss, *Master Builders*, 291. Elsewhere, disputes over the relative legitimacy of the two factions turned bitter. In South Carolina, tensions continued right up until the British unification of the two sides in 1813. The formation of state Grand Lodges following the Revolution generally obliterated all distinctions, though some states, e.g., Pennsylvania and Virginia, retained a strong adherence to Ancient doctrine. See Coil, *Freemasonry through Six Centuries*, 2:19.

16. John L. Brooke has increased the previous estimate of sixteen thousand provided by William P. Vaughn (*The Antimasonic Party in the United States, 1826–1843* [Lexington: University Press of Kentucky, 1983], 11), through a closer examination of lodge lists. Brooke, "Ancient Lodges and Self-Created Societies: Voluntary Association and the Public Sphere in the Early Republic," in *Launching the "Extended Republic": The Federalist Era*, ed. Ronald Hoffman and Peter J. Albert (Charlottesville: University of Virginia Press, 1996), 273–377. These twenty-five thousand lodge members constituted 2.3 percent of white males over age fifteen (1,088,241), or 3.6 percent of white males over twenty-five (695,476), in the 1800 Federal Census. United States Census Office, *Return of the Whole Number of Persons within the Several Districts of the United States: According to an Act Providing for the Second Census or Enumeration thereof . . .* (Washington, DC: Apollo, 1802). Since the youngest Masons entered the order in their early twenties, about 3 percent of the white male population that age or older were Masons.

17. See especially Gary B. Nash, *The Urban Crucible: Social Change, Political Consciousness, and the Origins of the American Revolution* (Cambridge, MA: Harvard University Press, 1979); Edward Countryman, *A People in Revolution: The American Revolution and Political Society in New York, 1760–1790* (Baltimore: Johns Hopkins Press, 1981); Eric Foner, *Tom Paine and Revolutionary America* (New York: Oxford University Press, 1976).

18. For an overview of the scholarship in this area, see Gregory H. Nobles, "Breaking into the Backcountry: New Approaches to the Early American Frontier, 1750–1800," *William and Mary Quarterly*, 3rd ser., 46, no. 4 (October, 1989): 641–70. For a discussion of scholarship on the link between cosmopolitanism and Freemasonry, see Harland-Jacobs, *Builders of Empire*, 66–73.

19. Bullock, *Revolutionary Brotherhood*, 10–114.

20. Ronald E. Heaton, *Masonic Membership of the Founding Fathers* (Bloomington, IL: Masonic Book Club, 1974), iii.

21. Jacob Hugo Tatsch, *Freemasonry in the Thirteen Colonies* (New York: Macoy Publishing and Masonic Supply, 1929), 202–27, lists all revolutionary-era military lodges. At a 1779 meeting of military lodges, delegates identified themselves first as representing particular states and secondly particular lodges. Henry J. Parker, *Army Lodges during the Revolution* (Boston: Press of the Liberal Freemason, 1884), 6, 11.

22. Howard Lewis Applegate, "Organization and Development of the American Chaplaincy during the Revolutionary War," *Picket Post* 68 (1960): 19–21, 37–41.

23. Charles H. Metzger, "Chaplains in the American Revolution," *Catholic Historical Review* 21 (1945–46): 37–38.

24. Howard Lewis Applegate, "Duties and Activities of Chaplains," *Picket Post* 61 (1958): 39; Metzger, "Chaplains in the American Revolution," 43.

25. Applegate, "Duties and Activities of Chaplains," 15.

26. Metzger, "Chaplains in the American Revolution," 49, 54–56.

27. Ibid., 34, 75–79 (a list of chaplains and their denominational and state affiliations).

28. Applegate, "Duties and Activities of Chaplains," 37.

29. Metzger, "Chaplains in the American Revolution," 40–41.

30. *Journal of the Rev. Ammi Robbins, a Chaplain in the American Army, in the Northern Campaign of 1776* (New Haven, 1850), 37, quoted in Jon Butler, *Awash in a Sea of Faith: Christianizing the American People* (Cambridge, MA: Harvard University Press, 1990), 211.

31. Applegate, "Duties and Activities of Chaplains," 12.

32. Robert W. Reid, "Little Britain No. 6 St. John's Regimental No. 1," *Transactions: The American Lodge of Research, Free and Accepted Masons* 4, no. 2 (October 20, 1944–December 18, 1945): 230.

33. Tatsch, *Freemasonry in the Thirteen Colonies*, 221.

34. Sidney Hayden, *Washington and His Masonic Compeers* (New York: Masonic Publishing and Manufacturing, 1867), 85–86.

35. Steven C. Bullock makes a similar argument for why men joined the military lodges, though he gives greater emphasis to the more elusive

motivation of public recognition for men "uncertain of their honor and fearful of their reputations." Bullock, *Revolutionary Brotherhood*, 123.

36. Parker, *Army Lodges*, 1–12.

37. Charles S. Plumb, *The History of American Union Lodge No. 1, Free and Accepted Masons of Ohio, 1776–1933* (Marietta, OH: American Union Lodge, 1934) 159, 24.

38. Ibid., 66–67.

39. Parker, *Army Lodges* 4; Plumb, *History of American Union Lodge*, 46–47.

40. Hayden, *Washington*, 52.

41. Norris S. Barratt and Julius F. Sachse, *Freemasonry in Pennsylvania, 1727–1907* (Philadelphia: Grand Lodge of Pennsylvania, 1908), 301.

42. Huss, *Master Builders*, 40–41. Smith's sermon was "dedicated to his Excellency George Washington, Esquire, General and Commander in Chief of all armies of the United States of America, the friend of his country and mankind, . . . in . . . brotherly affection and esteem of his merit." Smith, *Ahiman Rezon . . . to Which Is Added a Sermon Preached in Christ-Church, Philadelphia . . .* (Philadelphia: Grand Lodge of Pennsylvania, 1778).

43. Huss, *Master Builders*, 49.

44. Hayden, *Washington*, 51. For a discussion of Washington as a Masonic icon, see William D. Moore and John D. Hamilton, "Washington as the Master of His Lodge: History and Symbolism of a Masonic Icon," in *George Washington: American Symbol*, ed. Barbara J. Mitnick (New York: Hudson Hills, 1999), 71–90.

45. Hayden, *Washington*, 124–28.

46. Ossian Lang, *History of Freemasonry in the State of New York* (New York: Grand Lodge of New York, 1922), 80–82.

47. Hayden, *Washington*, 149–60. On the Masonic tradition of cornerstone ceremonies, see S. Brent Morris, *Cornerstones of Freedom: A Masonic Tradition* (Washington DC: Supreme Council, 1993). Corn, oil, and wine were used as Masonic symbols of the "necessities of life" as early as the laying of a foundation stone at the Edinburgh Royal Exchange in 1753. T.O. Haunch, "The Constitution and Consecration of Lodges under the Grand Lodges of England," *Ars Quatuor Coronatorum* 83 (1970): 14–15.

48. Hayden, *Washington*, 154–58.

49. *Proceedings of the Most Worshipful Grand Lodge . . . of Massachusetts, 1792–1815* (Boston: Massachusetts Grand Lodge, 1905), 75; William Moseley Brown, *Freemasonry in Virginia (1733–1936)* (Richmond, VA: Masonic Home, 1936), 100 n. 9, 128.

50. An 1817 edition of the *Ahimon Rezon* (Baltimore: Benjamin Edes, 1817) describes the "ceremony at the opening of a bridge" (103); *Albany Argus*, July 8, 1825; Thomas L. Parramore, *Launching the Craft: The First Half-Century of Freemasonry in North Carolina* (Raleigh: Grand Lodge of North Carolina, 1975), 127–31; *Proceedings of the Grand Annual Communication of the Grand Lodge of Virginia . . . 1817* (Richmond, VA: Grand Lodge, 1818), 5, 18–19; *New-England Galaxy and Masonic Magazine* (Boston), July 4, 1818.

51. *Masonic Mirror and Mechanics' Intelligencer* (Boston), September 23, 1826, 311.

52. See ch. 8, nn. 10, 17.

53. See T. O. Haunch, "Constitution and Consecration of Lodges," 1–62, for the ceremonies' British origins; William L. Cummings, "Ceremonial of Cornerstone Laying," *Transactions: The American Lodge of Research, Free and Accepted Masons* 1 (1930–33): 153–54, for their American transformation.

54. *Proceedings of the Most Worshipful Grand Lodge of Massachusetts . . . , 1815–1825* (Cambridge: Grand Lodge of Massachusetts, 1905), 541–49.

55. David Waldstreicher, *In the Midst of Perpetual Fetes: The Making of American Nationalism, 1776–1820* (Chapel Hill: University of North Carolina Press, 1997), 293. See also Simon P. Newman's *Parades and the Politics of the Street: Festive Culture in the Early American Republic* (Philadelphia: University of Pennsylvania Press, 1997), which shares Waldstreicher's view of the emerging postwar public sphere as a contested arena working to create a common public world.

56. Robert Shalhope gave republicanism conceptual identity in his historiographical essay "Toward a Republican Synthesis: The Emergence of an Understanding of Republicanism in American Historiography," *William and Mary Quarterly*, 3rd ser., 29, no. 1 (January 1972): 49–80. The understanding of the term here reflects its use in the three books that have most shaped its common meaning: Bernard Bailyn, *The Ideological Origins of the American Revolution* (Cambridge, MA: Harvard University Press, 1967); Gordon Wood, *The Creation of the American Republic, 1776–1787* (Chapel Hill: University of North Carolina Press, 1969); J. G. A. Pocock, *The Machiavellian Moment: Florentine Political Thought and the Atlantic Republican Tradition* (Princeton, NJ: Princeton University Press, 1975). Since the early 1970s, the term has been used so widely to fulfill a variety of interpretive needs—relating to, e.g., social class or gender differences—that some believe it has lost its explanatory power. See Daniel T. Rodgers, "Republicanism: The Career of a Concept," *Journal of American History* 79, no. 1 (June 1992): 11–38.

57. Thomas F. Oliver, *A Discourse Delivered at the Episcopal Church in Providence before the Society of Free and Accepted Masons . . .* (Providence, RI: John Carter, 1784), 12.

58. Washington, quoted in Frederick W. Hotchkiss, *A Sermon Delivered at the Installation of Pythagoras Lodge . . .* (New London, CT: Green, 1800), 21.

59. DeWitt Clinton, *An Address Delivered before Holland Lodge . . .* (New York: Francis Childs and John Swaine, 1793), 8.

60. Benjamin Green, *An Oration Delivered before the Right Worshipful Master, Wardens, and Brethren of the Philanthropic Lodge of Free and Accepted Masons* (Salem, MA: Thomas C. Cushing, 1797), 17.

61. Reinier John Vanden Broek, *Address Delivered at the Consecration of the Room, Accommodated for the Meetings of Independent Royal-Arch Lodge, No. 2 . . .* (New York: James Oram, 1796), 16; Clark Brown, *The Utility of Moral and Religious Societies, and of the Masonick in Particular . . .* (Keene, NH: John Prentiss, 1814), 16.

62. Clinton, *Address Delivered before Holland Lodge*, 8.

63. James Milnor, *Oration on Masonry*, (Philadelphia: n.p., 1811), 23.

64. Clinton, *Address Delivered before Holland Lodge*, 5.

65. John Crawford, *An Address Delivered at the Grand Convocation of the Free Masons of the State of Maryland* . . . (Baltimore: Thomas and George Dobbin, 1802), A.

66. See, e.g., Milnor, *Oration on Masonry*, 32.

67. Clinton, *Address Delivered before Holland Lodge*, 4.

68. John H. Sheppard, *An Address Delivered in Portland, at the Consecration of the Grand Lodge of Maine* (Portland, ME: A. Shirley, 1820), 5–6.

69. Ibid., 5–7.

70. Charles T. McClenachan, *History of the Most Ancient and Honorable Fraternity of Free and Accepted Masons in New York* . . ., 4 vols. (New York: Grand Lodge, 1888–94), 2:228–38; Lang, *History of Freemasonry in New York*, 91–95.

71. An article by a Masonic historian suggests greater follow-through by midcentury. "Starting in 1844 in Lexington, Missouri, at least 30 colleges and universities were started by American Masonic Lodges and Grand Lodges, mostly in the Southern Jurisdiction," though most of these "closed long ago." Cloyd J. Bumgardner, "The Educational Legacy of Somerset Lodge No. 111," *Scottish Rite Journal*, March–April 2010, http://scottishrite.org/journal/march-april-2010/.

72. For a similar discussion of the Masonic embodiment of republican values, see Bullock, *Revolutionary Brotherhood*, 137–50.

73. United States Bureau of the Census, with the Cooperation of the Social Science Council, *Historical Statistics of the United States, Colonial Times to 1957*, ser. A123–180 (Washington, DC: U.S. Government Printing Office, 1960), 3.

74. For membership statistics, see C.P. MacCalla, "Freemasonry in America," *Ars Quatuor Coronatorum* 3 (1890): 123; Bullock, *Revolutionary Brotherhood*, 371 n. 16. According to the 1820 Federal Census, the estimated eighty thousand lodge members constituted 4 percent of adult white males over the age of fifteen (2,015,801), or 6.3 percent of adult white males over the age of twenty-five (1,260,281). United States Census Office, *Population Schedules of the Fourth Census of the United States, 1820* (Washington, DC: National Archives and Records Service, General Services Administration, 1959). Again, since the youngest Masons entered the fraternity in their early twenties, approximately 5 percent of people that age or older were Masons. In Pennsylvania, the number of lodges rose from 19 in 1786 to 85 in 1800, 132 in 1811, and 165 in 1819. "Masonic Lodges in Pennsylvania from 1730 to 1880 . . .," in *The Grand Lodge . . . of Pennsylvania: Its Early History and Constitutions* (Philadelphia: Grand Lodge of Pennsylvania, 1877), 1–15. By 1825 there were more than five hundred lodges in New York alone. For rough comparative purposes, consider that according to the 1850 Census there were 3,625 Protestant churches in the state. See Edwin Scott Gaustad and Philip L. Barlow, *New Historical Atlas of Religion in America* (New York: Oxford University Press), 400. So in New York in 1825 there was probably at least one lodge for every seven or so churches.

75. William Fowler Brainard, *A Masonic Lecture, Spoken before the Brethren of Union Lodge, New-London* . . . (New London, CT: Samuel Green, 1825).

76. Helping shape this convergence were older Puritan views of spiritual redemption and religious community, as well as battles with tyrannical governments and the revolutionary experience. Bloch, "Religion and Ideological Change," 44–61.

77. James Anderson, *The Constitutions of the Free-Masons* (1723), reprint of Anderson's book by Benjamin Franklin (1734; repr., Bloomington, IL: Masonic Book Club, 1971), 48. Hereafter cited as *Constitutions*.

78. On the origins of Unitarianism, see Conrad Wright, *The Beginnings of Unitarianism in America* (Boston: Beacon, 1955); Daniel Walker Howe, *The Unitarian Conscience: Harvard Moral Philosophy, 1805–1861* (Cambridge, MA: Harvard University Press, 1970).

79. "Biographical Sketches of Grand Chaplains," in *Proceedings of the Grand Lodge of the Most Ancient and Honorable Fraternity of Free and Accepted Masons of the Commonwealth of Massachusetts* (Boston: Rockwell and Churchill, 1874), 216.

80. William B. Sprague, *Annals of the American Pulpit*, 8 vols. (New York: Robert Carter and Brothers, 1865), 8:154–57; "Biographical Sketches," 193–96.

81. "Biographical Sketches," 185–261; Sprague, *Annals of the American Pulpit*, 5:492–94, 575–80, 8:92–99, 112–19, 154–57, 215-21, 416–19.

82. "Biographical Sketches," 213.

83. Emerson, quoted in Sprague, *Annals of the American Pulpit*, 8:115–18.

84. "Biographical Sketches," 247.

85. Ibid., 220, 215.

86. Ezekiel L. Bascom, *The Opposition of "the World" to Religious and Moral Societies: A Sermon, Delivered at Westfield (Mass.), at the Request of the Officers and Members of Friendly Society Lodge* . . . (Hartford, CT: B. and J. Russell, 1815), 10.

87. Brown, *Utility of Moral and Religious Societies*, 12–13.

88. William Bentley, *An Address Delivered in the Essex Lodge, upon the Festival of St. John the Evangelist* (Salem, MA: Joshua Cushing, 1799), 16.

89. Joshua Bradley, *Accounts of Religious Revivals in Many Parts of the United States from 1815 to 1816* (Albany, NY: G.J. Loomis, 1819); Bradley, *Some of the Beauties of Freemasonry* . . . (Rutland, VT: Fay and Davison, 1816).

90. Solomon Sias, *An Address Delivered . . . before the Portland Lodge . . .* (Portland, ME: A. Shirley, 1820), 8–9.

91. Sprague, *Annals of the American Pulpit*, 6:66.

92. Schultz, *History of Freemasonry in Maryland*, 2:238. The records of Saint Albans Lodge, Bristol (Rhode Island), show that Dow was "raised to the degree of Master Mason on Sunday, December 26, 1824, after having twice preached in that town." Neither the Masons nor Dow saw the work of the lodge as "incompatible with the Lord's Day." *National Freemason* 1, no. 2 (July 1863), 27; *Historical Sketch of St. John's Commandery No. 1* . . . (Providence: Rhode Island Printing, 1875), 21. For additional Masonic clergymen, see Bullock, *Revolutionary Brotherhood*, 175–78; scattered references in Dorothy Ann Lipson, *Freemasonry in Federalist Connecticut* (Princeton, NJ: Princeton University Press, 1977).

93. Lipson, *Freemasonry in Federalist Connecticut*, 132–49, and Bullock, *Revolutionary Brotherhood*, 184–238, explore the socioeconomic and political reasons.

94. *Constitutions*, 48, 25. See also N. Barker Cryer, "The De-Christianizing of the Craft," *Ars Quatuor Coronatorum* 97 (1984): 38.

95. William Preston, *Illustrations of Freemasonry*, 1st American from 10th London ed. (Alexandria, VA: Cotton and Stewart, 1804), 16.

96. William Hutchison, *The Spirit of Masonry* (London: J. Wilkie, 1775), 18. See also Cryer, "De-Christianizing the Craft"; J.R. Clarke, "The Change from Christianity to Deisim in Freemasonry," *Ars Quatuor Coronatorum* 78 (1965): 49–73.

97. "Biographical Sketches," 185.

98. According to Dorothy Ann Lipson, "clergymen were sought in some parts of Connecticut or by some members of the lodges, in the same way that noble sponsorship had been sought in England. Since membership in Masonry was expensive, the fees for the clergy were usually waived." Lipson, *Freemasonry in Federalist Connecticut*, 128.

99. McClenachan, *Masons in New York*, 2:181, 426.

100. Avery Allyn, *A Ritual and Illustrations of Free-Masonry, and the Orange and Odd Fellows' Societies* . . . (Devon, England: S. Thorne, 1844), xiv–xv.

101. Crawford, *Address Delivered at the Grand Convocation*, 24.

102. While my focus here is on orthodox Calvinist opposition to Freemasonry, John L. Brooke has extended the discussion to include the Masonic Federalists' similarly futile resistance to Republican Freemasonry. In documenting the fact that Republican political leaders in every state were Freemasons, he argues that Masonry connected "men of moderate property who had been excluded from power by the Federalists . . . with men of prominence within the state and the nation, and it connected them with the symbols of nation-building charisma." Brooke, "Ancient Lodges," 359.

103. See Mark Noll, *A History of Christianity in the United States and Canada* (Grand Rapids, MI: Eerdmans, 1992), 114–19; extended discussion in Hatch, *Sacred Cause of Liberty*.

104. Gary B. Nash, "The American Clergy and the French Revolution," *William and Mary Quarterly*, 3rd ser., 22, no. 3 (July 1965): 392–412.

105. See David Lewis, "The Reformer as Conservative: Protestant Counter-subversion in the Early Republic," in *The Development of an American Culture*, ed. Stanley Cobden and Lorman Ratner (Englewood Cliffs, NJ: Prentice Hall, 1972), 64–91.

106. Jedidiah Morse, *A Sermon, Delivered at the New North Church in Boston, in the Morning, and in the Afternoon at Charlestown* . . . (Boston: Samuel Hall, 1798), 18–19.

107. Ibid., 20; John Robison, *Proofs of a Conspiracy against All the Religions and Governments of Europe, Carried On in the Secret Meetings of the Free Masons, Illuminati, and Reading Societies* (Edinburgh: William Creech; London, T. Cadell Jr. and W. Davies, 1797). Augustin Barruel, *The Anti-Christian and Anti-social Conspiracy* (Lancaster, PA: Joseph Ehrenfried, 1812), a partial

translation of a four-volume work published in French in 1797, made the Catholic case against Freemasonry. Morse's credulity also betrayed him when, in 1815, he employed similarly flimsy evidence to assert that a conspiracy of liberals was working to undermine orthodox teaching at Harvard. On Morse, see James K. Morse, *Jedidiah Morse: A Champion of New England Orthodoxy* (New York: Columbia University Press, 1939); Joseph W. Phillips, *Jedidiah Morse and New England Congregationalism* (New Brunswick, NJ: Rutgers University Press, 1983).

108. The campaign against the Illuminati touched on all the important themes common to later nineteenth- and twentieth-century American nativist crusades. Foreign, anti-Protestant, atheistic, and conspiratorial, the Illuminati were perceived as hiding behind the respectability of the Freemasons, who although already worrisome to some evangelicals were not subject to massive attack until the 1820s and 1830s. For the most detailed account of this controversy, see Vernon Stauffer, *New England and the Bavarian Illuminati* (New York: Columbia University Press, 1918).

109. Morse, *Sermon, Delivered at the New North Church*, 21, 22.

110. Jedidiah Morse, *A Sermon Delivered before the Grand Lodge of Free and Accepted Masons of the Commonwealth of Massachusetts, June 25th, 1798* (Leominster, MA: Charles and John Prentiss, 1798).

111. Timothy Dwight, *The Duty of Americans in the Present Crisis, Illustrated in a Discourse, Preached on the Fourth of July, 1798* (New Haven, CT: Thomas and Samuel Green, 1798), 11. On Dwight, see John R. Fitzmeir, *New England's Moral Legislator: Timothy Dwight, 1752–1817* (Bloomington: Indiana University Press, 1998).

112. *Massachusetts Mercury* (Boston), August 21, 1798, contains the full address of the Grand Lodge and President Adams's response.

113. William Bentley, *A Charge Delivered before the Morning Star Lodge, in Worcester, Massachusetts* . . . (Worcester, MA: Isaiah Thomas, 1798), 9, 31.

114. Stauffer, *New England and the Bavarian Illuminati*, 328, 338, 340–41.

115. Morse and his like-minded colleagues appealed to their parishioners and brother ministers but were not able to dramatically change the behavior of their fellow New Englanders. Such confrontations as the Illuminati row were part of the laborious process of separating church and state after the Revolution, and in time, the old-line Congregational clergy came to see their political concerns as out of step with the newly democratic society. See David Lewis, "The Reformer as Conservative."

116. Alexander Collins, *A Masonic Oration Pronounced on the Festival of St. John the Evangelist, December 26, 1799* (Middletown, CT: Dunning, 1800), 15.

3. A PRIVATE WORLD OF RITUAL, 1797–1825

1. Stephen C. Bullock's insightful treatment of these changes in the degree ceremonies and their implications informs my analysis. See *Revolutionary Brotherhood: Freemasonry and the Transformation of the American Social Order, 1730–1840* (Chapel Hill: University of North Carolina Press, 1996), 239–73.

2. Albert Gallatin Mackey, Robert Ingham Clegg, and William James Hughan, *Mackey's History of Freemasonry*, 7 vols. (New York: Masonic History, 1921), 5:1238.

3. Walter M. Callaway, foreword to William Preston, *Illustrations of Masonry*, 2nd ed. (London, 1775; repr., Bloomington, IL: Masonic Book Club, 1975), xv. Prior to the publication of this work, every eighteenth-century Masonic book included a lengthy appendix of songs for festive occasions. James Anderson's 1723 *Constitutions of the Free-Masons* had songs (see reprint of Anderson's book by Benjamin Franklin [1734; repr., Bloomington, IL: Masonic Book Club, 1971]; hereafter cited as *Constitutions*); the 1738 edition (Anderson, *The New Book of Constitutions of the Ancient and Honourable Fraternity of Free and Accepted Masons . . .* [Dublin: Edward Bate, 1751]) added others. The Ancients' 1756 *Ahiman Rezon*, by William Smith (Philadelphia: Hall and Sellers, 1783), had 128 pages of songs and poetry out of 224 total. In contrast, Preston studiously avoided such merriment, including but "a few songs" at the end of the second edition of his text. See A. C. F. Jackson, "Preston's England," in *The Collected Prestonian Lectures*, vol. 3, 1975–1987 (London: Lewis Masonic, 1988), 32.

4. Callaway, foreword to Preston, *Illustrations of Masonry*, xiv.

5. Preston, *Illustrations of Masonry*, 98.

6. The first appearance in print of this symbol in Freemasonry is in the second edition of Thomas Smith Webb's *Freemason's Monitor* (New York: Southwick and Crocker, 1802), 79. Its several purported origins are discussed in Jay Macpherson, "The Masons and the Great Seal," in *Freemasonry on Both Sides of the Atlantic: Essays Concerning the Craft in the British Isles, Europe, the United States, and Mexico*, ed. R. William Weisberger, Wallace McLeod, and S. Brent Morris (New York: Columbia University Press, 2002), 557–82. On the variety of Masonic aprons and their decorations, see Barbara Franco, *Bespangled, Painted and Embroidered: Decorated Masonic Aprons in America, 1790–1850* (Lexington, MA: Museum of Our National Heritage, Scottish Rite Masonic Museum and Library, 1980).

7. Avery Allyn, *A Ritual and Illustrations of Free-Masonry, and the Orange and Odd Fellows' Societies . . .* (Devon, England: S. Thorne, 1844), 30–31. For a detailed description of the three craft degrees, see Anthony D. Fels, "The Square and the Compass: San Francisco's Freemasons and American Religion, 1870–1900" (PhD diss., Stanford University, 1987), 143–201.

8. On rites of passage, see Victor Turner, *The Ritual Process: Structure and Anti-Structure* (Ithaca, NY: Cornell University Press, 1969).

9. Allyn, *Ritual*, 30.

10. John Vanderbilt Jr., *An Oration Delivered . . . before the Members of Trinity and Benevolent Lodges . . .* (New York: H. C. Southwick, 1808), 18.

11. Solomon Sias, *An Address Delivered . . . before the Portland Lodge . . .* (Portland, ME: A. Shirley, 1820), iii.

12. John H. Sheppard, *An Address Delivered in Portland, at the Consecration of the Grand Lodge of Maine* (Portland, ME: A. Shirley, 1820), 9.

13. Preston, *Illustrations of Masonry*, 68–69.

14. David Hartley, *Observations on Man* (London: S. Richardson, 1749). For a discussion, see Barbara Bowen Oberg, "David Hartley and the

Association of Ideas," *Journal of the History of Ideas* 37, no. 3 (July–September 1976): 441–54.

15. Allyn, *Ritual*, 38.

16. John Locke, *An Essay Concerning Human Understanding*, ed. A. S. Pringle-Pattison (London: Oxford University Press, 1953), 64–73.

17. So enamored of Locke was Preston that he appended to his *Illustrations* a 1696 letter in which Locke approves of the "principles of Masonry" as he understood them, based on his reading of an "old manuscript on the subject" that he had run across in Oxford's Bodleian Library. *Illustrations of Masonry*, 151–63. On the broad impact of Locke's educational ideas in America, see Lorraine Smith Pangle and Thomas L. Pangle, *The Learning of Liberty: The Educational Ideas of the American Founders* (Lawrence: University of Kansas Press, 1993).

18. Benjamin Gleason, *An Oration, Pronounced before the Bristol Lodge* . . . (Boston: Belcher and Armstrong, 1806), 13.

19. Mackey, Clegg, and Hughan, *Mackey's History of Freemasonry*, 4:1246–47.

20. For example, in Baltimore in 1810, a new Select Degree appeared, with one Philip Eckel claiming authority over it and its dissemination. Eugene E. Hinman, Ray Vaughn Denslow, and Charles Clyde Hunt, *A History of the Cryptic Rite*, vol. 1 (Tacoma, WA: n.p., 1931), 53. A later rite, the Knights of Three Kings, was "believed [to have been] . . . invented by some of our grand lecturers, who make it their business to travel from lodge to lodge and instruct men in the mysteries of ancient Freemasonry." Allyn, *Ritual*, 180.

21. Thomas Smith Webb, *The Freemason's Monitor, or Illustrations of Masonry: In Two Parts* (Albany, NY: [Fry and Southwick?], 1797).

22. Ibid., vi.

23. Ray Baker Harris, *History of the Supreme Council, 33rd Degree, Ancient and Accepted Scottish Rite of Freemasonry Southern Jurisdiction, U.S.A., 1801–1861* (Washington, DC: Supreme Council, 1964), 15–20.

24. This figure is for just the last four editions of *The Freemason's Monitor*. Herbert T. Leyland, *Thomas Smith Webb* (Dayton, OH: Otterbein, 1965), 388.

25. Bullock, *Revolutionary Brotherhood*, 251; Harris, *History of the Supreme Council*, 1–131.

26. C. P. MacCalla, "Freemasonry in America," *Ars Quatuor Coronatorum* 3 (1890): 123; Bullock, *Revolutionary Brotherhood*, 371 n. 16.

27. Leyland, *Thomas Smith Webb*, xii.

28. Isaiah Thomas, *An Address to the Most Worshipful Grand Lodge of Massachusetts . . . at the Close of the Constitutional Term of His Presiding as Grand Master* (Boston: John Elliot, 1811), 5.

29. Charles T. McClenachan, *History of the Most Ancient and Honorable Fraternity of Free and Accepted Masons in New York . . .*, 4 vols. (New York: Grand Lodge, 1888–94), 2:207–8.

30. Hinman et al., *History of the Cryptic Rite*, 161.

31. Thomas, *Address to the Grand Lodge of Massachusetts*, 5.

32. On print culture, see Richard R. John, *Spreading the News: The American Postal System from Franklin to Morse* (Cambridge, MA: Harvard University Press, 1995), ix; John, "Expanding the Realm of Communication," in *An*

Extensive Republic: Print, Culture, and Society in the New Nation, Robert A. Gross and Mary Kelley, eds., vol. 2 of *A History of the Book in America*, ed. David D. Hall (Chapel Hill: University of North Carolina Press, 2010), 211–20.

33. For more on these momentous developments in American Christianity, see Nathan O. Hatch, *The Democratization of Christianity* (New Haven, CT: Yale University Press, 1989); Roger Finke and Rodney Stark, *The Churching of America, 1776–1990: Winners and Losers in Our Religious Economy* (New Brunswick, NJ: Rutgers University Press, 1992), 54–108.

34. Hinman et al., *History of the Cryptic Rite*, 34; Mackey, Clegg, and Hughan, *Mackey's History of Freemasonry*, 4:1242.

35. Webb, *Freemason's Monitor*, 153.

36. William Morgan, *Illustrations of Freemasonry* (Rochester, NY, 1827) 69–103; Allyn, *Ritual*, 66–81; Fels, "The Square and the Compass," 180–185.

37. Allyn, *Ritual*, 109–40.

38. Webb, *Freemason's Monitor*, 153.

39. Ibid., 176.

40. For an overview of these developments, see Richard D. Brown, "The Emergence of Urban Society in Rural Massachusetts, 1760–1820," *Journal of American History* 61 (1974): 29–50; Alan Dawley, *Class and Community: The Industrial Revolution in Lynn* (Cambridge, MA: Harvard University Press, 1976), 11–41; Stuart Blumin, "Mobility and Change in Ante-Bellum Philadelphia," in *Nineteenth-Century Cities: Essays in the New Urban History*, ed. Stephen Thernstrom and Richard Sennett (New Haven, CT: Yale University Press, 1969), 165–208; George Rogers Taylor, *The Transportation Revolution, 1815–1860* (New York: Rinehart, 1951); Edward Pessen, *Jacksonian America: Society, Personality, and Politics* (Homewood, IL: Dorsey, 1969), 114–15; Paul E. Johnson, *A Shopkeeper's Millennium: Society and Revivals in Rochester, New York, 1815–1837* (New York: Hill and Wang, 1978), 37–61, 207–28.

41. Bullock reports that somewhere between a quarter and a half of the total membership held offices in the fraternity. *Revolutionary Brotherhood*, 247–52.

42. Alexis de Tocqueville, *Democracy in America*, ed. Harvey C. Mansfield and Delba Winthrop (Chicago: University of Chicago Press, 2000), 482.

43. The most extreme identification of women with private life is offered by Carroll Smith-Rosenberg, "The Female World of Love and Ritual," in her *Disorderly Conduct: Visions of Gender in Victorian America* (New York: Oxford University Press, 1985), 53–76.

44. Jan Lewis, *The Pursuit of Happiness: Family and Values in Jefferson's Virginia* (New York: Cambridge University Press, 1983), 209–30.

45. See Robert L. Griswold, *Family and Divorce in California, 1850–1890: Victorian Illusions and Everyday Realities* (Albany: State University of New York Press, 1982), 5; Carl N. Degler, *At Odds: Women and the Family in America from the Revolution to the Present* (New York: Oxford University Press, 1980), 8–25.

46. Webb, *Freemason's Monitor*, 153. Here he refers to the mysterious content of the Old Charges produced by guilds of stonemasons. See Douglas Knoop and G.P. Jones, *The Genesis of Freemasonry: An Account of the Rise and*

Development of Freemasonry in Its Operative, Accepted, and Early Speculative Phases (London: Quatuor Coronati Lodge No. 2076, 1978), 62–86.

47. See, e.g., "The First Masonic Discourse Delivered in America" (1733), *Freemason's Monthly Magazine* (Boston) 8, no. 10 (August 1, 1849): 293.

48. *Constitutions*, 7-46.

49. Thomas Paine, *An Essay on the Origin of Free Masonry* (London: R. Carlile, 1818), 5.

50. Webb, *Freemason's Monitor*, 19, 34–35, 21.

51. Hebrews 7:17 (King James Version); Webb, *Freemason's Monitor*, 199–200.

52. Webb, *Freemason's Monitor*, 244–61.

53. Jan Shipps, "The Reality of the Restoration and the Restoration Ideal in the Mormon Tradition," in *The American Quest for the Primitive Church*, ed. Richard T. Hughes (Champagne: University of Illinois Press, 1988), 182–83.

54. Edwin S. Gaustad, "Restitution, Revolution, and the American Dream," *Journal of the American Academy of Religion* 44 (1976): 78. David Edwin Harrell has gone further, suggesting that restoration "may be the most vital single assumption underlying the development of American Protestantism." Harrell, epilogue to Hughes, *The American Quest for the Primitive Church*, 239. Throughout the eighteenth and nineteenth centuries, a wide range of strategies appeared that sought to reform the present by juxtaposing it with some primeval past. In characterizing this broader outlook, Gaustad points to recurrent appeals to the classical worlds of the Greeks and Romans, the original "Laws of Nature," and ancient Christianity as models for envisioning the good society.

55. Scholarship on primitivism began with Arthur O. Lovejoy and George Boas, *Primitivism and Related Ideas in Antiquity: Contributions to the History of Primitivism* (Baltimore: Johns Hopkins Press, 1935; repr., New York: Octagon Books, 1965). Franklin H. Littell pioneered the study of Christian primitivism in America in his book on sixteenth-century Anabaptists, *The Anabaptist View of the Church: A Study in the Origins of Sectarian Protestantism* (2nd ed., Boston: Starr King, 1958). This was followed by a surge of scholarly interest led by Richard T. Hughes. See Hughes, ed., *American Quest for the Primitive Church;* Hughes and C. Leonard Allen, *Illusions of Innocence: Protestant Primitivism in America* (Chicago: University of Chicago Press, 1988); Theodore Dwight Bozeman, *To Live Ancient Lives: The Primitivist Dimension in Puritanism* (Chapel Hill: University of North Carolina Press, 1988); Hughes, ed., *The Primitive Church in the Modern World* (Urbana: University of Illinois Press, 1995). For a review of this scholarship, see W. Clark Gilpin, "Recent Studies of American Protestant Primitivism," *Religious Studies Review* 19, no. 3 (July 1993): 231–35.

56. Salem Town, *A System of Speculative Masonry* . . . (Salem, NY: Dodd and Stevenson, 1818), 30, 97–98.

57. Ibid., 24; Morgan, *Illustrations of Freemasonry*, 102. See also James Creighton Odiorne, *Opinions on Speculative Masonry* (Boston: Perkins and Marvin, 1830), 260.

58. Richard Bushman, *Joseph Smith: Rough Stone Rolling* (New York: Vintage, 2007), 133.

59. See John L. Brooke, *The Refiner's Fire: The Makings of Mormon Cosmology, 1644–1844* (New York: Cambridge University Press, 1994), 129–46.

60. David John Buerger, "The Development of the Mormon Temple Endowment Ceremony," *Dialogue: A Journal of Mormon Thought* 20 (Winter 1987): 35, 43–44.

61. Bushman, *Joseph Smith*, 450.

62. Cummings, quoted in Michael W. Homer, "Similarity of Priesthood in Masonry: The Relationship between Freemasonry and Mormonism," *Dialogue: A Journal of Mormon Thought* 27 (Fall 1994): 69.

63. Smith, quoted by Hebar Kimball in Bushman, *Joseph Smith*, 449.

64. Young, quoted in Homer, "Similarity of Priesthood in Masonry," 38.

65. Kimball, quoted in Buerger, "Mormon Temple Endowment Ceremony," 45.

66. Young also believed that Freemasons were behind the murder of Smith and were seeking to undermine Mormonism. Nevertheless, as Michael Homer has pointed out, some Mormons continued to practice Freemasonry and to clamor for the creation of a lodge after the arrival in Salt Lake City ("Similarity of Priesthood in Masonry," 97–98). This suggests the fraternity's attraction even after the creation of the endowment ceremony.

67. W. Clark Gilpin, "Recent Studies of American Protestant Primitivism," *Religious Studies Review* 19, no. 3 (July 1993): 234.

68. On Hume, see Ann Taves, *Fits, Trances, and Visions: Experiencing Religion and Explaining Experience from Wesley to James* (Princeton, NJ: Princeton University Press, 1999), 41–45.

69. On Scottish commonsense realism, see E. Brooks Holifield, *Theology in America: Christian Thought from the Age of the Puritans to the Civil War* (New Haven, CT: Yale University Press, 2003), 173–80.

70. Edmund Burke, *A Philosophical Inquiry into the Origins of Our Ideas of the Sublime and Beautiful* (London: R. and J. Dodsley, 1757).

71. For the eighteenth-century understanding of the sublime, see Patrick V. McGreevy, *Imagining Niagara: The Meaning and Making of Niagara Falls* (Amherst: University of Massachusetts Press, 1994), 10–11, 73. For an overview of the century's progression from reason to feeling as embodying the essential nature of humanity, see Walter Jackson Bate, *From Classic to Romantic: Premises of Taste in Eighteenth-Century England* (New York: Harper and Row, 1961), 129–59.

72. *Collected Letters of Samuel Taylor Coleridge*, ed. E.L. Griggs, 6 vols. (Oxford: Clarendon, 1956–71), 2:709. For the development of the romantic movement, see Morse Peckham, *The Triumph of Romanticism: Collected Essays* (Columbia: University of South Carolina Press, 1970), 36–57.

73. Allyn, *Ritual*, 118–40.

74. William G. McLoughlin, introduction to *Lectures on Revivals of Religion by Charles Grandison Finney*, ed. McLoughlin (Cambridge, MA: Harvard University Press, 1960), vii.

75. Ibid., x.

76. McLoughlin suggests that there was never a definitive list of the new measures, though many of them grew out of practices invented in the First

Great Awakening and by camp exhorters in the Second Great Awakening. Ibid., xxxvi. For more on the new measures, see Richard Carwardine, *Transatlantic Revivalism: Popular Evangelicalism in Britain and America, 1790–1865* (Westport, CT: Greenwood, 1978), 3–58; Keith J. Hardman, *Charles Grandison Finney, 1792–1875: Revivalist and Reformer* (Syracuse, NY: Syracuse University Press, 1987), 134–48.

77. Charles Grandison Finney, *Memoirs of Charles G. Finney* (New York: A. S. Barnes, 1876), 7.

78. Charles Grandison Finney, *The Character, Claims and Practical Workings of Freemasonry* (Cincinnati: Western Tract and Book Society, 1869), v–vi.

79. Finney, quoted in Mark C. Carnes, *Secret Ritual and Manhood in Victorian America* (New Haven, CT: Yale University Press, 1989), 69–73. See also Hardman, *Charles Grandison Finney*, 99–100.

80. Charles Grandison Finney, *Lectures on Revivals of Religion* (New York: Fleming H. Revell, 1868), 253–54.

81. For a discussion of the therapeutic culture, see pt. 2, "Private Life," in Robert N. Bellah, Richard Madsden, William M. Sullivan, Ann Swidler, and Steven M. Tipton, *Habits of the Heart: Individualism and Commitment in American Life*, updated ed. (Berkeley: University of California Press, 2008), 55–163.

82. See Philip Rieff, "The Emergence of Psychological Man," concluding chapter in his *Freud: The Mind of the Moralist*, 3rd ed. (Chicago: University of Chicago Press, 1979), 329–57. On the movement from self-denial to self-realization in Protestant theology, see E. Brooks Holifield, *A History of Pastoral Care in America: From Salvation to Self-Realization* (Nashville: Abingdon, 1983).

83. Hannah Mather Crocker, *A Series of Letters on Free Masonry* (Boston: John Eliot, 1815), 7–9. Portions first appeared in the *Boston Centinel* in 1810. Biographical information on Crocker can be found in Francis Samuel Drake, ed., *Dictionary of American Biography* (Boston: Houghton, Osgood, 1879), 231; Edward T. James, Janet Wilson James, and Paul S Boyer, eds., *Notable American Women, 1607–1950* (Cambridge, MA: Belknap Press of Harvard University Press, 1971), 406–7.

84. Linda K. Kerber and Ruth H. Bloch have led the way in exploring the "republican mother" as a transitional phase in the redefinition of women's ideals and roles from the late colonial to the early national periods. Kerber first coined the term *republican motherhood* to describe the indirect political role that revolutionary-era women had in "raising sons and disciplining husbands to be virtuous citizens of the republic." See "The Republican Mother: Women and the Enlightenment—An American Perspective," *American Quarterly* 28 (1976): 187–205, quotation on 203; *Women of the Republic: Intellect and Ideology in Revolutionary America* (Chapel Hill: University of North Carolina Press, 1980). Bloch first suggested the need to pay attention to the republican dimensions of motherhood from 1785 to 1815. See "American Feminine Ideals in Transition: The Rise of the Moral Mother, 1785–1815," *Feminist Studies* 4, no. 2 (1978): 125–26 n. 67. She explored the transition from masculine to feminine understandings of virtue in "The Gendered Meanings of Virtue in the Early Republic," *Signs: Journal of*

Women in Culture and Society 13 (1987–88): 37–88. In a later refinement, Kerber argued that "republican motherhood was a conceptualization which grafted the language of liberal individualism onto the inherited discourse of civic humanism," which could not by itself "effectively describe an active role for women in the republic." "The Republican Ideology of the Revolutionary Generation," *American Quarterly* 37, no. 4 (1985): 486, 484. She placed the idea of republican womanhood into the context of scholarship on women in American history in "Separate Spheres, Female Worlds, Woman's Place: The Rhetoric of Women's History," *Journal of American History* 75, no. 1 (1988): 9–39. For the implications of republican ideology for relations between men and women, see Jan Lewis, "The Republican Wife: Virtue and Seduction in the Early Republic," *William and Mary Quarterly*, 44, no. 4 (October 1987): 689–721; Mary Beth Norton, *Liberty's Daughters: The Revolutionary Experience of American Women, 1750–1800* (Boston: Little, Brown, 1980). Among the many reconsiderations of the gendered public-private argument, see especially Kerber, Nancy F. Cott, Robert Gross, Lynn Hunt, Carroll Smith-Rosenberg, and Christine Stansell, "Beyond Roles, Beyond Spheres: Thinking about Gender in the Early Republic," *William and Mary Quarterly* 46, no. 3 (July 1989): 565–85; Joan B. Landes, "The Public and the Private Sphere: A Feminist Reconsideration," in *Feminism, the Public and the Private*, ed. Landes (Oxford: Oxford University Press, 1998), 135–63; articles by Mary Kelley, Julie Roy Jeffrey, Laura McCall, and Carol Lasser in "Redefining Womanly Behavior in the Early Republic: Essays from a SHEAR Symposium," *Journal of the Early Republic* 21 (Spring 2001): 73–123; articles by Bloch, John L. Brooke, Christopher Looby, and David Waldstreicher in "Forum: Alternative Histories of the Public Sphere," *William and Mary Quarterly*, 3rd ser., 62, no. 1 (January 2005).

85. Crocker, *Letters on Free Masonry*, 8.

86. Hannah Mather Crocker, *Observations on the Real Rights of Women*, in *Women's Early American Historical Narratives*, ed. Sharon M. Harris (New York: Penguin, 2003), 230–31, 248. For the place of this pamphlet in the history of the women's rights movement, see Eleanor Flexner, *Century of Struggle: The Women's Rights Movement in the United States* (Cambridge, MA: Belknap Press of Harvard University Press, 1959; repr., 1996), 23; Anne Firor Scott, "Unfinished Business," *Journal of Women's History* 8, no. 2 (1996): 112.

87. Kerber, *Women of the Republic*, 185–231.

88. Steven C. Bullock makes a similar point in *Revolutionary Brotherhood*, 182. In contrast to the ephemerality of this American female lodge, Margaret C. Jacob has explored the significance of women's lodges in late eighteenth-century French Freemasonry. Reminiscent of how protofeminist women's rights advocates emerged from Protestant women's societies in the mid-nineteenth century—a development first identified by Nancy F. Cott, in *The Bonds of Womanhood: "Woman's Sphere" in New England, 1780–1835* (New Haven, CT: Yale University Press, 1977)—according to Jacob, late eighteenth-century French women grew in "confidence, power, and awareness" in the arena that Freemasonry provided. Through their women-led and women-centered rituals, these lodges furnished leading women with "their own rite of passage into the culture of Enlightenment." Jacob, *The Origins of Freemasonry* (Philadelphia: University

of Pennsylvania Press, 2006), 92–129. See also Janet M. Burke, "Leaving the Enlightenment: Women Freemasons after the Revolution," *Eighteenth-Century Studies*, 33, no. 2 (Winter 2000): 255–65; Burke, "Freemasonry, Friendship, and Noblewomen: The Role of the Secret Society in Bringing Enlightenment Thought to Pre-Revolutionary Women Elites," *History of European Ideas* 10 (1989): 283–94; Burke and Jacob, "French Freemasonry, Women, and Feminist Scholarship," *Journal of Modern History* 68 (1996): 513–49.

89. Several scholars have discussed the transition of elite women from colonial "tea table" matrons presiding over the manners and morals of polite society to republican mothers seeking to influence civil society more directly. See especially Frederika Teute, "Roman Matron on the Banks of Tiber Creek: Margaret Smith Bayard and the Politicization of Spheres in the Nation's Capital," and Jan Lewis, "Politics and the Ambivalence of the Private Sphere: Women in Early Washington, D.C.," in *A Republic for the Ages: The United States Capitol and the Political Culture of the Early Republic*, ed. Donald R. Kenon (Charlottesville: University Press of Virginia, 1999), 89–151; Mary Kelley, *Learning to Stand and Speak: Women, Education, and Public Life in America's Republic* (Chapel Hill: University of North Carolina Press, 2006), 8, 50–54; Linda K. Kerber, *No Constitutional Right to Be Ladies: Women and the Obligations of Citizenship* (New York: Hill and Wang, 1998), 3–46; Paula Baker, "The Domestication of' Politics: Women and American Political Society, 1780–1920," *American Historical Review* 89 (1984): 622–25.

90. Kelley, *Learning to Stand and Speak*, 7–8, 67.

91. Kelley coined this term, which she defined as "the discourse that took as its subject the role of women in the nation's public life." Ibid., 25.

92. Crocker, *Letters on Free Masonry*, 5–19.

93. Ibid., 4.

94. Most colonial European men and women in America traced their model of civil society to the family and the husband's power over his wife. This understanding derived from early seventeenth-century English thought and practice, particularly the theoretical model associated with Sir Robert Filmer. See Mary Beth Norton, *Founding Mothers and Fathers: Gendered Power and the Forming of American Society* (New York: Knopf, 1996), 8–14. For the Puritans, the helpmeet was the wifely ideal, justified by biblical patriarchs and buttressed by cultural assumptions that saw women as less rational, more emotional, and thus unfit for holding official positions in the formal public of colonial political and church life. See Bloch, "Gendered Meanings of Virtue," 37–88; Bloch, "American Feminine Ideals in Transition," 100–26. Because of this hierarchical relationship, women could not participate in the formal public of colonial life, but because of the close relationship between men and women in the family, they could still wield significant influence in the informal public of community life. This was particularly true of widows, who took their husband's place in some public dealings, and high-status women, who wielded greater influence than low-status men, but also of all women who mingled with men in taverns, in the streets, and at communal gatherings. See Catherine A. Brekus, *Strangers and Pilgrims: Female Preaching in America, 1740–1845* (Chapel Hill: University of North Carolina Press, 1998), 12–14, 27–28.

95. William Bentley, *A Discourse Delivered at Amherst . . . at the Installation of the Benevolent Lodge . . .* (Amherst, MA: Samuel Preston, 1797), 21. Dorothy Ann Lipson suggests that Masonic responses to women in this period "were all couched in language that emphasized the distance between the social roles of men and women." Lipson, *Freemasonry in Federalist Connecticut, 1789–1835* (Princeton, NJ: Princeton University Press, 1977), 191.

96. Ruth S. Bloch, "Gender and the Public/Private Dichotomy in American Revolutionary Thought," in her *Gender and Morality in Anglo-American Culture, 1650–1800* (Berkeley: University of California Press, 2003), 156.

97. Kathleen M. Brown, "Brave New Worlds: Women's and Gender History," *William and Mary Quarterly*, 3rd ser., 50, no. 2 (April 1993): 311. The origins of this dominant paradigm are most frequently traced to the works of Barbara Welter, Carroll Smith-Rosenberg, Kathryn Kish Sklar, Nancy F. Cott, and Mary P. Ryan. See Welter, "The Feminization of American Religion: 1800–1860," *American Quarterly* 18 (1966): 151–74; Smith-Rosenberg, *Religion and the Rise of the American City: The New York City Mission Movement, 1812–1870* (Ithaca, NY: Cornell University Press, 1971); Smith-Rosenberg, *Disorderly Conduct: Visions of Gender in Victorian America* (New York: Oxford University Press, 1985); Sklar, *Catharine Beecher: A Study in American Domesticity* (New Haven, CT: Yale University Press, 1973); Cott, *Bonds of Womanhood*; Ryan, *Cradle of the Middle Class: The Family in Oneida County, New York, 1790–1865* (New York: Cambridge University Press, 1981). *Women's sphere* describes a female-dominated household world of piety and domesticity. Emerging with the separation of the workplace from the home in the early nineteenth century, the ideology of separate spheres held a dichotomized view of male and female nature whereby men occupied a public sphere of economics and politics while women held sway over a private sphere of children, religion, and morality. For each of these authors, Protestantism played an important role in shaping the colonial ideal of the true woman. The perception of many nineteenth-century Americans that Christianity, and particularly liberal Protestantism, had been feminized was linked to the predominance of women in Protestant churches and new theological interpretations of a nurturing and self-sacrificing Christ, which were seen as feminine. Subsequent scholarship has demonstrated how Protestantism became a means of extending women's work outside the household, through their participation in a variety of reform movements. See, for example, Barbara Epstein, *The Politics of Domesticity: Women, Evangelism and Temperance in Nineteenth-Century America* (Middletown, CT: Wesleyan University Press, 1981); Ruth Bordin, *Women and Temperance: The Quest for Power and Liberty, 1873–1900* (Philadelphia: Temple University Press, 1982); Nancy A. Hewitt, *Women's Activism and Social Change: Rochester, New York, 1822–1872* (Ithaca, NY: Cornell University Press, 1984); Paula Baker, *The Moral Frameworks of Public Life: Gender, Politics and the State in Rural New York, 1870–1930* (New York: Oxford University Press, 1991). Building on these efforts, scholars have further elaborated these moral frameworks in their investigations of women's lives before 1800. See, e.g., Mary Beth Norton, "The Evolution of White Women's Experience in Early America," *American Historical Review* 89 (1984): 593–619.

98. Norton, *Founding Mothers and Fathers*, 10–11; Brekus, *Strangers and Pilgrims*, 72–73.

99. Bloch, "American Feminine Ideals in Transition," 114.

100. Robert G. Wetmore, *An Oration on the Festival of St. John, the Evangelist, Twenty-Seventh December, 5797* (Catskill, NY: M. Crosswell, 1797), 15.

101. Samuel Dana, *An Address Delivered in Amherst . . . at the Consecration of the Benevolent Lodge* (Amherst, MA: Samuel Preston, 1797), 10.

102. James Milnor, *Oration on Masonry, Delivered at St. John's Church, in the City of Philadelphia* . . . (Philadelphia: Grand Lodge of Pennsylvania, 1811), 34.

103. *Freemason's Magazine and General Miscellany* 1, no. 2 (May 1811): 128. Carroll Smith-Rosenberg was among the first scholars to articulate this well-known dichotomy, in "Beauty and the Beast and the Militant Woman: A Case Study in Sex Roles and Social Stress in Jacksonian America," *American Quarterly* 23 (1971): 562–84; "The Female World of Love and Ritual: Relations between Women in Nineteenth-Century America," *Signs: Journal of Women in Culture and Society* 1 (1975): 1–29. See also Mary P. Ryan, "The Power of Women's Networks: A Case Study of Female Moral Reform in Antebellum America," *Feminist Studies* 5 (1979): 66–85.

104. Crocker, *Real Rights of Women*, 230–31.

105. George Richards, ed., *Freemason's Magazine and General Miscellany* 1, no. 3 (June 1811): 204.

106. "A Lady in Worcester" [Abigail Lyon], *Observations on Freemasonry; With a Masonic Vision* (Worcester, MA: [Leonard Worcester?], 1798), 4–5.

107. Bloch, "American Feminine Ideals in Transition," 101–20.

108. S. B. T. Caldwell, *A Masonic Oration, Delivered at Middleburg, Va. . . .* (Leesburg, VA: Brother B. W. Sower, 1820), 17–19. See also Milnor, *Oration on Masonry*, 33–35.

109. Ann Douglas, *The Feminization of American Culture* (New York: Alfred A. Knopf, 1977).

4. ANTI-MASONRY AND THE PUBLIC SPHERE 1826–1850

1. Alexis de Tocqueville, *Democracy in America*, ed. and trans. Harvey C. Mansfield and Delba Winthrop (University of Chicago Press, 2000), 492. See also Mark A. Tabbert, *American Freemasons: Three Centuries of Building Communities* (New York: New York University Press, 2005), 70–71. A century later, Arthur M. Schlesinger Sr. observed that America had matured into "a nation of joiners," as seen in the multiplication and growth of benevolent associations, reform societies, business and professional societies, farmers' and laborers' cooperatives, "and fraternal associations." Voluntary organizations, he concluded, were "a great cementing force for national integration." Schlesinger, "Biography of a Nation of Joiners," *American Historical Review* 50, no. 1 (October, 1944): 1, 25. More recently, scholars have debated the relative role of local and translocal forces in the creation and duration of voluntary organizations while affirming their decisive role in American democracy. See Gerald Gamm and Robert D.

Putnam, "The Growth of Voluntary Associations in America, 1840–1940," *Journal of Interdisciplinary History* 29, no. 4 (Spring 1999): 511–57; Theda Skocpol, Marshall Ganz, and Ziad Munson, "A Nation of Organizers: The Institutional Origins of Civic Voluntarism in the United States," *American Political Science Review* 94, no. 3 (September 2000): 527–46.

2. Whitney Cross popularized the term *burned-over district* in his pathbreaking study *The Burned-Over District: The Social and Intellectual History of Enthusiastic Religion in Western New York State, 1800–1850* (Ithaca, NY: Cornell University Press, 1950). Charles Grandison Finney appears to have coined it, using *burnt district* in his 1876 autobiography to denote an area in central and western New York State that had been so heavily evangelized by antebellum revivalism as to have no "fuel" (unconverted population) left to "burn" (convert) in the Second Great Awakening. Charles Grandison Finney, *Memoirs of Charles G. Finney* (New York: A. S. Barnes, 1903), 95.

3. Tabbert, *American Freemasons*, 58–60, is the most recent recounting of this history. In his study of the Anti-Masonic Party in the United States, William Preston Vaughn found that "the southern states were no more receptive to Antimasonry than to antislavery or to other reform movements of the Age of Jackson." Vaughn, *The Antimasonic Party in the United States, 1826–1843* (Lexington: University Press of Kentucky, 1983), 170. For estimates of membership following the Anti-Masonic period, see ibid., 187.

4. On this fundamental transformation, see especially Sean Wilentz, *Chants Democratic: New York City and the Rise of the American Working Class, 1788–1850* (New York: Oxford University Press, 1984); Joyce Appleby, *Capitalism and a New Social Order: The Republican Vision of the 1790s* (New York: New York University Press, 1984).

5. Nathan Hatch, *The Democratization of American Christianity* (New Haven, CT: Yale University Press, 1989), 9. The "upstart sects," especially the Baptists and the Methodists, led this religious democratization. See Roger Finke and Rodney Starke, "How the Upstart Sects Won America," *Journal for the Scientific Study of Religion* 28, no. 1 (March 1989): 27–44.

6. Kathleen Smith Kutolowski, "Freemasonry Revisited: Another Look at the Grass-roots Bases of Antimasonic Anxieties," in *Freemasonry on Both Sides of the Atlantic: Essays Concerning the Craft in the British Isles, Europe, the United States, and Mexico*, ed. R. William Weisberger, Wallace McLeod, and S. Brent Morris (New York: Columbia University Press, 2002), 586–91. See also Ronald P. Formisano with Kutolowski, "Antimasonry and Masonry: The Genesis of Protest, 1826–1827," *American Quarterly* 29 (1977): 139–65.

7. Dorothy Ann Lipson, *Freemasonry in Federalist Connecticut, 1789–1835* (Princeton, NJ: Princeton University Press, 1977), 354.

8. John G. Stearns, *An Inquiry into the Nature and Tendency of Speculative Freemasonry* (Utica, NY: Northway and Bennett, 1827), 78.

9. Kutolowski, "Freemasonry Revisited," 589–90.

10. Lipson, *Freemasonry in Federalist Connecticut*, 7–8.

11. Paul Goodman, *Towards a Christian Republic: Antimasonry and the Great Transition in New England, 1826–1836* (New York: Oxford University Press, 1988), 11, 60.

12. Douglas Knoop and G. P. Jones, eds., "An Antimasonic Leaflet of 1698," *Transactions of the Quatuor Coronati Lodge No. 2076, London* 54 (1942): 152–54.

13. Samuel Prichard, *Masonry Dissected: Being an Universal and Genuine Description of All Its Branches* (London: Wilford, 1730).

14. In 1750, Joseph Green parodied the *Boston Gazette*'s description of Saint John's Lodge's Saint John's Day procession. Green, *Entertainment for a Winter's Evening* . . . (Boston, 1750). The *Boston Evening Post* offered cruder commentary. On January 7, 1751, "a scandalous" poem and drawing appeared in its pages that saw anal torture as the actual use of Masonic trowels.

15. David Bernard, *Light on Masonry: A Collection of All the Most Important Documents on the Subject of Speculative Free Masonry* . . ., 13th ed. (Dayton, OH: W. J. Shuey, 1871), iii.

16. Kutolowski, "Freemasonry Revisited," 592. The county's Masons numbered but three hundred men of a total 1820 population of more than fifty-eight thousand. U.S. Census Bureau, *Fourth Census of the United States, 1820*, vol. 1, ser. no. 7 (New York: N. Ross, 1990).

17. Jabez D. Hammond, *The History of Political Parties in the State of New York*, vol. 2 (Cooperstown, NY: H. and E. Phinney, 1846), 237–38.

18. Henry Brown, *A Narrative of the Anti-Masonick Excitement, in the Western Part of the State of New York, during the Years 1826, '7, '8, and a Part of 1829* (Batavia, NY: Adams and M'Cleary, 1829), 119.

19. Town of Eiba, Genesee County, 1827 declaration, reproduced in ibid., 117–18.

20. William Vaughn has estimated that one-quarter of western New York's ministers and one-twentieth of the laymen were Masons (*Antimasonic Party*, 22). A list of prominent Masonic clergymen and political leaders who publicly renounced Freemasonry is provided in Henry Dana Ward, ed., *Anti-Masonic Review* 1, no. 12 (1828): 359.

21. Bernard, *Light on Masonry*, 311.

22. Ibid., 2–9.

23. Here are the two oaths most disturbing to evangelicals:

Obligation of a Master Mason

To all which I do most solemnly and sincerely promise and swear, with a fixed and steady purpose of mind in me, to keep and perform the same, binding myself under no less penalty than to have my body severed in two in the midst, and divided to the north and south, my bowels burnt to ashes in the centre, and the ashes scattered before the four winds of heaven, that there might not the least track or trace of remembrance remain among men or Masons of so vile and perjured a wretch as I should be, were I ever to prove willfully guilty of violating any part of this my solemn oath or obligation of a Master mason. So help me God, and keep me steadfast in the due performance of the same. (Bernard, *Light on Masonry*, 47–48)

Obligation of a Royal Arch Mason

Binding myself under no less penalty, than that of having my skull smote off, and my brains exposed to the scorching rays of the sun, should I ever knowingly, or willingly, violate or transgress any part of this my solemn oath, or obligation, of a Royal Arch Mason. So help me God, and keep me steadfast in the performance of the same. (Ibid., 57)

In the best contemporaneous account of the Morgan affair, William L. Stone, a Mason, decried the hysteria of Anti-Masonry, particularly defending the Masonic punishments for the breaching of oaths as symbolic rather than real. Stone, *Letters on Masonry and Anti-Masonry, Addressed to the Hon. John Quincy Adams* (New York: O. Halsted, 1832), 67–71, appendix p. 2.

24. John G. Stearns's *Inquiry into the Nature and Tendency of Speculative Freemasonry* is the best contemporaneous Christian theological attack on the fraternity. First printed in 1826, this personal testimony led Bernard and other Masonic ministers across New York to contemplate renunciation.

25. Kutolowski found that a lodge in Bernard's village of Warsaw, a dozen miles from where Morgan had been abducted in Batavia, had "conducted at least two funerals without benefit of clergy although three churches existed in the village" ("Freemasonry Revisited," 590).

26. Stone, *Letters on Masonry and Anti-Masonry*, 391–92.

27. Ibid., 392.

28. Henry D. Ward, ed., *Antimasonic Review and Monthly Magazine* (New York: Vanderpool and Cole, 1828), 330–31, summarizes these proceedings.

29. Lebbeus Armstrong, *Masonry Proved to Be a Work of Darkness, Repugnant to the Christian Religion; and Inimical to a Republican Government*, 4th ed. (New York: J.A. Lewis, 1831); Armstrong, *The Men of Sin Revealed or the Total Overthrow of the Institution of Freemasonry Predicted by St. Paul* (New York: n.p., 1829), 1.

30. William H. Brackney recounts these events in "Religious Antimasonry: The Genesis of a Political Party" (PhD diss., Temple University, 1976), 133–80, 290–91. See also Vaughn, *Antimasonic Party*, 21–23.

31. Stone, *Letters on Masonry and Anti-Masonry*, 329, 336.

32. Cowell, quoted in Vaughn, *Antimasonic Party*, 23.

33. On the significance of public opinion to Anti-Masonry, see Stephen C. Bullock, *Revolutionary Brotherhood: Freemasonry and the Transformation of the American Social Order, 1730–1840* (Chapel Hill: University of North Carolina Press, 1996), 283–98.

34. Mary P. Ryan, "Gender and Public Access: Women's Politics in Nineteenth-Century America," in *Habermas and the Public Sphere*, ed. Craig Calhoun (Cambridge, MA: MIT Press, 1992), 259–88; Ryan, *Civic Wars: Democracy and Public Life in the American City during the Nineteenth Century* (Berkeley: University of California Press, 1997); Geoff Eley, "Nations, Publics, and Political Cultures," in Calhoun, *Habermas and the Public Sphere*, 289–333; David Waldstreicher, *In the Midst of Perpetual Fetes: The Making of American Nationalism, 1776–1820* (Chapel Hill: University of North Carolina Press, 1997), 289–339.

35. Brown, *Narrative of the Anti-Masonick Excitement*, 110.

36. Milton W. Hamilton, "Antimasonic Newspapers, 1826–1834," *Papers of the Bibliographical Society of America* 32 (1939): 71–97. On the expansion

of print media after the Revolution, see especially the essays by Robert A. Gross and Richard R. John in *An Extensive Republic: Print, Culture, and Society in the New Nation, 1790–1840*, ed. Gross and Mary Kelley, vol. 2 of *A History of the Book in America*, ed. David D. Hall (Chapel Hill: University of North Carolina Press, 2010), 1–50, 211–20.

37. Ronald P. Formisano, *The Transformation of Political Culture: Massachusetts Parties, 1790s–1840s* (New York: Oxford University Press, 1983), 197–221; Michael F. Holt, "Antimasonic and Know Nothing Parties," in *History of U.S. Political Parties*, ed. Arthur M. Schlesinger Jr., vol. 1 (New York: Chelsea House, 1973), 575–93.

38. For an assessment of the significance of political Anti-Masonry, see Donald J. Ratcliffe, "Antimasonry and Partisanship in Greater New England," *Journal of the Early Republic* 15 (1995): 199–240.

39. E. Brooks Holifield, *Theology in America: Christian Thought from the Age of the Puritans to the Civil War* (New Haven, CT: Yale University Press, 2003), 159–394.

40. Paul Goodman's discussion in *Towards a Christian Republic*, 60–73, 235, informs my argument here.

41. James Turner, *Without God, without Creed: The Origins of Unbelief in America* (Baltimore: Johns Hopkins University Press, 1985), 73.

42. Formisano, *Transformation of Political Culture*, 197.

43. *New York Baptist Register*, May 15, 1829. See Brackney, "Religious Antimasonry," 178.

44. "Report on the Effect of Freemasonry on the Christian Religion," in *Extracts from the Proceedings of the First U. States Antimasonic Convention . . .* (Boston: Young Men's Antimasonic Association for the Diffusion of Truth, 1833), 82–83.

45. For an overview of this transformation in one New York market town, see Mary P. Ryan, *Cradle of the Middle Class: The Family in Oneida County, New York, 1790–1865* (New York: Cambridge University Press, 1981).

46. David G. Hackett, *The Rude Hand of Innovation: Religion and Social Order in Albany, New York, 1652–1836* (New York: Oxford University Press, 1991), 85–86, 141–44; Ryan, *Cradle of the Middle Class*, 79–80, 257.

47. Nancy A. Hewitt, *Women's Activism and Social Change: Rochester, New York, 1822–1872* (Ithaca, NY: Cornell University Press, 1984). Hewitt identifies three successive networks of female activists—"benevolent" women (1820s), "perfectionists" (1830s), and "ultras" (1840s)— all of whom were white, Protestant, and roughly middle class yet retained distinctive qualities.

48. Neither Ryan's *Cradle of the Middle Class* nor Hewitt's *Women's Activism and Social Change* mentions women's role in Anti-Masonry, nor did I find any evidence of it in my study of Albany. To my knowledge, neither the period's most well-known Anti-Masonic journal, the *Anti-Masonic Review*, nor its best-known newspaper, Albany's *Anti-Masonic Enquirer*, discussed the effect of Masonry on women. Nevertheless, both Paul Goodman and Dorothy Ann Lipson assert that women had considerable influence on Anti-Masonry. See Goodman, *Towards a Christian Republic*, 16–17, 80–102; Lipson, *Freemasonry in Federalist Connecticut*, 9, 187–200, 329–31, 333–36. Certainly this finding

may be inferred from the new sexual division of labor, but I have found little hard evidence to support the contention that evangelical women were a significant force behind Anti-Masonry.

49. *Republican Advocate*, December 8, 1826. See Kutolowski, "Freemasonry Revisited," 587.

50. Vaughn, *Antimasonic Party*, 19.

51. "Women and Masonry," editorial in the Anti-Masonic *Ravenna (OH) Star* (1830), quoted in ibid.

52. On Hale's influential understanding of the role of women, see Mary Kelley, *Learning to Stand and Speak: Women, Education, and Public Life in America's Republic* (Chapel Hill: University of North Carolina Press, 2006), esp. 7–14, 52–55; Patricia Okker, *Our Sister Editors: Sarah J. Hale and the Tradition of Nineteenth-Century Women Editors* (Athens: University of Georgia Press, 1995).

53. George Washington Warren, *The History of the Bunker Hill Monument Association during the First Century of the United States of America* (Boston: James R. Osgood, 1877), 307–8. This fair was a forerunner of later ones run by Masonic women in support of the order. See William D. Moore, "Funding the Temples of Masculinity: Women's Roles in Masonic Fairs in New York State, 1870–1930," in *Freemasonry in Context: History, Ritual, Controversy*, ed. Arturo de Hoyos and S. Brent Morris (Lanham, MD: Lexington Books, 2004), 75–87.

54. Warren, *Bunker Hill Monument Association*, 285–314.

55. On Hale and Freemasonry, see Olive Burt, *First Woman Editor: Sarah J. Hale* (New York: Messner, 1960), 42–44; Ruth E. Finley, *The Lady of Godey's, Sarah Josepha Hale* (Philadelphia: J.B. Lippincott, 1931), 31–39; Isabelle W. Entrikin, *Sarah Josepha Hale and Godey's Lady's Book* (Philadelphia, Lancaster Press, 1946) 8, 9, 17; Goodman, *Towards a Christian Republic*, 96–102.

56. Kutolowski, "Freemasonry Revisited," 595.

57. Vaughn, *Antimasonic Party*, 190.

58. Tabbert, *American Freemasons*, 74.

59. Lynn Dumenil, *Freemasonry and American Culture, 1880–1930* (Princeton, NJ: Princeton University Press, 1984), 8.

5. GENDER, PROTESTANTS, AND FREEMASONRY, 1850–1900

1. Lynn Dumenil, *Freemasonry and American Culture, 1880–1930* (Princeton, NJ: Princeton University Press, 1984), app. A, 225, has a chart on the historical relationship between Masonic membership and the American population.

2. W. S. Harwood, "Secret Societies in America," *North American Review* 164 (May 1897): 620–23.

3. Gerald Gamm and Robert Putnam, "The Growth of Voluntary Associations in America, 1840–1940," *Journal of Interdisciplinary History* 29, no. 4 (Spring 1999): 529–30.

4. Theda Skocpol and Jennifer Lynn Oser, "Organization Despite Diversity: The Origins and Development of African American Fraternal Associations," *Social Science History* 28, no. 3 (Fall 2004): 374.

5. Rowland Berthoff, *An Unsettled People: Social Order and Disorder in American Society* (New York: Harper and Row, 1971), 272–74, 445, 447; Don H. Doyle, *The Social Order of a Frontier Community; Jacksonville, Illinois, 1825–70* (Urbana: University of Illinois Press, 1978), 178–93; Arthur M. Schlesinger, *The Rise of the City, 1878–1898* (New York: Macmillan, 1933), 287–89.

6. Daniel Soyer, *Jewish Immigrant Associations and American Identity in New York, 1880–1939* (Cambridge, MA: Harvard University Press, 1997), 1–9.

7. David T. Beito, *From Mutual Aid to the Welfare State: Fraternal Societies and Social Services, 1890–1967* (Chapel Hill: University of North Carolina Press, 2000), 2–3.

8. For an exhaustive list of every published exposé of Freemasonry, see Kent Logan Walgren, *Freemasonry, Anti-Masonry, and Illuminism in the United States, 1734–1850: A Bibliography* (Worcester, MA: American Antiquarian Society, 2003).

9. See Albert C. Stevens, comp. and ed., *The Cyclopaedia of Fraternities: A Compilation of Existing Authentic Information and the Results of Original Investigation as to . . . More than Six Hundred Secret Societies in the United States* (Detroit: E. B. Treat, 1907).

10. Mark A. Tabbert, *American Freemasons: Three Centuries of Building Communities* (New York: New York University Press, 2005), 71–74. In the Civil War, tens of thousands of Masons served in both the Union and the Confederate armies. Together they formed more than 225 military lodges. See Allen E. Roberts, *House Undivided: The Society of Freemasonry and the Civil War* (New York: Macoy, 1961); Dumenil, *Freemasonry and American Culture*, 101–2.

11. Harwood, "Secret Societies in America," 620–23, provides the following membership data (rounded to the nearest thousand) for 1896:

Odd Fellows	810,000
Freemasons	750,000
Knights of Pythias	475,000
Ancient Order of United Workmen	361,000
Knights of the Maccabees	244,000
Modern Woodmen of America	204,000
Royal Arcanum	189,000
United American Mechanics, Jr.	187,000
Improved Order of Red Men	165,000
Knights of Honor	118,000

Others have argued for even higher figures. Albert C. Stevens, for example, estimated that 40 percent of the adult male population belonged to a fraternal order in 1896 (*Cyclopaedia of Fraternities*, xvi).

12. Anthony D. Fels, "The Square and the Compass: San Francisco's Freemasons and American Religion, 1870–1900," (PhD diss., Stanford University, 1987), 8–9 n. 2.

13. Beito, *Mutual Aid to the Welfare State*, 1.

14. Soyer, *Jewish Immigrant Associations*, 36.

15. Each of these arose from the post-1820s Baltimore Mutual Aid Society to become a national organization. Monroe N. Work, "Secret Societies as Factors in the Social and Economical Life of the Negro," in *Democracy in Earnest*, ed. James E. McCulloch (Washington, DC: Southern Sociological Congress, 1918), 343.

16. Gamm and Putnam, "Voluntary Associations in America," 522; Anne Firor Scott, *Natural Allies: Women's Associations in American History* (Urbana: University of Illinois Press, 1991); Ruth Bordin, *Woman and Temperance: The Quest for Power and Liberty, 1873–1900* (Philadelphia: Temple University Press, 1981). On women's involvement in missionary societies, see Dana L. Robert, *American Women in Mission: A Social History of Their Thought and Practice* (Macon, GA: Mercer, 1997).

17. Tabbert, *American Freemasons*, 79–81.

18. Theodore A. Ross, *Odd Fellowship: Its History and Manual* (New York: M. W. Hazen, 1888), 2.

19. In his analysis of the occupations of Pennsylvania Masons between 1856 and 1873, Wayne A. Huss concludes that "similar to . . . earlier periods . . . Freemasonry in Pennsylvania appealed mostly to independent craftsmen, professionals, and men involved with commerce." *The Master Builders: A History of the Grand Lodge of Free and Accepted Masons of Pennsylvania*, vol. 1, *1731–1873* (Philadelphia: Grand Lodge of Pennsylvania, 1986), 229. Lynn Dumenil reported that between 1880 and 1900, the Live Oak Lodge of Oakland, California, was primarily white collar and middle class. *Freemasonry and American Culture*, 12–13, app. B-1. John Gilkeson found that about 60 percent of the Masons in Providence, Rhode Island, in the 1870s were professionals or white-collar workers. "A City of Joiners: Voluntary Associations and the Formation of the Middle Class in Providence, 1830–1920" (PhD diss., Brown University, 1981), 121. Earlier, Merle Curti noted that the members of the three Masonic lodges in Trempeleau County, Wisconsin, in the late nineteenth century were prominent and well-to-do citizens. *The Making of an American Community: A Case Study of Democracy in a Frontier County* (Stanford, CA: Stanford University Press, 1959), 126. In studying data from a more recent period, Roy Rosenzweig found that 77 percent of Boston Masons in 1900–35 were white-collar workers, compared with 36 percent of Boston's entire work force. Most of these, however, were salesmen, clerks, and petty proprietors, leading him to conclude that in this later period, Boston Masons came more from the lower middle class. "Boston Masons, 1900–1935: The Lower Middle Class in a Divided Society," *Nonprofit and Voluntary Sector Quarterly* 6, nos. 3–4 (July 1977): 121–22.

20. Both Mark C. Carnes and Dumenil make this point. Carnes, *Secret Ritual and Manhood in Victorian America* (New Haven, CT: Yale University Press, 1989), 4; Dumenil, *Freemasonry and American Culture*, 13.

21. The Grand Lodges of both Philadelphia and New York opened monumental edifices in 1873. Tabbert, *American Freemasons*, 134–35.

22. In her important study *Constructing Brotherhood: Class, Gender, and Fraternalism* (Princeton, NJ: Princeton University Press, 1989), the sociologist Mary

Ann Clawson presents fraternalism as a widely available resource for organizing social relations and responding to issues of class, gender, and racial difference. She holds that the cross-class membership of fraternal societies provided workers and employers with a refuge from the convulsions of capitalism. Against the disintegration wrought by the economic and social changes of late nineteenth-century America, fraternal orders "articulated a vision of unity and brotherhood among men of disparate social statuses" (6). Clawson's study makes the important point that fraternalism offered men both a critique of and an accommodation to powerful currents that tended to atomize individuals and impersonalize social relations. Her relative lack of empirical data on the class composition of mainstream lodges, however, weakens her claims. She offers occupational information on only a few Knights of Pythias, Odd Fellows, and Red Men lodges to argue that the lodges in general consisted of large numbers of both blue- and white-collar workers. Furthermore, she concedes that the Freemasons do not fit this claim, because they were indeed the "accepted elite" of the fraternal movement, with few blue-collar members (95–106). Although not a site for cross-class bonding, the Freemason's lodge provided nineteenth-century upwardly mobile bourgeois native white American men with a sanctuary where they might reestablish some sense of community based on social class and a shared set of values.

23. Mary Ann Clawson, "Nineteenth-Century Women's Auxiliaries and Fraternal Orders," *Signs: Journal of Women in Culture and Society* 12, no. 1 (1986): 40–61. This article and its reprisal in Clawson, *Constructing Brotherhood*, 178–210, inform my argument in this section.

24. Richard D. Shiels, "The Feminization of American Congregationalism, 1730–1835," *American Quarterly* 33, no. 1 (Spring 1981): 46–62. On women's church participation in the colonial period, see Amanda Porterfield, "Women's Attraction to Puritanism," *Church History* 60, no. 2 (June 1991): 196–209; Edmund Morgan, "New England Puritanism: Another Approach," *William and Mary Quarterly*, 3rd ser., 18 (April 1961): 236–42; Cedric B. Cowing, "Sex and Preaching in the Great Awakening," *American Quarterly* 20, no. 3 (Fall 1968): 624–44; Mary Maples Dunn, "Saints and Sisters: Congregational and Quaker Women in the Early Colonial Period," *American Quarterly* 30, no. 5 (Winter 1978): 583–601.

25. E. Brooks Holifield, "Toward a History of American Congregations," in *American Congregations*, ed. James P. Wind and James W. Lewis (Chicago: University of Chicago Press, 1994), 40. Statistics from *The Congregational Yearbook* show that 66.5 percent of all Congregational church members were women. National Council of the Congregational Churches Executive Committee, *The Congregational Yearbook for 1895* (Boston: Congregational Sunday School and Publishing Society, 1895), 469.

26. Ann Douglas, *The Feminization of American Culture* (New York: Knopf, 1977). For an expansion of Douglas's argument to include Catholics and a refinement of its application through object-relations theory, see Ann Taves, "Mothers and Children and the Legacy of Mid-Nineteenth-Century American Christianity," *Journal of Religion* 67, no. 2 (April 1987): 203–19.

27. Barbara Leslie Epstein, *The Politics of Domesticity: Women, Evangelism, and Temperance in Nineteenth-Century America* (Middletown, CT: Wes-

leyan University Press, 1981), 115–51; Carroll Smith-Rosenberg, "The Cross and the Pedestal: Women, Anti-ritualism, and the Emergence of the American Bourgeoisie," in her *Disorderly Conduct: Visions of Gender in Victorian America* (New York: Oxford University Press, 1975), 130.

28. T. Calvin McClelland, "Woman's Work in Our Churches," in *Minutes of the National Council of the Congregational Churches of the United States, at the Eleventh Session . . .* (Boston: National Council Publishing Committee, 1901).

29. On the efforts of women in this counterpublic to reclaim their subjectivity by making public that which had been designated private, see especially Nancy Fraser, "Rethinking the Public Sphere: A Contribution to the Critique of Actually Existing Democracy," in *Habermas and the Public Sphere*, ed. Craig Calhoun (Cambridge, MA: MIT Press, 1992), 109–42; Fraser, *Unruly Practices: Power, Discourse, and Gender in Contemporary Social Theory* (Minneapolis: University of Minnesota Press, 1989), 113–43. On the existence of counterpublics that foster cultural and political activities among working-class and other disenfranchised peoples who intend to reclaim their subjectivity and challenge the influence of the white male property holders whom Habermas identified as the members of his public sphere, see Oskar Negt and Alexander Kluge, *Public Sphere and Experience: Toward an Analysis of the Bourgeois and Proletarian Public Sphere*, trans. Peter Labanyi, Jamie Owen Daniel, and Assenka Oksiloff (Minneapolis: University of Minnesota Press, 1993).

30. Mary P. Ryan, *Women in Public: Between Banners and Ballots, 1825–1880* (Baltimore: Johns Hopkins University Press, 1990); Ryan, "Gender and Public Access: Women's Politics in Nineteenth-Century America," in Calhoun ed., *Habermas and the Public Sphere*, 259–88.

31. Clawson, *Constructing Brotherhood*, 187.

32. Gage, quoted in *Proceedings of the Sixth Anniversary of the National Christian Association* (Chicago: Ezra Cook, 1874), 126.

33. William Hunter, "Address," in *Freemason's Quarterly Magazine and Review for 1850* (London: Spencer, 1850), 440.

34. Rob Morris, *The Lights and Shadows of Freemasonry* (Louisville, KY: J. F. Brennan, 1852), 124.

35. "A Woman's Thoughts on Masonry," in *The Ashlar*, ed. Allyn Weston, vol. 2 (Detroit: Palmer, Luce and Fleming, 1857), 446.

36. C. P. Nash, "Why Women Cannot Be Masons," *Mystic Star* 6 (1868): 132.

37. "Women's Interest in Freemasonry," editorial, *Mystic Star* 4 (1866): 152.

38. "Woman's Thoughts on Masonry," 446–47.

39. Although there were no earlier female Masonic organizations in the United States, in Europe women had been part of the Masonic enterprise from at least the middle of the eighteenth century. For an overview of emerging scholarship in this area, see Alexandra Heidle and Jan A. M. Snoek, eds., *Women's Agency and Rituals in Mixed and Female Masonic Orders* (Leiden, Netherlands: Brill, 2008).

40. Barton, quoted in *New Age*, March 1924, 178.

41. Willis Engle, *The History of the Order of the Eastern Star*, 2nd ed. (Indianapolis: Engle, 1912), 106.

42. Carnes, *Secret Ritual and Manhood*, 88.

43. "Androgynous Masonry," *Masonic Review*, February 1869, quoted in ibid., 85.

44. Clawson, "Women's Auxiliaries and Fraternal Orders," 54.

45. Dudley Wright, *Woman and Freemasonry* (London: William Rider and Son, 1922), 134.

46. On the evolution of women's organizations in the nineteenth century, see Carolyn De Swarte Gifford, "Women in Social Reform Movements," in *Women and Religion in America*, ed. Rosemary Radford Reuther and Rosemary Skinner Keller, vol. 1 (San Francisco: Harper and Row, 1981), 294–340; Ellen Carol DuBois, *Feminism and Suffrage: The Emergence of an Independent Women's Movement in America, 1848–1869* (Ithaca, NY: Cornell University Press, 1978); Bordin, *Woman and Temperance*; Scott, *Natural Allies*.

47. Order of the Eastern Star, "Constitution of the General Grand Chapter," in *Proceedings of the General Grand Chapter of the Order of the Eastern Star, 1876-1895* (repr., Chicago: Galbraith, 1908; hereafter *Eastern Star Proceedings*), bk. 1876, 21–34.

48. Engle, *Order of the Eastern Star*, 36.

49. Elizabeth Butler, "Address of the M.W. Grand Matron," in *Eastern Star Proceedings*, bk. 1878, app., vi–vii.

50. Ibid., bk. 1892, 143.

51. Nettie Ransford, "Grand Matron's Address," in ibid., 21. Frances E. Willard included Ransford in her coedited four-volume compendium of notable American women, *A Woman of the Century* (Buffalo: Charles Wells Mouton, 1893), which recognizes her leadership role in the Women's Relief Corps and the Order of the Eastern Star (3:596–97).

52. *Eastern Star Proceedings*, bk. 1886, 15.

53. Ibid., bk. 1883, 10.

54. Engle, *Order of the Eastern Star*, 285.

55. *Eastern Star Proceedings*, bk. 1895, 150–51.

56. Ibid., bk. 1892, 56.

57. Wright, *Woman and Freemasonry*, 131. On the growing participation of women in the life of the lodge, see William D. Moore, "Funding the Temples of Masculinity: Women's Roles in Masonic Fairs in New York State, 1870–1930," in *Freemasonry in Context: History, Ritual, and Controversy*, ed. Arturo de Hoyos and S. Brent Morris (Lanham, MD: Lexington Books, 2004), 75–87; Moore, *Masonic Temples: Freemasonry, Ritual Architecture, and Masculine Archetypes* (Knoxville: University of Tennessee Press, 2006), 144–46.

58. From *A Brief History of the National Christian Association* (Chicago: Ezra A. Cook, 1875), 28–29:

Number of Pastors and Communicants in churches which prohibit fellowship with "secret" societies:

Denominational Name	No. of Preachers	No. of Communicants
Reformed Presbyterian	100	9,726
United Presbyterian	595	74,833

Associate Presbyterian	12	1,162
United Brethren	1,886	131,859
Free Methodist	145	6,113
German Baptists	1,048	200,000
LUTHERAN		
Norwegian Danish Conf.	48	[199,800]
Augustana Synod Swedish	93	30,127
Evangel. Synodical Conf.	930	187,873
Total:	4,857	641,693

We lack the statistics of the Wesleyan Methodists, Friend Quakers and others who do not fellowship with Masonry; but this table is sufficiently complete to show that a vast body of conscientious Protestant Christians are opposed to secret societies.

The number of Protestants in 1870 is estimated to have been 10,118,077. Extrapolated from Roger Finke and Rodney Starke, *The Churching of America, 1776–1990: Winners and Losers in Our Religious Economy* (New Brunswick, NJ: Rutgers University Press, 1992), 114, table 4.1.

59. I use the term *Midwest* primarily to refer to the newly incorporated territories of Ohio, Indiana, Illinois, Kentucky, and Michigan and to such older western areas as Whitney Cross's "burned-over district" of western New York (see ch. 4, n. 2) and the western Pennsylvania settlements of the seceding Scottish and Scots-Irish Presbyterians and the German United Brethren.

60. For more on these developments, see Timothy L. Smith, *Revivalism and Social Reform: American Protestantism on the Eve of the Civil War* (New York: Harper and Row, 1965); T. Scott Miyakawa, *Protestants and Pioneers: Individualism and Conformity on the American Frontier* (Chicago: University of Chicago Press, 1964).

61. For more on Blanchard, see Donald W. Dayton, *Discovering an Evangelical Heritage* (New York: Harper and Row, 1976), 7–14; Clyde Kilby, *Minority of One: The Biography of Jonathan Blanchard* (Grand Rapids, MI: Eerdmans, 1959); Richard S. Taylor, "Seeking the Kingdom: A Study in the Career of Jonathan Blanchard, 1811–1892" (PhD diss., Northern Illinois University, 1977).

62. George Marsden, *Fundamentalism and American Culture: The Shaping of Twentieth Century Evangelicalism, 1870–1925* (New York: Oxford, 1980), 28–29.

63. Jonathan Blanchard, "Editorial Correspondence," *Christian Cynosure,* September 13, 1877.

64. *History of the National Christian Association,* 6.

65. This came in 1874, with 4,780 subscribers, primarily from the Midwest. Taylor, "Seeking the Kingdom," 515.

66. Jonathan Blanchard, "A.H. Quint, Chairman of the National Committee Yet Is Today Grand Chaplain of Masons," *Christian Cynosure,* November 14, 1871.

67. Williston Walker, *A History of the Congregational Churches in the United States*, 6th ed. (Boston: Pilgrim, 1897), 398–400; "Declaration of Faith," *Congregational Quarterly* 10 (1868): 377–78.

68. *Proceedings of the Grand Lodge of the Most Ancient and Honorable Fraternity of Free and Accepted Masons of the Commonwealth of Massachusetts* (Boston: Rockwell and Churchill, 1874), 382–85. Throughout the 1870s, Quint was responsible for conducting the Sunday services at the North Congregational Church in New Bedford and, during the week, participating in and occasionally presiding over the devotional exercises of the Grand Lodge.

69. Jonathan Blanchard, *Christian Cynosure*, November 14, 1871.

70. *Proceedings of the Grand Lodge of Massachusetts* (Boston: Rockwell and Churchill, 1872), 477–84.

71. Carnes, *Secret Ritual and Manhood*, 80. My argument here differs from that of Carnes. He claims that the central reason for the growth of fraternal orders was that they "facilitated the young man's transitions to, and acceptance of, a remote and problematic conception of manhood in Victorian America" (ix). This intuitively attractive argument turns on the mid-nineteenth-century changes in fraternal rituals. In particular, Carnes holds that "the rituals' exclusion of references to Christ and their implicit refutation of liberal theology can best be understood as an indirect assault upon women and women's role in the church" (79). This assault is made more apparent when he argues that the rituals were "often written by liberal Protestant ministers" (61). Apparently these ministers preached a theology of love and nurturance to their largely female congregations on Sundays and created and participated in Calvinistic male rites of passage on weekdays. Finally, Carnes makes his case for the centrality of gender by emphasizing the role of evangelical women in the attacks on the lodges by the Anti-Masonic NCA (72–89), an idiosyncratic association that reflected neither the majority nor the variety of female perspectives. Although he significantly brings gender into the explanation for the growth of late nineteenth-century fraternal orders, he claims more than can be delivered. While it is likely that the desire for male rites of initiation was among the reasons for pursuing the higher degrees in such large middle-class white orders as the Freemasons and the Odd Fellows, the assertion that men joined lodges in response to an invariant psychological need for masculine guidance, regardless of their socioeconomic, racial, and ethnic diversity or their different situations and historical moments, does not sufficiently take into account the probable variety of their motives. And although it is plausible that the Victorian white middle-class ideology of the women's sphere led many mothers to have to raise their boys alone and some women to attack the lodges for undermining their and the Protestant churches' moral authority, this does not account for the many women who supported or simply accepted the lodges or whose poverty, race, or immigrant status provided them with a different perspective. Carnes's argument suffers from several other false assumptions. He asserts that "after the Civil War only a handful of rituals offered prayers to Christ" (60), wrongly implying that Christ was previously prominent in fraternal rituals. In Freemasonry at least, as I have argued in this book, Christianity had an ambiguous legacy. While Carnes may be right that there were few prayers to Christ in late nineteenth-century rituals, the same is

true for those of the fraternity's earlier (post-1717) speculative history. Moreover, as he asserts in his analysis of the Royal Arch degree, the forest of symbols and stories incorporated into fraternal rituals was "susceptible to contradictory interpretations" (47). Another difficulty is Carnes's identification of the disproportionate role that liberal Protestant ministers played in mid-nineteenth-century fraternal ritual life. As we have seen, throughout the eighteenth and nineteenth centuries, a substantial number of liberal Protestant clergy were Masons. Carnes nevertheless attributes this long-term characteristic of American fraternalism to the mid-nineteenth-century feminization of Protestantism and the resulting efforts of female-dominated clergy to chart a path to their and other mother-raised men's mature masculinity through involvement in the higher degree rites. Though Carnes makes an intriguing case for the attraction of fraternal rituals as an antidote to feminized Protestantism, their counter to liberal theology can also be interpreted as motivated by antimodernism.

72. *Proceedings of the Sixth Anniversary of the National Christian Association.*

73. "A Woman's Plea against Secret Societies," *Christian Cynosure*, June 3, 1875, 2; *Christian Cynosure*, August 9, 1883, 2.

74. Blanchard, quoted in Taylor, "Seeking the Kingdom," 547–73.

75. Ibid. See also Donald W. Dayton, *Discovering an Evangelical Heritage* (New York: Harper and Row, 1976).

76. Marsden, *Fundamentalism and American Culture*, 31.

77. Betty A. DeBerg, *Ungodly Women: Gender and the First Wave of American Fundamentalism* (Minneapolis: Fortress, 1990); Michael S. Hamilton, "Women, Public Ministry, and American Fundamentalism, 1920–1950," *Religion and American Culture* 3, no. 2 (Summer 1993): 171–96.

78. On the previously discussed early nineteenth-century Methodist responses to fraternal orders, see William Henry Brackney, "Religious Antimasonry: The Genesis of a Political Party" (PhD diss., Temple University, 1976), 133–37. One example of Methodism's deflection of Anti-Masonic agitation in this later period is found in Lucia C. Cook, *The Mystic Tie, or Freemasonry: A League with the Devil* . . . (Elkhart, IN: printed by author, 1869).

79. Carolyn De Swarte Gifford, *Writing Out My Heart: Selections from the Journal of Frances E. Willard* (Urbana: University of Illinois Press, 1995), 7–8.

80. *Christian Cynosure*, June 9, 1887, and discussion in July issues.

81. Ruth Bordin, *Frances Willard: A Biography* (Chapel Hill: University of North Carolina Press, 1986), 57; *Christian Cynosure*, July 11, 1871.

82. *Proceedings of the Sixth Anniversary of the National Christian Association*, 126.

83. Anna E. Stoddard, *The Foe in Hiding* (Chicago: Christian Cynosure, n.d.), 2.

84. On changes in late nineteenth-century Protestantism, see Paul Carter, *The Spiritual Crisis of the Gilded Age* (DeKalb: Northern Illinois University Press, 1971), 3–61; Paul Boyer, *Urban Masses and Moral Order in America, 1820–1920* (Cambridge, MA: Harvard University Press, 1978); Henry F. May, *Protestant Churches and Industrial America* (New York: Harper and Row, 1971). On the development of liberal Protestantism, see William Hutchison,

The Modernist Impulse in American Protestantism (Cambridge, MA: Harvard University Press, 1976). On the emergence of fundamentalism, see Marsden, *Fundamentalism and American Culture*.

85. Dumenil, *Freemasonry and American Culture*, 59.

86. Fels, "Square and the Compass," 480.

87. "By 1898, there were 998 commanderies and 114,540 Knights, or about one out of every seven Masons." Tabbert, *American Freemasons*, 95.

88. Fels, "Square and the Compass," 440–70.

89. Ibid., 417–19, 596–97.

90. "In 1880, for the United States as a whole, 22.1 percent of all Masons pursued York Rite, and only 8.9 percent were in Knights Templar. By 1900, the ratio had become smaller, and Knights Templar were more prevalent (26.5 and 14.9 percent, respectively). Scottish Rite was even more exclusive—only 1.6 percent of all Masons were Scottish Rite Masons in 1880, with the percentage rising to 4.6 in 1900." Dumenil, *Freemasonry and American Culture*, 240–41 n. 28.

91. Glenn Hughes, *A History of the American Theatre, 1700–1950* (London: Samuel French, 1951), 000–000.

92. Harwood, "Secret Societies in America," 621.

93. Jabez Richardson, *Richardson's Monitor of Free-Masonry* (New York: Fitzgerald, 1860), 64-80. Carnes, *Secret Ritual and Manhood*, 42–59, informs my argument.

94. Max Weber, *The Protestant Ethic and the Spirit of Capitalism*, trans. Talcott Parsons (New York: Charles Scribner's Sons, 1958).

95. T. J. Jackson Lears, *No Place of Grace: Antimodernism and the Transformation of American Culture, 1880–1920* (Chicago: University of Chicago Press, 1994), 32.

96. Lears, *No Place of Grace*, 176–77. See Albert Gallatin Mackey, Robert Ingham Clegg, and H. L. Haywood, *Encyclopedia of Freemasonry*, rev. ed. (London: Kessinger, 1946; first published 1905), 612, for a reference to "Brother" Carus.

97. Lears, *No Place of Grace*, 196–97. In an earlier work, Frederic proudly identified himself as a Mason: *The New Exodus: A Study of Israel in Russia* (New York: G. P. Putnam and Sons, 1892), 178.

98. Gerald Burnworth, "Brother Samuel Langhorne Clemens: A Missouri Freemason," paper presented to the Missouri Lodge of Research at the 178th Annual Communication of the Grand Lodge of Missouri, September 28, 1999.

99. Lears, *No Place of Grace*, 165.

100. Edgar F. Blanchard, *The Lodge Versus the Church* (Nashua, NH: Golden Rule, 1908), 1–16. This perceived fault of the church was signaled as early as the 1857–58 "businessmen's revival." See Kathryn Teresa Long, *The Revival of 1857–1858: Interpreting an American Religious Awakening* (New York: Oxford University Press, 1998).

101. Frank Graves Crossley, *The Church and Young Men* (Chicago: Fleming H. Revell, 1903), 113–39.

102. Clifford Wallace Putney, *Muscular Christianity: Manhood and Sports in Protestant America, 1880–1920* (Cambridge, MA: Harvard University Press, 2001), 84–87, 246 n. 65.

103. For more on this movement, see ibid., esp. 1–44.

104. As Gail Bederman explains, liberal Social Gospel leaders and conservative church members joined the Men and Religion Forward Movement for different reasons. Proponents of the Social Gospel used it to gain a broader audience for their controversial call for religiously inspired social reform. For them, social service activity was masculine church work. The more conservative members, in contrast, employed the movement for the narrower intent of defeminizing the church. The result was a Social Gospel inspired less by an awakened social conscience than by a search for masculinity. The M&RFM's official publications, Bederman observes, said nothing about the advancement of women yet addressed all of the other major issues of the day. Bederman, "'The Women Have Had Charge of the Church Work Long Enough': The Men and Religion Forward Movement of 1911–1912 and the Masculinization of Middle-Class Protestantism," *American Quarterly* 41, no. 3 (September 1989): 448–52. See also Susan Curtis, *A Consuming Faith: The Social Gospel and Modern American Culture* (Baltimore: Johns Hopkins University Press, 1991); Janet F. Fishburn, *The Fatherhood of God and the Victorian Family: A Study of the Social Gospel in America* (Philadelphia: Fortress, 1981). On the relationship between the M&RFM and the Promise Keepers of the late twentieth century, see L. Dean Allen, *Rise Up, O Men of God: The Men and Religion Forward Movement and Promise Keepers* (Macon, GA: Mercer University Press, 2002).

105. Bederman, "'Women Have Had Charge'," 432–65.

106. Nancy F. Cott, *The Grounding of Modern Feminism* (New Haven, CT: Yale University Press, 1987), 282.

107. Bederman argues that "if the Presbyterian experience is at all typical," the effect on women of the masculinization of churches "was devastating. Churchmen disbanded women's organizations: women church leaders lost their authority" ("'Women Have Had Charge'," 457). In a similar vein, Janette Hassey, Betty A. DeBerg, and Margaret L. Bendroth have reconstructed the changing role of women in conservative Evangelicalism. In 1986, Hassey reported that in the early twentieth century, evangelical women—identified with the Pentecostal, the Holiness, and other protofundamentalist movements—held significant positions in public ministry, only to be "squeezed out" of them by men as the century progressed. *No Time for Silence: Women in Public Ministry around the Turn of the Century* (Grand Rapids, MI: Zondervan, 1986). DeBerg analyzed the militant rhetoric and aggressive posturing of these male leaders, while Bendroth charted the marginalization of fundamentalist women in public roles. DeBerg, *Ungodly Women: Gender and the First Wave of American Fundamentalism* (Minneapolis: Fortress, 1990); Bendroth, *Gender and Fundamentalism, 1875–1980* (New Haven, CT: Yale University Press, 1993). These scholars' various explanations for this squeezing-out process include fundamentalism's withdrawal from social reform and separation from the mainline, hardening of beliefs about biblical inerrancy and premillennial dispensationalism, and growing male anxiety over an overly feminized Christianity.

108. Bederman, "'Women Have Had Charge'," 454.

6. THE PRINCE HALL MASONS AND THE AFRICAN AMERICAN CHURCH

In the interest of legibility, these notes use short citations for the minutes of the annual North Carolina conference of the AME Church (published in Raleigh, NC, by John Nichols) and the proceedings of the North Carolina Grand Lodge. For instance, Minutes of the Eleventh Session of the North Carolina Annual Conference of the African Methodist Episcopal Zion Church is Minutes 11 (1874), while Proceedings of the Most Worshipful Grand Lodge of Free and Accepted Ancient York Masons for the State of North Carolina is Proceedings (Raleigh, NC: Nichols and Gorman, 1872) and Proceedings of the Most Worshipful Grand Lodge of Free and Accepted Ancient York Masons for the State of North Carolina at Its Fifth Annual Communication is Proceedings 5 (Raleigh, NC: Nichols, 1874).

1. "Bishop James W. Hood," *Masonic Quarterly* 1, no. 3 (1919).

2. Sandy Dwayne Martin, "Biblical Interpretation, Ecclesiology, and Black Southern Religious Leaders, 1860–1920: A Case Study of AMEZ Bishop James Walker Hood," in *Ain't Gonna Lay My 'Ligion Down: African American Religion in the South*, ed. Alonzo Johnson and Paul Jerslid (Columbia: University of South Carolina Press, 1996), 111. I am indebted to Martin's fine biography of Hood for providing me with a great deal of information on his life and career: *For God and Race: The Religious and Political Leadership of AMEZ Bishop James Walker Hood* (Columbia: University of South Carolina Press, 1999).

3. W. E. B. DuBois, *The Philadelphia Negro* (Philadelphia: published for the university, 1899), 221–24.

4. Howard W. Odum, *Social and Mental Traits of the Negro: Research into the Conditions of the Negro in Southern Towns* (New York: Columbia University Press, 1910), 267. Booker T. Washington praised fraternal orders for teaching black businessmen how to create capital and thereby "greatly increase property in the hands of members of the race." *The Story of the Negro*, 2 vols. (New York: Doubleday, 1909), 2:169. By the 1930s, Carter Godwin Woodson found that two-thirds of all black physicians and lawyers were members of fraternal orders. *The Negro Professional Man and the Community, with Special Emphasis on the Physician and the Lawyer.* (Washington DC: Association for the Study of Negro Life and History, 1934), chs. 8 and 16. In 1967, John Hope Franklin asserted that the creation of independent fraternal organizations in the antebellum free black communities of the North was central to their struggle to achieve status in an evolving American society. *From Slavery to Freedom: A History of Negro Americans*, 3rd ed. (New York: Knopf, 1967), 165.

5. Frank Lincoln Mather., ed., *Who's Who of the Colored Race* (1915; repr., Detroit: Gale Research, 1976).

6. For the economic influence of black fraternal orders, see David M. Fahey, *The Black Lodge in White America: "True Reformer Brown" and His Economic Strategy* (Dayton, OH: Wright State University Press, 1994). William A. Muraskin's *Middle-Class Blacks in a White Society* (Berkeley: University of California Press, 1975) emphasizes class. Other studies that to some degree include black fraternal orders and an analysis that weaves together economics,

class, and politics are Earl Lewis, *In Their Own Interests: Race, Class, and Power in Twentieth-Century Norfolk, Virginia* (Berkeley: University of California Press, 1991); Joe William Trotter Jr., *Coal, Class, and Color: Blacks in Southern West Virginia, 1915–32* (Urbana: University of Illinois Press, 1990), esp. 198–213; Peter J. Rachleff, *Black Labor in Richmond, 1865–1890* (Urbana: University of Illinois Press, 1989; repr. of *Black Labor in the South: Richmond, Virginia, 1865–1890* [Philadelphia: Temple University Press, 1984]); David A. Gerber, *Black Ohio and the Color Line, 1860–1915* (Urbana: University of Illinois Press, 1976), esp. 162; the older yet still frequently cited Hylan Lewis, *Blackways of Kent* (Chapel Hill: University of North Carolina Press, 1955), esp. 259–76. On black masculinity, see Martin Summers, *Masculinity and Its Discontents: The Black Middle Class and the Transformation of Masculinity, 1900–1930* (Chapel Hill: University of North Carolina Press, 2004); Maurice Wallace, *Constructing the Black Masculine: Identity and Ideality in African American Men's Literature, 1775–1995* (Durham, NC: Duke University Press, 2002).

7. See Nick Salvatore, *We All Got History: The Memory Books of Amos Webber* (New York: Times Books, 1996); Joanna Brooks, *American Lazarus: Religion and the Rise of African-American and Native American Literatures* (New York: Oxford University Press, 2003), 115–50; Brooks, "The Early American Public Sphere and the Emergence of a Black Print Counterpublic," *William and Mary Quarterly*, 3rd ser., 62, no. 1 (January 2005): 67–93; Corey D. B. Walker, *A Noble Fight: African American Freemasonry and the Struggle for Democracy in America* (Urbana: University of Illinois Press, 2008).

8. Joseph A. Walkes Jr., the long-term editor of the Prince Hall research journal *Phylaxis*, frequently laments in its pages the absence of comprehensive state-by-state records. Moreover, more than once in my efforts to access a lodge, I was told that the building and whatever records it held were not available to me because they were secret. Nevertheless, a fairly large though hardly comprehensive public collection of Prince Hall materials can be found at the Iowa Masonic Library in Cedar Rapids. In recent years, however, substantially more material has been found and investigated. For recent scholarship on Prince Hall Freemasonry, see Peter Hinks and Stephen Kantrowitz, eds., *All Men Free and Brethren: Essays on the History of American Freemasonry* (Ithaca, NY: Cornell University Press, 2013).

9. "Black Print Counterpublic," 73.

10. *Minutes* 11 (1874), 37–47.

11. For studies of African American Christianity's expansion in the South during the Civil War and Reconstruction, see Daniel W. Stowell, *Rebuilding Zion: The Religious Reconstruction of the South, 1863–1877* (New York: Oxford University Press, 1998); Paul Harvey, *Redeeming the South: Religious Culture and Racial Identities among Southern Baptists, 1865–1925* (Chapel Hill: University of North Carolina Press, 1997); Reginald F. Hildebrand, *The Times Were Strange and Stirring: Methodist Preachers and the Crisis of Emancipation* (Durham, NC: Duke University Press, 1995); William E. Montgomery, *Under Their Own Vine and Fig Tree: The African-American Church in the South, 1865–1900* (Baton Rouge: Louisiana State University Press, 1993);

Katherine L. Dvorak, *An African-American Exodus: The Segregation of Southern Churches* (Brooklyn: Carlson, 1991); portions of Forrest G. Wood, *The Arrogance of Faith: Christianity and Race in America from the Colonial Era to the Twentieth Century* (Boston: Northeastern University Press, 1990).

12. *Minutes* 11: 23.

13. In an address to the North Carolina Grand Lodge in 1917, Hood stated that when he "was appointed by Bishop J. J. Clinton as Superintendent of Missions for the A.M.E. Zion Church, I also had an appointment by Most Worshipful G. W. Titus, Grand Master of Masons in New York, as Superintendent of the Southern Jurisdiction of the Grand Lodge of New York." *Proceedings* 48 (Nashville: AME Sunday School Union, 1917), 89.

14. *Proceedings* (Raleigh, NC: Nichols and Gorman, 1872), 53–55; *Minutes* 11: 37–47.

15. *Proceedings* 5 (Raleigh, NC: Nichols, 1874), 5–9; bylaws in *Proceedings* (1872), 14–21.

16. I compiled this statistical information from the following sources—for the AMEZ Church: *Minutes* 11–15 (1874–78); for the Prince Hall Grand Lodge: *Proceedings* (1872); *Proceedings* 5; Joseph C. Hill, *Proceedings of the Most Worshipful Grand Lodge of Free and Accepted Ancient York Masons for the State of North Carolina—Sessions of December 1875, 1876, and 1877* (Wilmington, NC: Hall, 1878); Hill, *Proceedings* 11 (Wilmington, NC: Warrock, 1881).

17. Both the conference and the Grand Lodge founded societies along the routes of the new railroads that crisscrossed the state following the Civil War. Hood often pointed to distance from railroad stations as a reason for a church or lodge's dormant state. In his 1874 report to the Grand Lodge, for example, he explained the slow growth of Rising Sun Lodge in Columbus County as due to its being "six or seven miles from the nearest railroad station." *Proceedings* 5: 8. For an insightful discussion of the relationship between the expansion of southern railroads and the development of African American social institutions, see John M. Giggie, *After Redemption: Jim Crow and the Transformation of African American Religion in the Delta, 1875–1915* (New York: Oxford University Press, 2007), 23–58.

18. *Minutes* 11; *Proceedings* 5.

19. *Proceedings* (1872), 54.

20. Albert J. Raboteau, "Richard Allen and the African Church Movement," in his *A Fire in the Bones: Reflections on African-American Religious History* (Boston: Beacon, 1995), 79–102. See also Gary B. Nash, *Forging Freedom: The Formation of Philadelphia's Black Community* (Cambridge, MA: Harvard University Press, 1988), 98–104. For a broader view, see Will B. Gravely, "The Rise of African Churches in America (1786–1822): Re-examining the Contexts," *Journal of Religious Thought* 41 (Spring–Summer 1984): 58–73.

21. Nash, *Forging Freedom*, 210.

22. James Oliver Horton, *Free People of Color: Inside the African American Community* (Washington DC: Smithsonian Institution Press, 1993), 153.

23. Monroe N. Work, "Secret Societies as Factors in the Social and Economical Life of the Negro," in *Democracy in Earnest*, ed. James E. McCulloch (Washington DC: Southern Sociological Congress, 1918), 343.

24. DuBois, *Philadelphia Negro*, 222.

25. James B. Browning, "The Beginnings of Insurance Enterprise among Negroes," *Journal of Negro History* 22 (1937): 421–29. For statistics on the origins and development of African American fraternalism, see Theda Skocpol and Jennifer Lynn Oser, "Organization Despite Diversity: The Origins and Development of African American Fraternal Associations," *Social Science History* 28, no. 3 (Fall 2004): 374.

26. The African origins of these mutual benefit societies remain speculative. Certainly in the South, some evolved from the "invisible" institutions and folk culture that slaves developed in their plantation communities. Melville J. Herskovitz probably extrapolated from too little evidence when he held in *The Myth of the Negro Past* (New York: Harper and Brothers, 1941) that they could be directly linked to African secret societies. Still, it is logical to assume that prior knowledge of African mutual aid systems would have been applied in the slave community. Several scholars have argued for structural similarities between the organization and rituals of the early mutual aid societies and their African counterparts. See Deborah Gray White's study of the "female slave network," which contributed to the collective care of children, the sick, and the elderly, as suggestive of the African origins of this mutual aid system. *Ar'n't I a Woman?: Female Slaves in the Plantation South* (New York: Norton, 1985), 119–41. Herbert Gutman believed that this web of social obligations reached back to family and gender responsibilities in Africa. See *The Black Family in Slavery and Freedom, 1750–1925* (New York: Pantheon, 1976). Betty M. Kuyk suggests an even more direct link, noting the African birth of several founders of these American societies, in "The African Derivation of Black Fraternal Orders in the United States," *Comparative Studies in Societies and History* 25, no. 4 (October 1983): 559–94. Susan D. Greenbaum argues that the earliest African American societies existed before European American organizations had much to offer in the way of models. See "A Comparison of African American and Euro-American Mutual Aid Societies in 19th Century America," *Journal of Ethnic Studies* 19, no. 3 (1991): 111. Michael A. Gomez has explicitly drawn parallels between Sierra Leonean secret societies and the Prince Hall Masons, suggesting that "it is plausible that African American freemasonry is an institution derived from West African, and specifically Sierra Leonian, origins." *Exchanging Our Country Marks: The Transformation of African Identities in the Colonial and Antebellum South* (Chapel Hill: University of North Carolina Press, 1998), 101. Similarly, Craig Steven Wilder has argued that the secrecy that the Prince Hall Masons and other early nineteenth-century black associations practiced originated in the efforts of West African societies to maintain boundaries allowing for autonomous self-expression. *In the Company of Black Men: The African Influence on African American Culture in New York City* (New York: New York University Press, 2001), 13. Still, the traditional emphasis on secrecy and the need to hide organized behavior from their masters has left scant evidence of the existence of these societies among slaves. In contrast, evidence for the existence of Northern societies such as the Free African Society of Philadelphia is much more visible. Sylvia Frey's "The Visible Church: Historiography of African American Religion since Raboteau," *Slavery and*

Abolition 29, no. 1 (March 2008): 83–110, summarizes what we know about the persistence of African religions in the United States.

27. Mary Ann Clawson, *Constructing Brotherhood: Class, Gender, and Fraternalism* (Princeton, NJ: Princeton University Press, 1989), 131–35.

28. Nash, *Forging Freedom*, 217.

29. See William B. Gravely, "The Dialectic of Double-Consciousness in Black American Freedom Celebrations, 1808–1863," *Journal of Negro History* 67, no. 4 (Winter 1982): 302–17.

30. Prince Hall, "A Charge, Delivered to the African Lodge, June 24, 1797, at Menotomy," in *Early Negro Writings, 1760–1837*, ed. Dorothy Porter (Baltimore: Black Classic, 1995), 77.

31. Martin Delaney, *The Origins and Objects of Ancient Freemasonry; Its Introduction into the United States, and Legitimacy among Colored Men* (Pittsburgh: W. S. Haven, 1853), 18. See also Hall, "A Charge Delivered to the Brethren of the African Lodge on the 25th of June, 1792," in Porter ed., *Early Negro Writings*, 63–69.

32. Brooks, "Black Print Counterpublic," 67–92. See also Regina Austin, "The Black Public Sphere and Mainstream Majoritarian Politics," *Vanderbilt Law Review* 50 (March 1997): 340; Michael C. Dawson, "A Black Counterpublic? Economic Earthquakes, Racial Agenda(s), and Black Politics," in *The Black Public Sphere: A Public Culture Book*, ed. the Black Public Sphere Collective (Chicago: University of Chicago Press, 1995), 199–228.

33. Joanna Brooks, "Prince Hall, Freemasonry, and Genealogy," *African American Review* 34, no. 2 (Summer 2000): 197–216. On the black Egyptian roots of Western civilization, see Martin Bernal, *Black Athena: The Afro-Asiatic Roots of Classical Civilization* (New Brunswick, NJ: Rutgers University Press, 1987).

34. John Marrant, "A Sermon Preached on the 24th Day of June 1789, Being the Festival of St. John the Baptist, at the Request of the Right Worshipful the Grand Master Prince Hall, and the Rest of the Brethren of the African Lodge of the Honourable Society of Free and Accepted Masons in Boston," in *Face Zion Forward: First Writers of the Black Atlantic, 1785–1798*, ed. Joanna Brooks and John Saillant (Boston: Northeastern University Press, 2002), 77–92. For analyses of Marrant's sermon, see Brooks, *American Lazarus*, 127–28; Laurie Maffly-Kipp, *Setting Down the Sacred Past: African-American Race Histories* (Cambridge, MA: Harvard University Press, 2010), 32–38. Several scholars have assessed Marrant's theology. See especially Peter P. Hinks, "John Marrant and the Meaning of Early Black Freemasonry," *William and Mary Quarterly* 64, no. 1 (January 2007): 105–16; Cedrick May, "John Marrant and the Narrative Construction of an Early Black Methodist Evangelical Author(s)," *African American Review* 38, no. 4 (Winter 2004): 553–70; Saillant, "'Wipe Away All Tears from Their Eyes': John Marrant's Theology in the Black Atlantic, 1785–1808," *Journal of Millennial Studies* 1, no. 2 (Winter 1999).

35. On race histories, see Maffly-Kipp, *Setting Down the Sacred Past*. On the emergence of African American Freemasonry in the Atlantic diaspora of African peoples, see especially Walker, *Noble Fight*, 45–85.

36. Cory D. B. Walker has described this "heterodox political language" that Prince Hall leaders developed in their early nineteenth-century orations. See "Nation and Oration: The Political Language of African American Freemasonry in the Early Republic," in Hinks and Kantrowitz eds., *All Men Free and Brethren*, 84–94.

37. See Brooks, "Black Print Counterpublic," 67–92.

38. *Proceedings* (1872), 27.

39. James Walker Hood, *One Hundred Years of the African Methodist Episcopal Zion Church* (New York: AME Book Concern, 1895), 85–86; Martin, *For God and Race*, 22–58.

40. Hood, *One Hundred Years*, 2–26.

41. Ibid., 10.

42. Ibid., 27–55. See also Martin, *For God and Race*, 74, 134.

43. By 1909, 2,600 of 3,336 Prince Hall lodges were in the South. For example, Alabama had 340 and Pennsylvania 70. W. H. Anderson, *Anderson's Masonic Directory* (Richmond, VA: W. H. Anderson, 1909). The order continued to grow in the twentieth century, with as many as 150,000 followers in the 1920s and 300,000 in the 1950s, before beginning to decline. See William A. Muraskin, *Middle-Class Blacks in a White Society* (Berkeley: University of California Press, 1975), 29. C. Eric Lincoln and Lawrence H. Mamiya confirm this decline in their *The Black Church in the African American Experience* (Durham, NC: Duke University Press, 1990), 152.

44. Moses Nathaniel Moore, "Orishatukeh Faduma and the New Theology," *Church History* 63, no. 1 (March 1994): 64–66.

45. Throughout his career, Hood remained committed to the belief that the Bible was the pure and infallible word of God. His commentary on the Book of Revelation, for example, reflects this literalist understanding. See *The Plan of the Apocalypse* (York, PA: P. Anstadt and Sons, 1900). His sermon "Creation's First Born, or The Earliest Gospel Symbol" takes issue with Darwinian science. See *The Negro in the Christian Pulpit* (Raleigh, NC: Edwards, Broughton, 1884), 105–21. For examples of his understanding of the nature of the Christian church in general and the mission of the black church in particular, see "The Polity of the A.M.E. Zion Church," *African Methodist Episcopal Zion Quarterly Review* 8, nos. 1–2 (1899): 1–9; "The Character and Power of the Christian Religion," *African Methodist Episcopal Zion Quarterly Review* 13 (January–March, 1904): 11–19; *Sketch of the Early History of the African Methodist Episcopal Zion Church*, vol. 2 (New York: AME Book Concern, 1914), 66–69. On Hood's position that Christianity is the unique pathway of salvation, see, e.g., *Negro in the Christian Pulpit*, 105–21.

46. Henry Louis Gates, "The Trope of a New Negro and the Reconstruction of the Image of the Black," *Representations* 24 (1988): 199–55; Laurie Maffly-Kipp, "Mapping the World, Mapping the Race: The Negro Race History, 1874–1915," *Church History* 64 (1995): 617–19.

47. Hood, "The Negro Race," in his *One Hundred Years*, 27–52.

48. Ibid., 51–55. For a discussion of similar race histories, see Maffly-Kipp, *Setting Down the Sacred Past;* Brooks, *American Lazarus*, 115–50.

49. See, for example, Benjamin T. Tanner, *The Descent of the Negro* (Philadelphia: AME Publishing House, 1898). For an insightful discussion of the influence of Darwinian science on conceptions of race and manhood, see Gail Bederman, *Manliness and Civilization: A Cultural History of Gender and Race in the United States, 1880–1917* (Chicago: University of Chicago Press, 1995).

50. James Walker Hood, *Star of Zion*, November 16, 1893, 2. The *AME Church Review* in January 1899 (631) listed *The Cushite, or The Descendants of Ham* (New York: Literary Union, 1887) as the fourth-most-important work of the race (*Narrative of the Life of Frederick Douglass* was first). James Melvin Washington believed not only that Perry was a Mason but that his history "shows signs of his Masonic influences." Washington, *Frustrated Fellowship: The Black Baptist Quest for Social Power* (Mercer, GA: Mercer University Press, 1986), 75, 131.

51. Delaney, *Origins and Objects of Ancient Freemasonry*, 16–19. For a discussion of Delaney's contribution to Prince Hall Masonry, see Maurice O. Wallace, "'Are We Men?': Prince Hall, Martin Delaney, and the Black Masculine Ideal in Black Freemasonry, 1775–1865," in his *Constructing the Black Masculine*, 53–81.

52. Hood, *Sketch*, 60, 62.

53. *Proceedings* (1880), 10.

54. Ibid., 11.

55. Ibid., 12–13.

56. William Spencer Carpenter, "Sermon Delivered to the Masons of the Second Masonic District, May 16th, 1920," *Mason Quarterly Review* 1, no. 3 (1920).

57. *Proceedings* (1872), 34; Hill, *Proceedings* (1878), 27–28.

58. Armstrong, quoted in Lawrence W. Levine, *Black Culture and Black Consciousness: Afro-American Folk Thought from Slavery to Freedom* (New York: Oxford University Press, 1977), 268–69.

59. Harrison L. Harris, *Masonic Visitor*, August 1887, 29.

60. *Proceedings* 19 (Goldsboro, NC: Argus, 1889), 87.

61. Hood, *Negro in the Christian Pulpit*, 115.

62. *Masonic Visitor*, June–July 1887, 9.

63. *Proceedings* 5: 7.

64. *Proceedings* (1886), 42–43.

65. *Proceedings* 48: 90.

66. On "respectability," see Evelyn Brooks Higginbotham, *Righteous Discontent: The Women's Movement in the Black Baptist Church, 1880–1920* (Cambridge, MA: Harvard University Press, 1993), 14–15; Montgomery, *Vine and Fig Tree*, 36–37.

67. *Masonic Visitor*, June–July 1887, 9.

68. On the emergence of the Holiness movement, see Montgomery, *Vine and Fig Tree*, 345–47. For its attack on fraternal orders, see Giggie, *After Redemption*, 184–85.

69. Jones, quoted in Otho B. Cobbins, *History of Church of Christ (Holiness) U.S.A., 1895–1965* (New York: Vantage, 1966), 18.

70. Martin, *For God and Race*, 17–18. For Hood's evangelical and Holiness views, see his *Negro in the Christian Pulpit*, esp. 33–48, 247–59.

71. Rev. Leonard of Olivet Baptist Church, paraphrased in "An Immense Congregation," *Indianapolis Freeman*, June 6, 1891.

72. H. T. Keating, "Secret Societies among the Negroes," *Christian Recorder*, April 12, 1883.

73. S. H. Coleman, "Freemasonry as a Secret Society Defended," *AME Church Review* 14, no. 3 (January 1898): 327, 337.

74. Knox, quoted in "An Immense Congregation."

75. *The History of the National Christian Association* (Chicago: Ezra Cook, 1875), 28–29. In contrast to white Masonry, there is no evidence of an Anti-Masonic campaign against Prince Hall Masons nor of a decline in membership in the 1830s. To the contrary, the order grew and prospered in that period. As one Prince Hall historian put it, "perhaps" the Prince Hall Mason's "subordinate and inconspicuous position permitted the storm [of Anti-Masonry] to pass over his head." Harry E. Davis, *A History of Freemasonry among Negroes in America* (published under the auspices of the Scottish Rite, Northern Jurisdiction, 1946), 187–88.

76. Salvatore, *We All Got History*, 262. See also James Oliver Horton, "Freedom's Yoke: Gender Conventions among Antebellum Free Blacks," *Feminist Studies* 12, no. 1 (Spring 1986): 51–76.

77. Montgomery, *Vine and Fig Tree*, 114–15.

78. Salvatore, *We All Got History*, 66, 162, 207, 275.

79. On the white Eastern Star, see *Proceedings* (1876); 29. Late in life, Hood stated that "there are three important organizations in this State in which I have taken special interest, namely: The A.M.E. Zion Church, the Masonic Fraternity, and the Eastern Star." *Proceedings* 48: 89. In the 1920s, the Prince Hall historian Harry A. Williamson remarked that "*unlike the whites* [his emphasis], Negroes do not appear to understand the great line of demarcation between the two [male and female orders]." "The Adoptive Rite Ritual," n.d., Williamson Papers, Schomburg Library, New York City. Other black orders, such as the True Reformers, incorporated women from the outset. See David M. Fahey, "Class, Gender and Race in Fraternal Ritualism: A Review Essay," *Old Northwest* 14 (Summer 1988), 161–69; Fahey, *Black Lodge in White America*, 7.

80. Martin, "The Women's Ordination Controversy, the AMEZ Church, and Hood's Leadership," *For God and Race*, 163–75.

81. Brittney C. Cooper has recently provided a closer study of gender relations between Prince Hall men and black women in "'They Are Nevertheless Our Brethren': The Order of the Eastern Star and the Battle for Women's Leadership, 1874–1926," in Hinks and Kantrowitz eds., *All Men Free and Brethren*, 114–30. Her findings of tensions and accommodations are similar to those that Evelyn Brooks Higginbotham has identified in the black Baptist church, in *Righteous Discontent*. See also Cheryl Townsend Gilkes, "The Politics of 'Silence': Dual-Sex Political Systems and Women's Traditions of Conflict in African-American Religion," in *African-American Christianity: Essays in History*, ed. Paul E. Johnson (Berkeley: University of California Press, 1994), 80–110.

7. FREEMASONRY AND NATIVE AMERICANS, 1776–1920

In the interest of legibility, these notes use short citations for the proceedings of the Indian Territory Grand Lodge. Thus, for example, Proceedings of the Most Worshipful Grand Lodge of the Indian Territory (1874) appears as Proceedings (1874) (Sedalia, MO: Democrat Steam Book and Job, 1881) and Proceedings of the Most Worshipful Grand Lodge of the Indian Territory, Third Annual Communication as Proceedings 3 (Sedalia, MO: Democrat Steam Book and Job, 1881).

1. I am aware that the term *Native American* can include Indians and non-Indian groups of indigenous peoples such as Native Hawaiians, Alaskan Eskimos, and Canadian Aleuts. Each of these terms derives from the experience of colonization and includes multiple societies with their own cultures and histories. I understand *Indian* as a subset of *Native American* that can identify all or any one of these groups. However, in this chapter, *Native* and *Native American* refer specifically to Native American Indians.

2. Patrick N. Minges, "The Spread of Freemasonry among the American Indians of the United States," *Proceedings of the Ohio Lodge of Research* (March 2004): 1–2; Philip Deloria, "White Sacheme and Indian Masons: American Indian Otherness and Nineteenth-Century Fraternalism," *Democratic Vistas* 1, no. 2 (Autumn 1993): 27–43; Jessica Harland-Jacobs, *Builders of Empire: Freemasonry and British Imperialism, 1717–1927* (Chapel Hill: University of North Carolina Press, 2007), 78–80. See also Isabel Thompson Kelsay, *Joseph Brant, 1743–1807, Man of Two Worlds* (Syracuse, NY: Syracuse University Press, 1984).

3. Minges, "Freemasonry among the American Indians," 4–5; Deloria, "White Sacheme," 36–38. Other notable Indian Masons appear in William R. Denslow, *Freemasonry and the American Indian* (Columbia: Missouri Lodge of Research, 1956); Albert Gallatin Mackey, Robert Ingham Clegg, and H. L. Haywood eds., *Encyclopedia of Freemasonry*, rev. ed. (London: Kessinger, 1946; first published 1905), 481–83.

4. Rachel Wheeler, *To Live upon Hope: Mohicans and Missionaries in the Eighteenth-Century Northeast* (Ithaca, NY: Cornell University Press, 2008), 10.

5. Thomas Jefferson to the Marquis de Chastellux, June 7, 1785, in *The Papers of Thomas Jefferson*, ed. Barbara Oberg (Princeton, NJ: Princeton University Press, 2009), 8:186.

6. William G. McLoughlin, *Cherokee Renascence in the New Republic* (Princeton: Princeton University Press, 1986), xv.

7. Jackson, quoted in Murray R. Wickett, *Contested Territory: Whites, Native Americans and African Americans in Oklahoma, 1865–1907* (Baton Rouge: Louisiana State University Press, 2000), 4. For earlier discussions of this ideological change, see Bernard Sheehan, *Seeds of Extinction: Jeffersonian Philosophy and the American Indian* (Chapel Hill: University of North Carolina Press, 1973); Ronald N. Satz, *American Indian Policy in the Jacksonian Era* (Lincoln: University of Nebraska Press, 1975).

8. Ross was one of many "mixed-bloods" whose fathers had been granted full tribal membership through their marriage to Cherokee women. See Theda Perdue, *"Mixed-Blood Indians": Racial Construction in the Early South* (Athens: University of Georgia Press, 2005).

9. Minges, "Freemasonry among the American Indians," 6–8.

10. The degree of their adaptation is a matter of debate. While some took on Western dress, houses, farming, English, and Christian schooling, many more retained their language, respected hereditary social structures, pursued government by consensus, and practiced the age-old rituals of communal solidarity. See Wickett, *Contested Territory*.

11. *Daily Oklahoman* (Oklahoma City), September 15, 1925, reproduced in "Notes and Documents," *Chronicles of Oklahoma* 22, no. 2 (June 1944): 213.

12. Mary M. Rogers, "Notes for a Talk to Kiowa Chapter No. 650 E.S.," *Chronicles of Oklahoma* 4, no. 3 (September 1926): 298. I have found few sources on Native American women's attitudes toward Freemasonry. On Cherokee women, see Theda Perdue, *Cherokee Women: Gender and Culture Change, 1700–1835* (Lincoln: University of Nebraska Press, 1998); Carolyn Ross Johnston, *Cherokee Women in Crisis: Trail of Tears, Civil War, and Allotment, 1838–1907* (Tuscaloosa: University of Alabama Press, 2003).

13. J. Fred Latham, *The Story of Oklahoma Masonry: The First Seventy-Five Years of Symbolic Masonry, 1874 to 1953* (Guthrie: Grand Lodge of Oklahoma, 1978), 6–7. See also George W. Moser, "A Brief History of Cherokee Lodge No. 10," *Cherokee Advocate*, July 23, 1879: "Most of the Lodge membership was Cherokee, including several ones of influence."

14. Latham, *Story of Oklahoma Masonry*, 59. See also Denslow, *Freemasonry and the American Indian*, 69.

15. The records of the Grand Lodge list these men throughout the following volumes: *Proceedings* (1874) and (1875) (Sedalia, MO: Democrat Steam Book and Job, 1881); *Proceedings* (Memphis: Publication Society, 1876); *Proceedings* 3 (Sedalia, MO: Democrat Steam Book and Job, 1881); *Proceedings* 4 (Muskogee, OK: Phoenix Steam Print, 1889); *Proceedings* 5 (Washington, DC: Office of the Masonic Eclectic, 1880); *Proceedings* 6–10 (Sedalia, MO: Democrat Steam Book and Job, 1880–84).

16. *Proceedings* (1876), 8.

17. *Proceedings* 5: 53. Other disparaging comments include the 1879 judgment of the Grand Lodge of Louisiana that the members of the Indian Grand Lodge were "tramps" because of their inability to pay their dues and the opinion of the general grand high priest of Royal Arch Masonry that they could not form a chapter in Indian Territory "because of the ethical tendencies of the Masons out in that wild country." Quoted in Denslow, *Freemasonry and the American Indian*, 84.

18. *Proceedings* 3: 4.

19. *Indian Journal* (Eufaula, Indian Territory), June 26, 1878, reproduced in "Notes and Documents," *Chronicles of Oklahoma* 22, no. 1 (March 1944): 109.

20. "Rev. Thomas Bertholf," *Chronicles of Oklahoma* 11, no. 4 (December 1933): 1019.

21. Paul D. Mitchell, *From Tepees to Towers: A History of the Methodist Church in Oklahoma* (Verden, OK: n.p., 1947), 36; *Proceedings* (1876), 21; John Bartlett Meserve, "Chief Samuel Checote, with Sketches of Chiefs Locher Harjo and Ward Coachman," *Chronicles of Oklahoma* 16, no. 4 (December 1938): 403.

22. Others included James McHenry and Forbis LeFlore. See Mitchell, *From Tepees to Towers*, 11–33; *Proceedings* (1876), 21, 24.

23. "Resolved, therefore, by the Conference, we disapprove of the course of our Brother, C. M. Slover, in neglecting to attend the present session to attend the sitting of the Grand Lodge [of Masons] at Little Rock, Arkansas, and that his Presiding Elder be requested to inform him of this action and admonish him." "1860 Annual Conference Minutes," quoted in Mitchell, *From Tepees to Towers*, 29. In 1874, Slover was appointed the first deputy grand master of the Grand Lodge of Indian Territory. *Proceedings* [1874], 3.

24. Latham, *Story of Oklahoma Masonry*, 58; Raymond L. Holcomb, *Father Murrow: The Life and Times of Joseph Samuel Murrow, Baptist Missionary, Confederate Indian Agent, Indian Educator, and Father of Freemasonry in Indian Territory* (Atoka, OK: Atoka County Historical Society, 1994).

25. *Proceedings* [1875], 3.

26. John Bartlett Meserve, "Chief Lewis Downing and Chief Charles Thompson (Oochalata)," *Chronicles of Oklahoma* 16, no. 3 (September 1938): 316.

27. McLoughlin, *Cherokee Renascence*, 350–65; McLoughlin, *Champions of the Cherokees: Evan and John B. Jones* (Princeton, NJ: Princeton University Press, 1990).

28. William G. McLoughlin, *The Cherokees and Christianity, 1794–1870: Essays on Acculturation and Cultural Persistence*, ed. Walter H. Conser Jr. (Athens: University of Georgia Press, 1994), 109–26.

29. Ibid., 188–218.

30. The Cherokee social ideal was to live in harmony in an interdependent web of relationships that extended to the natural and supernatural worlds. There was no central tribal authority. Members of all seven clans inhabited each town. Each town was self-governing and followed unwritten customs. Clan unity transcended town self-government, and kinship united all of the towns. When major issues of war or trade needed the attention of all the people, national councils were called and decisions made, but these were not binding on individual towns. For overviews of Cherokee life and history in the eighteenth century, see McLoughlin, *Cherokee Renascence*, 3–32; Russell Thornton, *The Cherokees: A Population History* (Lincoln: University of Nebraska Press, 1990), 5–46; Gary C. Goodwin, *Cherokees in Transition* (Chicago: University of Chicago Press, 1977); Charles M. Hudson, *The Southeastern Indians* (Knoxville: University of Tennessee Press, 1976); James Mooney, *Historical Sketch of the Cherokee* (Chicago: Aldine, 1975).

31. Fred S. Barde, "The Keetoowah or Nighthawk Society of the Cherokee Nation," 1, Fred S. Barde Collection, Oklahoma Historical Society, Oklahoma City.

32. Patrick N. Minges, *Slavery in the Cherokee Nation: The Keetoowah Society and the Defining of a People, 1855–1867* (New York: Routledge, 2003), 81–82. See also "Keetoowah Laws, 1859–1876," app. A, 102–20, in Howard Tyner, "The Keetoowah Society in Cherokee History" (MA thesis, University of Oklahoma, 1949), 102–20.

33. On the origins and development of the Keetoowah Society, see Minges, *Slavery in the Cherokee Nation*, 55–198; McLoughlin, *Cherokees and Christian-*

ity, 219–84. Both of these are indebted to Tyner's MA thesis (see previous note).

34. Philip J. Deloria, *Playing Indian* (New Haven, CT: Yale University Press, 1998). This insightful book builds on Roy Harvey Pierce, *Savagism and Civilization: A Study of the Indian and the American Mind* (1953; repr., Berkeley: University of California Press, 1988); Richard Slotkin, *Regeneration through Violence: The Mythology of the American Frontier* (Middletown, CT: Wesleyan University Press, 1973); Robert Berkhofer, *The White Man's Indian: Images of the American Indian from Columbus to the Present* (New York: Knopf, 1978).

35. John Higham, "The Reorientation of American Culture in the 1890's," in his *Writing American History* (Bloomington: Indiana University Press, 1970), 73–102. See also T. J. Jackson Lears, *No Place of Grace: Antimodernism and the Transformation of American Culture, 1880–1920* (Chicago: University of Chicago Press, 1981); Gail Bederman, *Manliness and Civilization: A Cultural History of Gender and Race in the United States, 1880–1917* (Chicago: University of Chicago Press, 1995).

36. This scholarship includes Jay Mechling, "'Playing Indian' and the Search for Authenticity in Modern White America," in *Prospects* 5, ed. Jack Salzman (New York: Burt Franklin, 1980), 17–54; Rayna Green, "The Tribe Called Wannabee: Playing Indian in America and Europe," *Folklore* 99 (1988): 50–55; George Lipsitz, "Mardi Gras Indians: Carnival and Counter-narrative in Black New Orleans," in his *Time Passages: Collective Memory and American Popular Culture* (Minneapolis: University of Minnesota Press, 1990), 233–56; Robert Baird, "Going Indian: Discovery, Adoption, and Renaming toward a 'True American' from *Deerslayer* to *Dances with Wolves*," in *Dressing in Feathers: The Construction of the Indian in American Popular Culture*, ed. S. Elizabeth Baird (Boulder, CO: Westview, 1996). 195–209. See also "Constructing Race," special issue, *William and Mary Quarterly* 3d series, 54, no. 1 (January 1997); Shari M. Huhndorf, ed., *Going Native: Indians in the American Cultural Imagination* (Ithaca, NY: Cornell University Press, 2001).

37. For a fuller discussion and similar argument about the relationship between Morgan and Parker, see Deloria, *Playing Indian*, 76–94; Joy Porter, *To Be Indian: The Life of Iroquois-Seneca Arthur Caswell Parker* (Norman: University of Oklahoma Press, 2001), 33–44. Porter's more recent *Native American Freemasonry* (Lincoln: University of Nebraska Press, 2011) particularly emphasizes European American and Native American Masons' appropriations of one another's performances and sacred spaces to create bonds and advance a variety of individual and communal ends.

38. Gilbert Herdt, *Secrecy and Cultural Reality: Utopian Ideologies of the New Guinea Men's House* (Ann Arbor: University of Michigan Press, 2003), 1–31, explores the relationship between Morgan's participation in male secret societies and the development of the field of anthropology.

39. Mark C. Carnes, *Secret Ritual and Manhood in Victorian America* (New Haven, CT: Yale University Press, 1989), 96.

40. Frederick E. Hoxie, *A Final Promise: The Campaign to Assimilate the Indians, 1880–1920* (Lincoln: University of Nebraska Press, 2001), 16–19.

41. Arthur C. Parker, "Ely S. Parker—Man and Mason," *Freemasons* 8, no. 2 (January–December 1961): 229–47. See also Denslow, *Freemasonry and the American Indian*, 142–51. For the most recent and extended treatment of Parker's life, see Porter, *To Be Indian*.

42. Deloria, "White Sacheme," 38.

43. Parker, quoted in Denslow, *Freemasonry and the American Indian*, 143–44.

44. Maureen Konkle makes this point in *Writing Indian Nations: Native Intellectuals and the Politics of Historiography, 1827–1863* (Chapel Hill: University of North Carolina Press, 2004), 261.

45. Joy Porter, personal communication.

46. William N. Fenton, introduction to *Parker on the Iroquois*, ed. Fenton (Syracuse, NY: Syracuse University Press, 1968), 2–9.

47. Hoxie, *Final Promise*, 41–81.

48. Fenton, introduction to *Parker on the Iroquois*, 4–8; Denslow, *Freemasonry and the American Indian*, 167–69.

49. Porter, *To Be Indian*, 3–25.

50. Fenton, introduction to *Parker on the Iroquois*, 9–47.

51. Porter, *To Be Indian*, 70, 84–90.

52. On Boas's influence on American racial thinking, see Vernon Williams Jr., *Rethinking Race: Franz Boas and His Contemporaries* (Lexington: University Press of Kentucky, 1996).

53. Hoxie, *Final Promise*, 134–45, 211–38.

54. This analysis draws on Porter, *To Be Indian*, 143–64.

55. Denslow, *Freemasonry and the American Indian*, 168.

56. Lynn Dumenil, *Freemasonry and American Culture, 1880–1930* (Princeton, NJ: Princeton University Press, 1984), 120–26.

57. Lears, *No Place of Grace*, xv–xx.

58. Kavanaugh, quoted in Denslow, *Freemasonry and the American Indian*, 3.

59. Deloria, "White Sacheme," 28–37.

60. Arthur C. Parker, "Freemasonry among the American Indians," *Builder* 6 (1920): 296; Parker, *American Indian Freemasonry* (Buffalo, NY: Buffalo Consistory, 1919), 10.

61. Parker, *"American Indian Freemasonry,"* 14.

62. Parker draws this parallel in his biography of his granduncle Ely. There he also closely ties his family to Masonic history by asserting that William Morgan, the flashpoint of the 1920s Anti-Masonic crusade, had hidden books revealing the secrets of Freemasonry in the Parker home on the Tonawanda Reservation. "Ely S. Parker—Man and Mason," 229–47.

63. Parker, "Freemasonry among the American Indians," 297.

64. Frederick Hoxie, "Exploring a Cultural Borderland: Native American Journeys of Discovery in the Early Twentieth Century," *Journal of American History* 79 (December 1992): 969–95.

65. Frederick Hoxie, introduction to *Talking Back to Civilization: Indian Voices of the Progressive Era*, ed. Hoxie (Boston: Bedford/St. Martin's, 2001), 1–28.

66. Deloria, *Playing Indian*, 188.
67. Hoxie, introduction to *Talking Back to Civilization*, 26.

8. JEWS AND CATHOLICS, 1723–1920

1. The text (James Anderson, *The Constitutions of the Free-Masons* [1723], reprint of Anderson's book by Benjamin Franklin [1734; repr., Bloomington, IL: Masonic Book Club, 1971], 48) reads as follows:

Concerning GOD and RELIGION.

A Mason is oblig'd by his Tenure, to obey the moral Law; and if he rightly understands the Art, he will never be a stupid Atheist, nor an irreligious Libertine. But though in ancient Times Masons were charg'd in every Country to be of the Religion of that Country or Nation, whatever it was, yet 'tis now thought more expedient only to oblige them to that Religion in which all Men agree, leaving their particular Opinions to themselves; that is, to be good Men and true, or Men of Honour and Honesty, by whatever Denominations or Persuasions they may be distinguish'd; whereby Masonry becomes the Center of Union, and the Means of conciliating true Friendship among Persons that must else have remain'd at a perpetual Distance.

2. David Stevenson has noted that Anderson's Presbyterian sermons around the time of his writing the constitution did not approve of even Deists or Unitarians. However, as mentioned in ch. 1, n. 58, in his "professional capacity" as the author of the constitution, Anderson reflected the more inclusive views of his fellow Masons. Stevenson, "James Anderson: Man and Mason," *Heredom* 10 (2002): 116.

3. Jacob Katz, *Jews and Freemasons in Europe 1723–1939*, trans. Leonard Oschry (Cambridge, MA: Harvard University Press, 1970), 13–15, 198–99.

4. John M. Shaftesley, "Jews in English Freemasonry in the 18th and 19th Centuries," *Ars Quatuor Coronatorum* 92 (1979): 25–63. On English Jews and Anglicization, see Todd M. Endelman, *The Jews of Georgian England, 1714–1830: Tradition and Change in a Liberal Society* (Philadelphia: Jewish Publication Society of America, 1979).

5. Katz, *Jews and Freemasons*, 16.
6. Ibid., 2–3, 17–25, 212.
7. Bill Williams, *The Making of Manchester Jewry, 1740–1875* (Manchester: Manchester University Press, 1976), 25.
8. Shaftesley, "Jews in English Freemasonry," 30.
9. Katz, *Jews and Freemasons*, 200–201.
10. Ibid., 16.
11. Shaftesley, "Jews in English Freemasonry," 37–39.
12. Ira Rosenswaike, "An Estimate and Analysis of the Jewish Population of the United States in 1790," in *American Jewish History*, ed. Jeffrey S. Gurock, vol. 1 (New York: Routledge, 1998), 349.
13. Jonathan D. Sarna, *American Judaism: A History* (New Haven, CT: Yale University Press, 2004), 1–30.
14. Bernard Kusinitz, "Masonry and the Colonial Jews of Newport," *Rhode Island Jewish Historical Notes* 9, no. 2 (November 1984): 183–84.

15. "Gershom Mendes Seixas (1745–1816)," Jewish Virtual Library, accessed October 13, 2011, www.jewishvirtuallibrary.org/jsource/biography/Seixas.html.

16. Kusinitz, "Colonial Jews of Newport," 183–85. Washington was a member of Virginia's Fredericksburg Lodge No. 4, as was Hezekiah Levy. Samuel Oppenheim, *The Jews and Masonry in the United States before 1810*, Publications of the Jewish Historical Society no. 19 (New York: American Jewish Historical Society, 1910), 58.

17. "'To Bigotry No Sanction, to Persecution No Assistance': George Washington's Letter to the Jews of Newport, Rhode Island (1790)," Jewish Virtual Library, accessed October 13, 2011, www.jewishvirtuallibrary.org/jsource/US-Israel/bigotry.html.

18. Oppenheim, *Jews and Masonry*, 41–42. The Sublime Lodge of Perfection was a body of the Order of the Royal Secret, which later transformed into the Scottish Rite. See Arturo de Hoyos, *Scottish Rite Ritual Monitor and Guide* (Washington DC: Supreme Council, Southern Jurisdiction, 2007). The 1781 minutes of Philadelphia's Masonic Lodge No. 2 note that most of the Jewish members of the Sublime Lodge "were identified with Lodge No. 2." Norris S. Barratt and Julius F. Sachse, eds., *Freemasonry in Pennsylvania, 1727–1907* (Philadelphia: New Era, 1908), 424.

19. Sarna, *American Judaism*, 44–45.

20. In 1788, Bush was instrumental in bringing about fraternal relations between the Pennsylvania Grand Lodge and the two rival Grand Lodges of England's Ancients and Moderns. Oppenheim, *Jews and Masonry*, 47.

21. Ibid., 58.

22. Oppenheim, *Jews and Masonry*, 43–48, 79.

23. James William Hagy, *This Happy Land: The Jews of Colonial and Antebellum Charleston* (Tuscaloosa: University of Alabama Press, 1993), 50; Albert Gallatin Mackey, *The History of Freemasonry in South Carolina, from Its Origins in the Year 1736 to the Present Time . . .* (Columbia: South Carolinian Steam Power Press, 1861), 75; Charles Reznikoff, *The Jews of Charleston: A History of an American Jewish Community* (Philadelphia: Jewish Publication Society of America, 1950), 50.

24. Oppenheim, *Jews and Masonry*, 5–8, 41–42. See also Ray Baker Harris, *History of the Supreme Council, 33rd Degree, Ancient and Accepted Scottish Rite of Freemasonry, Southern Jurisdiction, U.S.A., 1801–1861* (Washington DC: Supreme Council, 1964), 13–14.

25. Reznikoff, *Jews of Charleston*, 95.

26. *Official Bulletin of the Supreme Council, Ancient and Accepted Scottish Rite, Southern Jurisdiction, for 1889*, 625, discussed in Oppenheim, *Jews and Masonry*, 38.

27. Sarna, *American Judaism*, 52–61, 83.

28. The best source for this ceremony is Lewis F. Allen, "Founding of the City of Ararat on Grand Island by Mordecai M. Noah," *Publications of the Buffalo Historical Society* 1 (1879): 305–28.

29. The proclamation is reproduced in Joseph L. Blau and Salo W. Baron, eds., *The Jews of the United States 1790–1840: A Documentary History* (New York: Columbia University Press, 1963), 3:894–900.

30. Allen, "Founding of the City of Ararat," 317–22.

31. Henry Samuel Morais, *The Jews of Philadelphia* (Philadelphia: Levytype, 1894), 16.

32. Oppenheim, *Jews and Masonry*, 1.

33. Jonathan D. Sarna, *Jacksonian Jew: The Two Worlds of Mordecai Noah* (New York: Holemes and Meier, 1981), 9.

34. M.M. Noah, *Oration, Delivered by Appointment, before Tammany Society of Columbian Order* . . . (New York: J.H. Sherman, 1817), 20–22.

35. Mordecai M. Noah, *Discourse, Delivered at the Consecration of the Synagogue of K.K. Shearith Israel* . . . (New York: C.S. Van Winkle, 1818), 6.

36. Sarna, *Jacksonian Jew*, 119.

37. Donald E. Pitzer, ed., *America's Communal Utopias* (Chapel Hill: University of North Carolina Press, 1997).

38. Jacob R. Marcus, *The Colonial American Jew, 1492–1776*, vol. 1 (Detroit: Wayne State University Press, 1970), 361–66. On American Jewish colonies in the later nineteenth century, see Tobias Brinkman, "Between Vision and Reality: Reassessing Jewish Agricultural Colony Projects in Nineteenth-Century America," *Jewish History* 21 (2007): 305–24.

39. Jonathan D. Sarna, "The American Jewish Response to Nineteenth-Century Christian Missions," *Journal of American History* 68 (1981): 35–51; Joshua Kohn, "Mordecai Manual Noah's Ararat Project and the Missionaries," *American Jewish Historical Quarterly* 55, no. 2 (December 1965): 162–96.

40. For an overview of the several articulations of this belief in the early modern period, see Lynn Glaser, *Indians or Jews? An Introduction to a Reprint of Manasseh ben Israel's "The Hope of Israel"* (Gilroy, CA: Roy V. Boswell, 1973).

41. Richard Bushman, *Joseph Smith: Rough Stone Rolling* (New York: Vintage, 2007), 94–99.

42. In an 1825 letter, Noah disclosed that he based this on the views of the Sephardic rabbi Menasseh Ben Israel, who had published his *Mikveh Israel* (The hope of Israel) in Amsterdam in 1650; the Indian trader James Adair's *History of the American Indian* (London: Dilly, 1775); and Elias Boudinot's *A Star in the West, or A Humble Attempt to Discover the Long Lost Ten Tribes of Israel, Preparatory to Their Return to Their Beloved City, Jerusalem* (Trenton, NJ: D. Fenton, S. Hutchinson, and J. Dunham, 1816). See I. Harold Sharfman, *Jews on the Frontier* (Chicago: Henry Regnery, 1977), 214. On colonial Jewish views of the Indians' Hebrew origins, see Marcus, *Colonial American Jew*, 40–42.

43. On March 7, 1831, less than a year after the founding of the Mormons' Church of Christ in upstate New York, David Staats Burnet, a Dayton, Ohio, newspaper editor and an admirer of the religious reformer Alexander Campbell, published this remark:

> [The Mormons believe] that treasures of great amount were concealed near the surface of the earth, probably by the Indians, whom they were taught to consider the descendants of the ten lost Israelitish tribes, by the celebrated Jew who a few years since promised to gather Abraham's sons on Grand Island, thus to be made a Paradise. (*Evangelical Inquirer* 1, no. 10: 218)

44. *Niles' Weekly Register* (Baltimore), October 1, 1825, 69.

45. Grand Rabbi De Cologne to the Paris *Journal des débats*, letter partially reproduced in "Re-assemblage of the Jews," *Niles' Weekly Register*, January 21, 1826, 330–31.

46. Mordecai M. Noah, *Discourse on the Restoration of the Jews* (New York: Harper, 1845), 4. Since the late nineteenth century, American Zionists have identified Noah as a precursor of their movement. See Michael Weingrad, "Messiah, American Style: Mordecai Manuel Noah and the American Refuge," *American Jewish Studies Review* 31, no. 1 (April 2007): 75–108.

47. Sarna, *American Judaism*, 83–84, 54–61.

48. Charles W. Moore, "Jewish Opinions of Christ," *Freemason's Monthly Magazine* 15, no. 5 (March 1856), quoted in Oppenheim, *Jews and Masonry*, 1.

49. Isaac M. Wise, *Israelite* (Cincinnati) 2, no. 7 (August 17, 1855): 52.

50. Anthony D. Fels, "The Square and the Compass: San Francisco's Freemasons and American Religion, 1870–1900" (PhD diss., Stanford University, 1987), 481–87. Fels found that a further benefit of the fraternity was its mixing of members from San Francisco's Polish and German Jewish communities, who early on had kept apart. Fels, "Religious Assimilation in a Fraternal Organization: Jews and Freemasonry in Gilded Age San Francisco," *American Jewish History* 74, no. 4 (June 1985): 373–76.

51. Albert M. Friedenberg, *A List of Jews Who Were Grand Masters of Masons in Various States of the Country*, Publications of the Jewish Historical Society no. 19 (New York: American Jewish Historical Society, 1910), 95.

52. *Boston Daily Times* article, reprinted without date in Isaac M. Wise, "Intolerance and Insolence," *Israelite* (Cincinnati) 2, no. 4 (August 3, 1855): 28.

53. Ibid.

54. Deborah Dash Moore, *B'nai B'rith and the Challenge of Ethnic Leadership* (Albany: State University of New York, 1981), 1–34; Edward E. Grusd, *B'nai B'rith: The Story of a Covenant* (New York: Appleton-Century, 1966), 12–24. Though both of these accounts suggest discrimination against Jewish members of the Masons and the Odd Fellows as a reason for the formation of B'nai B'rith, Cornelia Wilhelm has argued that this was not the case. Wilhelm, *Deutsche Juden in Amerika: Bürgerliches Selbstbewusstsein und jüdische Identität in den Orden B'nai B'rith und Treue Schwestern, 1843–1914* (Stuttgart: Franz Steiner, 2007). For a discussion, see Jonathan D. Sarna, "The Halakha According to B'nai B'rith," in *Rav Chesed: Essays in Honor of Rabbi Dr. Haskel Lookstein*, ed. Rafael Medoff (Jersey City, NJ: KTAV, 2009), 165–66. I am grateful to Sarna for bringing Wilhelm's work to my attention.

55. Moore, *B'nai B'rith*, ch. 1.

56. Moore, *B'nai B'rith*, 12.

57. Leo N. Levi, *Memorial Volume* (Chicago: Hamburger, 1905), 261.

58. Grusd, *B'nai B'rith*, 45.

59. Levi, *Memorial Volume*, 305.

60. See Hannah Kliger's discussion and replication of the original text, "Jewish Landsmanschaften and Family Circles in New York," in her *Jewish Hometown Associations and Family Circles in New York* (Bloomington: Indiana University Press, 1992).

61. Ibid., 35–55.

62. Daniel Soyer, *Jewish Associations and American Identity in New York, 1880–1939* (Cambridge, MA: Harvard University Press, 1997), 38–39. See also his "Entering the 'Tent of Abraham': Fraternal Ritual and American-Jewish Identity, 1880–1920," *Religion and American Culture* 9, no. 2 (July 1999): 159–82.

63. Leo Wolfson, "Jewish Fraternal Organizations," in *The Jewish Communal Register of New York City, 1917–1918*, (New York: Kehillah [Jewish Community] of New York City, 1918), 866.

64. My intention here is to emphasize the appropriation of fraternal rituals by immigrant Jews in general. One can, however, make a helpful distinction, Daniel Soyer has suggested, between Jews who were members of Reform synagogues and joined the Masons or other non-Jewish societies as part of their assimilation into American society and more traditional Jews, for whom fraternal ritual was decidedly strange and so might have provided an alternative to traditional Judaism (personal communication).

65. Kliger, *Jewish Hometown Associations*, 52–53.

66. Soyer, "Entering the 'Tent of Abraham,'" 162. This work exemplifies recent scholarship on European immigration to the United States, which has moved from telling a straightforward story of assimilation to giving growing attention to immigrant resistance to Americanization. These studies emphasize the processes whereby newcomers become less foreign yet never completely American. For two discussions, see Elliott R. Barkan, Rudolph J. Vecoli, Richard Alba, and Olivier Zunz, "Race, Religion, and Nationality in American Society: A Model of Ethnicity—From Contact to Assimilation," *Journal of American Ethnic History* 14, no. 2 (Winter 1995): 38–101; Cathleen Neils Conzen, David A. Gerber, Ewa Morawska, George E. Pozzetta, and Vecoli, "The Invention of Ethnicity: A Perspective from the U.S.A.," *Journal of American Ethnic History* 12, no. 1 (Fall 1992): 3–41.

67. Soyer, "Entering the 'Tent of Abraham,'" 174.

68. Douglas Knoop and G.P. Jones, *A Short History of Freemasonry to 1730* (Manchester: Manchester University Press, 1940), 23–26.

69. William J. Whalen, *Christianity and American Freemasonry* (Milwaukee: Bruce, 1958), 36.

70. *Gould's History of Freemasonry throughout the World*, ed. Dudley Wright, vol. 1 (New York: Charles Scribner's Sons, 1936), 221–58.

71. Alec M. Ellor, "The Roman Catholic Church and the Craft," *Ars Quatuor Coronatorum* 89 (1976): 60–64; W.J. Chetwode Crawley, "The Old Charges and the Papal Bull," *Ars Quatuor Coronatorum* 24 (1911), 114; Albert C. Stevens, *Cyclopedia of Fraternities* (New York: E.B. Treat, 1907), 10.

72. Chetwode Crawley, "Old Charges," 58–60.

73. Ellor, "Roman Catholic Church and the Craft," 60.

74. Jay Dolan, *The American Catholic Experience* (New York: Doubleday, 1985), 101–26.

75. Carroll, quoted in Peter Guilday, *The Life and Times of John Carroll, Archbishop of Baltimore (1735–1815)* (New York: Encyclopedia Press, 1922), 781.

76. Whalen, *Christianity and American Freemasonry*, 103–4. The Masonic historian Richardson Wright reported that in the colonial period, "Masonic burials were held in Roman Catholic cemeteries and Roman Catholic priests served as chaplains to lodges." Wright, "The American Masonic Sermon," *Transactions of the American Lodge of Research* 3 (1937): 215.

77. *Catholic Historical Review* 4, no. 3 (October 1918): 277–78.

78. "Notes from the Old Records," written by "A Catholic Mason," *Masonic Review* 18, no. 5 (February 1858): 283.

79. Fels, "Square and the Compass," 356–93. Other anti-Catholic, nativist organizations that likely drew some Masonic interest include the Order of United American Mechanics, the Protestant Association, the Patriotic Order Sons of America, and the Junior Order United American Mechanics. In contrast to the mainstream Masonic bodies, the York Rite's Knights Templar and the Southern Jurisdiction of the Scottish Rite were known to actively attack the Catholic Church. On the Protestant identity of the Knights Templar and their opposition to Catholicism, see William D. Moore, *Masonic Temples: Freemasonry, Ritual Architecture, and Masculine Archetypes* (Knoxville: University of Tennessee Press, 2006), 63–64. On anti-Catholicism and the Scottish Rite, see Whalen, *Christianity and Freemasonry*, 2, 88–99.

80. "Notes from the Old Records" and its editorial note by C. Moore, 283–84.

81. Charles Moore, "Freemasonry and Romanism," *Freemasons' Monthly Magazine* 19, no. 6 (April 1860): 163.

82. Fels, "Square and the Compass," 393.

83. Leo XIII, *Humanum Genus*, quoted in H.L. Haywood, *Freemasonry and Roman Catholicism* (Chicago: Masonic History, 1943), 77–102.

84. Albert Pike, "Allocution of the Grand Commander of the Supreme Council of the 33d Degree for the Southern Jurisdiction of the United States of America," delivered in Supreme Council, October 1884, reproduced in Haywood, *Freemasonry and Roman Catholicism*, 103.

85. Whalen, *Christianity and Freemasonry*, 105.

86. Stevens, *Cyclopedia*, 10. As recently as the November 26, 1983, declaration of the Sacred Congregation for the Doctrine of the Faith, issued by the then-cardinal Joseph Ratzinger (later Pope Benedict XVI) and Jerome Hamer, the Catholic Church has continued attacking the "serious sin" of Masonic affiliation.

87. Henry J. Browne, *The Catholic Church and the Knights of Labor* (Washington, DC: Catholic University of America Press, 1949), 64–68. On the rituals of the Knights of Labor and their meaning, see Robert E. Weir, *Beyond Labor's Veil: The Culture of the Knights of Labor* (University Park: Pennsylvania State University Press, 1996).

88. Christopher J. Kauffman, *Faith and Fraternalism: The History of the Knights of Columbus*, rev. ed. (New York: Simon and Schuster, 1992), 1–9.

89. Ibid., xxvii.

90. Ibid., 152.

91. Ibid., 113.

92. Colleen McDannell, "'True Men as We Need Them': Catholicism and the Irish-American Male," *American Studies* 26 (Fall 1986): 19–36.

93. Amy Koehlinger, "'Let Us Live for Those Who Love Us': Faith, Family, and the Contours of Manhood among the Knights of Columbus in Late Nineteenth-Century Connecticut," *Journal of Social History* 38, no. 2 (Winter 2004): 464.

94. John Higham, "The Reorientation of American Culture in the 1890s," in *The Origins of Modern Consciousness*, ed. John Weiss (Detroit: Wayne State University Press, 1965), 30–31.

95. Margaret Marsh, "Suburban Men and Masculine Domesticity, 1870–1915," in *Meanings for Manhood: Constructions of Masculinity in Victorian America*, ed. Mark C. Carnes and Clyde Griffen (Chicago: University of Chicago Press, 1990), 111–27.

96. Moore, *B'nai B'rith*, 78; Linda Gordon Kuzmack, "B'nai B'rith Women," in *Jewish Women: A Comprehensive Historical Encyclopedia*, published March 1, 2009, Jewish Women's Archive, accessed December 9, 2009, http://jwa.org/encyclopedia/article/bnai-brith-women. Jonathan Sarna notes that the earliest female organization parallel to B'nai B'rith was the short-lived United Order of True Sisters, founded in 1846. Sarna, *American Judaism*, 90.

97. Kauffman, *Faith and Fraternalism*, xv, 138, 305; Carol Dorr Clement, *Daughters of Isabella: Our Legacy, Our Future, 1897–2007* (New Haven, CT: Daughters of Isabella, 2008).

98. William D. Moore has demonstrated middle-class Protestant women's involvement in raising funds for the construction of Masonic temples in New York State between 1870 and 1930 and concluded that turn-of-the-century "Freemasonry was not just a male resource for the construction of masculinity, but a societal resource that reinforced values supported by both men and women alike." Moore, "Funding the Temples of Masculinity: Women's Roles in Masonic Fairs in New York State, 1870–1930," in *Freemasonry in Context: History, Ritual, and Controversy*, ed. Arturo de Hoyos and S. Brent Morris (Lanham, MD: Lexington Books, 2004), 75–76.

99. Anthony Fels, "Square and Compass," 480.

100. Paula E. Hyman, "Gender and the Immigrant Jewish Experience in the United States," in *Jewish Women in Historical Perspective*, ed. Judith R. Baskin (Detroit: Wayne State University Press, 1991), 224.

101. Soyer, *Jewish Immigrant Associations*, 78–79.

102. Hyman, "Gender and the Immigrant Jewish Experience," 237.

103. In his study of Toronto's late nineteenth-century Irish Catholic community, Brian P. Clarke found that parish devotional organizations enjoyed almost universal support among Catholic women. Clarke, *Piety and Nationalism: Lay Voluntary Associations and the Creation of an Irish-Catholic Community in Toronto, 1850–1895* (Montreal: McGill-Queens University Press, 1993), 72.

104. Colleen McDannell, *The Christian Home in Victorian America, 1840–1900* (Bloomington: Indiana University Press, 1986), 52–75.

105. Robert A. Orsi, *Thank You, St. Jude: Women's Devotion to the Patron Saint of Hopeless Causes* (New Haven, CT: Yale University Press, 1996).

106. Paula M. Kane, "The Pulpit of the Hearthstone: Katherine Conway and Boston Catholic Women, 1900–1920," *US Catholic Historian* 5, nos. 3–4 (Sum-

mer–Fall 1986): 355. See also her *Separatism and Subculture: Boston Catholicism, 1900–1920* (Chapel Hill: University of North Carolina Press, 1994).

EPILOGUE

1. See Lynn Dumenil, *Freemasonry and American Culture, 1880–1930* (Princeton, NJ: Princeton University Press, 1984), app. A, 225, for data on Masonic membership and the United States adult native white male population between 1850 and 1970. For post-1970 numbers, see the Masonic Service Association of North America, "Membership Totals since 1924," accessed August 13, 2013, www.msana.com/msastats.asp#totals.

2. Robert D. Putnam, *Bowling Alone: The Collapse and Revival of American Community* (New York: Simon and Schuster, 2000), app. 3, 15–28.

3. See Benjamin R. Barber, *A Place for Us: How to Make Society Civil and Democracy Strong* (New York: Hill and Wang, 1998); Robert N. Bellah, Richard Madsden, William M. Sullivan, Ann Swidler, and Steven M. Tipton, *Habits of the Heart: Individualism and Commitment in American Life*, updated ed. (Berkeley: University of California Press, 2008); Amitai Etzioni, *The New Golden Rule: Community and Morality in a Democratic Society* (New York: Basic Books, 1996). For discussions of Putnam's argument, see Scott L. McLean, David A. Schutz, and Manfred B. Steger, eds., *Social Capital: Critical Perspectives on Community and "Bowling Alone"* (New York: New York University Press, 2002).

4. See Jürgen Habermas, "The Public Sphere: An Encyclopedia Article (1964)," *New German Critique* 3 (1974): 54; Habermas, *The Structural Transformation of the Public Sphere: An Inquiry into a Category of Bourgeois Society*, trans. Thomas Burger, with the assistance of Frederick Lawrence, from the 1962 German original (Cambridge, MA: MIT Press, 1989), 195.

5. Between 1860 and 1900, the growth of lodge numbers kept pace with the growth of the national population, while membership more than tripled. Gerald Gamm and Robert D. Putnam, "The Growth of Voluntary Associations in America, 1840–1940," *Journal of Interdisciplinary History* 29, no. 4 (Spring 1999): 523–29, 545–47.

6. David T. Beito, *From Mutual Aid to the Welfare State: Fraternal Societies and Social Services, 1890–1967* (Chapel Hill: University of North Carolina Press, 2000), 5–16; Mark A. Tabbert, *American Freemasons: Three Centuries of Building Communities* (Lexington, MA: National Heritage Museum, 2005), 106–13; Anthony D. Fels, "The Square and the Compass: San Francisco's Freemasons and American Religion, 1870–1900" (PhD diss., Stanford University, 1987), 589–95.

7. Tabbert, *American Freemasons*, 111–17.

8. Masonic Lodge of Education, "Masonic Insurance," accessed August 13, 2013, www.masonic-lodge-of-education.com/masonic-insurance.html.

9. Tabbert, *American Freemasons*, 128–32.

10. One Masonic response to these developments was the increasingly theatrical Scottish Rite. This purportedly elite and esoteric progression of degree rituals, culminating in the celebrated thirty-third degree, boomed in popularity between 1880 and 1920 (from 9,000 to 374,000 members), when the site for

their enactment expanded by need or design to the auditorium stage. Tabbert, *American Freemasons*, 141–46.

11. Clifford Putney, "How Lodge Style Fraternalism Yielded to Men's Service Clubs," in *Freemasonry in Context: History, Ritual, and Controversy*, ed. Arturo de Hoyos and S. Brent Morris (Lanham, MD: Lexington Books, 2004), 105–16; Tabbert, *American Freemasons*, 163–64; Mark C. Carnes, *Secret Ritual and Manhood in Victorian America* (New Haven: Yale University Press, 1989), 153–54.

12. Dumenil, *Freemasonry and American Culture*, 120–26. The classic explanation of nativism in this period is John Higham, *Strangers in the Land: Patterns of American Nativism, 1860–1925* (New Brunswick, NJ: Rutgers University Press, 1955).

13. Wyn Craig Wade, *The Fiery Cross: The Ku Klux Klan in America* (New York: Simon and Schuster, 1987), 141.

14. Mark David Chalmers, *Hooded Americanism: The History of the Ku Klux Klan* (Durham, NC: Duke University Press, 1987), 191, 149.

15. Dumenil, *Freemasonry and American Culture*, 122.

16. Chalmers, *Hooded Americanism*, 254.

17. Dumenil, *Freemasonry and American Culture*, 147.

18. Robert E. Weir, "Prince Hall Masons," in *Organizing Black America: An Encyclopedia of African American Associations*, ed. Nina Mjagkij (New York: Garland, 2001), 593–94.

19. William A. Muraskin, *Middle-Class Blacks in a White Society* (Berkeley: University of California Press, 1975), 29.

20. Ibid., 221–36. See also Tabbert, *American Freemasons*, 206.

21. Muraskin, *Middle-Class Blacks*, 30–31; Weir, "Prince Hall Masons," 594; Tabbert, *American Freemasons*, 214–15.

22. Deborah Dash Moore, *B'nai B'rith and the Challenge of Ethnic Leadership* (Albany: State University of New York, 1981), 102–34.

23. Christopher J. Kauffman, *Faith and Fraternalism: The History of the Knights of Columbus*, rev. ed. (New York: Simon and Schuster, 1992), 166–67.

24. Norman Cohn, *Warrant for Genocide: The Myth of the Jewish Conspiracy and the Protocols of the Elders of Zion* (London: Penguin Books, 1971); Warren Jacob Katz, *Jews and Freemasons in Europe, 1723–1939* (Cambridge, MA: Harvard University Press, 1970), 171–96.

25. Kauffman, *Faith and Fraternalism*, 182–89.

26. Tabbert, *American Freemasons*, 211–15, 161. The occasional eruptions of the fraternity onto the public stage today suggest renewed refrains of evangelical Protestant or Catholic accusations of its evil intentions or links to various conspiracies.

27. Masonic Service Association of North America, "U.S. Grand Lodges," http://msana.com/msastats_02to03.asp#us, http://msana.com/msastats_04to05.asp#us; "U.S. Grand Lodges 2007 Membership," http://msana.com/msastats_06to07.asp#us; "U.S. Grand Lodges Membership," http://msana.com/msastats_08to09.asp#us, http://msana.com/msastats.asp#us.

28. Adam Tschorn, "Freemasons in Midst of Popularity, Membership Boom," *Los Angeles Times*, May 18, 2008, www.latimes.com/features/image/la-ig-masons18-2008may18,0,42602.story.

29. California Grand Lodge, "California Masons in the 21st Century," 2008–9 annual report, www.freemason.org/doc/California%20Masons%20in%20the%2021st%20Century%20(2%20MB).pdf?id=267.

30. Tschorn, "Freemasons in Midst of Popularity, Membership Boom." Some critics of Robert D. Putnam's thesis of weakening social capital (*Bowling Alone: The Collapse and Revival of American Community* [New York: Simon and Schuster, 2000]) have pointed to similar signs of revival as the growth of the U.S. Soccer League (twentyfold in the past twenty years), Little League Baseball, and even the PTA, which continues, though far below its membership peak. See, e.g., Nicholas Lemann, "Kicking in Groups," *Atlantic Monthly* 227, no. 4 (April 1996): 22–26 (available online at www.theatlantic.com/past/docs/issues/96apr/kicking/kicking.htm).

31. Information on the Masonic Restoration Foundation can be found at http://traditionalobservance.com/.

32. Dennis V. Chornenky, "The Traditional Observance Lodge," accessed August 13, 2013, http://traditionalobservance.com/wp-content/uploads/2011/02/DVC_-_The_Traditional_Observance_Lodge.pdf.

33. Masonic Restoration Foundation, "List of Lodges," accessed August 13, 2013, http://traditionalobservance.com/traditional-lodges/.

Index

Abiff, Hiram, 92
abolition movement, 122, 135, 138,
  144, 182
Abraham (biblical figure), 24, 195
Accounts of Religious Revivals (J. Bradley),
  76
Adam (biblical figure), 95–96
Adams, John, 81, 82
Adams, Zabdiel, 46, 47, 51
African American Improved Order of the
  Elks, 221
African Americans: in fraternal organiza-
  tions, 128, 152, 157–58, 271n15,
  280n4 (*see also* Prince Hall Masons
  and the AMEZ Church); gender tensions
  among, 173; identity of, 159; in
  post-revolutionary social institutions,
  156–57, 283–84n26; print culture of,
  159, 160; Reconstruction-era migration
  of, 223, 224
African Methodist Episcopal Zion Church.
  See Prince Hall Masons and the AMEZ
  Church
African Union Church (New York City),
  161
The Age of Reason (Paine), 81
Ahiman Rezon (Dermott), 57–58, 59,
  255n3
Ahlstrom, Sydney, 3
Albany (New York): Anglican church in,
  40; British rule opposed in, 41; colonial

lodges in, 40–41; colonial Masonry in,
  36, 37–42; commercial growth of, 21,
  40; Dutch Reformed church in, 38,
  39–40; as a Dutch settlement, 37–38;
  officers quartered in, 39–40; polite
  society in, 37–41; Presbyterian church
  in, 40; Scotch Irish and English
  immigrants in, 40; Tory sympathizers
  in, 42
Albany Commission for Detecting and
  Defeating Conspiracies, 42
Albany Committee of Correspondence, 41,
  54
Allen, Richard, 156–57, 161
Allestree, Richard: *The Whole Duty of
  Man*, 47
"All-Seeing Eye" of God, 86, 255n6
AME Church Review, 163
American Bible Society, 91
American Catholic Church, 210, 213
American Colonization Society, 202
American Education Society, 75
American Philosophical Society, 50
American Protective Association, 210
American religious history, 2–3
American Society for Ameliorating the
  Conditions of the Jews, 202
American Sunday School Union, 91
American Union Lodge, 62–64
AMEZ Church. *See* Prince Hall Masons and
  the AMEZ Church

145; introduction of, 89; and Mormon rites, 99; mysticism of, 116; number of members, 144; Scottish Rite, 89–90, 95–96, 144; spread of, 89, 90; symbolism/mystery/hermeticism of, 84, 95; and the York Rite, 144
Royal Society (England), 23, 27
Ryan, Mary P., 131

Sabbatarianism, 138
Sachse, Julius T., 9
Sacred Congregation for the Doctrine of the Faith, 298n86
Saint Andrew's, 33
Saint Ann's Lodge (Boston), 103–6
Saint George's, 33
Saint George's Methodist Church, 156–57
Saint John's Day sermons, 44–45, 47, 51
Saint John's Lodge (Boston), 235n12
Saint John's Lodge (New York City), 65
Saint John's Lodge (Philadelphia), 49
Saint John's Lodge No. 1 (Newport), 196–97
Saint Mary's Church (Albany), 210
Saint Peter's Church (Albany, N.Y.), 41
saints, visible, 80
Salvatore, Nick, 11–12, 172–73
San Francisco, Freemasonry in, 142–43, 204, 215
Santa Monica–Palisades Lodge No. 307, 226
Sarah (biblical figure), 24
Sarna, Jonathan, 202, 299n96
Savanna, 21
Schaw, William, 27, 237n34
Schlesinger, Arthur M., Sr., 264n1
Schmidt, Leigh Eric, 237n42
The School of Good Manners, 47
Schultz, Edward T., 9
Schuyler, Catalina, 38–39, 53–54
Schuyler, Philip, 39
Schuyler family, 37, 38–39. *See also* Flatts
Scottish Reformation (1560), 26
Scottish Rite, 89–90, 95–96, 144, 198, 294n18, 300–301n10
scripture as the Word, 25
Seabury, Samuel, 44
Searle, Addison, 199–200
Searle, Roger, 79
Second Great Awakening, 13, 85, 199, 259–60n76, 265n2
secrecy, value of, 236n32
Secret Ritual and Manhood in Victorian America (Carnes), 11

secret tablets, search for, 27
Seixas, Abraham Mendes, 197
Seixas, Gershom Mendes, 197
Seixas, Isaac Mendes, 197
Seixas, Moses, 197
self as illusory, 146
Seminole Nation, 177
Seneca Iroquois Indian Nation, 187
Seneca Nation, 184, 189, 292n62
separation of church and state, 70, 72–73, 254n115
service clubs, 222
Seward, William H., 185
Shaftesbury, Anthony Ashley Cooper, Third Earl of, 1, 30, 33, 43, 68; "An Essay on the Freedom of Wit and Humour," 30–31
Shakespeare, William, 100
Shalhope, Robert, 250n56
Shepherd, Thomas, 19
Sheppard, John H., 71, 87
Sheraith Israel (New York City), 197
Shields, David S., 8, 22, 34, 36
Shriners (Ancient Arabic Order of the Nobles of the Mystic Shrine), 127, 221
Sias, Solomon, 76–77
Simmel, Georg, 236n32
Simmons, R. H., 155
Simmons, William Joseph, 223
Six Nations of the Iroquois Confederacy, 184
Skocpol, Theda, 11
slaves, discipline/respectability for, 171
Slover, C. M., 290n23
Smith, J. E., 186
Smith, Jonathan Z., 3
Smith, Joseph, 97–99, 203, 259n66
Smith, Josiah, 243–44n130
Smith, William, 44, 59, 64, 249n42, 255n3
Smith-Rosenberg, Carroll, 264n103
social Darwinism, 183
Social Gospel, 147, 279n104
social reforms, 119–20, 138, 221–22. *See also specific movements*
society: hierarchical, 29–31, 68; private (*see* polite societies)
Society for the Promotion of Christian Knowledge, 43
Society for the Propagation of the Gospel (SPG), 43–44, 75
Solomon, King (biblical figure), 24, 95, 99, 158
Solomon's Lodge (Savannah), 44
Solomon's Temple, 24–26, 66, 86, 97, 99, 166–67, 188

DATE DUE
